# Journal of Biblical Literature

Volume 136
2017

GENERAL EDITOR
ADELE REINHARTZ
University of Ottawa
Ottawa, ON K1N 6N5

A Quarterly Published by
SBL Press

## EDITORIAL BOARD

WILLIAM ADLER, North Carolina State University
ELIZABETH BOASE, Flinders University
JO-ANN A. BRANT, Goshen College
DAVID M. CARR, Union Theological Seminary
RICHARD J. CLIFFORD, Boston College
KELLEY COBLENTZ BAUTCH, St. Edwards University
COLLEEN CONWAY, Seton Hall University
TOAN DO, Australian Catholic University
GEORG FISCHER, Leopold-Franzens-Universität Innsbruck
PAULA FREDRIKSEN, Hebrew University
WIL GAFNEY, Brite Divinity School
FRANCES TAYLOR GENCH, Union Presbyterian Seminary
SHIMON GESUNDHEIT, Hebrew University of Jerusalem
MARK GOODACRE, Duke University
MARTIEN A. HALVORSON-TAYLOR, University of Virginia (Charlottesville)
RACHEL HAVRELOCK, University of Illinois at Chicago
ELSE K. HOLT, Aarhus Universitet
DAVID G. HORRELL, University of Exeter
L. ANN JERVIS, Wycliffe College
JONATHAN KLAWANS, Boston University
JENNIFER KNUST, Boston University
BRUCE W. LONGENECKER, Baylor University
MICHAEL A. LYONS, Simpson University
DANIEL MACHIELA, McMaster University
CHRISTL M. MAIER, Philipps-Universität Marburg
JOHN W. MARSHALL, University of Toronto
SHELLY MATTHEWS, Brite Divinity School
NAPHTALI MESHEL, Hebrew University
CHRISTINE MITCHELL, St. Andrew's College, University of Saskatchewan
KEN M. PENNER, St. Francis Xavier University
PIERLUIGI PIOVANELLI, University of Ottawa
MARK REASONER, Marian University
ANNETTE YOSHIKO REED, University of Pennsylvania
THOMAS RÖMER, Collège de France and University of Lausanne
DALIT ROM-SHILONI, Tel Aviv University
JEAN-PIERRE RUIZ, St. John's University (New York)
SETH L. SANDERS, University of California, Davis
KONRAD SCHMID, University of Zurich
WILLIAM M. SCHNIEDEWIND, University of California Los Angeles
CLAUDIA SETZER, Manhattan College
ABRAHAM SMITH, Perkins School of Theology, Southern Methodist University
JOHANNA STIEBERT, University of Leeds
JOHN T. STRONG, Missouri State University
D. ANDREW TEETER, Harvard Divinity School
MATTHEW THIESSEN, Saint Louis University
STEVEN TUELL, Pittsburgh Theological Seminary
EMMA WASSERMAN, Rutgers University
LAWRENCE M. WILLS, Episcopal Divinity School

*Managing Editor:* Christopher Hooker, Society of Biblical Literature
*Editorial Assistant:* Caitlin J. Montgomery, Society of Biblical Literature

### EDITORIAL MATTERS OF THE *JBL*

1. Prospective contributors should first review the *JBL* submission guidelines available at https://submissions.scholasticahq.com/sites/journal-of-biblical-literature/for-authors. If a manuscript is submitted in a form that departs in major ways from these instructions, it may be returned to the author for revision prior to being considered for publication.
2. Manuscripts may be submitted using our online platform at https://submissions.scholasticahq.com/sites/journal-of-biblical-literature.
3. Communications regarding the *Journal* should be addressed to Adele Reinhartz at jbleditor@gmail.com.
5. Permission to quote more than 500 words may be requested from the Rights and Permissions Department, Society of Biblical Literature, 825 Houston Mill Road, Suite 350, Atlanta, GA 30329, USA (E-mail: sblpressp@sbl-site.org). Please specify volume, year, and inclusive page numbers.

### BUSINESS MATTERS OF THE SBL
(not handled by the editors of the *Journal*)

1. All correspondence regarding membership in the Society, subscriptions to the *Journal*, change of address, renewals, missing or defective issues of the *Journal*, and inquiries about other publications of the Society should be addressed to Society of Biblical Literature, Customer Service Department, 825 Houston Mill Road, Atlanta, GA 30329. Phone: 866-727-9955 (toll-free) or 404-727-9498. E-mail: sblservices@sbl-site.org.
2. All correspondence concerning the research and publications programs, the Annual Meeting of the Society, and other business should be addressed to the Executive Director, Society of Biblical Literature, The Luce Center, 825 Houston Mill Road, Atlanta, GA 30329. (E-mail: sblexec@sbl-site.org).
3. Second Class postage paid at Atlanta, Georgia, and at additional mailing offices.

## Presidential Address

by

BEVERLY ROBERTS GAVENTA

President of the Society of Biblical Literature 2016
Annual Meeting of the Society of Biblical Literature
19 November 2016
San Antonio, Texas

*Introduction given by Michael V. Fox*
*Vice President, Society of Biblical Literature*
doi: http://dx.doi.org/10.15699/jbl.1361.2017.1361

Professor Gaventa was born Beverly Roberts in a small town in western Tennessee. Her parents were factory workers, and she would be the first in her family to go to college. You might think of this background as a disadvantage that Beverly overcame, but she insists that she had a *privileged* upbringing, for she had a supportive family that was determined to see her educated.

Beverly went to Phillips University, where she fell in love with academia. She did a double major in religious studies, which she made her vocation, and English literature, which she made her avocation. She is an avid, serious reader of English literature, which clearly enriches her reading of the literature of the New Testament. There was only one subject she disliked in college—the Bible, Old Testament and New, in which she had required courses.

She decided to become a professor, because that looked like a neat job, as it is. She went to Union Theological Seminary to pursue graduate work in religious studies. There she found that the undergraduate New Testament courses she had disliked qualified her to enter advanced New Testament exegesis, which she loved, and advanced New Testament exegesis is what she has done ever since. Her main teachers in New Testament, who remained a source of personal and intellectual inspiration, were Raymond Brown and Louis Martyn. Martyn's most powerful quality as scholar and teacher was *attentiveness:* his attention to the text and to his students. He conveyed to his students that they were doing something very important, something worthy of an enormous investment of work. Beverly does the same for her students.

After receiving her doctorate from Duke in 1979, she taught at several universities and seminaries, joining the faculty at Princeton Theological Seminary in

1992, where she became Helen H. P. Manson Professor of New Testament. In 2013 she went to Baylor as Distinguished Professor of New Testament.

Her publications include fourteen books, authored or edited, and scores of articles. She has also been active as an editor of journals and essay collections. She also writes for lay and clerical audiences, for she considers Christian education an important component of her vocation. She has written a study on conversion;[1] commentaries on Acts[2] and on 1 and 2 Thessalonians;[3] and essays on a great variety of other topics. She is currently writing a commentary on Romans for the New Testament Library. You can find her curriculum vitae and her ever-developing bibliography at http://www.baylor.edu/religion/doc.php/280629.pdf.

Time constraints allow me only to summarize the achievements of two of her books. I am sure that the New Testament scholars present are familiar with them, but these works have much to offer Old Testament scholars too, as models of lucidity, careful methodology, and fresh insights.

When I learned that I was to introduce Beverly Gaventa, a scholar I did not know in a field I was barely acquainted with, I resolved to do my duty and read some of her writings. I began with her book *Our Mother Saint Paul*.[4] Duty immediately became pleasure, then fascination. It is a pleasure to read what Beverly writes. Her style is direct and clear, and her argumentation beautifully reasoned. She addresses and evaluates earlier scholarship but quickly cuts to the heart of the matter. In this book, Beverly first gives us a vivid vignette of a community of Christians gathering to hear one of Paul's newly arrived letters. She asks us to think in particular about how the women in the audience would have heard his words, which at first seem directed only to men and men's concerns. One feature of the letters that may have spoken in a special way to the women present was Paul's use of maternal metaphors.

Paul sometimes speaks of himself as a woman in labor and as a nursing mother and even applies the birthing metaphor to all creation, which labors to give birth to Christ, but in vain. These strange and striking metaphors had earlier received almost no scholarly attention, but they are not just piquant rhetoric. They are essential expressions of Paul's self-image and sense of mission, and they help to communicate his theology. They are also a challenge to typical Roman machismo, for Paul is placing himself in a role of the female-identified male, which was considered

---

[1] Beverly Roberts Gaventa, *From Darkness to Light: Aspects of Conversion in the New Testament*, OBT (Philadelphia: Fortress, 1986).

[2] Beverly Roberts Gaventa, *The Acts of the Apostles*, ANTC (Nashville: Abingdon, 2003).

[3] Beverly Roberts Gaventa, *I and II Thessalonians*, IBC (Louisville: Westminster John Knox, 1998).

[4] Beverly Roberts Gaventa, *Our Mother Saint Paul* (Louisville: Westminster John Knox, 2007).

shameful in Roman society. Paul violates hierarchical expectations because they have no place in his apocalyptic theology.

In the second part of the book Beverly discusses this apocalyptic theology. This is the belief that, by the crucifixion, God has "invaded" human history, for God is in the final battle with the powers of evil and cannot rely on humans to direct history aright.

Beverly argues that "Paul's letters are of urgent importance for the lives of women."[5] This assertion runs counter to the suspicion and hostility that many women feel toward Paul. Beverly argues that Pauline theology is not, as she puts it, "just a guy thing."

Beverly's book *Mary: Glimpses of the Mother of Jesus*[6] is a great rarity, a study of Mary by a Protestant, a Protestant woman at that, and Beverly explains how this perspective, as well as her own experience as a mother, helped shape her encounter with the text. Earlier studies of Mary were historical or theological in orientation. Beverly chooses a literary approach. She is interested in the images of Mary as a literary character. She compares four portrayals of Mary in early Christianity—those of Matthew, Luke-Acts, John, and the Protevangelium of James—and shows the different purposes of each portrayal. In a sentence that catches the essence of the book, Beverly writes, "John's Mary is no more interchangeable with Luke's than a painting of the Virgin of Guadalupe is with an icon of the Queen of Heaven."[7] In other words, Mary is a multifaceted character who is remembered in different ways and who lives on as recalled and recounted.

Beverly is on all accounts an exemplary teacher, one whose scholarly strengths permeate her teaching. I have interviewed some of her former students, and they all agree, in almost the same words, that as a teacher she is very professional, clear, and demanding—repeat demanding—as well as gracious, friendly, and generous with her time, certainly to her own students but to others as well. Beverly is a devoted undergrad instructor but is especially rigorous with her grad students. She expects them to be professionals and trains them to that end. They respond by working hard, because they do not want to disappoint her. She listens carefully to her students, even responding to some of their questions in her publications. But she is not all niceness. She is a tough grader and is notorious for her intolerance of tardiness and jargon. If a student comes late—well, it doesn't happen again. If she catches a whiff of jargon in student essays, she writes things like "ugh" or "barf" in the margins.

---

[5] Ibid., 63.
[6] Beverly Roberts Gaventa, *Mary: Glimpses of the Mother of Jesus,* Studies on Personalities of the New Testament (Columbia: University of South Carolina Press, 1995; Minneapolis: Fortress, 1999).
[7] Ibid., 2.

When I asked her what her greatest accomplishment was, she immediately answered, "my students." She has received many honors, including two honorary doctorates, but she mentioned only one—the festschrift in her honor, *The Unrelenting God: God's Action in Scripture; Essays in Honor of Beverly Roberts Gaventa*, ed. David J. Downs and Matthew L. Skinner (Grand Rapids: Eerdmans, 2013). This volume is so important to her because it came from her students and colleagues.

I have come to know Beverly over the past year, both directly and through the eyes of some of her colleagues and students, who helped me prepare these remarks. I immediately came to like and respect her as a person and a scholar. I am honored to present Beverly Roberts Gaventa to give the Society of Biblical Literature Presidential Address for 2016, "Reading Romans 13 with Simone Weil: Toward a More Generous Hermeneutic."

# Reading Romans 13 with Simone Weil: Toward a More Generous Hermeneutic

BEVERLY ROBERTS GAVENTA
Beverly_Gaventa@baylor.edu
Baylor University, Waco, TX 76798

Simone Weil's interpretation of the *Iliad* as a "poem of force" has resonances with Rom 1–8, reinforcing the question of how Rom 13:1–7 belongs in the larger argument of Romans. Seeking a generous reading of 13:1–7 along the lines of the generosity Weil extends to the *Iliad*, I first take Pharaoh as an example of Paul's understanding of the relationship between God and human rulers and then propose that Paul's treatment of human rulers coheres with his refusal in this letter to reify lines between "insider" and "outsider." I conclude with a reflection on the need for generosity in scholarly research and pedagogy.

---

Among the few works French intellectual Simone Weil published during her lifetime is a 1941 essay entitled "The *Iliad*, or The Poem of Force."[1] The title of the essay contains the thesis *in nuce*, which is that the "true hero, the true subject matter, the center of the *Iliad* is force." She goes on to define force, or perhaps we would say "power," as "that which makes a thing" of whoever is subjected to it.[2]

---

I am grateful to John M. G. Barclay, Alexandra R. Brown, Alan Jacobs, and Jonathan A. Linebaugh for conversations about this project. I wish also to thank Susan G. Eastman, Jacqueline E. Lapsley, Carey Newman, and Mikeal C. Parsons for their constructive comments on earlier versions. And I benefitted significantly from the research assistance of Ryan Harker and Natalie Webb.

[1] The original, "L'*Ilise*, ou le Poème de la Force," was published in *Cahiers du Sud*, December 1940 and January 1941. It was later translated by Mary McCarthy and published in English as *The Iliad, or the Poem of Force* (Wallingford, PA: Pendle Hill, 1956). More recently James P. Holoka has published a critical edition containing the French, an English translation and notes, and the Greek text of those portions of the *Iliad* quoted by Weil (*Simone Weil's The* Iliad *or The Poem of Force: A Critical Edition* [New York: Lang, 2003]). All references to Weil's essay and to the *Iliad* itself are to the Holoka edition. I am grateful to my colleague Jonathan Tran for introducing me to this remarkable essay and to Eric O. Springsted for corresponding with me about Simone Weil and for his own work on Weil.

[2] Holoka, *Simone Weil's The* Iliad, 45.

7

That "force" is crucial to the *Iliad* is, in one sense, so obvious a statement as to be trivial. The literal use of force runs throughout the epic and results in death time and again. Noble chariot drivers lie on the ground "much dearer to the vultures than to their wives" (*Il.* 11.162).³ As the wife of Hector orders water heated for his return from battle, the poet comments:

> ... She knew not that far indeed from warm baths
> Achilles' arm had beaten him down. (*Il.* 22.445–446)⁴

Death is only the first, most obvious instance of force that Weil finds in the *Iliad*. There is also force that does not kill immediately but already transforms human beings into "things." The human being is turned "into stone," when the warrior who is "disarmed and exposed … becomes a corpse before being touched." This is force "which does not kill, or rather does not kill just yet. It will kill for a certainty, or it will kill perhaps, or it may merely hang over the being it can kill at any instant."⁵ Even when force does not kill, it paralyzes.

Force can make human beings into things off the battlefield as well. Agamemnon insists that he will not return the young woman he has taken as a prize of war:

> I will not return her. Before that old age will seize her,
> in my home, in Argos, far from her homeland,
> moving along the loom and lying in my bed. (*Il.* 1.29–31)⁶

Later a mother anticipates her child's future of "degrading labor, toiling under the eyes of a pitiless master" (*Il.* 24.733–734).⁷ This is, Weil comments, life "that death has frozen long before putting an end to it."⁸ "The mind [of the victim of force] should devise a way out but has lost all ability to devise such a thing. It is occupied entirely in violating itself." "Each morning [the soul] amputates itself of all aspiration."⁹

Force devastates its victims without pity, but the wielder of force scarcely escapes. Force may crush the victim, but it intoxicates those who possess it, leading each side to regard the other as so alien as to belong to a different species.¹⁰ As a result, force destroys everyone: both those who use force and those who endure it are destroyed.¹¹ Yet no one actually "possesses" force in the *Iliad*, since every agent is subject to it at one time or another. Weil describes war in the *Iliad* as having the movement of a seesaw.¹² The work breathes throughout such "an extraordinary

---

³ Ibid.
⁴ Ibid., 46.
⁵ Ibid.
⁶ Ibid., 49.
⁷ Ibid.
⁸ Ibid.
⁹ Ibid., 59.
¹⁰ Ibid., 51, 53.
¹¹ Ibid., 61.
¹² Ibid., 54.

sense of equity" between the Greeks and the Trojans that readers are scarcely aware the author is Greek, observes Weil.[13]

This remarkable essay is cast entirely as a study of the *Iliad*. Although it was published in 1941, there is not a single reference to Adolf Hitler, to Germany, or to the French occupation. At the same time, every line bears the marks of the period in which it was written. Weil might well have cited the apostle Paul, "Whatever was written earlier was written to instruct us" (Rom 15:4).

This brief summary provides a glimpse into the depths of Weil's essay. Classicists have occasionally quibbled with it, noting its neglect of the poem's preoccupations with glory, with heroism, with the gods.[14] Nonetheless, many readers have recognized the intensity of Weil's insight into the *Iliad*, indeed into human life.[15] To read Weil's essay is to be caught up in the destructive folly of the human quest for power.

Turning from Simone Weil's essay on the *Iliad* to Rom 13:1–7 creates the readerly equivalent of whiplash. In that notorious passage, Paul admonishes followers of Christ in Rome to be ordered under human authority. He contends that such authority as exists does so by virtue of God's action. The rulers, presumably both local and empirewide, are installed for the doing of good.[16] They are meant to reward the good, and they bear the sword in order to punish wrongdoing. Resisting them is tantamount to resisting God.

Little imagination is required to conclude that Simone Weil would be mystified, even repulsed, by such naïve assertions about governing authorities. It does not appear that she ever commented on Rom 13; her references to Paul's letters are infrequent. She would be mystified by Rom 13 because her own argument about the *Iliad* resonates deeply with Paul's understanding of the human situation prior to the apocalypse of God's saving power in Jesus Christ articulated elsewhere in Romans. Sentences in her essay read like paraphrases of sections in Romans.

To begin with, in Rom 1–8 Sin is a central character, as force is for the *Iliad*. Paul employs the noun ἁμαρτία and related words eighty-one times in the

---

[13] Ibid., 66. The complicated question of Homeric "authorship" does not come into Weil's discussion.

[14] See Sheila Murnaghan, review of *Simone Weil's The Iliad or The Poem of Force: A Critical Edition*, by James P. Holoka, *Bryn Mawr Classical Review* 2004.02.24, as well as John Mackinnon's response (*Bryn Mawr Classical Review* 2004.02.37).

[15] See esp. Eric O. Springsted, *Simone Weil and the Suffering of Love* (Cambridge: Cowley, 1986), 17–35.

[16] Earlier proposals that Paul refers both to human authorities and to angelic powers behind them have been abandoned (see Martin Dibelius, *Die Geisterwelt im Glauben des Paulus* [Göttingen: Vandenhoeck & Ruprecht, 1909], 200; Oscar Cullmann, *The State in the New Testament* [New York: Scribner's Sons, 1956], 50–70, 95–114). More recently, Mark D. Nanos has argued that Paul has in mind synagogue authorities to whom gentile Christians should be subordinate (*The Mystery of Romans: The Jewish Context of Paul's Letter* [Minneapolis: Fortress, 1996], 289–336), but that view also has not been widely adopted.

undisputed letters, and sixty of those instances occur in Romans.[17] The role of ἁμαρτία is understated at the outset of the letter (1:18–32), but in 3:9 Paul discloses its power over all people, both Jew and gentile. Later, as the argument spirals down, the power known as Sin comes into view: it entered the world through Adam and made its way among all people (5:12).[18] It increased in power; it ruled over all people (5:20–21). Its power was such that it could bend even God's holy, right, and good law to its purposes, deceiving the infamous "I" of Rom 7, producing enslavement and even death.[19] Here Weil's comments about the relentless character of force seem lifted from Paul's prose.

Less directly, Sin in Romans, like force in the *Iliad*, is also delusional. Throughout the *Iliad*, the wielder of force imagines that each conflict will be the controlling event, that their side in the conflict will prevail. In Romans also, Sin produces delusion, explicitly so in Rom 7 ("Sin deceived me," 7:11) and implicitly earlier in the letter, where the "worthless mind" results in evil (1:28).

In addition, as force in the *Iliad* produces death, both physical death and death-within-physical life, Sin in Romans produces death of several sorts. The warrior in the *Iliad* lives with death as he waits for the final blow; the warrior's family lives with death as it also waits for the final blow. Sin's intertwining with Death is similarly relentless and inescapable in Rom 5. Sin and Death rule the whole of human life, producing what Paul finally terms a body possessed by Death (7:24).[20]

When this resonance between Weil's essay and Paul's letter to the Romans is recognized, the challenge of Rom 13:1–7 comes into focus. The problem is not only that the text conflicts with our observations of actual governments across the ages. The text seems to conflict with the first half of the letter as regards the human being, who is subject to the power of Sin, who does not do what is right, who may desire the good but produces evil.[21] At least as this passage is usually read, there is in

---

[17] See the discussion in my *Our Mother Saint Paul* (Louisville: Westminster John Knox, 2007), 125–36, 198–200.

[18] The notion of the argument of Romans as a spiral comes from Leander E. Keck, "What Makes Romans Tick?," in *Romans*, vol. 3 of *Pauline Theology*, ed. David M. Hay and E. Elizabeth Johnson (Minneapolis: Fortress, 1995), 25.

[19] On the role of Sin in Rom 7, see esp. Paul W. Meyer, "The Worm at the Core of the Apple," in *The Word in This World: Essays in New Testament Exegesis and Theology*, ed. John T. Carroll (Louisville: Westminster John Knox, 2004), 57–77.

[20] On Simone Weil and Romans, see further my "The Powers and Paul's Letter to the Romans," in *Life amid the Principalities: Identifying, Understanding, and Engaging Created, Fallen, and Disarmed Powers Today*, ed. Michael Root and James J. Buckley (Eugene, OR: Cascade, 2016), 24–37.

[21] Neil Elliott finds a similar tension in Romans, but he restricts the tension to Paul's comments about the "pagan world" in 1:18–32 and his more optimistic view of governing authorities in 13:1–7 ("Romans 13:1–7 in the Context of Imperial Propaganda," in *Paul and Empire: Religion and Power in Roman Imperial Society*, ed. Richard A. Horsley [Harrisburg, PA: Trinity Press International, 1997], 184–204, here 186–87).

Rom 13 an expectation that rulers both know and serve the good, an expectation hard to reconcile with Paul's insistence in chapters 1–8 that all human beings are subject to the power of Sin. To state my question directly: how is it possible for the person who wrote Rom 1–8 also to have written Rom 13:1–7?[22]

For the most part, despite the complex history of interpreting this passage, the dominant questions have concerned the relationship between the passage and the actual experience of government, and those questions have been with us almost as long as the text itself.[23] Beginning with Origen (*Comm. Rom.* 9.27), commentators have attempted to moderate Paul's words by balancing them with Acts 5:29 ("We must obey God rather than humans") and insisting that Paul does not have in mind those who persecute the church.[24] To be sure, Paul's remarks have also many defenders—including notably Queen Elizabeth I,[25] the apartheid regime in South

---

[22] The question is heuristic, although some scholars have argued that the passage is an interpolation, including Ernst Barnikol, "Der nichtpaulinische Ursprung der absoluten Obrigkeitsbejahrung von Römer 13,1–7," in *Studien zum Neuen Testament und zur Patristik: Erich Klostermann zum 90. Geburtstag dargebracht*, TUGAL 77 (Berlin: Akademie, 1961), 65–133; J. Kallas, "Romans XIII.1–7: An Interpolation," *NTS* 11 (1965): 365–74; J. C. O'Neill, *Paul's Letter to the Romans*, PNTC (Baltimore: Penguin, 1975), 207–9; Winsome Munro, "Romans 13:1–7: Apartheid's Last Biblical Refuge," *BTB* 20 (1990): 161–68; and William O. Walker Jr., *Interpolations in the Pauline Letters*, JSNTSup 213 (London: Sheffield Academic, 2001), 221–31. In the judgment of most scholars, the lack of manuscript evidence has undermined this argument.

[23] For surveys of the history of interpretation, see K. H. Schelkle, "Staat und Kirche in der patristischen Auslegung von Rm 13:1–7," *ZNW* 44 (1952): 223–36; Fritzhermann Keienburg, *Die Geschichte der Auslegung von Römer 13,1–7* (Gelsenkirchen: W. Hertel, 1956); Valentin Zsifkovits, *Der Staatsgedanke nach Paulus in Röm 13, 1–7 mit Besonderer Berücksichtigung der Umwelt und der patristischen Auslegung*, WBTh 7 (Vienna: Herder, 1964); Ulrich Wilckens, *Der Brief an die Römer 12–16*, EKKNT 6.3 (Zurich: Benziger, 1982), 43–74; Bernard Lategan, "Reading Romans 13 in a South African Context," in *The Reader and Beyond: Theory and Practice in South African Reception Studies* (Pretoria: Human Sciences Research Council, 1992), 115–33; Lategan, "Romans 13:1–7: A Review of Post-1989 Readings," *Scriptura* 110 (2012): 259–72; Mitsuo Miyata, *Authority and Obedience: Romans 13:1–7 in Modern Japan*, trans. Gregory Vanderbilt, AmUStTR 294 (New York: Lang, 2009); Ron Cassidy, "The Politicization of Paul: Romans 13:1–7 in Recent Discussion," *ExpTim* 121 (2010): 383–89; Stefan Krauter, *Studien zu Röm 13,1–7: Paulus und der politische Diskurs der neronischen Zeit*, WUNT 243 (Tübingen: Mohr Siebeck, 2009), 4–54; Víctor Manuel Morales Vásquez, *Contours of a Biblical Reception Theory: Studies in the Rezeptionsgeschichte of Romans 13.1–7* (Göttingen: V&R Unipress, 2012).

[24] J. Patout Burns Jr. notes that all the early commentators tried to nuance Paul's comments on similar grounds (*Romans: Interpreted by Early Christian Commentators*, The Church's Bible [Grand Rapids: Eerdmans, 2012], 314). Interestingly, Irenaeus draws on Rom 13:1–7 as evidence that Satan lied when he claimed to control all the earth's kingdoms (in Matt 4:8–9 and Luke 4:5–7; *Haer.* 5.24).

[25] "Sententiae," in *Elizabeth I: Translations 1544–89*, ed. Janel Mueller and Joshua Scodel (Chicago: University of Chicago Press, 2009), 331–94.

Africa,[26] and the late Supreme Court justice Antonin Scalia[27]—but many readers of Paul have sought to correct, to limit, to situate his comments, often by recourse to other parts of the New Testament or to some reconstruction of the historical situation.[28] Yet, as Leander Keck astutely observed, this passage has been "more successful in thwarting a convincing explanation than the experts" have been in finding one.[29]

What we need is another entry point or angle of vision. I think that alternative comes if we turn my own question around. Instead of asking how it is possible for the person who wrote Rom 1–8 to write 13:1–7, what happens if we read 13:1–7 *with the assumption that it does continue Paul's argument*? How does 13:1–7 read differently if we look for its coherence with what has preceded? That strategy

---

[26] Allan A. Boesak, "What Belongs to Caesar? Once Again Romans 13," in *When Prayer Makes News*, ed. Allan A. Boesak and Charles Villa-Vicencio (Philadelphia: Westminster, 1986), 138–57; Jan Botha, *Subject to Whose Authority? Multiple Readings of Romans 13*, ESEC 4 (Atlanta: Scholars Press, 1993), xv–xvi. See also Lategan, "Romans 13:1–7: A Review of Post-1989 Readings," 259–72.

[27] Antonin Scalia, "God's Justice and Ours," *First Things* 123 (2002): 17–21; see further the discussion by Jay Twomey, "Antonin Scalia v. Jonathan Edwards: Romans 13 and the American Theology of State," in *Sacred Tropes: Tanakh, New Testament, and Qur'an as Literature and Culture*, ed. Roberta Sterman Sabbath; BibInt 98 (Leiden: Brill, 2009), 493–503.

[28] Some commentators limit the effect of Rom 13 by pairing it with Acts 5:29, as Origen did (e.g., Albert Barnes, *Notes on the New Testament, Explanatory and Practical: Romans* [1834; repr., Grand Rapids: Baker, 1949], 290–91); others connect Rom 13 with Matt 22:21 (e.g., the anonymous commentator known as Ambrosiaster, *Comm. Rom.* 13.1–7 [CSEL 81.1:417.23–423.14]; Augustine, *Commentary on Statements in the Letter to the Romans*, 64–66 [CSEL 84:44.12–47.3]). Karl Barth declared the importance for Christians of reading both Rom 13 and Rev 13 ("The Christian Community in the Midst of Political Change," in *Against the Stream: Shorter Post-War Writings, 1946–52*, ed. Ronald Gregor Smith [New York: Philosophical Library, 1954], 51–124, here 97). At least as early as Erasmus, interpreters also appeal to some element in the historical setting (Erasmus, *Annotations on Romans*, ed. Robert D. Sider, trans. John B. Payne et al., vol. 56 of *Collected Works of Erasmus* [Toronto: University of Toronto Press, 1994], 347). Calvin opines that this passages seems "to have been forced on [Paul] by some great necessity," involving those "restless spirits" who identify Christ's kingdom with the abolition of "earthly powers" (*The Epistles of Paul the Apostle to the Romans and to the Thessalonians*, trans. Ross Mackenzie [Grand Rapids: Eerdmans, 1960], 280). A more recent strategy for muting Rom 13 is to find in it the use of either irony (as in T. L. Carter, "The Irony of Romans 13," *NovT* 46 [2004]: 209–28) or a "hidden transcript" (as in James R. Harrison, *Paul and the Imperial Authorities at Thessalonica and Rome: A Study in the Conflict of Ideology*, WUNT 273 [Tübingen: Mohr Siebeck 2011], 313).

[29] Leander E. Keck, *Romans*, ANTC (Nashville: Abingdon, 2005), 325. Also of note is Ernst Käsemann's comment regarding the discussion of Rom 13: "It is becoming continually more difficult to know what is really happening in the guerilla warfare of the specialists, in which there are so many shots fired and so few targets hit, so many issues confused and so few decided" ("Principles of the Interpretation of Romans 13," in *New Testament Questions of Today* [Philadelphia: Fortress, 1969], 196–216, here 207).

produces a more generous reading of Rom 13, one that shares some of Weil's generosity toward the *Iliad*.

I. ROMANS 13:1–7: PRELIMINARY OBSERVATIONS

Two preliminary observations about Rom 13 are in order. First, Paul writes Rom 13—indeed Paul writes this entire section of the letter (12:1–15:13)—to strengthen what he perceives to be fragile communities in Rome. I take that statement to be uncontroversial. Regardless of whether Paul knows of particular difficulties in Rome, he hopes to promote the corporate good, as is evident as early as his introduction of the "body of Christ" image in chapter 12 and as late as his admonitions about welcoming one another in chapter 15. We can reasonably assume, then, that 13:1–7 also intends to protect believing communities from harm of some sort. The specific warnings in vv. 3–4 about the consequences of wrongdoing reinforce that observation.[30] In addition, the repeated commands related to the paying of taxes, located at the end of the passage, may suggest, as a number of scholars have argued, that Paul fears specifically the involvement of Roman believers in some form of tax revolt. Concerned about the potentially harmful result of such behavior, Paul urges the communities to respect the authorities and pay their taxes.[31]

A second preliminary observation follows: Paul is not addressing the authorities themselves, whether those authorities are thought to be the local magistrates or the emperor. Paul is addressing communities of believers about their own attitudes and conduct, which means that treating this passage under headings such as "Paul's doctrine of the state" misleads from the outset. Paul is not instructing authorities regarding their roles; neither is he licensing their activities.[32] This is not

---

[30] So also Botha, *Subject to Whose Authority?*, 210. At just this point, commentators sometimes affirm the need for "order" in human relations, as when Erasmus claims that, even if rulers are evil, "order is still good" (*Romans*, 347), or when James D. G. Dunn comments on the "normal circumstances of social order" (*Romans 9–16*, WBC 38B [Dallas: Word, 1988], 771–72). Such endorsements of order as a social good overlook the fact that what one group regards as "order" may well be experienced by others as repression. See the impassioned discussion of William Stringfellow in *Conscience and Obedience: The Politics of Romans 13 and Revelation 13 in Light of the Second Coming* (Waco, TX: Word, 1978), 35–63.

[31] Among others, see Johannes Friedrich, Wolfgang Pöhlmann, and Peter Stuhlmacher, "Zur historischen Situation und Intention von Röm 13,1–7," *ZTK* 73 (1976): 131–66.

[32] This is a point that Dietrich Bonhoeffer made several times in his discussion of Rom 13:1–7 in his *Discipleship*, vol. 4 of *Dietrich Bonhoeffer Works*, ed. Wayne Whitson Floyd Jr., trans. Martin Kuske and Ilse Tödt (Minneapolis: Fortress, 1996), 240–42. Here I differ with Robert Jewett, who contends that Paul is appealing to officials or their workers in the congregations in Rome because he needs their support for the Spanish mission (*Romans: A Commentary*, Hermeneia [Minneapolis: Fortress, 2007], 788, 790, 792, 794).

an essay on rulership, which means that it differs substantially from *De Clementia*, the roughly contemporaneous treatise by Seneca.[33] Queen Elizabeth I implicitly recognizes this point when she begins her "sentences" on rulers by quoting from Rom 13 but immediately follows Rom 13 with quotations from a variety of sources warning about unwise and unjust rulers. She takes our passage as directed to her subjects, yet for her own instruction and formation as a ruler she looks elsewhere.[34]

Those observations about the audience and the goal of Rom 13 are reasonable; they keep us safe at the shallow end of the interpretive pool. They may convince, but they scarcely satisfy. Is there something more to be learned from Romans that may prove instructive?

## II. Romans 13:1–7 Read Generously

### *The Authority Known as Pharaoh*

To address the preceding question, we first need to linger over Paul's statements about the authorities. Although he does not address the authorities themselves, he does write to the Romans *regarding* them. Following the initial call for submission comes the crucial assertion: "There is no authority except the authority that comes from God, and those that exist have been set up by God" (13:1). Paul reinforces this introductory remark when he goes on to assert that resisting authority amounts to resisting God (13:2) and later still that the authority is the διάκονος (agent) of God, God's λειτουργός (servant, 13:4).

This text has no parallels elsewhere in the Pauline corpus. To the contrary, the hardship catalogue of 2 Cor 11 indicates that Paul's own encounters with some authorities have scarcely provided evidence of their goodwill: imprisonment, beatings, and stonings are not tokens of goodwill.[35] Indeed, when Paul identifies the "rulers of this age" in 1 Cor 2:8 as those who unwittingly put to death the Lord of glory, he is far from associating them with the doing of good and the prevention of evil.[36]

Although 13:1–7 has no parallel elsewhere in Paul's letters, there is nonetheless a specific human authority standing close by in Romans, namely, the Egyptian ruler Pharaoh, who makes a brief appearance in Rom 9.[37] As Paul recasts the

---

[33] See the discussion in Harrison, *Paul and the Imperial Authorities*, 292–99; as well as *De Clementia*, ed. and trans. Susanna Braund (Oxford: Oxford University Press, 2009). Her discussion of the genre of *De Clementia* is particularly instructive (17–23).

[34] Note the shift in the *Sententiae* at sentence 10.

[35] As Steve Friesen observed, "When [Paul] composed these lines he had scars on his body from unjust floggings by rulers and authorities" ("Government, NT," *NIDB* 2:641).

[36] The "rulers of this age" may well refer to those suprahuman powers who are in conflict with God, but they make use of earthly "rulers" to accomplish the death of Jesus.

[37] Studies of Rom 13 neglect the connection to Pharaoh, apart from passing references by

history of Israel, he first narrates God's creation of Israel through the birth of Isaac, then God's unilateral choice of Jacob over Esau, a choice God makes before the twins are born and on the basis of nothing whatever except God's will.[38] In response to the possible claim that God acts unjustly, Paul cites Exod 33:19: God has mercy on whom God pleases.

Paul next turns not to yet another of Israel's ancestors brought into being by God but to the quintessential outsider, the "ruler" Pharaoh. Drawing again from Exodus, Paul cites selectively from God's words to Pharaoh:

> I have raised you up for this reason—so that I might demonstrate in you my power and so that my name might be spread throughout the whole earth. (Rom 9:17; Exod 9:16 LXX)

In keeping with the peculiar history he has been tracing, Paul emphasizes God's role in putting this particular authority in place. Where the LXX reads "you have been kept" (διετηρήθης), Paul reads "I raised you up" (ἐξήγειρά σε).[39] The Exodus account suggests that Pharaoh exists already and God preserves him, but that is not how Paul reads the story. In Paul's presentation, God brings Pharaoh into existence. Further, by contrast with the Exodus account, which says both that God hardened Pharaoh's heart (4:21; 7:3; 10:1, 27; 14:4, 8) and that Pharaoh hardened his own heart (9:34–35, 13:15; see also 1 Sam 6:6),[40] here the action is entirely one-sided. Paul observes: "[God] has mercy on whom he wills to have mercy, and God hardens the one whom he hardens."

In addition, God puts Pharaoh in place for a reason: "that I might make my power known through you and that my name might be spread through the whole earth." Instead of the LXX's ἰσχύς, or "strength," Paul uses δύναμις, or "power." That minor change may be unintentional, although the use of δύναμις coheres nicely with Paul's emphasis from the beginning of the letter on God's power, which is reflected in the resurrection of Jesus from the dead ἐν δυνάμει (1:3) as well as in Paul's identification of the gospel with God's salvific δύναμις (1:16). Pharaoh is an

---

Keck (*Romans,* 316) and Frank J. Matera (*Romans,* Paideia [Grand Rapids: Baker Academic, 2010], 303).

[38] On the divine initiative in this passage, see John M. G. Barclay, "Unnerving Grace: Approaching Romans 9–11 from the Wisdom of Solomon," in *Between Gospel and Election: Explorations in the Interpretation of Romans 9–11,* ed. Florian Wilk and J. Ross Wagner, WUNT 257 (Tübingen: Mohr Siebeck, 2010), 91–109; and, in the same volume, Gaventa, "On the Calling-into-Being of Israel: Romans 9:6–29," 255–69.

[39] For careful explication of these differences, see J. Ross Wagner, *Heralds of the Good News: Isaiah and Paul "In Concert" in the Letter to the Romans,* NovTSup 101 (Leiden: Brill, 2002), 55–56.

[40] As Dennis Olson observes, "The plague stories suggest a complex interplay of divine sovereignty and human responsibility, not entirely reducible to either divine determinism or human freedom" ("Exodus," in *Theological Bible Commentary,* ed. Gail R. O'Day and David L. Petersen [Louisville: Westminster John Knox, 2010], 27–40, here 30).

implement of God's power, which Paul would clearly identify with the "good." Paul treats Pharaoh as an agent of God for the good.

None of this has anything to do with Pharaoh's capacity or disposition or intention to do what is good. Paul pays no attention whatever to Pharaoh's own inclinations, or to his actions. They are not important.

Other interpreters of Pharaoh read the story differently. The author of 3 Maccabees faults Pharaoh for his arrogant treatment of Israel, making no reference to God's hardening (2:6, 6:4). In his *Life of Moses*, Philo introduces Pharaoh as one "whose soul from his earliest years was weighed down with the pride of many generations" (*Mos.* 1.88 [Colson, LCL]); later Philo suggests that God only wanted to instruct Pharaoh and his people, not to destroy them (*Mos.* 1.110, 134). Similarly, Josephus's retelling in the *Antiquities* consistently faults Pharaoh for his unwillingness to yield to God's demand for the Israelites' release (*Ant.* 2.293–310). None of these texts remembers God's hardening of Pharaoh's heart. Paul flips the script at this point, making Pharaoh into God's passive instrument.

Paul's use of one authority, Pharaoh, helps us see Rom 13 more clearly. First, to say that authority is established by God is to make a statement about God rather than about any authority or ruler. Pharaoh is of no interest to Paul apart from God's action in him, and the same would be said of the authorities in Rom 13. Taking Pharaoh into account confirms that, when Paul identifies the authorities as established by God, Paul is not exalting the authorities—he is instead putting them in their place, their subordinate place.[41]

Second, informed by Paul's remarks about Pharaoh, we see that asserting the role of the authorities "for the good" need not mean either that they themselves will the good or that they will do the good.[42] To be sure, they are said to reward the good and to punish evil, but they do so *as* God's servants.

Further, Paul's identification of the human ruler as God's διάκονος or God's λειτουργός says nothing of the rightness of their own intentions or actions. The designations set them out only in relation to God. This point does not pertain only to rulers; it pertains also to Paul himself. Paul has a διακονία (11:13) and calls himself a λειτουργός of Jesus Christ (15:16), but that says nothing about his qualifications for the position. Elsewhere he makes clear that his curriculum vitae is more liability than asset, when he reports in 1 Cor 15 that he was unfit to be an apostle because he resisted the gospel itself. Neither does being a διάκονος or a λειτουργός mean that the governing authorities will do what is right.[43] It is most unfortunate

---

[41] As N. T. Wright observes, 13:1–7 "constitutes a severe demotion of arrogant and self-divinizing rulers" ("Romans," *NIB* 10:395–770, here 719).

[42] On different grounds, Dorothea H. Bertschmann draws a similar conclusion in *Bowing before Christ—Nodding to the State? Reading Paul Politically with Oliver O'Donovan and John Howard Yoder*, LNTS 502 (London: Bloomsbury T&T Clark, 2014), 161.

[43] In 2 Cor 11:23, Paul refers to the "superapostles" with whom he is in conflict as Christ's διάκονοι.

if we bring to these terms an expectation that puts the persons so identified out of the way of wrongdoing or divine judgment, whether the terms are used in reference to Christian leaders or to those outside the community of believers.[44] These designations indicate not character but relationship.

### The Authorities, the Powers, and the Community

Although Pharaoh is the only human being in Romans who might be identified as a ruler or an authority, other powers are at work in the letter, powers that turn out to be far more dangerous. Most obviously, the powers are those of Sin and Death, mentioned above by way of noting the resonance between Simone Weil's reading of the *Iliad* and the early chapters of Romans. While Paul does not refer to Sin and Death as ἐξουσίαι or as ἄρχοντες, the terms found in Rom 13, he does speak of them in kingly terms. In 5:17, he announces that Death "ruled as a king" (ἐβασίλευσεν) and in 5:21 that Sin ruled as a king through Death (again ἐβασίλευσεν). They even ruled over Jesus, as is implied when Paul declares in 6:9–10 that Death no longer "lords it over" him (κυριεύει). The language of ruling and lording it over continues in 6:12–14, where Paul warns the Romans against submitting again to Sin. Sin and Death have been defeated in the case of Jesus Christ, but their destruction is not yet complete.

Sin and Death are not the only powers at work in the world. The end of Rom 8 acknowledges that suprahuman powers continue to assault the "us," that they attempt to separate the "us" from the love of God. They manifest themselves in tribulation, hardship, persecution, famine, nakedness, peril, and the sword, experiences brought on by the powers named in 8:38–39. They persist in their attack, but they will not prove able to separate humanity from its lord.[45] Paul's highly rhetorical list of the powers is matched by his words of assurance: Who will separate "us"? "We" are "supervictors."[46] Paul returns to this assurance at the close of the letter: "God will quickly put Satan under your feet" (16:20). In other words, God has real enemies, even "rival rulers," as Dorothea Bertschmann ably puts it,[47] but they are not human authorities or powers.[48] The enemies of God may use human rulers,

---

[44] In one of his several treatments of this passage, Karl Barth commented that the work of the state "can be perverted just as the divine service of the Church itself is not exempt from the possibility of perversion" ("The Christian Community and the Civil Community," in *Community, State, and Church: Three Essays* [Garden City, NY: Doubleday, 1960], 149–89, here 157).

[45] On the powers, see further my "Neither Height nor Depth: Discerning the Cosmology of Romans," *SJT* 64 (2011): 265–78.

[46] Jewett, *Romans*, 531.

[47] Bertschmann, *Bowing before Christ*, 140.

[48] This conclusion seems consistent with John M. G. Barclay's observation that Paul "does not assign [the Roman empire] to one side or the other of the battle lines created by the Christ-event" ("Why the Roman Empire Was Insignificant to Paul," in *Pauline Churches and Diaspora Jews*, WUNT 275 [Tübingen: Mohr Siebeck, 2011], 363–87, here 385).

especially in the case of the reference to the "sword" in 8:35 (see also 1 Cor 2:8), but the human rulers are not identified as God's enemies.

This treatment of the powers of Sin and Death, as well as the other powers invoked at the end of Rom 8, puts 13:1–7 into perspective. The human rulers are not God's enemies; instead, they are God's agents (however good or bad they may be). Their role is limited to God's intent, as we saw in the case of Pharaoh.

What does this conclusion about human rulers suggest about their relationship to the assemblies of believers? The context of Paul's remark, especially in chapter 12, could suggest that human powers are both outside of and even at enmity with the community. Paul opens that chapter by reprising the analogy of the body from 1 Cor 12 to urge that members of the community employ their charismatic gifts in service of one another. At some length he itemizes desirable features of the community and warns against arrogance. Then he admonishes against repaying evil for evil and urges the members of the community to seek peace with all people (vv. 17–18). They are not to seek revenge, even in the case of an enemy.

In the middle of chapter 12, it *appears* that Paul turns from addressing concerns about life in the congregations to addressing relationships between believers and outsiders. It is by no means clear, however, where—or even whether—such a shift between inside and outside occurs. Does the warning against returning evil for evil refer to evildoers outside the community or inside? Are the ones who persecute the community believers or unbelievers? Perhaps Paul has in mind those human rulers who work evil against believers, but he may be anticipating chapter 14 and the conflict over dietary practices, so that all of chapter 12 addresses matters internal to the congregations.

My aim is not to propose a solution to this thicket of exegetical dilemmas just now. My aim is simply to notice the difficulty of discerning the lines between inside and outside in Rom 12; they are less clear than is often assumed. In fact, the firm drawing of such lines between the inside and the outside is inimical to the letter.[49] That observation returns us to the human rulers: Paul does not present them as members of the community, but he also does not treat them as enemies.[50] This refusal to reify the human authorities—even the authorities—as "others," to classify them as "enemies," is not an incidental point; it goes to the muscle and bone of this letter.

At crucial moments in the letter, Paul introduces "othering" discourse only to undermine it. One of those moments comes at the beginning of chapter 2. The second half of Rom 1 notoriously attacks "those people,"[51] the ones who refused to

---

[49] As Paul W. Meyer astutely observed, "The whole of [Romans] is but a single massive argument against the conventional uses of this distinction [between 'godly' and 'ungodly']" ("Worm at the Core of the Apple," 65).

[50] On different grounds, Karl Barth comes to similar conclusions regarding Rom 13:1–7 in *The Doctrine of God*, vol. 2.2 of *Church Dogmatics* (London: T&T Clark, 1957), 720–21.

[51] So also Bernadette J. Brooten, *Love between Women: Early Christian Responses to Female*

acknowledge God and who were, in turn, handed over. Paul invites his Roman auditors to join in the castigation of those "others," the gentiles who rejected God, who participated in idolatry, and whose rebellion produced a laundry list of misconduct, sexual and otherwise. In 2:1 he pivots sharply, calling out the "you" who dares to judge that "other person" while engaging in the same deeds. Paul deliberately generalizes on gentile conduct in order to entice the auditors to imagine themselves as separate from, indeed above, the "they," only to reveal that "you" and "they" are both liable to judgment. (Recall Weil's observation about the way in which force invites its temporary possessor and its victim to regard themselves as so different from one another as to be part of another species.)

A similar move takes place in Rom 11. In his lengthy argument about God's faithfulness to Israel, Paul encourages his Roman auditors to conclude that the subject matter of his discourse is the "problem" of "Israel's unbelief." This is especially the case in Rom 10: Israel has tripped on a stumbling stone that God put in place. Israel has acted out of ignorance: they have zeal for God, but they lack knowledge. They should know better, as there have been divinely commissioned preachers. They do not know, however, despite the fact that God has continually stretched out God's hands to receive them. Throughout chapter 10, Paul speaks of Israel as a whole, as a single unit.

Paul glances at gentiles from time to time, yet Rom 9–11 generally has to do with Israel, and with Israel *in the third person*. Paul speaks of himself at several crucial junctures, when he makes himself both a brother to Israel and a supplicant on "their" behalf. The audience is led to understand Israel—*some* or perhaps *most* of Israel—as the problem. Then comes 11:13, "I am speaking to you gentiles." With verse 18 he becomes more emphatic. To paraphrase: "Do not boast! God has brought you in, and God can take you out again." "I am speaking to you gentiles." In 11:26–28, Paul announces the conclusion of this long consideration of God's dealings with Israel: "all Israel will be saved." The point is extended in 11:32: "God has confined all to disobedience that God might have mercy on all." Many questions plague any reading of Rom 9–11; my point at present is a simple one: what appears to be a discourse "othering" Israel becomes a discourse confronting gentiles with their arrogance.

Romans 13 differs from both 2:1 and 11:13. Paul does not treat the authorities as part and parcel of the "we" of faith. Paul also declines to make them into enemies. Making the powers that be into enemies, understanding them as enemies, risks exactly the problems so well articulated by Simone Weil. Even to warn about them is to build them up as "other," which undermines the letter's persistent claim that God has acted for all people.

---

*Homoeroticism,* Chicago Series on Sexuality, History, and Society (Chicago: University of Chicago Press, 1996), 230.

## III. Conclusion

Anyone who tackles Rom 13:1–7 should drink deeply from the bottle labeled "modesty," yet I think I have made a contribution here. Paul writes Rom 13 to protect fragile Roman communities from the harm that might ensue should they reject or rebel against human authority, but his argument is not simply pragmatic. These authorities do not belong to themselves. They are meant for good, and they should be treated as such. To say that the rulers are set up by God is no more than what Paul says of Pharaoh in Rom 9, and to say that they are God's "servants" does not mean that they always do the good (any more than God's servants in the congregations always do the good).

Paul is not concerned only to protect these fragile communities from human rulers. He may also fear the harm they do to themselves, if they make the "rulers" into the enemy. They are not the "us" of the letter, but they are also not other than "us." I think that reading coheres with chapter 12. In common with the rhetorical turns we find in 2:1 and 11:13, Rom 13 prevents (or hopes to prevent) believers from misunderstanding the relationship between "we" and "they." Paul's protection of the community from outsiders—from the human rulers—is also protection from themselves, from their own proclivity to hubris, to making more of their own judgments than is appropriate. He will go on at the end of the chapter to characterize this as the obligation to love, an obligation made more urgent by the gospel with its declaration that God's saving action is at hand (13:11–14).[52]

This is admittedly a generous reading of Rom 13. For me as for many others, the words and especially the reception history of the chapter make such generosity difficult to come by, and I chose the passage for tonight to test the possibility of a generous reading. It is the kind of reading Simone Weil undertakes when she reads the *Iliad*.[53] She lingers over the vast, sprawling *poiēsis* that is the *Iliad* and finds in it something other than an epic account of honor, something other than a story of the gods' dealings with humanity, something other than a glorification of warfare.

---

[52] On the relationship between 13:1–7 and 13:11–14, see esp. Luise Schottroff, "'Give to Caesar What Belongs to Caesar and to God What Belongs to God': A Theological Response of the Early Christian Church to Its Social and Political Environment," in *The Love of Enemy and Nonretaliation in the New Testament*, ed. Willard M. Swartley, Studies in Peace and Scripture 3 (Louisville: Westminster John Knox, 1992), 223–57.

[53] Weil was not always a generous reader of texts. Her comments about the Hebrew Bible in particular and ancient Judaism in general have generated considerable criticism. For a judicious and illuminating review of Weil's life in its historical context, see Maud S. Mandel, "Simone Weil (1909–1943)," in *Makers of Jewish Modernity: Thinkers, Artists, Leaders, and the World They Made*, ed. Jacques Picard et al. (Princeton: Princeton University Press, 2016), 466–79. On the idiosyncrasy of Weil's thought, see David Tracy, "Simone Weil: The Impossible," in *The Christian Platonism of Simone Weil*, ed. E. Jane Doering and Eric O. Springsted (Notre Dame, IN: University of Notre Dame Press, 2004), 229–41.

Reading generously, she probes the *Iliad* on the assumption that there is a unified angle of vision, that the text has integrity, even that she has something to learn from it. Elsewhere she writes that giving genuine attention to something or someone begins with the question, "What are you going through?"[54] That is to say, it begins with a patient attempt to hear the other person or, in this case, the other text. Her work on the *Iliad* exemplifies that engagement, and my reading of Rom 13 hopes to follow her lead.

## Afterword

Romans 13:1–7 will continue to be difficult, especially for those of us who have responsibilities to communities of faith. I think the interpretation I have offered has some traction for Christians, and I will explore that possibility elsewhere. For our guild, my conclusion moves in another direction.

I offer this reading of a single text by way of suggesting that we need to make room for a more generous hermeneutic in our scholarly discourse, one that reads both the primary texts and the work of other scholars as we ourselves wish to be read. This is a deeply unfashionable proposal, that we should approach the texts we study with generosity. It is also susceptible of misunderstanding, as if addressed only to certain scholars and certain approaches. That is in no way my intent.

This risky plea is needed for the flourishing of our discipline, our students, even our larger society. We have become exceedingly good at what some refer to as "interrogating" our texts. Our hermeneutic of suspicion works very well indeed. Much instructive work has emerged in recent decades as a result of those reading strategies. They are not the only strategies we need, however. We also need to ask, to borrow from Weil, "What is this text going through?" What does this text wish to say? What might it contribute to our understanding of the world and its workings?

This is the argument of a committed reader. I have skin in the game. As a scholarly community, we all have something at stake, whatever our religious commitments may or may not be. To be highly pragmatic and self-interested, if the only words our students hear from us about our texts are words of distrust and suspicion, it is hard to see a long-term future for our enterprise.

My concern extends beyond the hermeneutic we use for ancient texts. I am even more concerned by the way in which we characterize and too often caricature one another's work. When we find ourselves dismissing out of hand approaches that are different from our own, what are we contributing to our discipline? If we denigrate those scholars who participate in a particular faith tradition, or if we

---

[54] Simone Weil, *Waiting for God*, trans. Emma Craufurd (New York: Harper & Row, 1951), 115.

denigrate those who participate in no faith tradition, what has become of our own generosity? When a scholar's character is impugned in print or in social media, and when we in turn find such blood sport amusing, we offer an example to our students that none of us wants to set. Nothing good comes from these practices, as our public life is making achingly clear.

Simone Weil's reading of the *Iliad* may offer one starting point in the direction of a more generous hermeneutic. She leaves to others questions of sources, critiques of the characters, warnings of the dangers of warfare; instead, she asks this vast text what it is "going through." It is a simple question, naïve really, yet it has the potential to draw us into a constructive, generous listening and learning, both of our texts and of one another. That is what I have treasured about this Society for decades, and what I hope will obtain for decades to come.

# Joseph the Infiltrator, Jacob the Conqueror? Reexamining the Hyksos–Hebrew Correlation

RONALD A. GEOBEY
geobeyr@tcd.ie
Meath, Ireland

The anachronisms in the story of Exodus have long complicated claims to its historicity, yet some of the "usual suspects" endure. Scholarly tradition has generally argued that the expulsion of the so-called Hyksos rulers of Egypt in the sixteenth century BCE was the foundation for the Israelite cultural memory of liberation from Egypt. With the shift in biblical scholarship toward the Persian and Hellenistic periods regarding the crystallization of the biblical texts, scholarship has moved away from extrabiblical correlations pertaining to more ancient contexts. This trend, combined with locating earliest Israel within a generic "Canaanite" milieu, has led to the devaluation of the place of Egypt in discussions of Israel's origins. In this article, I reexamine the "Hebrew–Hyksos" correlation, with a view to defending the great antiquity of memories of interaction with Egypt that were appropriated by developing Israel.

In the context of the ongoing debate surrounding the historicity of the exodus, there are a number of potentially relevant ethnic groups and historical figures that go unmentioned in the Bible. Whether their absence is due to a lack of awareness or to a dismissal of their relevance on the part of the biblical authors, we cannot be entirely sure. I will argue, however, that they cannot simply be overlooked in a discussion that should first and foremost be concerned with the memories preserved in the Bible of Israel's interaction with Egypt (as well as all things deemed Egyptian) that lie behind the crystallization of the written accounts of the same.

Proponents of the historicity of the transition between Genesis and Exodus—the Joseph story—often see the so-called Hyksos rulers of the Egyptian Fifteenth Dynasty (ca. 1640–1550[1]) as ethnically analogous to the earliest "Israelites." This

[1] J. Maxwell Miller and John H. Hayes, *A History of Ancient Israel and Judah*, 2nd ed. (Louisville: Westminster John Knox, 2006), 46. Lester L. Grabbe gives a date of 1650–1550 (*Ancient Israel: What Do We Know and How Do We Know It?* [London: T&T Clark, 2007], 62–63),

view places the "sons of Israel" (or "Hebrews") in Egypt in preparation for the exodus and views their subsequent migration from Egypt as a memory of the Egyptian expulsion of the Hyksos recorded in ancient texts.[2]

## I. Manetho via Josephus

The "Hyksos–Hebrew" correlation entered discussion on the origins of Israel as early as the first century CE and possibly earlier.[3] Flavius Josephus dealt with these "shepherd kings" rather comfortably. In his view, their alignment with his ancestors (*C. Ap.* 1.74) upheld his claims of antiquity for the Jews.[4] Despite

---

while Amihai Mazar locates the Fifteenth Dynasty a century later ("The Patriarchs, Exodus, and Conquest Narratives in Light of Archaeology," in Israel Finkelstein and Amihai Mazar, *The Quest for the Historical Israel: Debating Archaeology and the History of Early Israel; Invited Lectures Delivered at the Sixth Biennial Colloquium of the International Institute for Secular Humanistic Judaism, Detroit, October 2005*, ed. Brian B. Schmidt, ABS 17 [Atlanta: Society of Biblical Literature, 2007], 57–65, here 58). Based on the textual and archaeological evidence, David O'Connor is more precise, suggesting circa 1648–1540 ("The Hyksos Period in Egypt," in *The Hyksos: New Historical and Archaeological Perspectives*, ed. Eliezer D. Oren, University Museum Monograph 96 [Philadelphia: University Museum, University of Pennsylvania, 1997], 45–67, here 48–56). Marc Van de Mieroop states that the mid-seventeenth century saw the Hyksos ruling some of "a number of principalities" into which Egypt had been split (*A History of the Ancient Near East ca. 3000–323 BC* [Oxford: Blackwell, 2007], 131–32). Israel Finkelstein dates the expulsion of the Hyksos to the sixteenth century ("Patriarchs, Exodus, Conquest: Fact or Fiction?" in Finkelstein and Mazar, *Quest for the Historical Israel*, 41–65, here 52).

[2] See, e.g., *ANET*, 233–34, relating to the participation of Ah-mose, captain of a vessel on the Nile, in the campaigns to defeat the Hyksos. For a collection of texts contemporary to and following the expulsion, see James B. Pritchard, ed., *The Ancient Near East: An Anthology of Texts and Pictures* (Princeton: Princeton University Press, 2011), 226–28; and Donald B. Redford, "Textual Sources for the Hyksos Period," in Oren, *Hyksos*, 11–20.

[3] Josephus's polemic (*Contra Apionem*, passim) against the details of Jewish origins in Manetho's *Aegyptiaca* is the oldest surviving testament to the existence of the *Aegyptiaca*. Without contemporary texts confirming the contents of Manetho's writings, we cannot be completely confident that Josephus was recounting precisely what Manetho wrote. Donald B. Redford suggests a fourth-century BCE date for Manetho's sources and even goes so far as to say that Josephus's citations constitute "a fortunately surviving excerpt quoted *in extenso*" (*Egypt, Canaan, and Israel in Ancient Times* [Princeton: Princeton University Press, 1992], 98–101). For a discussion of the veracity of both Manetho's words and Josephus's citations, see Lucia Raspe, who locates Josephus's polemic within a wider context of Greco-Roman attacks (and Jewish apologetics) on the antiquity and credibility of Judaism ("Manetho on the Exodus: A Reappraisal," *JSQ* 5 [1998]: 124–55). See also John Van Seters, *The Hyksos: A New Investigation* (New Haven: Yale University Press, 1966), 121–26.

[4] Raspe cautions against concluding that Manetho actually referred to the Jews in his original text (which we do not have); thus, the alignment of the Hyksos with the Jews may be attributable to Josephus himself ("Manetho on the Exodus," 124–25). I believe that the truth lies somewhere

"quoting" Manetho's understanding of the word *Hycsos* (where *Hyc* meant "king" and *Sos* meant "shepherd"; *C. Ap.* 1.82), Josephus favors his own interpretation, "captive shepherds" (with *Hyc* now meaning "shepherds"), for the sake of accommodating the biblical narrative or "ancient history" (*C. Ap.* 1.83), the context within which Manetho's account is assessed.[5] The term *Hyksos*, however, is best understood as "foreign ruler" or "ruler of foreign lands" and was in use as early as the Middle Kingdom (ca. 2040–1650 BCE) to designate "foreign princes," primarily Amorites or Canaanites.[6] As such, it was not a term associated with a specific ethnic group that descended into Egypt from Syria-Palestine; rather, it was a common designation that came to be used to describe this new regime—and not the people—so that their status as outsiders was maintained.[7] The term *Asiatics* appears to

---

between the two positions: Josephus dealt with a widely held belief that Manetho—whose "history" likely bore authority (see Zuleika Rodgers, "Introduction," in *Making History: Josephus and Historical Method*, ed. Zuleika Rodgers, JSJSup 110 [Leiden: Brill, 2006], 1–22, here 11)—had actually referred to the Jews. Using Manetho's account of the Hyksos as Josephus does allows the latter to maintain the biblical claim that the "Israel" that came up out of Egypt was previously in the land. His assertion, however, that this "deliverance" "preceded the siege of Troy almost a thousand years" (*C. Ap.* 1.104) is decidedly anachronistic.

[5] Josephus cites "another copy" as his reasoning behind this alternative translation (*C. Ap.* 1.83), without clarifying the reference. Is this another copy of Manetho or just another Egyptian history? Josephus deals with this interpretation of Jewish history within the constraints of the biblical text (and, of course, his own *Antiquities*), so it is acknowledged that the Israelites came from another country into Egypt (*C. Ap.* 1.104, 223; cf. *Ant.* 2.177). Amid what appears to be the intellectual jostling for the greater antiquity of one's nation (or simply the need to tackle established opinions regarding the antiquity of the Jews), Josephus has to (in this matter, at least) "stick to the script." In arguing for a specifically Roman audience for the *Bellum Judaicum*, Steve Mason relates an awareness of "presumed" information—that which is excluded—to matters of audience identification ("Of Audience and Meaning: Reading Josephus' *Bellum Judaicum* in the Context of a Flavian Audience," in *Josephus and Jewish History in Flavian Rome and Beyond*, ed. Joseph Sievers and Gaia Lembi, JSJSup 104 [Leiden: Brill, 2005], 71–100, here 91–95).

[6] Eliezer D. Oren, "The Hyksos Enigma: Introductory Overview," in Oren, *Hyksos*, xix–xxviii, here xxi. *Hyksos* is a Greek translation of the Egyptian term *Heqau-Khasut*, meaning "rulers of foreign lands" (Manfred Bietak, "The Center of Hyksos Rule: Avaris (Tell el-Dab'a)," in Oren, *Hyksos*, 87–139, here 113). Transliterations of the Egyptian term vary, but the phonetics are relatively consistent. Bietak also concludes that "an Amorite attribution of the dynasty is far more likely [than Hurrian]" (ibid.). Cf. Van Seters, who notes the use of ꜥꜣmw (for *Amurrite*) to "designate the foreign population of Egypt in the Hyksos period" (*Hyksos*, 188). See also E. A. Speiser, "Ethnic Movement in the Near East in the Second Millennium B.C.: The Hurrians and Their Connections with the Habiru and the Hyksos," *AASOR* 13 (1931): 13–54, here 34, http://dx.doi.org/10.2307/3768469.

[7] Van Seters, *Hyksos*, 187; Redford, *Egypt, Canaan, and Israel*, 100; Grabbe, *Ancient Israel*, 45. The titles of the Hyksos rulers conflated Egyptian royal epithets with Semitic personal names. In presenting the Hyksos onomasticon, Redford suggests that the condition of the script may be testament to the scribes' lack of knowledge of these "strange names" ("Textual Sources for the Hyksos Period," 20–21).

have been used for people who had descended into Egypt and either took control after a long period of gradual settlement or in the wake of a sudden invasion, but "Asiatics," "foreign rulers," and "princes of Retenu" are terms that maintain a sense of cultural disconnection and are contrary to a theory of integration or acculturation over a long period of time. The evidence shows that these people, although "Egyptianized" in their behavior, did not see themselves as Egyptian.[8] In this light, Manetho's (or Josephus's) claim that the Hyksos dominated Egypt for 511 years (*C. Ap.* 1.84) is drawn either from a misunderstanding of Manetho's schematic king list or from a need to accommodate biblical chronology.[9] It would appear, rather, that little more than a century passed between the ascension of the first Hyksos king (of which there were six) and the expulsion of their dynasty.[10]

There were Asiatics in Egypt before the Hyksos came to power (the archaeological record has preserved architecture at Tell ed-Dab'a/Avaris similar to that in Syria-Palestine); the people living there from the late Twelfth Dynasty onward were likely "subordinate to Egyptian officials."[11] The Thirteenth Dynasty palace constructed above the earlier Canaanite settlement at Tell ed-Dab'a appears to have accommodated officials favoring Asian burial customs.[12] Yet, despite another

---

[8] Redford, *Egypt, Canaan, and Israel*, 102. Notably, Retenu is used of the tribal chief under whom Sinuhe finds success in a foreign (Canaanite) land. The Tale of Sinuhe seems concerned with asserting that there is "no place like home," and Retenu, therefore, may be a generic appellation to refer to people in the Syria-Palestine region. In other words, the story is not about where Sinuhe has been but where he has come from and, ultimately, where he will return to. See further *The Tale of Sinuhe and Other Ancient Egyptian Poems 1940–1640 B.C.*, trans. R. B. Parkinson, Oxford World's Classics (London: Oxford University Press, 1999); also Garrett Galvin, *Egypt as a Place of Refuge*, FAT 2/51 (Tübingen: Mohr Siebeck, 2011), 21–22. The Tale is echoed both in the story of Joseph's success in Egypt and in that of Moses in Midian, but the sentiment of belonging is quite poignantly expressed in Jacob's request that his bones be brought up out of Egypt (Gen 47:29–30).

[9] Redford notes the difficult situation in which Manetho found himself (*Egypt, Canaan, and Israel*, 107). The Egyptian priest listed "Shepherd Kings" for two dynasties (Sixteenth and Seventeenth) following Hyksos dominance, rather than presenting them as contemporaneous regimes; thus he was forced to expand his linear scheme. The Sixteenth and Seventeenth Dynasties—although O'Connor is unaware of a reason to distinguish the two—ruled from Thebes and produced the kings (Kamose and Ahmose, respectively) who besieged and eventually expelled the Hyksos from Avaris ("Hyksos Period in Egypt," 45, 52).

[10] One hundred eight years, according to the Turin Canon of Kings (O'Connor, "Hyksos Period in Egypt," 48). See also Grabbe, *Ancient Israel*, 45; Redford, *Egypt, Canaan, and Israel*, 107; and Bietak, "Center of Hyksos Rule," 114.

[11] O'Connor, "Hyksos Period in Egypt," 56. For a discussion of the Canaanite settlement in the late Twelfth Dynasty (ca. 1800 BCE), see Bietak, "Center of Hyksos Rule," 97–100; James K. Hoffmeier, *Israel in Egypt: The Evidence for the Authenticity of the Exodus Tradition* (New York: Oxford University Press, 1996), 63–65; and Israel Finkelstein and Neil Asher Silberman, *The Bible Unearthed: Archaeology's New Vision of Ancient Israel and the Origin of Its Sacred Texts* (New York: Touchstone, 2002), 55.

[12] Bietak, "Center of Hyksos Rule," 103.

Canaanite settlement atop the abandoned palace, Bietak argues against seeing the officials at Tell ed-Dab'a at this time as the predecessors of the Hyksos.[13] This settlement ended abruptly with an epidemic of what appears to have been bubonic plague (Egyptian texts refer to it as the "Asian disease"), and the Fourteenth Dynasty seems to have begun following this, with Nehesy taking control.[14] Nehesy appears to have been Egyptian, but Asian cultural influence played a significant role in his court. His short reign was ended by a "local Asian dynasty," following which the Fifteenth (Hyksos) Dynasty came to power.[15]

## II. Was Joseph a Hyksos Scout?

When all of this information is aligned with the biblical story of Joseph's rise to power and the descent of Jacob (Israel) and his family into Egypt (including the subsequent migration of the Hebrews), the temptation to assign at least some level of credence to the biblical narrative is wholly understandable. We should ask, however, whether the Joseph story truly reflects memories of the Hyksos rise to power, given the suggestion that it corresponds to an authentic Israelite memory of "a Semitic prince in the Egyptian court."[16] Some immediate problems from a biblical point of view are that Joseph's rise to power occurred prior to the descent of his father and brothers into Egypt and that there is no corresponding (extrabiblical) evidence for a Hyksos boy being sold into slavery and ending up in Egypt as a precursor for an invasion thirteen years later (which would certainly have made a wonderfully romanticized narrative reminiscent of the impetus for the Greek war against Troy).[17] The biblical text also maintains that Joseph's position, taking charge of "all the land of Egypt" (Gen 41:41), still kept him second to Pharaoh with regard

---

[13] See also Hoffmeier, *Israel in Egypt*, 63. This does not mean, of course, that the presence of Semitic peoples did not facilitate the peaceful infiltration of the Hyksos rulers at the site, considering that there is no evidence of military conquest at the crucial transitional phase (ibid., 65).

[14] Bietak, "Center of Hyksos Rule," 105, 108; O'Connor, "Hyksos Period in Egypt," 56.

[15] Bietak, "Center of Hyksos Rule," 109.

[16] Mazar maintains that such a story may "contain kernels of old traditions ... rooted in second-millennium B.C.E. realia" ("Patriarchs, Exodus, and Conquest Narratives," 58–59). See also Ronald Hendel, "The Exodus in Biblical Memory," *JBL* 120 (2001): 601–22, here 607, http://dx.doi.org/10.2307/3268262; and Redford, *Egypt, Canaan, and Israel*, 422–29. An early alignment of the Joseph story with the historical realia of New Kingdom Egypt can be found in Jozef Vergote's *Joseph en Égypte: Genèse chap. 37–50 à la lumière des études égyptologiques récentes*, OBL 3 (Leuven: Publications Universitaires, 1959). Vergote reaffirmed his conclusions in his "'Joseph en Égypte': 25 Ans Après," in *Pharaonic Egypt: The Bible and Christianity*, ed. Sarah Israelit-Groll (Jerusalem: Magnes, 1985), 289–306.

[17] Joseph is seventeen when he is sold by his brothers (Gen 37:2) and thirty when he is elevated to his high position under Pharaoh (Gen 41:46).

to the throne (Gen 41:40b).¹⁸ We are dealing, then, with a solely administrative position, not one to be aligned with Hyksos rule.¹⁹ The evidence for so-called Asian influence in the administration of the Thirteenth Dynasty palace at Tell ed-Dab'a (above) tells us that the Egyptian elite permitted the elevation of Asiatics to such high positions. The argument that the memory of one specific (named) ancestor held such a position survived for over a thousand years is something of a stretch, for the archaeological record shows how relatively commonplace the appointment could be.²⁰ Even those who argue that this memory has some historical value must concede that the details are so skewed as to render the alignment tentative at best.

In addition, there is the matter of ethnic differentiation; if Joseph's rise to power corresponds to that of the Hyksos, why should we read his subservience to a clearly Egyptian king in the biblical narrative as corresponding to Hyksos administrative control if Joseph were ethnically identical to the ruling elite, as the Hyksos alignment would require? Instead, the Bible is clear that the Egyptians "abhorred" shepherds (in Gen 46:34 the Hebrew term translated as "shepherds," רעה צאן, shares no phonetic affinity with *Hyksos*). This strange statement might be part of the biblical writers' construction of the Egyptian perspective on the Hebrews in preparation for the shift away from Egyptian favor that opens Exodus.²¹ Equally, it might belong to a context of sociopolitical debates regarding immigration or a more specific sociological clash between urban life and nomadic culture.²² In either case, distinction—even cultural polarity—informs the biblical text, and, despite the hints that Joseph had been Egyptianized during his time in Egypt (Gen 41:42–43, 45; 42:23;

---

¹⁸ Genesis 44:18 should be read in the context of a supplicant addressing an obvious superior. What the brothers see is a man as powerful as Pharaoh (and what would they know of the Egyptian court?), but the comparison is part of the ideology of the tale. As for Gen 45:8, while Joseph appears magnanimous in his forgiveness, he also appears to be enjoying his success in front of his brothers, since now he can provide everything for them in the role of a father (see esp. 45:13).

¹⁹ BDB suggests that the noun שַׁלִּיט in Gen 42:6, "having mastery, domineering," is a later substitution for an earlier (unknown) word. The NJPS renders "vizier," while the NRSV has "governor." Still, it is a leap to read Joseph's position as a memory among Canaanites of the "political primacy" of an ancestor (so Redford, *Egypt, Canaan, and Israel*, 412).

²⁰ Hoffmeier, *Israel in Egypt*, 93–95.

²¹ The new king of Exod 1 either does not know anything about the favor shown to the ancestor(s) of the Hebrew slave population, as suggested by the text, or simply does not care.

²² Grabbe notes that the first half of the second millennium was a time of great urbanization (esp. in Palestine), with urban populations outnumbering those in rural settings (*Ancient Israel*, 40). F. V. Greifenhagen reads Joseph's instruction to his family in the context of ensuring Israel's separation from the Egyptians by settling his family outside Egypt proper (i.e., in Goshen), although he goes on to deal with the problem arising from Pharaoh's instructing the family to settle "in the land of Rameses," "in the land of Egypt" (Gen 47:11, directly contradicting 47:6, but cf. Hoffmeier, *Israel in Egypt*, 121), and the subsequent ideological dichotomy of separation and assimilation (*Egypt on the Pentateuch's Ideological Map: Constructing Biblical Israel's Identity*, JSOTSup 361 [Sheffield: Sheffield Academic, 2002], 39–40).

43:32),[23] the Bible clearly maintains his status as a son of Israel, with Jacob asserting his patriarchal dominance from his deathbed. Even the children of Joseph, "adopted" by Jacob prior to bestowing his blessing upon them (Gen 48:5–6), bear Hebrew names (Gen 41:51–52), despite the apparent dissociation from Joseph's homeland implied by the accompanying etymologies of the names (and this also despite Joseph's inability to understand Hebrew in Gen 42:23!).[24] With all of this going on, there is no hint in the biblical text that the family envisage a rise to power over Egypt or that Joseph heralds the coming invasion of Jacob and his family/army. Subservience and indebtedness to Pharaoh as a result of his permitting their immigration and settlement cannot correspond to an influx of Asiatics who rise to dominate Egypt for a little more than a century prior to their expulsion, especially when the biblical text would have the "sons of Israel" living (or "dwelling"; Hebrew ישב) in Egypt for either 400 (Gen 15:13) or 430 years (Exod 12:40) prior to the exodus.[25]

Other anachronisms arise in Gen 41:43 and 46:29 concerning the use of chariots, with Pharaoh using one in the earlier verse and Joseph in the latter. If the Hyksos first introduced the chariot into Egypt[26] and its appearance in the archaeological record is to be aligned with the Hyksos invasion, what are we to make of

---

[23] Note especially Gen 42:23, in which Joseph understands the conversation between his brothers only through an interpreter.

[24] Many factors stand out as contradictory, highlighting for the most part the irrelevance of many details of a story concerned less with historical fact than with didactic theology (YHWH will provide and bring success in a foreign land). The problems with the chronology of the story can sometimes elicit humor, especially when we note that Joseph's sons were born "before the years of famine" (Gen 41:50), Jacob spent seventeen years in Egypt before he died (Gen 47:28)—counting them at least from the time the famine began—and Joseph's sons, at least in their late teens, sat on poor old Jacob's knees (Gen 48:12) as he blessed them (he was 147 years old; Gen 47:28)!

[25] Granted, the maintenance of cultural dissociation from the Hyksos on the part of the Egyptian sources is also found in Exodus, not only in casting Egypt as the "other" but also in Egypt separating itself from the "people of the sons of Israel" (Exod 1:9), a clear affirmation of ethnic distinction. Ascribing this act of separation to the nameless pharaoh (representative of Egypt) lends weight to having Israel as a nation recognized—and thus legitimized—by another (nation). Pharaoh's "rhetoric of differentiation" (Greifenhagen, *Egypt on the Pentateuch's Ideological Map*, 53) sets the stage for enslaving the entire עם בני ישראל.

[26] See James K. Hoffmeier, "Observations on the Evolving Chariot Wheel in the 18th Dynasty," *JARCE* 13 (1976): 43–45, here 43, http://dx.doi.org/10.2307/40001117; also Hoffmeier, *Israel in Egypt*, 64. Redford notes the "fixation" on the use of the chariot with regard to arguing for the Indo-European origins of the Hyksos (*Egypt, Canaan, and Israel*, 99). Cf. Van Seters, who argues that "the question of chariots ... ought to be dropped from the discussion" (*Hyksos*, 185). Paula Wapnish states, "The role of Asiatics ... in the introduction of the horse and [chariot] to Egypt is still an open question" ("Middle Bronze Equid Burials at Tell Jemmeh and a Reexamination of a Purportedly 'Hyksos' Practice," in Oren, *Hyksos*, 335–67, here 355). Despite a number of equine burials in Egypt during the Hyksos period (ibid.), however, it appears (at present) that there were no chariots buried with them.

Pharaoh using one prior to Joseph's appointment and, more importantly, prior to Jacob's descent into Egypt? Of course, the biblical writers may simply have had no memory of an Egypt without the chariot, so it is possible that all we are seeing here is a vision of Egypt from the time of the composition of the Joseph story (a solution that can apply to practically everything in the story, for there is no prohibition on using names and places long after either cease to exist).

### III. The Plot Thickens

The anachronisms are not restricted to the biblical account, for even Josephus's defense of the antiquity of his people with regard to the Hyksos expulsion and the exodus leaves much to be desired when it comes to relative chronology. It serves the chronological pattern of Josephus's argument to have the Hyksos (kings) establishing Jerusalem following their expulsion from Egypt, but letters from the Amarna period (fourteenth century BCE) mention a king of Jerusalem with a Hurrian name (Abdi-Heba), a king clearly subordinate to Egyptian rule.[27] If it was the Hurrian expansion into and dominance of Syria-Palestine that had initially created these Hyksos in forcing some of the indigenous people southward into Egypt (see below), it is highly unlikely that the Hyksos are to be equated with the progenitors of Israel in terms of their establishing Jerusalem if we encounter a Hurrian king in the city some two centuries later. This would suggest a hiatus in Israelite control of Jerusalem (or Israelite descent from Hurrians) to which no ancient source refers and to which archaeology bears no witness.

There are also some hints in Josephus's "Manethonian" quotations that the latter's historical retrospective was chronologically askew. Take, for example, the account of Salatis, the first of the Hyksos kings, foreseeing the ascendancy of the Assyrians (*C. Ap.* 1.77). To which period of Assyrian expansionism was Manetho referring? Assyrian military power in the thirteenth century was significant, but it

---

[27] EA 286 and EA 287 both have Abdi-Heba stating that it was the Egyptian king who put him in power in Jerusalem. See further Miller and Hayes, *History of Ancient Israel and Judah*, 32–35; Grabbe, *Ancient Israel*, 42–43; Redford, *Egypt, Canaan, and Israel*, 270; and Finkelstein and Silberman, *Bible Unearthed*, 238–40. The Jebusite rulers of Jerusalem, to whom the Bible refers (Josh 15:8, 63; 2 Sam 5:6; 1 Chr 11:4), are likely to have descended from the Hurrians. See Peter C. Craigie "Ugarit, Canaan, and Israel," Tyndale Biblical Archaeology Lecture 1982, *TynBul* 34 (1983): 145–67, esp. 160–61; and Billie Jean Collins, "The Bible, the Hittites and the Construction of the Other," in *Tabularia Hethaeorum: Hethitologische Beiträge; Silvin Košak zum 65. Geburtstag*, ed. Detlev Groddek and Maria Zorman, Dresdner Beiträge zur Hethitologie 25 (Wiesbaden: Harrassowitz, 2007), 153–61, esp. 154–55. Notably the Bible claims that the "Judahites" lived alongside the Jebusites in Jerusalem, because the Judahites could not remove the former inhabitants from the city (Josh 15:63). This would not correspond to the descendants of Jacob leaving Egypt and attacking Jerusalem or with the Hyksos *establishing* Jerusalem.

had not brought them near Egypt.[28] Not until the seventh century were there successful incursions that saw first Memphis and then Thebes fall into Assyrian hands.[29] Clearly, any reference by Manetho to the Assyrians disrupts the chronology with regard to the Hyksos and "casts suspicion on the whole account."[30] In a similar vein, a lot of the sacrilegious activity Manetho uses to demonize the Hyksos—directed (for Josephus, at least) at the Jews—belongs at the earliest to a fifth-century BCE context in the wake of the Persian conquest of Egypt.[31]

It would appear that the alignment of the stories of Jacob and Joseph with either the Hyksos invasion of or expulsion from Egypt entered the debate as a result of Josephus's having to deal with the details of Manetho's *Aegyptiaca*, which appeared to both corroborate and contradict some elements of the biblical narrative. If we are to take Josephus's Manethonian quotations as genuine, however, the direction of dependence should be considered. For example, Manetho's claims that "those who came from Jerusalem ... got the granaries of Egypt into their possession and perpetrated many of the most horrid actions there" (*C. Ap.* 1.275) brings to mind Joseph's control of the grain rations and the ensuing debt slavery of the Egyptians (Gen 47:19). In addition to the confusion arising from attempting to align the biblical chronology with Manetho's clearly muddled attack on Jewish "history" (in the Bible, Joseph was put in charge of the grain before Jacob and his family came down to Egypt; and, according to Manetho, the Hyksos had been expelled, had established Jerusalem, and then came back down to Egypt!), Manetho's account appears suspiciously dependent on the biblical narrative in his reconstruction of this period in Egyptian history, almost as if he purposely sought to find a period in Egyptian history best suited to his cause. We might imagine Josephus's frustration with the whole matter, but his acceptance of the veracity of Hyksos ancestors for the Jews may rightly be called a "fortunate mistake" for our understanding of the great antiquity of memories of the Hyksos, as will become clear.[32]

## IV. KING JACOB?

Josephus appears unaware of the most interesting onomastic correlation regarding the name of one of the kings of this period. Scarabs bearing the name

---

[28] Van de Mieroop, *History of the Ancient Near East*, 181–82.
[29] Ibid., 256–57.
[30] Van Seters, *Hyksos*, 123.
[31] Raspe suggests that the tensions between the Jewish soldiers at the Elephantine garrison and their Egyptian counterparts belong to this context ("Manetho on the Exodus," 153). Redford notes the successive invasions of Egypt by the Assyrians, Babylonians, and Persians that likely influenced Manetho's historical reflection (*Egypt, Canaan, and Israel*, 101). See also Van Seters, *Hyksos*, 123.
[32] See A. H. Sayce, "The Hyksos in Egypt," *JR* 21 (1903): 347–55, here 349, http://dx.doi.org/10.1086/473176.

*Yaʿaqob-har* have been found in Egypt, Nubia, and Palestine, a fact that would surely prompt proponents of the Hebrew–Hyksos alignment to boast of triumph.[33] Granted, we should not be so swift to dismiss as mere coincidence the presence of a king in Egypt during the Second Intermediate (Hyksos) period bearing among his royal titles the (West) Semitic name Jacob. When combined with all of the pertinent data, the memory preserved in the Bible of a Semitic Jacob in Egypt could be for some a keystone to the historicity of the presence there of the family of "Israel," but it could just as easily be argued that Jacob is a name so common in Syria-Palestine that to find correlations with the Hyksos is presumptuous.[34] One name does not settle an argument, and, by comparison, the name Joseph is not found in the Egyptian record at this time. The biblical writers not only show no awareness of a Jacob assuming power in Egypt—they do not even imagine such a thing.

As for the presence of people from Syria-Palestine—or Asiatics—in Egypt at times that would accommodate the Hyksos correlation, there is so much evidence of the presence of such people in Egypt throughout the second millennium that the thread of certainty unravels.[35] The Syro-Palestinian population of Tell ed-Dabʿa (Avaris) may have maintained its distance from its Egyptian neighbors,[36] but this does not necessarily fit with the segregation of the Israelite (Hebrew) population in Exodus, particularly when the Hyksos were in political ascendancy and the Hebrews were slaves of the regime. Further, the Hyksos dominated the region for

---

[33] Redford, *Egypt, Canaan, and Israel*, 108, 113. Other titles with the personal name Jacob appear in the record, but this form, belonging to a king and containing the epithet meaning "mountain deity," is of particular interest for anyone concerned with the origins of Israel's adoption of the deity YHWH (Redford, "Textual Sources for the Hyksos Period," 20). Interestingly, Bietak suggests that the name "*Yʿakub-Haddu*," found on a scarab in a grave near Haifa and thought to predate the Hyksos period, should be seen as "an actual forerunner of the Hyksos dynasty" ("Center of Hyksos Rule," 115). If this is the case, then a Semitic ruler named Jacob in Egypt might mark the latter stages of the Fourteenth Dynasty. See K. S. B. Ryholt, *The Political Situation in Egypt during the Second Intermediate Period, c. 1800–1550 B.C.* (Copenhagen: Museum Tusculanum Press, 1997), 96. Redford, on the other hand, positions "*Yaʿkob-har*" as the second (Hyksos) king of the Fifteenth Dynasty, attaching the *praenomen* Meruserre (*Egypt, Canaan, and Israel*, 110), which Ryholt uses to argue against such a conclusion. While Redford aligns Sheshy with Manetho's Salitis, Jan Assmann begins his king list with Salitis and follows with "Sheshi," placing "*Yaqub-Har*" third in Dynasty Fifteen (*The Mind of Egypt: History and Meaning in the Time of the Pharaohs*, trans. Andrew Jenkins [Cambridge: Harvard University Press, 2003], 480).

[34] It is also interesting to consider whether proponents of a Jacob–Hyksos alignment would have tried to identify historical contexts for any of the other eponymous ancestors of ethnic groups and nations featured in Genesis. To dismiss these ancestors as mere personifications of those groups, nations, or cultural norms would conflict with their own refusal to see the biblical Jacob in this light.

[35] Mazar, "Patriarchs, Exodus, and Conquest Narratives," 59; Grabbe, *Ancient Israel*, 85; Hoffmeier, *Israel in Egypt*, 52–68.

[36] Redford, *Egypt, Canaan, and Israel*, 115.

over a century, while the Hebrews "sojourned" as a subservient people for over four hundred years! The main problem with the alignment of Joseph's rise to power, Jacob's descent into Egypt, and the Hebrews' sojourn with the Hyksos period comes from the Bible itself—and not only from a chronological point of view. The writers simply do not recall this period as proponents of the alignment would prefer. That does not mean, of course, that we cannot see in the biblical text some faint echoes of the Hyksos period. Regardless of the chain of events that led to the Hyksos era and the Fifteenth Dynasty, forces external to Egypt clearly rose to ascendancy.[37] Yet, in light of the Bible's obvious demonization of Egypt from Exodus onward, should we not expect awareness on the part of the biblical writers of this dominance over their (perceived) ancient archenemy if indeed we are dealing with the earliest components of "Israel"? Is it really likely that the biblical writers, clearly concerned with telling stories of ethnic differentiation and great antiquity, would not eulogize both a conquest over the greatest enemy their ancestors had ever known and their dominance over that land that their ancient neighbors (not to mention the historical and archaeological record) could verify? Instead, there is no evidence of Egypt being defeated by "Israel" or the "Hebrews," while Hyksos dominance over Egypt actually occurred, could be verified, and was preserved in the record by the Egyptians themselves.[38] Is this not a story great enough to claim for one's ancestors? Why would the people who became Israel not shout this tale from the rooftops for generations to come? Perhaps a detailed preservation of the expulsion would have meant an embarrassing or shameful end to a triumphant tale, but the biblical writers appear to have had no problem justifying other "shameful ends" when it came to reflecting on the conquests of Samaria and Jerusalem. If the expulsion of the Hyksos was in fact the wholesale expulsion of a population of Hebrews, the skilled writers of the

---

[37] Redford advocates for the "invasion" hypothesis (*Egypt, Canaan, and Israel*, 111). Finkelstein and Silberman suggest that Manetho's memories of the seventh- and sixth-century invasions of Egypt prompted a presentation of the Hyksos' rise to power in terms of an invasion (*Bible Unearthed*, 55). Van de Mieroop sees the Asiatic incursion into Egypt in terms of the movement southward of people from Syria-Palestine in the wake of the military campaigns of the Hurrians, but he does not clarify whether he understands this as long-term immigration permitting gradual political ascension or the rapid influx of a hostile force (*History of the Ancient Near East*, 123; cf. Grabbe, *Ancient Israel*, 45).

[38] Assmann marks the "wars of liberation" to expel the Hyksos as foundational for the foreign policy of the New Kingdom (*Mind of Egypt*, 197–99). See also Kenton L. Sparks, *Ethnicity and Identity in Ancient Israel: Prolegomena to the Study of Ethnic Sentiments and Their Expression in the Hebrew Bible* (Winona Lake, IN: Eisenbrauns 1998), 84–85. Similarly, Nahum M. Sarna observes that the Hyksos' experience "had a profound effect upon the national psychology [of Egypt]" ("Exploring Exodus: The Oppression," *BA* 49.2 [1986]: 68–80, here 70). In contrast, the biblical claim that close to half the entire population of Egypt left that country occurs without note! See Redford, *Egypt, Canaan, and Israel*, 408. On how Egypt's ensuing domination of Canaan might have affected perceptions of interaction with Egypt, thus laying the foundations for the ideologies of Exodus, see esp. Nadav Na'aman, "The Exodus Story: Between Historical Memory and Historiographical Composition," *JANER* 11 (2011): 39–69.

Bible could easily have justified the event. Donald B. Redford suggests a subconscious modification of the details of the domination of Egypt by the Hyksos and their subsequent expulsion to dissociate from a memory of conquest as opposed to a "peaceful descent" into Egypt leading to political control.[39] The semantics, however, somewhat disarm the biblical writers in their literary retrospective, in that Redford would have them slaves to monolithic collective memories rather than affording them the ability to shape their memories accordingly.

Although Redford may be correct to suggest that "face saving" plays a part in the biblical recollection, we can be certain only of locating the modification of any details remembered (that is, remembered by Israel) in a much later historical context than Redford suggests.[40] In addition, we should consider the likelihood that we are witnessing in the Bible the purposeful recollection of only one (major) aspect of the Hyksos story—expulsion. While it cannot be stated with certainty that the biblical writers had no awareness of the domination of these ancestors over Egypt, there should be little doubt that their concern was with a (dislocated) memory of expulsion with which correlating information from ancient Egypt can be confidently associated. To assert, however, that the story of Joseph's success relates to a memory of the precursor to the Hyksos conquest is to misinterpret the story of Joseph, which—though addressing in its ideological context the dichotomous concerns of diaspora communities regarding the potential for success in an alien land and a (perceived) desire to return to their ancestral home—is best understood in its literary context as a device bolstering the motif of political (and historical) transition.[41]

What the writers are concerned with "remembering" is a migration from Egypt, recast in terms of divine intervention and liberation from oppression. This is clearly not the story of driving out the Hyksos kings of the Eighteenth Dynasty,

---

[39] Redford, *Egypt, Canaan, and Israel*, 413.

[40] Of course, Redford is speaking generally of a survival of these memories "in the folklore of the Canaanite population of the southern Levant," and he refers to the Phoenician legend of Io (significantly preserving a connection with the last Hyksos king, Apophis) as well as other relevant stories preserved, for example, by Strabo and Diodorus (*Egypt, Canaan, and Israel*, 412–13).

[41] This is not the place to elaborate on this motif, which I shall do in a forthcoming work. On the Joseph story as a late (exilic or postexilic) "novella" (albeit for some a redaction of an earlier version), see Rainer Albertz, *Israel in Exile: The History and Literature of the Sixth Century B.C.E.*, trans. David Green, SBLStBL 3 (Atlanta: Society of Biblical Literature, 2003); also Hans-Christoph Schmitt, *Die Nichtpriesterliche Josephsgeschichte: Ein Beitrag zur neuesten Pentateuchkritik*, BZAW 154 (Berlin: de Gruyter, 1980). An important textual analysis of the Joseph story (including an extensive German-language bibliography) can be found in Konrad Schmid, "The So-Called Yahwist and the Literary Gap between Genesis and Exodus," trans. Anselm C. Hagedorn, in *A Farewell to the Yahwist? The Composition of the Pentateuch in Recent European Interpretation*, ed. Thomas B. Dozeman and Konrad Schmid, SymS 34 (Atlanta: Society of Biblical Literature, 2006), 29–50.

something that must have been a tumultuous event for the people both of Egypt and of Palestine (especially since it eventually led to Egyptian dominance of Syria-Palestine). What became important for the Asiatic (or Canaanite) elements who became or were incorporated into developing Israel was the act of leaving Egypt—no matter the reason—and settling in the highlands of Palestine (a settlement to which conquest narratives were later attached).[42] This is the only truth that resonated, especially when Egypt came to dominate the region for centuries afterward. Perhaps in this context any idea of reversing the situation in earthly terms (that is, physically dominating Egypt) faded away until it was relegated to the realm and the will of the divine; but when it comes to the biblical recollection of leaving Egypt, we are dealing with a composite retrospective of a number of identifiable historical contexts in which the (latent) memory is purposefully recalled and shaped in a specific way to complement the context of recollection.[43] In other words, it is the combination of many (later) contextual reflections historically (and ideologically) disconnected from the Hyksos experience, an experience that is simply one of the pieces contributing to this composite retrospective.[44] Faint and piecemeal memories of the Hyksos' rise to power in Egypt may certainly have survived in general terms among the people of Canaan (who would have reason to appropriate stories of Asiatics dominating Egypt), but any transmission to "Israelite" lore that may have occurred is conspicuously ignorant of their very own Jacob as a king or any

---

[42] It is certainly possible, as Redford suggests, that it is to the memory of the expulsion of the Hyksos that we owe many legends not only of military encounters with Egyptian forces but also of origins in Egypt (*Egypt, Canaan, and Israel*, 412). But while the former may be memories of any number of encounters with Egypt spanning the fifteenth to twelfth centuries' dominance over Canaan, the latter may be interpreted in the contexts of popular claims to Egypt's great antiquity, particularly from the times of Hellenistic and Roman hegemony over that ancient nation. On Diodorus, see, e.g., Erich S. Gruen, *Rethinking the Other in Antiquity*, Martin Classical Lectures (Princeton: Princeton University Press, 2011), 90–99. It should also be borne in mind, however, that, when it comes to external reflections during these later periods on the origins of Israel or "the Jews," there might be some dependence on the (earlier) biblical traditions themselves (ibid., 251).

[43] This application of latent memories seems to draw from Sigmund Freud's theories on latency (for convenience, see the extract from "Moses and Monotheism" in *The Collective Memory Reader*, ed. Jeffrey K. Olick, Vered Vinitzky-Seroussi, and Daniel Levy [New York: Oxford University Press, 2011], 85–88); and Friedrich Nietzsche's imagery of "islands" of "embellished facts" (*On the Advantage and Disadvantage of History for Life*, trans. Peter Preuss [Indianapolis: Hackett, 1980], 17) surviving due to their importance for the perpetuation of the identity of a given group.

[44] See Donald B. Redford, "Some Observations on the Traditions Surrounding 'Israel in Egypt,'" in *Judah and the Judeans in the Achaemenid Period: Negotiating Identity in an International Context*, ed. Oded Lipschits, Gary N. Knoppers, and Manfred Oeming [Winona Lake, IN: Eisenbrauns, 2011], 279–364, here 309): "References to the Hyksos ought to be treated as tangential and in no way indicative of anything other than false association."

sort of political or military leader.[45] This would be a momentous omission for the biblical writers to make of the man who assumes the eponym Israel and is father of the twelve tribes.

## V. Conclusion

Perhaps, then, the considerably hazy memories of the Hyksos' control of and expulsion from Egypt were indeed incorporated into the biblical story of Joseph's rise to power and Jacob's descent into Egypt. If so, I would argue that this was purposefully done with a view to lending credence to a story of Israel's origins for which there was no other evidence in the ancient world. The historical truth claims of the writers would have needed something of note to which they could attach their foundation myths. The fact that we can see in these stories the echoes of the Hyksos' experience suggests the resonance of a memory of that experience in the collective memory of (all of) the people of Palestine.[46] The details were surely lost (they would otherwise have had considerable ideological weight for the biblical writers), but there was enough information of which to assume ownership in the right context. In this regard, there is ample reason to identify the Hyksos' sojourn in and subsequent expulsion from Egypt as contributing to the evolution of the exodus myth—if not as the point of origin of that myth—but only in the shadowy realms of embryonic memory. The Hyksos' experience in Egypt was an event completely irrelevant to the composers of the Jacob *toledot* and one completely unknown to their mid-first-millennium BCE audience. Had they been aware of it, it would have both disrupted the chronology of the Pentateuch and overshadowed the didactic and theological purpose of stories relevant to their contemporary experience(s). It is to Josephus that we owe the explicit alignment of the Hyksos in Egypt with the ancestors of Israel, although later compilers of Manetho's work might have drawn the same conclusions independently. Certainly, the evidence of this Asiatic dynasty in Egypt would have been uncovered in due course, but, without either a Bible or a copy of Josephus in one hand, the motivations for excavation and the ensuing interpretations of finds would likely have been quite different.

---

[45] See Assmann, *Mind of Egypt*, 198.

[46] Similar to the argument made by Na'aman that "the supposition that such early and deeply entrenched common Israelite religious consciousness could have grown from the experience of a small group does not make sense"—and here he is speaking of the "memory" of coming out of Egypt—any memories of the Hyksos expulsion should be understood in a wider context of its (lasting) effect on the people of ancient Palestine *from whom Israel emerged and developed* ("Exodus Story," 43). While Assmann states that the Hebrews "inherited" the traditions of the Hyksos (*Mind of Egypt*, 283), we should be careful not to marginalize any such inheritance in terms of a transition from one ethno-religious identity to another.

While the critical analysis of the accounts of the expulsion of these Asiatics may not be necessary for appreciating the origins of the ethnic identity of Israel, it is nonetheless fundamental for understanding how those accounts shaped the cultural memory of Israel.[47]

---

[47] The term *cultural memory* is becoming so popular in studies of the Hebrew Bible that sometimes its meaning can be confused, particularly when it is used alongside the term *collective memory*. It is important to recognize that the latter does not necessarily inform expressions of cultural distinction. A cultural memory is a codified or "sacralized" account of a past event through which a group defines and distinguishes itself. Cultural memory is that which makes the past present, and its most tangible manifestations can be seen in ritual, ceremony, and (religious) festivals. An excellent volume on the subject is Jan Assmann's *Religion and Cultural Memory: Ten Studies,* trans. Rodney Livingstone (Stanford, CA: Stanford University Press, 2006). Memory studies in general is the subject of an important collection of essays and extracts compiled in Olick, Vinitzky-Seroussi, and Levy, *Collective Memory Reader.*

# New in Biblical Studies

### A HANDBOOK TO
## OLD TESTAMENT EXEGESIS
### WILLIAM P. BROWN

Paper • $35.00

Designed for both Hebrew and non-Hebrew students, this book offers a fresh, hands-on introduction to exegesis of the Old Testament. William P. Brown walks students through a variety of interpretive approaches, including modern methodologies—feminist, womanist, Latino/a, queer, postcolonial, disability, and ecological approaches—alongside more traditional methods.

## Also Available

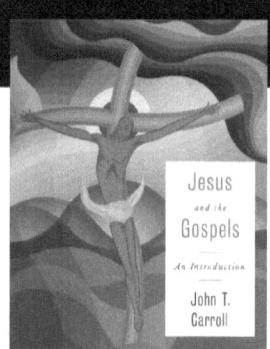

**Jesus and the Gospels**
*An Introduction*

John T. Carroll
Paper • $40.00

**Ancient Apocryphal Gospels**

Markus Bockmuehl
Hardback • $40.00

**Heaven on Earth**
*God's Call to Community in the Book of Revelation*

Michael Battle
Paper • $25.00

**WJK** WESTMINSTER JOHN KNOX PRESS
www.wjkbooks.com | 1.800.523.1631

# Joshua (and Caleb) in the Priestly Spies Story and Joshua's Initial Appearance in the Priestly Source: A Contribution to an Assessment of the Pentateuchal Priestly Material

ITAMAR KISLEV
ikislev@gmail.com
University of Haifa, Mount Carmel, Haifa 3498838, Israel

Scholars usually agree that it is relatively simple to distinguish between the Priestly and non-Priestly materials in the story of the spies in Num 13–14. It is generally acknowledged that the passages in which Joshua and Caleb appear together do not belong to the non-Priestly thread, where Caleb appears alone. Yet to deduce from this that the passages in which both characters appear are therefore part of the Priestly thread is not so easy. A number of scholars have suggested that in some cases the references to Joshua together with Caleb are not part of the original Priestly account. There are good reasons to believe that this is indeed the case and that in fact all of the passages in which the two men appear together are secondary in their context. The question thus arises whether these passages are part of a late stratum in the Priestly source or whether they belong to a redaction of the combined account. This in turn has bearing on the portrayal of the figure of Joshua, the determination of his initial appearance in the Priestly source, and the assessment of the pentateuchal Priestly material.

According to the scholarly consensus, the story of the spies in Num 13–14 is a composite text that contains Priestly and non-Priestly elements. Consideration of its Priestly component, especially the appearances of Joshua and Caleb there, not only sheds light on its compositional history but also has ramifications for our understanding of the character of P.

Recent decades have seen the renewal of a scholarly debate regarding the nature of the Priestly writings. Some scholars view them as a reworking of earlier, non-Priestly texts rather than an independent source. Others maintain that a continuous, originally independent source can be identified in the Priestly writings.¹ Among those who argue for a continuous, independent source, some propose a more limited scope of the original P narrative than previously assumed, and several scholars suggest that P ends at some point in Exodus or Leviticus—rather than in Joshua, as was once thought.² For the latter, the P-like sections in the remainder of the Pentateuch constitute very late redactional strata, not forming part of P^g, the core of the Priestly source.³ This debate raises questions regarding the nature of the Priestly parts in the story of the spies in Num 13–14 that render it a disputed matter.

The main question at hand is whether these Priestly elements form an independent story. In the traditional scholarly treatment of Num 13–14, a distinction is made between at least two independent narrative threads, one of them Priestly.⁴ Another approach considers the Priestly (or P-like) material as supplementing the non-Priestly narrative.⁵

---

¹ For reviews of these contemporary approaches, see Ernest Nicholson, *The Pentateuch in the Twentieth Century: The Legacy of Julius Wellhausen* (Oxford: Clarendon, 1998), 197–218; David M. Carr, "Changes in Pentateuchal Criticism," in *The Twentieth Century: From Modernism to Post-Modernism*, vol. 3.2 of *Hebrew Bible/Old Testament: The History of Its Interpretation*, ed. Magne Sæbø (Göttingen: Vandenhoeck & Ruprecht, 2015), 433–66, here 456–58. For a detailed argument in light of the Sinai P pericope, see Baruch J. Schwartz, "The Priestly Account of the Theophany and Lawgiving at Sinai," in *Texts, Temples, and Traditions: A Tribute to Menahem Haran*, ed. Michael V. Fox et al. (Winona Lake, IN: Eisenbrauns, 1996), 103–34. See also Itamar Kislev, "P: Source or Redaction; The Evidence of Numbers 25," in *The Pentateuch: International Perspectives on Current Research*, ed. Thomas B. Dozeman, Konrad Schmid, and Baruch J. Schwartz, FAT 78 (Tübingen: Mohr Siebeck, 2011), 387–99.

² See Thomas Römer, "Das Buch Numeri und das Ende des Jahwisten: Anfragen zur 'Quellenscheidung' im vierten Buch der Pentateuch," in *Abschied vom Jahwisten: Die Komposition des Hexateuch in der jüngsten Diskussion*, ed. Jan Christian Gertz, Konrad Schmidt, and Markus Witte, BZAW 315 (Berlin: de Gruyter, 2002), 215–32, here 216–18; Reinhard G. Kratz, *The Composition of the Narrative Books of the Old Testament*, trans. John Bowden (London: T&T Clark, 2005), 100–114; Christophe Nihan, *From Priestly Torah to Pentateuch: A Study in the Composition of the Book of Leviticus*, FAT 2/25 (Tübingen: Mohr Siebeck, 2007), 20–68; Carr, "Changes in Pentateuchal Criticism," 457–58.

³ See Kratz, *Composition of the Narrative Books*, 113–14; Carr, "Changes in Pentateuchal Criticism," 456–58, 461–62.

⁴ According to some critics, there are two separate sources (J and E) in the non-Priestly material; for a brief survey, see Philip J. Budd, *Numbers*, WBC 5 (Waco, TX: Word, 1984), 142. The more accepted view considers the non-Priestly material to be more or less unified, with some optional additions; see, e.g., Martin Noth, *Numbers: A Commentary*, trans. James D. Martin, OTL (London: SCM, 1968), 101; Joel S. Baden, *J, E, and the Redaction of the Pentateuch*, FAT 68 (Tübingen: Mohr Siebeck, 2009), 114–30; and recently Gili Kugler, "The Divine Threat to Destroy Israel during the Wandering in the Desert" [in Hebrew] (PhD diss., Hebrew University of Jerusalem, 2013), 20–38.

⁵ Budd considers this supplementarian to be the author of Numbers (*Numbers*, 141–44); Reinhard Achenbach attributes the redactional process of the story to several stages: Hexateuchredaktion, Pentateuchredaktion, and Theokratische Bearbeitung ("Die Erzählung von der

## I. The Character of the Composition of Numbers 13–14

The significant contradictions that make it difficult to read Num 13–14 as a literary unity also help to differentiate between the materials of which the unit is constructed and to characterize its Priestly component. I briefly note four of these discrepancies. One relates to the starting point of the spies' journey: מדבר פארן ("the wilderness of Paran") according to Num 13:3 and 26, whereas קדש ("Kadesh") appears as well in verse 26.[6] A second contradiction concerns the territory scouted: according to Num 13:2, 17a, this was ארץ כנען ("the land of Canaan"). In contrast, the area to which Moses dispatches the spies in verse 17b is more restricted: the Negev and the hill country. In the actual tour of the spies as described in verse 21, we find the comprehensive borders of the entire land of Canaan, but the account in verses 22–24 mentions only the Negev, Hebron, and Wadi Eshcol, namely, just southern Canaan.[7]

A third contradiction relates to the identity of the spy who was excluded from the penalty not to enter the land. According to Num 13:30, Caleb alone opposed the spies' report; consequently, Caleb alone was exempted from the fate of his generation and entered the land (14:24). But, according to 14:6–9, Joshua joined Caleb in opposing the people and in 14:30, 38 both were exempted from the harsh decree.[8]

Whereas there is general scholarly agreement regarding the existence of the three contradictions mentioned above, the following one is disputed. This fourth contradiction relates to the spies' report on the agricultural quality of the land. Numbers 13:27 clearly states that their report included an evaluation of the land as flowing with milk and honey, whereas in verse 32 the land is described as ארץ אכלת יושביה, one that "devours its inhabitants." The connotation of the phrase ארץ אכלת יושביה as the manifestation of דבת הארץ, the discrediting report spread by the spies,

---

gescheiterten Landnahme von Kadesch Barnea [Numeri 13–14] als Schlüsseltext der Redaktionsgeschichte des Pentateuch," *ZABR* 9 [2003]: 56–123). See also the critical review of the supplementary theories regarding the spies story by Ludwig Schmidt, "Die Kundschaftererzählung in Num 13–14 und Dtn 1,19–46: Eine Kritik neuerer Pentateuchkritik," *ZAW* 114 (2002): 43–57.

[6] Kadesh, also known as קדש ברנע, is in the wilderness of Zin (Num 20:1, 27:14, Deut 32:51; cf. Num 34:3–4; Josh 15:1, 3). This contradiction was observed, for example, by George Buchanan Gray, *A Critical and Exegetical Commentary on Numbers*, ICC (Edinburgh: T&T Clark, 1903), 129; Noth, *Numbers*, 101; but cf. Jacob Milgrom, *Numbers* במדבר: *The Traditional Hebrew Text with the New JPS Translation*, JPS Torah Commentary (Philadelphia: Jewish Publication Society, 1990), 104, who locates Kadesh on the border of these two wildernesses. This explanation, however, seems artificial, as Kadesh-Barnea is on the border of the promised land (Num 34:4; cf. Josh 15:3), namely, on the northern border of the wilderness of Zin, whereas the wilderness of Paran is probably farther south.

[7] As noted, e.g., by Noth, *Numbers*, 101; Schmidt, "Die Kundschaftererzählung in Num 13–14," 40.

[8] E.g., Gray, *Numbers*, 129; Schmidt, "Die Kundschaftererzählung in Num 13–14," 40.

is debated. Literally, it means that numerous human beings are dying there. Many scholars interpret this phrase as referring to the fertility of the land; others relate it to different features, the military aspect in particular.[9] I point out that, syntactically, the expression ארץ אכלת יושביה, which describes the land, must refer to the quality of the land itself. Its interpretation as possessing a military element relates not to the land itself but to its inhabitants; this, therefore, cannot be the meaning of דבת הארץ, "the discrediting report of the *land*." Moreover, because a state of war in the land prior to conquest is not necessarily detrimental to the Israelites, it is not applicable to the negative tone of the noun דבה in this context.[10] Further evidence for the view that the phrase in question refers to the land is the similar phrase אכלת אדם את (a land that devours men) in Ezek 36:13. This verse clearly has an agricultural meaning, as the verse is contrasted with the beautiful vision in verse 8 there: "but you, O mountains of Israel, shall put forth your branches, and bear your fruit for my people Israel."[11] This parallel suggests that the expression ארץ אכלת יושביה also has agricultural significance. This interpretation reveals a tension between Num 13:32bα and 32bβ–33, which characterize the land as a place of giants, as it seems unlikely that an infertile land would produce giants.[12] Accordingly, the phrase ארץ אכלת יושביה contradicts both the spies' report of a land flowing with milk and honey and the description of the land as one that breeds giants.

In addition to these contradictions, I note the presence of some doublets in this story. A notable one is the double divine response to the refusal of the people to continue the journey to Canaan (Num 14:11–25 and 26–35): the first refers to Moses alone and the second, to Moses and Aaron. It is difficult to view these responses as part of a single ongoing discussion between Moses and the Lord because verse 25 is a sentence of conclusion and verse 26 seems to open a new

---

[9] E.g., Noth, *Numbers*, 107; Horst Seebass, *Numeri*, 3 vols., BKAT 4 (Neukirchen-Vluyn: Neukirchener Verlag, 1995), 2:112; Kugler, "Divine Threat," 28–29. They rely on Lev 26:38, but there the devouring is not portrayed as a characteristic of the land. Furthermore, the context of Lev 26:38 clarifies that the Israelites will not die in battle, because the verses repeatedly state that there will be no pursuer and no sword (Lev 26:36–37).

[10] That דבה has negative connotations is evidenced by other occurrences of this noun in the Hebrew Bible (e.g., Jer 20:10, Ps 31:14 [Eng. 13]). In the context of the story of the spies, דבה appears with the explanatory adjective רעה in relation to the same report (Num 14:37; cf. Gen 37:2); see H. J. Fabry, "דבה," *TDOT* 3:75–76.

[11] See H. Holzinger, *Numeri*, KHC (Tübingen: Mohr Siebeck, 1903), 56; Gray, *Numbers*, 151, who is supported by the passage in Ezekiel. Note that the appearance of the noun דבה in this Ezekielian passage (v. 3) reinforces the connection between this passage and the (Priestly) story of the spies.

[12] See Holzinger, *Numeri*, 50; David Frankel, *The Murmuring Stories of the Priestly School: A Retrieval of Ancient Sacerdotal Lore*, VTSup 89 (Leiden: Brill, 2002), 133–35. Suzanne Boorer has suggested that the land is described as killing its inhabitants, "so that the only inhabitants left in the land are giants" ("The Place of Numbers 13–14* and Numbers 20:2–12* in the Priestly Narrative [Pg]," *JBL* 131 [2012]: 45–63, here 54); and cf. Nahmanides ad loc. Although this suggestion does harmonize the contradictory parts of 13:32, it seems forced.

conversation. From a synchronic perspective, one could argue that God wants to add something. Undermining this argument, however, is the fact that the "bottom line" of this second passage is more or less the same as the first: that the sinful generation would die in the wilderness (14:22–23, 29, 32, 35).[13]

One interpretation attributes the lack of uniformity in this unit to the interweaving of two independent narrative threads, Priestly and non-Priestly; another views the contradictions and doublets as late additions to a basic story. The former interpretation seems preferable in this case. It seems unlikely that an interpolator would create such sharp discrepancies and meaningless doublets, whereas a redactor attempting to attain maximum preservation of his sources while interweaving them might produce such literary difficulties. On the other hand, similarities in structure and narrative outline, alongside the presence of analogous elements in these assumed strands, cast doubt on their independence.[14] Thus, the figure of Caleb appears in both presupposed narratives. Furthermore, Joshua and Caleb, whose joint arrival on the scene belongs to only one of the surmised threads, respond to the military argument (14:9), as does Caleb alone in the other assumed version (13:30). Moreover, Joshua and Caleb use the phrase זבת חלב ודבש ("flowing with milk and honey") to describe the land (14:8), and the exact phrase occurs in the other supposed thread (13:27). In light of these similarities, it is difficult to sustain the independence of the conjectured versions.

These contradictory considerations suggest that an intermediate path may be viable.[15] One possibility is that composer of the Priestly version was familiar with the non-Priestly version and that this circumstance resulted in the similar details.[16] It appears, however, that the literary situation here is more complex, necessitating a separate, detailed analysis of the Priestly material. Whereas the salient contradictions and doublets point to the existence of independent, parallel threads in the spies story, the similarities suggest that the sources do not appear in their original form but were developed in the gradual process of textual composition. In the following, I examine and attempt to arrive at a more precise description of this conjectured process regarding the Priestly parts.[17]

---

[13] See, e.g., Schmidt, "Die Kundschaftererzählung in Num 13–14," 40; Kugler, "Divine Threat," 20–22.

[14] See the detailed comparison of both outlines in Sean E. McEvenue, *The Narrative Style of the Priestly Writer*, AnBib 50 (Rome: Biblical Institute Press, 1971), 92–93.

[15] See Frankel, *Murmuring Stories*, 120–22.

[16] This is the view held, e.g., by McEvenue, *Narrative Style of the Priestly Writer*, 90–96.

[17] The spies story has a parallel in Deut 1:22–40. This parallel story's relationship with Num 13–14 has been examined in detail by several scholars; see, e.g., Achenbach, "Die Erzählung von der gescheiterten Landnahme," 56–123; Baden, *J, E, and the Redaction of the Pentateuch*, 114–29; Aaron Schart, "The Spy Story and the Final Redaction of the Pentateuch," in *Torah and the Book of Numbers*, ed. Christian Frevel, Thomas Pola, and Aaron Schart, FAT 2/62 (Tübingen: Mohr Siebeck, 2013), 164–200. These studies, however, make no essential contribution to the analysis of the Priestly material in Num 13–14.

## II. The Priestly Thread

As an initial step, I isolate the independent Priestly version of the spies story from the threads that compose this unit. The contradictions and doublet mentioned above, together with the use of characteristic Priestly vocabulary and consideration of plot sequence, facilitate this process. In large part the shape and most of the details of the Priestly version are elements of an overall scholarly consensus.[18] As my focus is on this narrative, it is presented in its entirety below, but I preface this presentation of the text with two comments. First, as mentioned earlier, I perceive a contradiction between the phrase ארץ אכלת יושביה and the continuation of the verse, which deals with the giants native to the land of Canaan. On that basis I attribute only 13:32abα to the Priestly strand and interpret the negative element in the Priestly report of the spies as referring to the infertility of the land alone and not to the fear of war.[19] The second comment relates to the absence of a scholarly consensus regarding the exact attribution of every word in 14:1–10; accordingly, at this stage I present only some of the Priestly elements in this passage, those more definitively Priestly and more germane to the discussion:[20]

---

[18] The following vocabulary is characterized as Priestly: ארץ כנען ("land of Canaan," 13:2, 17), מטה ("tribe," 13:2, 4–15), נשיא ("leader," 13:2), עדה ("congregation," 13:26; 14:1–2, 5, 7, 10, 27, 35). In addition, in sentences that use the phrase ארץ כנען we find the unusual verb תור ("spy out"). Thus, the other instances in which this verb appears (13:21, 25, 32; 14:6–7, 36, 38) can be added to the Priestly thread. In line with this vocabulary, we can conclude that the second divine response (14:26–35) is Priestly. These are some of the lexical considerations that assist identification of the Priestly material in this story.

[19] Some scholars attribute verses 32bβ–33 to the non-Priestly version, e.g., Gray, *Numbers*, 151. Others consider them later than verse 32abα, e.g., Achenbach, "Die Erzählung von der gescheiterten Landnahme," 99–100. The claim of lateness for these verses is not decisive, but their exact attribution does not influence my discussion, as my focus is only on the Priestly thread.

[20] The presentation of the Priestly thread generally follows the proposals suggested by most scholars, e.g., Gray, *Numbers*, 130–32; Noth, *Numbers*, 102. It seems that four main points distinguish the various analyses with respect to the Priestly strand. The first is the question of the meaning of אכלת ישביה and its connection to the subsequent verses, discussed above. The second is the attribution of verse 26, discussed briefly in the next note. The third is the differentiation of the Priestly material in 14:1–10, which is treated at the end of this article. The fourth is the exact attribution of every verse and word in the second divine response (14:26–35), to which I refer in part later in this article and in the notes.

13: ¹The LORD said to Moses, ²"Send men to spy out the land of Canaan, which I am giving to the Israelites; from each of their ancestral tribes you shall send a man, everyone a leader among them." ³So Moses sent them from the wilderness of Paran, according to the command of the LORD, all of them leading men among the Israelites. ⁴These were their names: From the tribe of Reuben, Shammua son of Zaccur; ⁵from the tribe of Simeon, Shaphat son of Hori; ⁶from the tribe of Judah, Caleb son of Jephunneh; ⁷from the tribe of Issachar, Igal son of Joseph; ⁸from the tribe of Ephraim, Hoshea son of Nun; ⁹from the tribe of Benjamin, Palti son of Raphu; ¹⁰from the tribe of Zebulun, Gaddiel son of Sodi; ¹¹from the tribe of Joseph, that is, from the tribe of Manasseh, Gaddi son of Susi; ¹²from the tribe of Dan, Ammiel son of Gemalli; ¹³from the tribe of Asher, Sethur son of Michael; ¹⁴from the tribe of Naphtali, Nahbi son of Vophsi; ¹⁵from the tribe of Gad, Geuel son of Machi. ¹⁶These were the names of the men whom Moses sent to spy out the land. And Moses changed the name of Hoshea son of Nun to Joshua. ¹⁷Moses sent them to spy out the land of Canaan. ²¹So they went up and spied out the land from the wilderness of Zin to Rehob, near Lebo-hamath. ²⁵At the end of forty days they returned from spying out the land. ²⁶And they came to Moses and Aaron and to all the congregation of the Israelites in the wilderness of Paran.²¹

13: (1) וידבר יהוה אל משה לאמר:
(2) שלח לך אנשים ויתרו את ארץ כנען אשר אני נתן לבני ישראל איש אחד איש אחד למטה אבתיו תשלחו כל נשיא בהם:
(3) וישלח אתם משה ממדבר פארן על פי יהוה כלם אנשים ראשי בני ישראל המה:
(4) ואלה שמותם למטה ראובן שמוע בן זכור:
(5) למטה שמעון שפט בן חורי:
(6) למטה יהודה כלב בן יפנה:
(7) למטה יששכר יגאל בן יוסף:
(8) למטה אפרים הושע בן נון:
(9) למטה בנימן פלטי בן רפוא:
(10) למטה זבולן גדיאל בן סודי:
(11) למטה יוסף למטה מנשה גדי בן סוסי:
(12) למטה דן עמיאל בן גמלי:
(13) למטה אשר סתור בן מיכאל:
(14) למטה נפתלי נחבי בן ופסי:
(15) למטה גד גאואל בן מכי:
(16) אלה שמות האנשים אשר שלח משה לתור את הארץ ויקרא משה להושע בן נון יהושע:
(17) וישלח אתם משה לתור את ארץ כנען
(21) ויעלו ויתרו את הארץ ממדבר צן עד רחב לבא חמת:
(25) וישבו מתור הארץ מקץ ארבעים יום:
(26) וילכו ויבאו אל משה ואל אהרן ואל כל עדת בני ישראל אל מדבר פארן

---

[21] In the continuation of the verse, the phrase ואת כל העדה ("and to all the congregation") appears, which seems Priestly. It is likely that this is an editorial intervention, which aims to underscore the presence of the עדה in that episode. It seems reasonable that the opening of the verse, וילכו ויבאו אל משה ("and they came to Moses"), is shared, at least in part, by both P and non-P; see Baden, *J, E, and the Redaction of the Pentateuch*, 115, in contrast to, e.g., George W. Coats (*Rebellion in the Wilderness: The Murmuring Motif in the Wilderness Traditions of the Old Testament* [Nashville: Abingdon, 1968], 138), who attributes the entire verse to P, and to Siegfried Mittmann (*Deuteronomium 1:1–6:3: Literarkritisch und traditionsgeschichtlich Untersucht*, BZAW 139 [Berlin: de Gruyter, 1975], 46) and Frankel (*Murmuring Stories*, 132, 182), who consider the verse an editorial creation.

| | |
|---|---|
| ³²So they brought to the Israelites an unfavorable report of the land that they had spied out, saying, "The land that we have gone through as spies is a land that devours its inhabitants." | (32) ויוציאו דבת הארץ אשר תרו אתה אל בני ישראל לאמר הארץ אשר עברנו בה לתור אתה ארץ אכלת יושביה הוא |
| 14: ¹Then all the congregation raised a loud cry. ²And all the Israelites complained against Moses and Aaron; the whole congregation said to them, "Would that we had died in the land of Egypt! Or would that we had died in this wilderness!…" | 14: (1) ותשא כל העדה ויתנו את קולם (2) וילנו על משה ועל אהרן כל בני ישראל ויאמרו אלהם כל העדה לו מתנו בארץ מצרים או במדבר הזה לו מתנו … |
| ⁵Then Moses and Aaron fell on their faces before all the assembly of the congregation of the Israelites. ⁶And Joshua son of Nun and Caleb son of Jephunneh, of those who had spied out the land, tore their clothes ⁷and said to all the congregation of the Israelites, "The land that we went through as spies is an exceedingly good land…." ¹⁰But the whole congregation threatened to stone them. Then the glory of the Lord appeared at the tent of meeting to all the Israelites. | (5) ויפל משה ואהרן על פניהם לפני כל קהל עדת בני ישראל: (6) ויהושע בן נון וכלב בן יפנה מן התרים את הארץ קרעו בגדיהם: (7) ויאמרו אל כל עדת בני ישראל לאמר הארץ אשר עברנו בה לתור אתה טובה הארץ מאד מאד … (10) ויאמרו כל העדה לרגום אתם באבנים וכבוד יהוה נראה באהל מועד אל כל בני ישראל: |
| ²⁶And the Lord spoke to Moses and to Aaron, saying: ²⁷"How long shall this wicked congregation complain against me? I have heard the complaints of the Israelites, which they complain against me. ²⁸Say to them, 'As I live', says the Lord, 'I will do to you the very things I heard you say: ²⁹your dead bodies shall fall in this very wilderness; and of all your number, included in the census, from twenty years old and upwards, who have complained against me, ³⁰not one of you shall come into the land in which I swore to settle you, except Caleb son of Jephunneh and Joshua son of Nun. ³¹But your little ones, who you said would become booty, I will bring in, and they shall know the land that you have despised. ³²But as for you, your dead bodies shall fall in this wilderness.³³And our children shall be shepherds in the wilderness for forty years, and shall suffer for your faithlessness, until the last of your dead bodies lies in the wilderness. ³⁴According to the number of the days in which you spied out the land, forty days, | (26) וידבר יהוה אל משה ואל אהרן לאמר: (27) עד מתי לעדה הרעה הזאת אשר המה מלינים עלי את תלנות בני ישראל אשר המה מלינים עלי שמעתי: (28) אמר אלהם חי אני נאם יהוה אם לא כאשר דברתם באזני כן אעשה לכם: (29) במדבר הזה יפלו פגריכם וכל פקדיכם לכל מספרכם מבן עשרים שנה ומעלה אשר הלינתם עלי: (30) אם אתם תבאו אל הארץ אשר נשאתי את ידי לשכן אתכם בה כי אם כלב בן יפנה ויהושע בן נון: (31) וטפכם אשר אמרתם לבז יהיה והביאתי אתם וידעו את הארץ אשר מאסתם בה: (32) ופגריכם אתם יפלו במדבר הזה: (33) ובניכם יהיו רעים במדבר ארבעים שנה ונשאו את זנותיכם עד תם פגריכם במדבר: (34) במספר הימים אשר תרתם את הארץ ארבעים יום יום לשנה יום לשנה תשאו את עונתיכם ארבעים שנה וידעתם את תנואתי: (35) אני יהוה דברתי אם לא זאת אעשה לכל העדה הרעה הזאת הנועדים עלי במדבר הזה יתמו ושם ימתו: (36) והאנשים אשר שלח משה לתור את |

for every day a year, you shall bear your iniquity forty years, and you shall know my displeasure.' ³⁵I the LORD have spoken; surely I will do thus to all this wicked congregation gathered together against me: in this wilderness they shall come to a full end, and there they shall die." ³⁶And the men whom Moses sent to spy out the land, who returned and made all the congregation complain against him by bringing a bad report about the land— ³⁷the men who brought an unfavorable report about the land died by a plague before the LORD. ³⁸But Joshua son of Nun and Caleb son of Jephunneh alone remained alive, of those men who went to spy out the land.²²

הארץ וישבו וילונו [וילינו קרי] עליו את כל העדה להוציא דבה על הארץ: (37) וימתו האנשים מוצאי דבת הארץ רעה במגפה לפני יהוה: (38) ויהושע בן נון וכלב בן יפנה חיו מן האנשים ההם ההלכים לתור את הארץ:

As outlined above, the Priestly story contains the following elements: it first recounts that God commands Moses to send twelve spies to scout the land of Canaan. The starting point of their expedition is the wilderness of Paran, whence they proceed to scout the entire land. On their return, they report that the land is infertile,²³ and as a result the Israelites refuse to continue the journey to the promised land. While Joshua and Caleb are engaged in an unsuccessful attempt to change the people's minds, God decides not to let the current generation enter the land, exempting Caleb and Joshua from this decree. Finally the evil spies die in a plague, whereas Joshua and Caleb survive. This account can be read smoothly and all the contradictions and the doublet mentioned above are resolved.

An in-depth study of this Priestly story, however, reveals a lack of internal unity. Here I single out for examination the four pericopae in which Joshua appears (13:4–16; 14:6–10, 26–35, 36–38). Significantly, in all of them he appears together with Caleb. I consider the arguments and conclusions of the scholars who have noted that some or all of these occurrences are secondary, and I suggest a new, plausible picture of the formation of the Priestly spies story.

---

²² For the English translation, see http://www.devotions.net/bible/00old.htm. Most scholars consider 14:39 non-Priestly; see, e.g., Bruno Baentsch, *Exodus–Leviticus–Numeri*, HKAT (Göttingen: Vandenhoeck & Ruprecht, 1903), 532; Baden, *J, E, and the Redaction of the Pentateuch*, 117. Gray, however, attributes verse 39a to the Priestly thread (*Numbers*, 164); cf. Frankel, *Murmuring Stories*, 128 n. 20.

²³ Some scholars connect this description of the land as infertile to the condition in Yehud in the Persian period as reflected in Haggai, Zechariah, Ezra, and Nehemiah; see Julius Welhausen, *Prolegomena to the History of Ancient Israel, with a Reprint of the Article Israel from the Encyclopaedia Britannica*, trans. J. Sutherland Black and Allan Menzies, Meridian Library (1878; Cleveland: World, 1961), 354; Holzinger, *Numeri*, 56; Norbert Lohfink, *Theology of the Pentateuch: Themes of the Priestly Narrative and Deuteronomy*, trans. Linda M. Maloney (Edinburgh: T&T Clark, 1994), 159–60.

## III. Joshua and Caleb: The Second Priestly Stratum

One salient episode is the Priestly version of the report of the spies in Num 13:32, in which the land is characterized as infertile. That verse, however, contains no hint that only some of the scouts conveyed this negative portrayal. Surprisingly, Joshua and Caleb do not immediately speak out against the false report, as we might expect, but wait until the people's complaint in 14:1–3. The absence of an immediate response by Joshua and Caleb implies that, in the original Priestly version, all the scouts, without exception, portrayed the land in negative terms.[24]

A second significant episode is in Num 14:6–9. Following the voicing of a complaint by the עדה (vv. 1–3), Moses and Aaron fall on their faces (v. 5), while Joshua and Caleb attempt to change the Israelites' minds. Consequently, the congregation wants to pelt them with stones (v. 10). According to the narrative sequence as it stands, the word אתם ("them") in verse 10 refers to Joshua and Caleb, leaving the reader to ponder: what about Moses and Aaron, who remain prone on the ground from verse 5? Why did the people not seek to stone them, the actual leaders? The abandonment of Moses and Aaron in the narrative and the shift to Joshua and Caleb without reporting what Moses and Aaron did after they fell on their faces seems odd.[25] Furthermore, at the end of the scene כבוד יהוה, the presence of the Lord, appears and prevents the Israelites from attacking them. Note that we find כבוד יהוה appearing in relation to Moses and Aaron in similar circumstances, either to protect them or to help them resolve a problem, as in the manna story in Exod 16:10 and also in other episodes of the people's complaints (Num 17:7, 20:6).[26] This suggests that Moses and Aaron were the original targets and it was they whom the people wanted to pelt with stones, which means that, originally, verse 10 immediately followed verse 5, making the intervening speech by Joshua and Caleb a secondary addition, as some scholars note.[27] Significantly, the superfluous phrase in verse 6—מן התרים את הארץ ("of those who had spied out the land"), which describes Joshua and Caleb—conveys the impression of a particular effort to portray the pair as belonging to the delegation of spies.

---

[24] Frankel, *Murmuring Stories*, 124.

[25] Ibid.

[26] The most similar instance is found in Num 20:6, where Moses and Aaron fall on the ground and כבוד יהוה appears. Note that the existence of the threat of danger there makes Moses and Aaron enter the tabernacle מפני הקהל ("from the assembly"). This phrase resembles לפני כל קהל עדת ישראל ("before all the assembly of the congregation of the Israelites") in Num 14:5.

[27] Frankel, *Murmuring Stories*, 124. Others connect verse 5a with verse 10b; see Olivier Artus, *Etudes sur le livre des Nombres: Récit, histoire et loi en Nb 13,1–20,13*, OBO 157 (Fribourg: Editions Universitaires; Göttingen: Vandenhoeck & Ruprecht, 1997), 128; Achenbach, "Die Erzählung von der gescheiterten Landnahme," 104–5. The evidence cited for detaching verse 10a from verse 10b is not convincing given the contrastive use of the *qatal* form in verse 10b, most likely in relation to the people's threatening intentions in verse 10a.

Joshua and Caleb also appear in the second divine response (Num 14:26–35). Clearly, this is a stacked pericope, in which God swears twice or even three times that the people will die in the wilderness and not enter the land (vv. 28, 30, 35); the dropping of the Israelites' carcasses in the wilderness appears twice (vv. 29, 32), as does the reference to the next generation (vv. 31, 33). This divine speech, however, can be read in sequence until verse 29, whereas in verse 30 a second oath appears.[28] This redundant oath, which is syntactically loosely connected to the preceding verse, appears to be a secondary addition.[29] The next verse relates to the fear of war which, as already noted, does not belong to the original Priestly report. Verse 32, ופגריכם אתם יפלו במדבר הזה ("your dead bodies shall fall in this wilderness"), repeats the beginning of verse 29, במדבר הזה יפלו פגריכם ("your dead bodies shall fall in this very wilderness"), and seems to be a kind of resumptive repetition that eases the insertion of the addition in verses 30–31. The speech continues smoothly in the subsequent verses.[30] Thus, the original passage included verses 26–29 and 33–35. The intervening verses add two elements: the exemption of Joshua and Caleb from punishment and the fear of war.[31]

Joshua and Caleb make yet another appearance in Num 14:38. In this case, it is the formulation of the verse that sparks unease. The expression האנשים ההם ("those men") in relation to the spies instead of the expected האנשים האלה ("these men") or merely האנשים ("the men") generates a sense of distance, creating suspicion that the author who formulated this verse did not compose the previous verses. The continuation of the verse ההולכים לתור את הארץ ("who went to spy out the land"), like the similar phrase in verse 6 on which I commented earlier, is part of a comprehensive effort to insert Joshua and Caleb into the delegation of spies.[32]

This brings us to the first occurrence of the two in the narrative, in the enumeration of the spies in Num 13:4–16. The evidence suggests that the entire list is secondary. First of all, the list seems to come on the scene a bit too late—after,

---

[28] Some scholars consider the words וכל פקדיכם לכל מספרכם מבן עשרים שנה ומעלה ("and of all your number, included in the census, from twenty years old and upwards") a secondary gloss, inserted under the influence of Num 1–2; see Frankel, *Murmuring Stories*, 173–74; Achenbach, "Die Erzählung von der gescheiterten Landnahme," 119. Although the influence of Num 1 is evident, the lateness of these words in their context is unproven.

[29] See Noth, who supports this argument with the unusual mention of Caleb before Joshua (*Numbers*, 110).

[30] Some scholars have recognized verse 34 as later than verse 33; see Noth, *Numbers*, 110; Artus, *Etudes sur le livre des Nombres*, 150; Frankel, *Murmuring Stories*, 179 (and see also his interesting comment about the connection between this verse and Ezek 4:6, n. 122). The notion that there is no literary connection between the detail that the scouts' expedition lasted forty days (13:25) and the punishment of forty years (14:33) as articulated in verse 34, however, seems unlikely.

[31] See Frankel, *Murmuring Stories*, 196–99, for a comprehensive effort to explain all the details in the additional verses.

[32] See Mittmann, *Deuteronomium 1:1–6:3*, 52; Frankel, *Murmuring Stories*, 124, 174.

instead of before, Moses sends them on their mission, following the words וישלח אתם משה ("and Moses sent them") in verse 3. If the list was part of the Priestly story from the beginning, we would expect a formulation like *ויקח משה אנשים כאשר צוה ה' ואלה שמותם ("so Moses took men, by the Lord's command, and these were their names") or similar wording and only then וישלח אתם משה. Another consideration is that, because the list's literary function is only to introduce Joshua and Caleb, who will later take part in the story, and because we postulated that all the references to the pair in the story are secondary, there is no place in the original story for the entire list. Moreover, removing the list does not harm the narrative flow. Verse 17a represents a sort of resumptive repetition that duplicates verse 3a and could have functioned to facilitate the list's insertion. In addition, the noticeable effort throughout the story to include Joshua and Caleb in the scouting delegation (14:6, 38) can serve as further indication that, in the original form of the Priestly story, they did not belong to the delegation of spies. It appears likely that the list of the scouts, which includes Joshua and Caleb, is a secondary addition aimed at making this pair part of the delegation.[33]

This discussion suggests that Joshua and Caleb were completely absent from the original Priestly spies story and were introduced into the Priestly strand only at a later stage.[34] This raises the question of what motivated the addition of this pair to the story. It seems obvious that Caleb was added in line with the non-Priestly thread that exempted him from divine punishment. But why was Joshua, who receives no mention in the non-Priestly story, added? I propose that his insertion into this story was influenced by the references to Joshua in the non-Priestly material of the Pentateuch, such as his function in the war against Amalek in Exod 17:8–16 and the stories in which he accompanies Moses (Exod 24:13, 32:17, 33:11, Num 11:28). A consideration of these stories highlights their tension with Joshua's well-known role in the conquest of Canaan. If, as in some of the non-Priestly stories, Joshua participated in the events at the start of the Israelites' wandering in the wilderness, he must then die in the wilderness in accord with the punishment of the exodus generation in the wake of the spies story. In other words, his outstanding survival throughout the wandering in the wilderness demands explanation, and

---

[33] This addition includes verse 3b too, since the resumptive repetition marks its borders. Verse 3b interprets the word אנשים in verse 1, which simply means men, as important figures. This interpretation bestows on the people in the list the title of leader, probably because of the mention of Joshua and perhaps of Caleb too; see Frankel, who proposes that this addition "sought to present the scouts as a sort of microcosm of the community at large" (*Murmuring Stories*, 194–95). As a result, we can surmise that verse 2b, which includes the demand to include a leader of each tribe in the divine commandment, also belongs to this activity of insertion. Many researchers have argued that the list is secondary; see, e.g., Noth, *Numbers*, 103–4; Coats, *Rebellion in the Wilderness*, 137; Mittmann, *Deuteronomium 1:1–6:3*, 42.

[34] The insertions of Joshua and Caleb to the story could have taken place in a gradual process. The change in the order of this pair's names in 14:30 may imply such a notion, but reaching a decision on this matter is beyond the scope of this article.

Joshua's addition to the spies story and portrayal as one of the positive spies explain this survival.[35]

## IV. Tracing the Formation of the Priestly Version of the Spies Story

Simply recognizing the addition of Joshua and Caleb to the story and its possible motivation does not resolve the question of at what stage they were interpolated into the account. One possibility is that they were inserted into the combined story of the Priestly and non-Priestly threads and that their appearance can therefore be attributed to the redactor (R) or to an even later glossator (post-R). Another is that they were added to the Priestly source while it was still in an independent form and that this version should therefore be referred to as supplements to P (P$^s$). Siegfried Mittmann considers these passages part of the compositional process,[36] whereas Frankel attributes them to a posteditorial stage, admitting, however, that they are Priestly in nature.[37] Examination of the evidence leads to another conclusion, according to which Joshua and Caleb were introduced into the Priestly text before it was interwoven with the non-Priestly narrative.

I note first that the motivation proposed for explaining Joshua's survival influenced only the Priestly thread and that Joshua always joins Caleb only there. In the non-Priestly thread Joshua is missing, and Caleb both acts on his own (13:30) and is alone exempted from divine punishment (14:24). Another point relates to the comment regarding Joshua's name change from הושע to יהושע. Many scholars have noted the Priestly assumption that the name YHWH was revealed to Moses only shortly before the exodus (Exod 6:2) and that therefore no member of the first generation could bear the component יה or יהו in his name. As there are no theophoric names compounded with the divine name YHWH in the list of the scouts (13:4–15), the exceptional case of Joshua has to be explained. The solution provided by the list's interpolator is that the component יהו became part of his name just before the scouting expedition and that it was not his original name.[38]

Yet, based on my assumption that the appearance of Joshua in the Priestly spies story depends on the non-Priestly references to him in earlier stories, we

---

[35] See Samuel E. Loewenstamm, "The Death of Moses," in *From Babylon to Canaan: Studies in the Bible and Its Oriental Background,* Publication of the Perry Foundation for Biblical Research in the Hebrew University of Jerusalem (Jerusalem: Magnes, 1992), 136–66, here 138–39; Frankel, *Murmuring Stories,* 194.

[36] Mittmann, *Deuteronomium 1:1–6:3,* 55.

[37] Frankel, *Murmuring Stories,* 172–81. Cf. Artus, who considers 14:32–33 part of an early Priestly layer, 13:3b–16 a late Priestly layer, and 14:5–10a, 38 a post-Dtr layer (*Etudes sur le livre des Nombres,* 95–97, 131–32, 146–51).

[38] E.g., Gray, *Numbers,* 136–37; Milgrom, *Numbers,* 101.

would expect the comment on the change of Joshua's name to appear earlier, when it is first mentioned in Exod 17:9. The name change at this late stage is senseless and misses the point. Why, then, does this comment appear so late in the pentateuchal story? The straightforward answer is that the author who added Joshua to the story acted only within the independent Priestly source. The change of Joshua's name at this late point indicates that the earlier non-Priestly stories in which Joshua is mentioned were not included in the composition worked on by the interpolator. This interpolator was, however, familiar with the non-Priestly stories and took them into account in his editorial activity and when he made his additions to the Priestly spies story. At this stage, the Priestly source was still independent and not yet interwoven with the other sources. This proposal, which locates this literary activity within the independent Priestly source, explains not only why Joshua is missing from the non-Priestly spies story but also why the comment on Joshua's name change appears so late in the pentateuchal story; this is the first appearance of Joshua in the independent Priestly source.

Two additional points of evidence back this claim. The first is that these late passages contain Priestly vocabulary, as found in other Priestly texts or the Priestly spies story: מטה (13:4–15), תור (13:16; 14:6, 7, 38), עדה (14:7). The second is that these interpolations are located only in Priestly passages: the first passage, 13:3b–16, is inserted into the Priestly text of 13:1–3a, 17a; the second, 14:6–9, interrupts the Priestly sequence of 14:5 + 10; the third, 14:30–32, is part of the Priestly divine response (14:26–35); and the fourth, 14:38, is attached to the end of the Priestly story (14:36–37). In the latter case, the addition is not enclosed on both sides since it comes at the end of the story. This cumulative evidence indicates that Joshua and Caleb were interpolated into the Priestly story while it was still independent.[39]

We can now outline the original Priestly version of the spies story: When the Israelites were in the wilderness of Paran, God commanded Moses to send spies to scout the entire promised land. On their return after forty days of scouting, they all stated that the land is infertile, which caused the people to complain. Moses and Aaron fell on their faces and the people intended to pelt them with stones, but then כבוד יהוה (divine glory) appeared and determined that not the members of the sinful generation but their sons would enter the land. Finally, the spies died in a plague.

The second Priestly layer added some significant features to this basic layer. The spies are now twelve tribal leaders, and their report on the land of Canaan includes two defamatory aspects: the land is infertile and the local residents are

---

[39] Some scholars have noted the lack of uniformity within the Priestly spies thread. For example, Gerhard von Rad differentiates between two separate Priestly threads (*Die Priesterschrift im Hexateuch literarisch untersucht und theologisch gewertet* [Stuttgart: Kohlhammer, 1934], 103–9). His division, however, differs from mine. Noth recognized the list of the spies and 14:30–32 (34) as interpolations within the Priestly strand (*Numbers*, 103, 110–11) but not the other Joshua and Caleb appearances, 14:6–9, 38.

strong.⁴⁰ Also inserted into this additional layer are the two positive spies, Joshua and Caleb, who try to convince the people that the land is fertile and that they can overcome its inhabitants. Consequently, Joshua and Caleb were exempted from the punishment of the people and the plague that killed the evil spies.

This outlining of both layers facilitates attribution of the elements in Num 14:1–10 to source and layer, as there is some scholarly disagreement regarding this passage. Most scholars correctly consider verse 1b non-Priestly, since this is a doublet of verse 1a, which is usually attributed to P.⁴¹ Similarly, it is agreed that verse 2 is Priestly,⁴² but there are differences of opinion regarding verse 3.⁴³ Because this latter verse accentuates the fear of war, which I have concluded is secondary in the Priestly version, this verse can then be attributed to the second Priestly layer. Indeed, the wording of verse 3a is very similar to that of verse 31a, which was already attributed to this late layer.⁴⁴ Verse 4 is usually rightly accepted as non-Priestly,⁴⁵ whereas verses 5–7 are identified as Priestly. I have concluded, however, that Joshua and Caleb are part of the second Priestly layer, and verses 6–7 therefore also belong to this layer. The status of verses 8–9 is a matter of scholarly debate: whereas many attribute verse 8 to the non-Priestly thread and others include verse 9 (or only 9aα) in this thread as well, still others consider both Priestly.⁴⁶ It could be argued that these verses should be excluded from the Priestly thread because of the allusion to the fear of war in verse 9 and the use of the phrase זבת חלב ודבש ("flowing with milk and honey," v. 8), which the spies reported earlier in the non-Priestly version (13:27). But if the second Priestly layer knew the non-Priestly strand, then these elements were introduced into the Priestly story under the influence of the non-Priestly one. Moreover, these verses have no place in the non-Priestly thread; they do not continue the sequence of the last non-Priestly passage, and one struggles to find an appropriate location for them in the

---

⁴⁰ The interpolator did not add the strength of the people in Canaan in the spies' report but rather in the people's complaint (14:3), Joshua and Caleb's response (14:9), as well as in the divine speech (14:31). As an interpolator, and not an author, he did not do his job perfectly and missed the opportunity to add that information to the spies' report.

⁴¹ E.g., Coats, *Rebellion in the Wilderness*, 141–42; McEvenue, *Narrative Style of the Priestly Writer*, 90–93. This attribution is reasonable, but there are some doubts in this regard; see Gray, *Numbers*, 152.

⁴² See Baentsch, *Exodus-Leviticus-Numeri*, 524; Noth, *Numbers*, 108; but cf. the nuances in Mittmann, *Deuteronomium 1:1–6:3*, 47.

⁴³ See the brief review of the research in Boorer, "Place of Numbers 13–14*," 50 n. 16.

⁴⁴ The similarity between the end of verse 3 and that of verse 4 can be explained by the Priestly interpolator's awareness of the non-Priestly thread.

⁴⁵ See Noth, *Numbers*, 108; Kugler, "Divine Threat," 30; but see also Ludwig Schmidt, *Studien zur Priesterschrift*, BZAW 214 (Berlin: de Gruyter, 1993), 87–88.

⁴⁶ For a succinct survey of this issue, see Boorer, who includes only verse 9aβb in P ("Place of Numbers 13–14*," 50 n. 16).

non-Priestly sequence.⁴⁷ Thus, it seems preferable to attribute these verses to the late Priestly layer.⁴⁸ Since verse 10 is Priestly,⁴⁹ we can summarize that verses 1a, 2, 5, and 10 probably belong to the basic Priestly story, whereas verses 3 and 6–9 were inserted into the Priestly passage at a second stage.

## V. Conclusions

The present discussion shows that an independent Priestly thread can be identified in the current spies story (Num 13–14), and this indicates that P continued at least to the book of Numbers.⁵⁰ Moreover, we can speak of two stages for the independent Priestly source before it was interwoven with other materials. In the first stage, the Priestly source went its own way without considering—and maybe even without awareness of—the non-Priestly material. In the second stage, additions were made to this independent source in light of the non-Priestly material, but this account was still not part of the larger project of the composition of the Pentateuch. Most of the similarities between the Priestly and non-Priestly threads stem from this secondary layer. It stands to reason that nonrecognition of this important late stage led to some incorrect assessment of the Priestly writing in general and the Priestly spies story in particular.

We must now inquire as to the place of Joshua in the original stratum of the Priestly source, before the additions were made to the Priestly spies story. The next mention of Joshua in the Priestly material is in Num 26:65; there too in connection with the spies story and because the formulation is very close to the addition in Num 14:30, we can conclude that this reference was not part of the original layer of the Priestly source. Joshua also appears in the pericope on his investiture as Moses's successor in Num 27. There God says to Moses, "Take Joshua son of Nun, a man in whom the spirit is" (v. 18). This statement may be considered as presenting Joshua, and it is possible that this is the reader's first encounter with the figure of Joshua in the original stratum of the Priestly source. If so, we cannot rule out the possibility that, in the ancient layer of the Priestly source, Joshua was originally perceived as part of the second generation. If so, his appearance as the leader of the

---

⁴⁷ See Gray, *Numbers*, 153; and Baentsch, who suggests that either it was addressed by Moses to the people or formed the conclusion of Caleb's speech (13:30) (*Exodus–Leviticus–Numeri*, 524–25).

⁴⁸ Quite a few scholars consider verses 5–10 Priestly; see, e.g., Noth, *Numbers*, 107–8; Coats, *Rebellion in the Wilderness*, 138; Baden, *J, E, and the Redaction of the Pentateuch*, 116–17.

⁴⁹ See Holzinger, *Numeri*, 51; Seebass, *Numeri*, 2:96, 113; and n. 27 above.

⁵⁰ See my recent discussion, "Num 36:13: The Transition between Numbers and Deuteronomy, and the Redaction of the Pentateuch," in *From Author to Copyist: Essays on the Composition, Redaction, and Transmission of the Hebrew Bible in Honor of Zipi Talshir*, ed. Cana Werman (Winona Lake, IN: Eisenbrauns, 2015), 113–24.

conquest of Canaan would not require explanation. It is the consideration of the early appearance of Joshua in the non-Priestly material that creates the problem of Joshua's survival.

Thus, the first stratum of the independent Priestly source did not include Joshua in the spies story. His first appearance there was his appointment as Moses's successor in Num 27, where it seemed reasonable that he belonged to the second generation, and his involvement in the conquest of Canaan therefore raised no questions. In the second stratum of the independent Priestly source, Joshua and Caleb were added to the spies story as part of the delegation of scouts in light of the non-Priestly material, creating the need to harmonize the newer with the older material. I therefore conclude that not every sign of awareness by the Priestly writer of non-Priestly material should be interpreted as a compositional act involving the combination of sources or as proof of the dependence of the Priestly material in general on the non-Priestly sources. A careful analysis of the text may suggest another option, according to which a later Priestly author made additions in light of the non-Priestly material but not necessarily as part of a process of combination with this material. This may reflect not a process of full redaction but rather one of partial adaptation of a still independent source.

# SBL PRESS

## New and Recent Titles

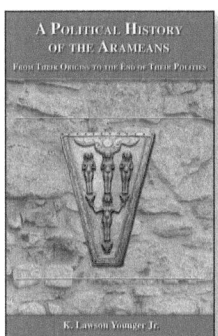

**A POLITICAL HISTORY OF THE ARAMEANS**
From Their Origins to the End of Their Polities
K. Lawson Younger Jr.
Paperback $97.95, 978-1-58983-128-5   886 pages, 2016   Code: 061713
Hardcover $117.95, 978-1-62837-080-5   E-book $97.95, 978-1-62837-084-3
Archaeology and Biblical Studies 13

**STONES, BONES, AND THE SACRED**
Essays on Material Culture and Ancient Religion in Honor of Dennis E. Smith
Alan H. Cadwallader, editor
Paperback $44.95, 978-1-62837-166-6   388 pages, 2016   Code: 064522
Hardcover $59.95, 978-0-88414-210-2   E-book $44.95, 978-0-88414-209-6
Early Christianity and Its Literature 21

**ALLUSIVE SOUNDPLAY IN THE HEBREW BIBLE**
Jonathan G. Kline
Paperback $27.95, 978-1-62837-144-4   170 pages, 2016   Code: 062630
Hardcover $42.95, 978-0-88414-171-6   E-book $27.95, 978-0-88414-170-9
Ancient Israel and Its Literature 28

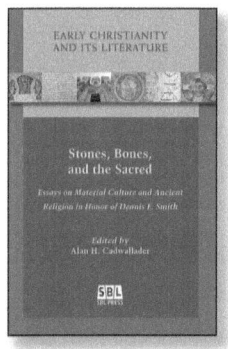

**THE BOOK OF GENESIS**
Composition, Reception, and Interpretation
Craig A. Evans, Joel N. Lohr, and David L. Petersen, editors
Paperback $99.95, 978-1-62837-169-7   788 pages, 2017   Code: 069578
Brill Reprints 78   Vetus Testamentum Supplements 152

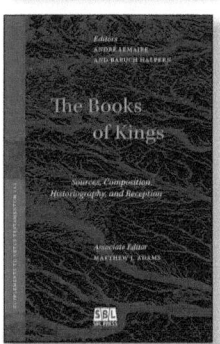

**THE BOOKS OF KINGS**
Sources, Composition, Historiography, and Reception
André Lemaire and Baruch Halpern, editors
Paperback $92.95, 978-1-62837-170-3   728 pages, 2017   Code: 069579
Brill Reprints 79   Vetus Testamentum Supplements 129

SBL Press • P.O. Box 2243 • Williston, VT 05495-2243
Phone: 877-725-3334 (toll-free) or 802-864-6185 • Fax: 802-864-7626
Order online at www.sbl-site.org/publications

# Remarks on a Coptic Sahidic Fragment of 3 Kingdoms, Previously Described as an Apocryphon of Solomon

ALIN SUCIU
asuciu@uni-goettingen.de
Akademie der Wissenschaften zu Göttingen, 37073 Göttingen, Germany

FELIX ALBRECHT
felix.albrecht@uni-goettingen.de
Akademie der Wissenschaften zu Göttingen, 37073 Göttingen, Germany

The subject of this article is a Sahidic manuscript fragment kept in the Coptic Museum in Cairo (inv. no. 9253), which was edited by Henri Munier as an unknown apocryphon about King Solomon. According to the *editio princeps*, the text would be based on 3 Kgdms 3:3–13. Munier's description of the content of the fragment led other scholars to mention it in their studies on the apocryphal literature related to King Solomon. A closer examination of the Cairo fragment, however, reveals that Munier was wrong in attributing the text to an unknown apocryphal writing. The authors of this article argue that it actually features portions of the Sahidic version of 3 Kgdms 3:4–6, 8–10. The Coptic biblical text is analyzed in relation with the parallel passage in the Septuagint.

---

In his catalog of the Sahidic manuscripts kept in the Coptic Museum in Cairo, Henri Munier offered the edition of a literary fragment that he entitled "Conte (?) sur le roi Salomon" ("Story [?] about king Solomon").[1] Munier's description influenced other scholars, who in their turn suggested that the Cairo fragment might belong to an apocryphal writing about Solomon. As we will show in this brief article, however, a more careful inspection reveals that the text edited by Munier is a fragmentary witness of the Sahidic version of 3 Kgdms 3:4–6, 8–10. Notably, this passage has not been attested in Coptic until now.

---

[1] Henri Munier, *Manuscrits coptes*, CGAE 74, nos. 9201–9304 (Cairo: Imprimerie de l'IFAO, 1916), 67–68.

57

## I. The Fragment Cairo, Coptic Museum 9253

The manuscript fragment treated here bears the inventory number Cairo, Coptic Museum, inv. no. 9253. It is a damaged parchment leaf tentatively dated by Munier to the twelfth century. According to the description provided in the *editio princeps*, in the current state of preservation the fragment measures ca. 17.5 × 12.5 cm. As we did not have access to the original manuscript, we give below a tentative reedition based on the text published by Munier.[2] In addition, we supply the parallel Greek text of the LXX in the second column.[3]

Cairo, Coptic Museum no. 9253 = 3 Kgdms 3:4–6, 8-10

Recto

```
3   4    ]ⲛⲉⲥ[                    3  4-ὅτι αὐτὴ
         ⲙⲛ̄]ⲛⲟ[ϭ ?                    ὑψηλοτάτη καὶ μεγάλη.
         ]ⲛ ⲛ̄ϭⲗ[ⲓⲗ                    χιλίαν ὁλοκαύτωσιν
         ⲥⲟ]ⲗⲟ[ⲙⲱⲛ ⲁϥ ?]              ἀνήνεγκεν Σαλωμων
    5  ⲧⲁⲗⲟⲟⲩ ⲉϩⲣⲁⲓ· ⲉϫⲙ̄ⲡⲉⲑⲩ-        ἐπὶ τὸ θυ-
       ⲥⲓⲁⲥⲧⲏⲣⲓⲟⲛ· ⲉⲧϩⲛ̄ⲅⲁⲃⲁⲱ(ⲛ):–    σιαστήριον ἐν Γαβαων.
       ⁵ⲁⲩⲱ ⲡϫⲟⲉⲓⲥ ⲁϥⲟⲩⲱⲛϩ̄ ⲉⲥⲟ-      ⁵καὶ ὤφθη κύριος τῷ Σα-
       ⲗⲟⲙⲱⲛ· ϩⲛ̄ⲟⲩⲣⲁⲥⲟⲩ ⲛ̄ⲧⲉⲩϣⲏ      λωμων ἐν ὕπνῳ τὴν νύκτα,
       ⲁⲩⲱ ⲡⲉϫⲉ ⲡϫⲟⲉⲓⲥ ⲛ̄ⲥⲟⲗⲟ-        καὶ εἶπεν κύριος πρὸς Σαλω-
    10 ⲙⲱⲛ· ϫⲉ ⲁⲓⲧⲉⲓ ⲛⲁⲕ ⲛⲟⲩ         μων Αἴτησαί τι
       ⲁⲓⲧⲏⲙⲁ ⲛⲧⲟⲟⲧ· ⁶ⲡⲉϫⲉ ⲥⲟⲗⲟ-     αἴτημα σαυτῷ. ⁶καὶ εἶπεν Σαλω-
       ⲙⲱⲛ ⲙ̄ⲡϫⲟⲉⲓⲥ· ϫⲉ ⲛ̄ⲧⲟⲕ ⲁⲕⲉⲓ-   μων Σὺ ἐποίη-
       ⲣⲉ ⲙⲛ̄ⲡⲉⲕϩⲙ̄ϩⲁⲗ· ⲉⲧⲉ ⲇⲁⲩⲉⲓⲇ ⲡⲉ σας μετὰ τοῦ δούλου σου Δαυιδ
       ⲡⲁⲓⲱⲧ ⲛⲟⲩⲛⲟϭ ⲛ̄ⲛⲁ-            τοῦ πατρός μου ἔλεος μέγα,
```

3 ⁴[…] [and] great […] burnt offerings […] [Solomon] offered them up on the altar which is in Gabaon. ⁵And the Lord appeared to Solomon in a dream at night. And the Lord said to Solomon, "Ask for yourself a request from me." ⁶Solomon said to the Lord, "You did with your servant, which is David, my Father, great mercy […]"

---

[2] Photographs of Cairo no. 9253 are not available in the main photographic archives of Coptic manuscripts (*Corpus dei manoscritti copti letterari* in Hamburg and *Digitale Gesamtedition und Übersetzung des koptisch-sahidischen Alten Testamentes* in Göttingen). Moreover, accessing manuscripts in the Coptic Museum is a notoriously difficult task.

[3] *Septuaginta: Id est Vetus Testamentum graece iuxta LXX interpretes; Editio altera*, ed. A. Rahlfs and R. Hanhart, 2nd ed., 2 vols. in 1 (Stuttgart: Deutsche Bibelgesellschaft, 2006), 633.

*Verso*

| | |
|---|---|
| ⁸[ ϩⲛ̄]<br>[ⲧⲙⲏⲏ]ⲧⲉ ⲙ̄ⲡⲉ[ⲕⲗⲁⲟⲥ]<br>[ⲛ̄ⲧⲁ]ⲕⲥⲟⲧⲡ[ϥ̄· ⲟⲩⲗⲁⲟⲥ ⲉⲛⲁ]<br>[ϣⲱϥ] ϩⲉⲛⲁ[ⲧⲏⲡⲉ· ⁹ⲉⲕⲉϯ ⲟⲩ]<br>5 [ϩⲏⲧ] ⲙ̄ⲙⲟⲧ[ⲛ̄ ⲙ̄ⲡⲉ]ⲕ[ϩⲙϩⲁⲗ ⲉϥ]<br>ⲛⲁϣⲥⲱⲧⲙ̄· ⲁⲩⲱ ⲉⲧⲉ[ⲣⲉϥ]<br>ϯϩⲁⲡ ⲉⲡⲉⲕⲗⲁⲟⲥ· ϩⲛ̄ⲟⲩⲇⲓ<br>ⲕⲁⲓⲟⲥⲩⲛⲏ· ⲁⲩⲱ ⲉⲧⲣⲉϥⲛⲟⲉⲓ<br>ϩⲛ̄ⲧⲙⲏⲧⲉ ⲛ̄ⲧⲙⲓⲛⲉ· ⲛⲟⲩⲁ<br>10 ⲅⲁⲑⲟⲛ ⲙ̄ⲛⲟⲩⲡⲉⲑⲟⲟⲩ<br>ϫⲉ ⲛⲓⲙ ⲡⲉⲧⲛⲁϣϭⲙϭⲟⲙ ⲉ<br>ⲕⲣⲓⲛⲉ ⲙ̄ⲡⲉⲕⲗⲁⲟⲥ ⲡⲁⲓ ⲉⲧ<br>ⲛⲁϣⲱϥ· ¹⁰ⲁⲩⲱ ⲥⲟⲗⲟⲙⲱⲛ· | ⁸-ἐν<br>μέσῳ τοῦ λαοῦ σου,<br>ὃν ἐξελέξω, λαὸν πολύν,<br>ὃς οὐκ ἀριθμηθήσεται. ⁹καὶ δώσεις<br>τῷ δούλῳ σου καρδίαν<br>ἀκούειν καὶ<br>διακρίνειν τὸν λαόν σου ἐν δι-<br>καιοσύνῃ τοῦ συνίειν<br>ἀνὰ μέσον ἀ-<br>γαθοῦ καὶ κακοῦ.<br>ὅτι τίς δυνήσεται<br>κρίνειν τὸν λαόν σου<br>τὸν βαρὺν τοῦτον; ¹⁰καὶ ἤρεσεν<br>ἐνώπιον κυρίου ὅτι ᾐτήσατο<br>Σαλωμων |

⁸[...] [in the midst] of [your people], [whom] you have chosen, [a numerous people, uncountable. ⁹You shall give a] sound [mind to] your [servant so that he] will be able to hear and to judge your people with righteousness and to discern between good and bad sort, for who will be able to judge your people, this which is great? ¹⁰And Solomon [...]

Although the Sahidic translation is not literal throughout, it is generally very accurate, without any rephrasing or significant adaptations of the Greek. On the recto, in those places where the text is clearly readable and does not require the intervention of the editors, the only notable differences are the following:

1. lines 10-11 (= 3 Kgdms 3:5): ⲁⲓⲧⲉⲓ ⲛⲁⲕ ⲛⲟⲩⲁⲓⲧⲏⲙⲁ ⲛ̄ⲧⲟⲟⲧ, "Ask for yourself a request from me." This sentence renders well the LXX Αἴτησαί τι αἴτημα σαυτῷ, but the Sahidic adds "from me" (ⲛ̄ⲧⲟⲟⲧ) at the end. Additionally, it uses the indefinite article ⲟⲩ-, whereas the Greek employs the singular pronoun τι.
2. lines 11-12 (= 3 Kgdms 3:6): ⲡⲉϫⲉ ⲥⲟⲗⲟⲙⲱⲛ ⲙ̄ⲡϫⲟⲉⲓⲥ, "Solomon said to the Lord." The LXX has a different clause, καὶ εἶπεν Σαλωμων, which translates the Hebrew ויאמר שלמה.[4] The Sahidic omits the conjunction καί and adds ⲙ̄ⲡϫⲟⲉⲓⲥ, "to the Lord," after ⲥⲟⲗⲟⲙⲱⲛ. This reading is not mentioned in the common editions that we checked.

According to Munier, the first four surviving lines of the recto preserve only some letters and strings of letters, which renders their reconstruction challenging. Nevertheless, at least the noun ϭⲗ[ⲓⲗ seems safe to restore in line 3 (3 Kgdms 3:4).

---

[4] A. Jepsen, in *BHS*, 5th ed., 564.

This word usually translates the Greek ὁλοκαύτωμα. One would expect to have here ογϣο ⲛ̄ϭⲗⲓⲗ ("a thousand burnt offerings"), which would harmonize with the LXX χιλίαν ὁλοκαύτωσιν. This is unlikely, however, since Munier notes that ⲛ̄ϭ[ⲗⲓⲗ is preceded by the letter ⲛ. Finally, in line 4 Munier gives as certain two letters, ]ⲇⲇ[, proposing the reconstruction ]ⲇⲇ[ⲩⲉⲓⲇ ("David"). This disagrees with the text of 3 Kgdms 3:4, which does not mention David but rather his son, Solomon. Such a corruption would be notable indeed, as it is not supported by any ancient version. It is possible, however, that Munier's suggestion is based on a misreading of the manuscript. Consequently, we cautiously suggest the reading ⲥⲟ]ⲗⲟ[ⲙⲱⲛ on recto, line 4. The examination of the visible traces of letters on the manuscript will help to check further the validity of this hypothesis.

On the verso of the fragment can be detected a few other variant readings compared to the Greek model. On lines 2–5 are preserved some strings of letters that are beyond a reasonable doubt the vestiges of 3:8. The reconstruction of the text, however, remains doubtful, as most of it is lost in the lacunae. Our proposal, ϩⲛ̄]|[ⲧⲙⲏⲏ]ⲧⲉ ⲙ̄ⲡⲉ[ⲕⲗⲁⲟⲥ]| [ⲛ̄ⲧⲁ]ⲕⲥⲟⲧⲡ[ϥ̄· ⲟⲩⲗⲁⲟⲥ ⲉⲛⲁ][ϣⲱϥ] ϩⲉⲛⲁ[ⲧⲏⲡⲉ, is a literal translation of the Greek ἐν μέσῳ τοῦ λαοῦ σου, ὃν ἐξελέξω, λαὸν πολύν, ὃς οὐκ ἀριθμηθήσεται, being supported both by the surviving letters and by the estimated length of the lines in the manuscript.

The beginning of verse 3:9 (lines 4–5) is even more difficult to conjecture because Munier transcribed only a few letters from it, ⲙ̄ⲙⲟⲧ[ ]ⲕ[. The string of four letters is relevant, however, because it indicates that the Coptic text must be restored as [ⲟⲩϩⲏⲧ] ⲙ̄ⲙⲟⲧ[ⲛ̄ ("sound mind"). This is congruent with a minority of Greek codices, which have at this point the lection καὶ δώσεις τῷ δούλῳ σου καρδίαν φρονίμην τοῦ ἀκούειν, instead of the more common καὶ δώσεις τῷ δούλῳ σου καρδίαν ἀκούειν.[5] The same reading appears in Theodoret of Cyrrhus's *Commentary on the Books of Kings and Chronicles* (CPG, 6201; PG 80:677). Similarly, the Vetus Latina version, as quoted by Ambrosius, *In Psalm. 118*, 18.47 (CPL, 141), has *cor prudens audire*.[6] Note also the morphological transformation of ἀκούειν, which in Sahidic uses the future tense and joins to the verbal auxiliary -ϣ-, "will be able to hear."

Leaving aside, therefore, the lacunose sections whose reconstruction is debatable and the normal amount of *variae lectiones*, the text edited by Munier represents a good translation of the LXX version of 3 Kgdms 3:4–10.

---

[5] See Frederick Field, *Genesis–Esther*, vol. 1 of *Origenis Hexaplorum quae supersunt*, 2 vols. (Oxford: Clarendon, 1875), 597. Field mentions that this reading occurs in codices 19, 82, 93, and 108.

[6] Michael Petschenig, *Expositio Psalmi CXVIII*, part 5 of *S. Ambrosii Opera*, CSEL 62 (Vienna: F. Tempsky, 1913), 421.

## II. Provenance of the Fragment

As with the other Sahidic manuscript fragments catalogued by Munier, no. 9253 once belonged to the Monastery of Apa Shenoute, or the White Monastery, as it is usually called, situated in Upper Egypt near Sohag. Around the year 1000 CE, the library of the White Monastery held copies of most of the biblical, liturgical, and literary works extant in Sahidic, and it is our main source of documentation on Coptic literature. Unfortunately, virtually no White Monastery codex has survived intact. Beginning in the second half of the eighteenth century, the White Monastery manuscripts emerged from their cache as dismembered leaves and fragments that were spread in different repositories all over the world.

Because the source of the fragment is known, we tried to identify the manuscript to which it originally belonged. It should be stressed from the outset that our task could not be completed properly without the paleographic inspection of the fragment. Therefore, the conclusions below depend entirely on the short description of the fragment in Munier's catalog.

Study of the collections containing White Monastery fragments has brought to light vestiges of only one codex featuring the Sahidic version of 3 Kingdoms. This is "sa 182," a tenth- to eleventh-century parchment manuscript.[7] But the possibility that Cairo no. 9253 would belong to this codex is excluded from the outset because the text of our fragment is arranged in one column, whereas "sa 182" is a two-column manuscript. Princeton AM 11249 is an unpublished Sahidic fragment of 3 Kgdms 20:24–26, 21:1–3 of unknown provenance. Although written in a single column, supposedly like the Cairo fragment under scrutiny here, AM 11249 is a paper manuscript, not parchment.

Yet another possibility is that the fragment actually came from a lectionary. Portions of 3 Kgdms are attested in the White Monastery lectionaries "sa 108[L]," "sa 148[L]," and "sa 212[L]."[8] None of these texts, however, conforms to the paleographical description provided by Munier for the Cairo fragment of 3 Kingdoms, which are all written in two columns. In conclusion, the fragment edited by Munier does not seem to correspond to any of the aforementioned White Monastery codices, although the fact that we are not able to examine the manuscript leaves this question open.

---

[7] Karlheinz Schüssler, *Biblia Coptica: Die koptischen Bibeltexte* (Wiesbaden: Harrassowitz, 2012), 2.1:132–39.

[8] See "Sa 108[L]" in Schüssler, *Biblia Coptica,* 1.4: 49–69; "sa 148[L]" in Schüssler, *Biblia Coptica,* 2.1:79–81; "sa 212[L]" will be introduced in the next fascicle of *Biblia Coptica* (vol. 2.2).

## III. An Apocryphon on Solomon?

Although the text can be identified with precision, Munier mistakenly asserted that it belonged to a "récit—inspiré du texte biblique (III Rois III, 3–15)—d'un songe du Salomon (ⲥⲟⲗⲟⲙⲱⲛ) pendant lequel le Seigneur apparaît et tient un long discours" ("story—based on the biblical text [3 Kgdms 3:3–13]—of a dream of Solomon during which the Lord appears and has a long discourse").[9] This description suggests that Munier neither read the Coptic text carefully nor compared it with the Greek version of 3 Kgdms 3:3–15. Had he done so, he would have realized that it is not God who speaks at length there but rather Solomon.

The wrong description of the text by Munier caused Albert-Marie Denis to refer repeatedly in his publications on Jewish pseudepigrapha to an apocryphon that actually never existed. Thus, in a list of apocryphal works on Solomon preserved in various ancient languages, Denis mentioned Cairo no. 9253.[10] Wolfgang Kosack was slightly more cautious, saying that the fragment is so short that the character of the work to which it belonged is hard to evaluate.[11] He wrote concerning this issue,

> Von der gleichen Kunst, eine Bibelstelle zu "umspielen," legt ein anderer Pergamentschnipsel Zeugnis ab, der leider so klein ist, dass er keinen Zusammenhang mehr ergibt. Die dazugehörige Bibelstelle, von der die Erzählung ihren Ausgang nahm, ist vielleicht 2. Könige 3,3 f, doch der Textumfang ist zu winzig, um etwas Sicheres darüber zu sagen.[12]

Kosack even offered a German translation of the text based on Munier's edition, without noticing what he actually translated. As the comparison against the Greek text of the Septuagint clearly shows, the fragment edited by Munier provides an accurate translation into Sahidic of a portion of 3 Kingdoms.

The identification of this fragment warns us once again that the fragmentary state of most of the surviving Coptic manuscripts often aims to subvert our research. Therefore, care is to be taken lest we invent texts that have never existed.[13]

---

[9] Munier, *Manuscrits coptes*, 67.

[10] Albert-Marie Denis, *Introduction aux pseudépigraphes grecs d'Ancien Testament*, SVTP 1 (Leiden: Brill, 1970), 68–69 n. 41; Denis, *Introduction à la littérature religieuse judéo-hellénistique*, 2 vols. (Turnhout: Brepols, 2000), 1:542 n. 135.

[11] Wolfgang Kosack, "Märchen und Lieder um König Salomo," *Armant* 4 (1969): 225–64, here 228–29.

[12] Ibid., 228 ("2. Könige" may be a typo for "3. Könige.").

[13] Enzo Lucchesi has demonstrated in several studies that many Coptic fragments have been attributed in the past either to the wrong author or to writings that never existed. See, e.g., his articles "Une évangile apocryphe imaginaire," *OLP* 28 (1997): 167–78; "Fausses attributions en hagiographie copte," *Mus* 119 (2006): 243–54, http://dx.doi.org/10.2143/MUS.119.3.2017947; and "Identification de P. Vindob. K 4856: À propos de Démas et Kestas," *Or* 78 (2009): 421–22.

# The Persianized Liturgy of Nehemiah 8:1-8*

MARK WHITTERS
mwhitters@emich.edu
Eastern Michigan University, Ypsilanti, MI 48197

The historicity of the ceremony recounted in Neh 8:1-8 is fiercely debated, but it is clear that the narrative presents Ezra and his Torah as clothed with the highest authority. While there is scant literary evidence for an "imperial authorization" of a Jewish commonwealth by Xerxes or Artaxerxes, I argue that Neh 8:1-8 represents various genuine correspondences with the Achaemenid Empire as it is known from Persian sources. In particular, there are some striking and heretofore unnoticed parallels between the performative actions described in the biblical text and the performative actions illustrated at Persepolis. Thus, while the depiction of Ezra may involve editorial flourish and calculated projection, there is no doubting the narrative's Persian context. The textual picture of the liturgy over which Ezra presides is dependent on cultural expressions such as those depicted in images at Persepolis. The biblical text is important as a political statement of the restoration of Israel after the Babylonian captivity. It also serves as a religious justification for such things as rabbinic authority, the synagogue service, the canonization of the Scriptures, and even a communal festal calendar. The passage claims to represent the milieu of the Achaemenid Empire, and correspondence between the images of Persepolis and the ceremony of Neh 8:1-8 appears to validate the claim. Contextualizing Neh 8:1-8 as a Persianized liturgy leads to many new insights about the restorationist agenda of Ezra and the Jews who returned from Babylon.

---

The Roman Empire and its subsidiary clients and partners often serve as the textbook case for illustrating the sociological principles of the diffusion of power and acculturation in the premodern era before the dawn of European colonization.[1] Through the dominance of the Caesars, Rome became the center of influence,

* Ago gratias consiliariis: Larry Lahey, Margaret Cool Root, JoAnn Scurlock, and Phil Schmitz.
[1] Historians have adapted several anthropological models to explain cultural reception and interpenetration, often called "diffusion" or "acculturation." The most common model since the 1970s is the "center-periphery" approach, which assumes a dominant group that influences

and its imperial subjects all over the Mediterranean world Romanized themselves in public art and ceremonies. There are, however, many other historical cases that teach similar lessons about how dominant civilizations propagated their prestige over subordinate cultures.[2]

One less-investigated case involves the return of the Judeans to their homeland in the fifth century BCE. The returnees found in Cyrus II a new kind of patron, who sent back their compatriots to their homeland and to their religious way of life.[3] For these liberated exiles, the influential cultural roads led to Persepolis instead of to Rome. The biblical books of Ezra and Nehemiah chronicle this rebirth of the nation, and one passage in particular, Neh 8:1–8, describes a public service that enshrined the spirit of their mission.[4] In this article, I compare the performative actions surrounding this service with what the art and inscriptions of fifth-century Persepolis portray as performative expressions of the Achaemenid Empire. The resemblance between these two sources points to some kind of dependence either in actual contact or in cultural milieu. I will suggest in conclusion that this relationship between the two performances leads to new understandings about the Second Temple enterprise as told by Ezra-Nehemiah. There are two presuppositions here on which the value of the comparison depends: first, that a performance is being described in both cases; and, second, that the biblical text and the Persian art and inscriptions reflect a contemporary and congruent world.

---

remote and subsidiary groups. This model is especially suited to an empire, where there is a well-defined political center and outlying colonial or imperial holdings; hence the Roman Empire is often offered as an example of this dynamic. The subsidiary group emulates the center to obtain prestige or status. The subsidiary unit does not disintegrate under this power of the center or, conversely, adopt every alien but hierarchical influence but often selects traits that allow it to identify with the center. For background and documentation on how this concept applies to the fifth century BCE, see Margaret C. Miller, *Athens and Persia in the Fifth Century B.C.: A Study in Cultural Receptivity* (Cambridge: Cambridge University Press, 1997), 244–46.

[2] For pre-Roman peoples, Irene J. Winter finds that ninth-century Hansanlus adopted centralized Assyrian symbols in their funerary art ("Perspective on the 'Local Style' of Hansanlu IV B: A Study in Receptivity," in *Mountain and Lowlands: Essays in the Archaeology of Greater Mesopotamia*, ed. Louis D. Levine and T. Cuyler Young, BMes 7 [Malibu, CA: Undena, 1977], 371–86); and Gerald L. Mattingly shows how ninth-century Moabites selectively adopted certain art forms of the dominant Egyptians without accepting their concomitant Egyptian religion ("Moabite Religion and the Meshaʿ Inscription," in *Studies in the Mesha Inscription and Moab*, ed. Andrew Dearman, ABS 2 [Atlanta: Scholars Press, 1989], 211–38, esp. 224–27). For later Jewish examples of acculturation, see Ephraim Shoham-Steiner, "The Virgin Mary, Miriam, and Jewish Reactions to Marian Devotion in the High Middle Ages," *AJSR* 37 (2013): 75–91, http://dx.doi.org/10.1017/S0364009413000044; and Katrin Kogman-Appel, "Jewish Art and Cultural Exchange: Theoretical Perspectives," *MedEnc* 17 (2011): 1–26, esp. 20–21, http://dx.doi.org/10.1163/157006711X561703.

[3] Isaiah 45:1; cf. Cyrus Cylinder, lines 30–34.

[4] The label often used for Ezra-Nehemiah is "restorationist literature." For a sampling of its nationalist rhetoric, see Ezra 1:1–4, 2:68–70, 3:1, 7:11–26, 9:8–9, Neh 1:5–10, 8:1–18, 9:7–37, 11:1–2.

Both sources are important in their own right. Scholars of Second Temple Judaism understand Neh 8:1–8 as foundational for the restoration of Israel as a nation after the Babylonian captivity. Iranologists, on the other hand, look to Persepolis as the equivalent of Athens for Greek civilization or Rome for the Roman Empire. Both images, therefore, serve to communicate on the level of real-world authorities and events, while simultaneously conveying a timeless aura of reverence and institution.

This comparison will depend on a repertoire of rituals or ceremonies that later Hellenistic literature would call liturgies.[5] There are two dimensions of liturgy: first, "performative rubrics" employing publicly recognizable gestures or rehearsed activities that comprise the mechanics of social communication;[6] and, second, the message of social cohesion that the participants experience.[7] In the case of the

---

[5] A liturgy brings together elements of public expression and forges community consensus. In the original sense it was a performance or presentation paid for by some civic benefactor. Thus, its background is in the Greek world of citizens and *polis*, an appropriate context for Ezra's and Darius's goals of nation building.

[6] Art historians and archaeologists increasingly recognize the role of performance in the functioning of society. In general, see Zainab Bahrani, "Performativity and the Image: Narrative, Representation, and the Uruk Vase," in *Leaving No Stones Unturned: Essays on the Ancient Near East and Egypt in Honor of Donald P. Hansen*, ed. Erica Ehrenberg (Winona Lake, IN: Eisenbrauns, 2001), 15–22; Elin Diamond, ed., *Performance and Cultural Politics* (London: Routledge, 1996), 1–12; Gary Palmer and William R. Jankowiak, "Performance and Imagination: Toward an Anthropology of the Spectacular and the Mundane," *Cultural Anthropology* 11 (1996): 225–98, http://dx.doi.org/10.1525/can.1996.11.2.02a00040; Takeshi Inomata and Lawrence S. Coben, "Overture: An Invitation to the Archaeological Theater," in *Archaeology of Performance: Theaters of Power, Community and Politics*, ed. Takeshi Inomata and Lawrence S. Coben (Lanham, MD: Altamira, 2006), 11–44. For a discussion of Persian culture specifically, see Margaret Cool Root, "Achaemenid Imperial Architecture: Performative Porticoes of Persepolis," in *Persian Kingship and Architecture: Strategies of Power in Iran from the Achaemenids to the Pahlavis*, ed. Sussan Babaie and Talinn Grigor (London: I. B. Taurus, 2015), 1–64.

Biblical scholars deal with texts, so it is more difficult to "visualize" the role of performance. For the prophets, it is clear that some messages were acted out before they were written down, and prophetic performances enhanced the effectiveness of the message. Even for legal materials, there is abundant evidence that covenant renewal texts assume some kind of drama involving superiors and inferiors. For the narratives coming from the Achaemenid era, there has been less investigation. See, however, Helen Dixon, "Writing Persepolis in Judah: Achaemenid Kingship in Chronicles," in *Images and Prophecy in the Ancient Eastern Mediterranean*, ed. Martti Nissinen and Charles E. Carter, FRLANT 233 (Göttingen: Vandenhoeck & Ruprecht, 2009), 163–94; Gary N. Knoppers and Paul B. Harvey Jr., "The Pentateuch in Ancient Mediterranean Context: The Publication of Local Lawcodes," and Joachim Schaper, "The 'Publication' of Legal Texts in Ancient Judah," both in *The Pentateuch as Torah: New Models for Understanding Its Promulgation and Acceptance*, ed. Gary N. Knoppers and Bernard M. Levinson (Winona Lake, IN: Eisenbrauns, 2007), 105–41 and 225–36, respectively. Yet a thoroughgoing comparative analysis of Near Eastern cultures is lacking as a background for Ezra-Nehemiah.

[7] The common patristic maxim, though a good deal later, still applies: *ut legem credendi lex*

returning Jews, we might call this "theology" or religious ideals, but it is not far removed from what historians of the Achaemenids might term "ideology." The discussion below will focus, first, on performative rubrics, and, second, on interpretations of the liturgies as depicted in the Jewish Scriptures and at Persepolis. Finally, it will be argued that these parallels point to significant Persianizing in society and government among returning Jews as they organize and establish institutions in the early Second Temple period.

## I. The Rubrics of Nehemiah 8:1–8

The story behind Neh 8:1–8 is culled from both the book of Ezra and the book of Nehemiah, though scholars disagree about how to untangle its definite outline and sequence of events, since the books have a complicated and confusing interdependence.[8] I will limit my remarks to the bare bones of the context for Ezra's public service in order to focus on how pervasive the Persian influences were, without trying to sort out the text's literary history.[9] For present purposes, I will accept the text's authorial claim to represent what happened.[10]

The simple antecedent event that led up to the service probably goes back to Ezra 7:10–26. There Ezra receives a letter from the king, presumably Artaxerxes I, authorizing him to restore Jerusalem's temple and Moses's Torah. At first glance, this "imperial authorization" is astounding:[11] Ezra is given the right not only to

---

*statuat supplicandi*, "So that the law of prayer ['rubrics'] grounds the law of belief [theology/ideology]."

[8] The Masoretes read the two as one book. The LXX tradition similarly presents the two as a single unit of twenty-three chapters. The Talmud makes reference only to biblical Ezra and subsumes the whole of Ezra-Nehemiah under the title Ezra. See Michael W. Duggan, *The Covenant Renewal in Ezra-Nehemiah (Neh 7:72b–10:40): An Exegetical, Literary, and Theological Study*, SBLDS 164 (Atlanta: Society of Biblical Literature, 2001), 35.

[9] For a critical commentary on the passage, see the standard handbooks, e.g., H. G. M. Williamson, *Ezra, Nehemiah*, WBC 16 (Waco, TX: Word, 1985), 275–99, esp. 279–86; Juha Pakkala, *Ezra the Scribe: The Development of Ezra 7–10 and Nehemiah 8*, BZAW 347 (Berlin: de Gruyter, 2004), 136–79; Jacob M. Myers, *Ezra, Nehemiah: Introduction, Translation, and Notes*, AB 14 (Garden City, NY: Doubleday, 1964), 149–54; and Joseph Blenkinsopp, *Judaism, the First Phase: The Place of Ezra and Nehemiah in the Origins of Judaism* (Grand Rapids: Eerdmans, 2009), 44–116, esp. 61–63.

[10] Even Jacob L. Wright's contention that Neh 8:1–8 represents the last "primary compositional layer" wedged into the canonical text does not rule out either its possible Achaemenid origins or its Persianized worldview (see Wright, *Rebuilding Identity: The Nehemiah-Memoir and Its Readers*, BZAW 348 [Berlin: de Gruyter, 2004], 315–40).

[11] Many scholars view the idea of "imperial authorization," first proposed by Peter Frei ("Die persische Reichsautorisation: Ein Überblick," *ZABR* 1 [1995]: 1–35), as a post-factum editorial fiction. See Pakkala, *Ezra the Scribe*, 75; and Joseph Blenkinsopp, "Footnotes to the Rescript of

reestablish the cultic activities of the temple but also to promulgate and impose divine (Torah) and royal (Achaemenid) laws on both those who already know them (the Jews of Ezra's ilk) and those who do not know them (the other residents of the land) (7:25). Ezra's jurisdiction is the region of Yehud, the area arguably corresponding to Judea. It is possible that he had authority over the whole fifth satrapy of "Ebar-Nehara" (Trans-Euphrates region), which Herodotus says includes Samaria, Lebanon, Cyprus, and western Syria (*Hist.* 3.91). Modern scholars question the authenticity of this rescript on the basis of Ezra's unprecedented authority to impose the Torah on a miscellaneous group of subjects who did not have much in common, certainly not religion.

Ezra 7:10–26 clears the way for Ezra to make his debut in the book of Nehemiah in the narrative at the heart of that book. His unexpected and abrupt placement in the text forces the reader to rethink his role, not only as an official sanctioned by Persia but as a great hero of national and religious transformation.

Form-critical studies emphasize that the narrative comprising Neh 8:1–8 and beyond describes a covenant renewal and that this particular scene describes a liturgy initiating the renewal.[12] The passage reads as follows:

> ¹All the people gathered together into the square before the Water Gate. They told the scribe Ezra to bring the book of the Torah of Moses.... ²Ezra the priest brought the Torah before the assembly, both men and women and all who could hear with understanding [מבין לשמע]. ³He read from it facing the square ... from early morning until midday in front of the men and the women and the interpreters [המבינים], and all the people were attentive to the book of Torah. ⁴Ezra the scribe stood on a wooden platform that had been made for the purpose; and beside him stood Mattithiah [and five others] on his right; and Pedaiah [and six others] on his left. ⁵And Ezra opened the book in the sight of all the people; ... and when he opened it, all the people stood up. ⁶Then Ezra blessed the LORD ... and all the people answered, "Amen, Amen," lifting up their hands. Then they bowed down ... and worshiped the LORD with their faces to the ground. ⁷Then the ... [thirteen] Levites helped the people to understand [מבינים] the Torah, while the people remained in their places. ⁸So they read from the book, from the Torah of God, with interpretation [מפרש]. They gave the sense [שום שכל], making the reading comprehensible [ויבינו במקרא]. (Neh 8:1–8)[13]

---

Artaxerxes (Ezra 7:11–26)," in *The Historian and the Bible: Essays in Honour of Lester L. Grabbe*, ed. Philip R. Davies and Diana V. Edelman, LHBOTS 530 (New York: T&T Clark, 2010), 150–57, esp. 157.

[12] See Duggan, *Covenant Renewal*, 21; and Williamson, *Ezra, Nehemiah*, 276, 279–80, 287, for a list of scholars who notice the elements of covenant renewal in this section of Ezra-Nehemiah, including Klaus Baltzer, Dennis J. McCarthy, and U. Kellermann.

[13] Biblical translations throughout this article are from the NRSV, sometimes with slight modifications.

Some of the liturgical rubrics that stand out are listed below in sequence:

| Verse | Rubric |
|---|---|
| 1 | Popular gathering into a public square |
| 1–3 | Designated day and time[14] |
| 2 | Ceremonial procession of the Torah |
| 3 | Public recitation of Torah |
| 4 | Wooden platform for ceremony and recognition |
| 5 | Designated trustees (on the right and left) |
| 5 | Opening (= elevation?) of the book |
| 5 | People standing at attention |
| 6 | Blessing and response to blessing |
| 6 | People lift up their hands |
| 6 | People's prostration |
| 7 | Transmission of teaching authority |
| 8 | Interpretation/instruction in alternative languages (?) |

What are the origins of such a liturgy and its focus on nation building and integrated leadership? Where do its rubrics come from, and whence its resolution for the problems facing the community?[15] The self-conscious claim of the books of Nehemiah and Ezra derives from special permissions granted the Babylonian and Persian exiles. Given the narrative's historical claims of imperial authorization (whether fact or fiction) and the lessons of acculturation, the natural place to begin an investigation would be the Jewish community in Yehud and the Achaemenid Empire. Although a direct link through an "imperial authorization" seems far from certain, there is no reason why returning Jews would not have cloaked their foundational documents in Persian trappings to advance a nationalist agenda. They were after all in a tenuous position, since they could not set up a sovereign government in Yehud. For the occupation forces and resident Persian sympathizers in the land, it was necessary that the Jewish returnees seem as closely allied with the superpower as possible. On this basis, then, there is justification for looking at the art and inscriptions of Persia for at least some of the context of Ezra's public service.

---

[14] For the event as a "nonspontaneous" ritual, see Sara Japhet, "The Ritual of Reading Scripture (Nehemiah 8:1–12)," in *New Perspectives on Old Testament Prophecy and History: Essays in Honour of Hans M. Barstad*, ed. Rannfrid I. Thelle, Terje Stordalen, and Mervyn E. J. Richardson, VTSup 168 (Leiden: Brill, 2015), 175–90, esp. 176 n. 5.

[15] Japhet concludes that the ceremony described in Neh 8 "remains a unique event in the history of Israel, with no attested precedents and no attested follow-ups" ("Ritual of Reading," 190).

## II. The Rubrics of Persepolis

Persepolis and Achaemenid images present a national perspective that would have dominated Ezra's time and space, if the authorial claims to authenticity are accepted. Here the performance rubrics are constructed largely from subjective interpretations of Persian propaganda art, although there are a few terse texts that accompany the reliefs to supplement the visual impressions. The power of the visual does offer an advantage over the text, in that it forces the observer to come to grips with the objective reality of the public event whatever it may be. That is, we do not seem to be dealing with an imaginative event staged *de novo* in an author's (or editor's) mind.

As with Neh 8:1-8, one must first reckon with the historical context of Persepolis. Darius has a task similar to Ezra's because he has to reinvent the Achaemenid nation-state after he forcibly takes power from his predecessor. One particularly effective (and traditional) way of establishing a *novum ordinem* is by founding a new capital,[16] wherein lie the remains of his nation-building efforts that offer a comparison to Neh 8:1-8.

The Greeks called this city "Persepolis," but the Persians referred to it as Parsa, also the name given to the entire homeland. This newly dedicated capital was the center of Darius's Achaemenid world—as Ezra's newly rebuilt Jerusalem was the "true pole of the earth" for Jews.

Most important of all for Parsa was its huge palace complex known as the Apadana. Between the palace's plaza and the porticoed hall were magnificent staircases adorned with friezes depicting the king and his royal courtiers in some official mode of governance. The stairways of the Apadana met in the center, the platform of which extended some one hundred yards along the east and north sides of the building. In addition to the Apadana façades, there are two other contemporary monuments to consider for constructing a list of performative rubrics that Persians

---

[16] The bibliography on the foundation of new cities in the ancient world is vast. One well-known example from antiquity is Akhenaten's efforts to establish a new capital at Tel el-Amarna with an explicitly different theological and political agenda. See Ian Shaw, "Building a Sacred Capital: Akhenaten, El-Amarna, and the 'House of the King's Statue,'" and Fritz Vokmar, "Planning a Capital: Akhetaten and Akhenaten," both in *Capital Cities: Urban Planning and Spiritual Dimensions; Proceedings of the Symposium Held on May 27-29, 1996, Jerusalem, Israel*, ed. Joan Goodnick Westenholz, Bible Lands Museum Jerusalem Publications 2 (Jerusalem: Bible Lands Museum, 1998), 55-64 and 117-28, respectively. Iron-Age Jerusalem itself is another case in point. See Joe Uziel and Itzhaq Shai, "Iron Age Jerusalem: Temple-Palace, Capital City," *JAOS* 127 (2007): 161-70, esp. 166-68. Concerning Jerusalem, see Alexei M. Sivertsev, *Judaism and Imperial Ideology in Late Antiquity* (Cambridge: Cambridge University Press, 2011), 45-124. Similarly, the ancient Chinese and the Aztecs built new capital cities when they asserted their civilizational dominance.

followed around the same time: Naqsh-i Rustam, the tomb complex nearby, and the legendary Bisitun carving in western Iran.

FIGURE 1. "Persepolis: Hypostyle Hall of Xerxes; Perspective View." From Charles Chipiez, *History of Art in Persia* (London: Chapman & Hall, 1892), opposite p. 300.

FIGURE 2. Persepolis Apadana, east façade, showing the section of gift-bearing delegations. Note also the lion–bull combat in the triangular frieze at the left base, the astrological symbol of the feast day. Photo courtesy of M. C. Root, 1973.

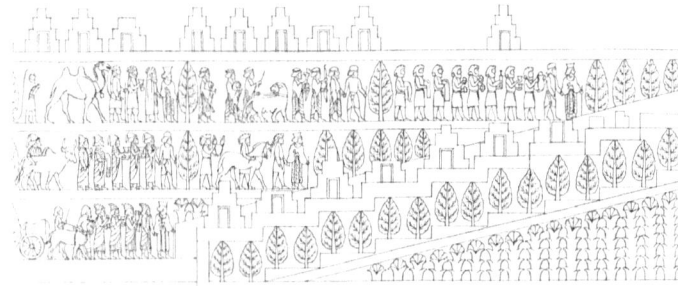

FIGURE 3. Drawing of delegate groups, Apadana staircase, east façade. Gift-bearing subject peoples proceed up the platform toward the king, each delegation led by a Persian usher. Adapted from Gerald Walser, *Die Volkerschaften auf den Reliefs von Persepolis* (Berlin: Mann, 1966), folding pl. 2.

FIGURE 4. Apadana platform, east façade. Persian nobles process in the ceremony of gift bearing, looking backward and forward. Photo courtesy of M. C. Root, 1973.

FIGURE 5. Apadana platform, east façade. Detail of Persian nobles, linked together, processing on platform. From Pierre Briant, *From Cyrus to Alexander: A History of the Persian Empire* [Winona Lake, IN: Eisenbrauns, 2002], 221). Used by permission of the author.

Figure 6.1. Apadana staircase, north façade: gift-bearing delegation (no longer *in situ*). The Persian usher takes the lead delegate by the hand and looks back possibly as if to instruct him, while following delegates resolutely look ahead. Photograph © 2017 Museum of Fine Arts, Boston.

Figure 6.2. Persepolis Apadana, east façade. Detail of usher taking lead figure of a foreign gift-bearing delegation by the hand. Photo courtesy of M. C. Root, 1973.

FIGURE 7. Apadana, reconstruction of central panel. King on platform with footstool (Greek δίφρος), surrounded by retinue of courtiers on either side (not shown in the illustration). The closest noble in front gestures respect with mouth covered. Adapted from A. B. Tilia, *Studies and Restorations at Persepolis and Other Sites of Färs*, 2 vols., Istituto italiano par il Medio ed Estremo Oriente, Centro studi e scave archeologici in Asia, Reports and Memoirs 16 (Rome: IsMEO, 1972–1978), fig. 3, following p. 194.

FIGURE 8. Naqsh-i Rustam, tomb façade of Darius I, full view. Photo courtesy of M. C. Root, 2011.

Figure 9. Naqsh-i Rustam, drawing of the tomb façade of Darius I. Detail showing central relief. Royal platform blessing and instruction (?) in the presence of Ahuramazda in the air. Representatives of the subject lands hold up the platofrm with their fingertips. See the translation of related panels below. Drawing from Root, adapted from Amélie Kuhrt, *The Persian Empire: A Corpus of Sources from the Achaemenid Period*, 2 vols. (London: Routledge, 2007), vol. 2, fig. 11.14. Used by permission.

*Inscription, behind the king*: "By the favour of Ahuramazda these are the countries which I seized outside Persia; I ruled over them; they bore me tribute; what was said to them by me, that they did; my law (OP: *data*)—that they held firm...." Translation by Amélie Kuhrt, *The Persian Empire: A Corpus of Sources from the Achaemenid Period* (London: Routledge, 2010), 502.

*Inscription below the figural representation* (originally from tomb of Darius, copied later for foundation text in the reign of Xerxes): "A great god is Ahuramazda ... who created happiness for man; who bestowed wisdom and energy upon Darius.... [who] proclaims: ... I am a friend to what is right, I am no friend to what is wrong. [It is] not my wish that to the weak is done wrong because of the mighty, it is not my wish that the mighty is hurt because of the weak. What is right, that is my wish. I am no friend of the man who is a follower of the Lie.... The man who cooperates, him do I reward.... He who does harm, him I punish.... What a man says, that does not convince me, until I have heard testimony from both parties." Translation from Kuhrt, *Persian Empire: A Corpus of Sources*, 502–3.

In the Darius inscription a moralistic exhortation for young men to listen to the words of the inscription follows. These lines are translated into Aramaic on the Naqsh-i-Rustam text, and many more copies of this text were found in diverse places throughout the empire (Egypt, Persepolis, possibly Susa).

Figure 10. Bisitun: Darius gestures (toward Ahuramazda above) while instructing bound opponents. Trilingual inscriptions accompany relief. Photo courtesy of the George G. Cameron Archives, Kelsey Museum of Archaeology, University of Michigan.

Figure 11. Bisitun. Detail of Darius blessing or instructing with hand gesture. Photo courtesy of the George G. Cameron Archives, Kelsey Museum of Archaeology, University of Michigan.

Figure 12. Babylon Monument. Reconstruction of stela of Darius I, once set up along the Sacred Way (now in Berlin); an abbreviated rendition of the Bisitun Monument for Babylonian audiences. Darius has his foot on his subdued rival Gaumata. Adapted from Ursula Seidl, "Ein Monument Darius' I aus Babylon," ZA 89 (1999): 101–14, fig. 2.

On the basis of the Persian art and inscriptions presented above, it is possible to list some performative rubrics that Darius and his line may have adopted for reconstituting the state. There are numerous ceremonial actions taking place in all these scenes, and the silent messages convey their power primarily to ancient spectators who were already immersed in the empire. Here are some possible acts being performed across the gamut of the scenes:

| Figure | Actions |
| --- | --- |
| 1 | Popular gathering in a public square |
| 1–2 | Designated day and time (frieze, storeroom, courtyard implications) |
| 2–7 | Ceremonial procession |
| 7 | Public audience with the king |
| 1–3; cf. 8–9 | Platform for ceremony and recognition |
| 2–5, 7 | Designated trustees (on the right and left) |
| 8–9 | Proclamation of the king; tribute to the king |
| 7–11 | People standing at attention |
| 7–11 | Blessing and response to blessing |
| 7 | People lift up their hands to their mouths |
| 7–12 | Submission to king (or people's prostration) |
| 2–5 | Transmission of government authority |
| 8–10 | Interpretation/instruction in alternate languages (?) |

## III. Meaning of the Rubrics: Theology and Ideology

Assuming that the performative rubrics express meanings that Jewish audiences and Persian spectators would grasp, I turn to the task of deciphering them. This is a difficult venture since it reaches out beyond the text and visuals and constructs meaning out of a patchwork of historical interpretations. Nonetheless, the circumstances surrounding both groups, returning Jews and reigning Persians, suggest parallel meanings and influences for their public services.

Nehemiah 8:1–8 describes a dramatic moment when the Jewish community gathers in a public square to affirm the religious tenets that hold them together. The Torah is paraded into the assembly as if it were returning to its rightful place, and the crowd recognizes the Torah as the foundation of the community. The leading returnees from Babylon (represented by Ezra) elevate and recite the Torah for all the others to recognize and accept. It is significant that the crowd coheres around a book, though Ezra is the central agent of the ceremony. The broader narrative also provides a festal occasion (8:2, 11) and an institutional expansion of that occasion (see 8:13–18).[17]

---

[17] Some scholars suggest that the observance of Sukkot here predates the textual precedent and commandment found in the Pentateuch. See Pakkala, *Ezra the Scribe*, 157–60; and Alexander

Larger theological and ideological forces are at work in these ceremonial actions. First and foremost, the books' editors see the need to restore the covenant, once and for all, between God and the reconstituted people after the period of turmoil surrounding the Babylonian exile.[18] A few centuries later, the rabbis also find in this "Great Assembly" the consecration of Judaism in its inchoate elements (see, e.g., m. Avot 1:1).[19] Alternatively, the astute reader of the biblical canon instinctively recognizes that Ezra's service symbolically ends a stream of biblical historiography, illustrated by the grim lessons of the Babylonian captivity, and simultaneously begins a new era (see 2 Chr 36:17–23; Ezra 1:1–4).

Closer to the context of the document and the narrative are at least two other thematic tensions within the Jewish community that this liturgy seeks to address as the Ezra-Nehemiah narrative lays out Ezra's task. First, the ceremony has to represent and mobilize a highly diversified collection of Israel's survivors. What Ezra needs to do is join the core city dwellers with the country folk, the advocates of cult with the believers in lay leadership, the "old guard" from Babylon with the native population. Facing such a wide range of interests and priorities, Ezra undertakes a colossal task.[20]

Second, looming in the narrative background is the Persian hegemony with

---

Fantalkin and Oren Tal, "The Canonization of the Pentateuch: When and Why? (Part II)," *ZAW* 12 (2012): 201–12, esp. 201 n. 1. Thomas Römer suggests that the gathering of the law codes and narratives into one "book" with five parts, the Pentateuch, actually goes back to the time of Ezra's mission in Jerusalem (*The So-Called Deuteronomistic History: A Sociological, Historical and Literary Interpretation* [London: T&T Clark, 2005], 179–83).

[18] It is at least possible that, in the imagination of the readers, this event is a formal one that has been staged over and over again in the history of the people of Israel. For example, it is a gathering of a cross-section of the people in a symbolic place represented by a recognized leader, and a document describes the duties entailed by the relationship between the superior (God) and the inferiors (the people of Israel). The context speaks of this people coming together after a period of flux and turmoil, and thus there is a need to restore the covenant between God and the reconstituted people. The reconstitutions of Israel under heroes and kings—Moses (Exod 24:7), Joshua (Josh 8:34), Josiah (2 Kgs 23:1–3, 2 Chr 34:29–32)—mean that Ezra's efforts fit a liturgical pattern.

[19] Ismar Elbogen describes the connections between this passage and rabbinic foundations in *Jewish Liturgy: A Comprehensive History,* trans. Raymond P. Scheindlin (Philadelphia: Jewish Publication Society, 1993; German original, 1913), 130–31.

[20] Erhard S. Gerstenberger finds historical precedent for this critical juncture of Israel's restoration in the Greek concept of *synoikia,* the bonding of residents presumably through a constitution (*politeia*) (*Israel in the Persian Period: The Fifth and Fourth Centuries B.C.E.,* trans. Siegfried Schatzmann, BibEnc 8 [Atlanta: Society of Biblical Literature, 2011], 108). For a discussion of Jewish *politeia* in the Hellenistic world, see Shaye J. D. Cohen, *The Beginnings of Jewishness: Boundaries, Varieties, Uncertainties,* HCS 31 (Berkeley: University of California Press, 1999), 125–29. While this is a suitable parallel, it is not a case of "acculturation" between Greek civilization and the Judean subsidiary culture. There is little historical basis for the *politeia*'s organic connection to Yehud at this stage of its development. The Greek term, nonetheless, is suitable for describing what Ezra must do.

which Jewish nationalism must reckon. Neither Ezra nor any of the venerable returnees can assume King David's office, for there already is "the king of kings" in Persepolis. The Jews, in short, must figure out another model of identity and leadership. The ceremony gives readers clues to the means by which Israel's leadership is to be reconstituted without threatening the imperial political hierarchy. The narrative begins with Ezra as the speaker, but then it gradually changes focus to his thirteen companions on the left and right (8:4) and then to his assistant teachers (8:7). As the account goes on, Ezra fades into the literary background.[21] His initial actions blend in with the actions of others in the book of Nehemiah who are part of the transitional team: Nehemiah and the Levites (8:9–12), the heads of households (8:13–15), and, finally, the entire people (9:3). It is an odd picture: the covenant renewal ceremony starts with Ezra, but the execution of the legal interpretation of the Torah involves a procession of helpers. In this context, then, power is distributed to others, and hierarchy is less elevated.

Yet there are many liturgical rubrics that remain unexplained by this conventional biblical exegesis. What is the nature of the platform to lift up Ezra (8:4–5)? Why are there confreres on Ezra's right and left (8:5)? Why is there a transmission of teaching rather than a univocal declaration? And why is there an emphasis on variegated interpretations (8:8) or perhaps even alternate translations or transcriptions?[22] Even a return to the remote sources of the covenant renewal ceremonies among the more ancient Near Eastern models fails to provide good answers to these questions. The performative elements surrounding this event conclusively go well beyond any imaginative interpretations of Neo-Assyrian imperial covenants with vassal subjects.[23]

---

[21] After the episode, Ezra's name in the book appears infrequently, and even then it seems to be "propped up" by a supporting cast (8:9, 13; 12:1, 13, 26, 33, 36).

[22] Four centuries later, 4 Ezra [2 Esdras] 14:42 says that Ezra and his scribal helpers wrote "in characters which they did not know," probably referring to the conversion from Hebrew characters to the Aramaic block script. See Karina Martin Hogan, *Theologies in Conflict in 4 Ezra: Wisdom, Debate, and Apocalyptic Solution*, JSJSup 130 (Leiden: Brill, 2008), 225 n. 55; Michael Stone, *Fourth Ezra: A Commentary on the Book of Fourth Ezra*, Hermeneia (Philadelphia: Fortress, 1990), 440. The rabbinic Jewish exegetical tradition, however, finds a justification in this passage for the targumim: "'They read from the book, from the Law of God' (Neh 8:8)—this refers to the Scripture; 'clearly' [*mĕpōrāš*]—this refers to targum" (y. Meg. 74d). Compare b. Meg. 3a; b. Ned. 37b; Gen. Rab. 36:8. The targumim were not simply translations but thoroughgoing and distinctive interpretations that continued to be recited even when the Aramaic dialect of the text died out.

[23] Two other biblical accounts—Deut 27:1–14 and Josh 8:30–35—seem to interrupt their respective narratives with their performances reflecting covenant renewal. Along with Neh 8:1–8, these passages involve witnesses to the covenants on or near elevated places. The witnesses seem to represent the twelve tribes gathered around the law. While Neh 8:1–8 has thirteen witnesses to the book, the explanation for this discrepancy could be that the ceremony recognizes that the tribe of Joseph has divided into Ephraim and Manasseh. All of the aforementioned accounts involve a written text, an assembly, a public reading, and even a provision for what the latter rabbis saw as the targumim (Neh 8:3, 7–8; Deut 27:8; Josh 8:34–35). One other account (2 Kgs 23:1–3)

The immediate impression of the Persian reliefs is more equivocal, but the accompanying inscriptions (at Nashq-i-Rustam and Bisitun), as well as other ancient commentaries, help to decipher the meaning. When Darius extends his hand over his subjects from his royal platform at Nashq-i-Rustam, the accompanying Old Persian inscription declares that his reign will extend his dominion in the form of *dāt*, the same word used five times for Ezra's mission to the region assigned to him by the Persian king.[24] The Semitic word *dāt* in the sources means something like general policy or approaches to life rather than the specific force of a legal code. For Jews, Ezra's Torah is a reasonable analogy for *dāt*; and for Darius, the word epitomizes his effort to reform the system of law among his twenty satrapies.[25] Religion is not left out of Darius's intentions, as the inscriptions and images clearly invoke divine powers for the legitimacy of Darius's rule.

Was there a particular festal occasion that the façades at Apadana depicted? Scholars are sometimes willing to speculate that a festal occasion such as the opening of the New Year or the annual presentations of pledges or gifts explained the popular convocation pictured in the reliefs.[26] It is clear that the Apadana courtyard permitted massive gatherings of people and that probably there were occasions where subject peoples paraded tribute. Even if there are no explicit literary

---

describes the master of ceremonies, King Josiah, standing על־העמוד ("on the dais") in order to renew the covenant for all the people of Israel, and later translations (Targum, Peshitta, Vulgate, and Josephus) all envision something like a dais, platform, or bema.

[24] This is the same word that is found in Persian sources and seems to signify a general approach to civic living rather than a specific legal code, such as the Greek and Roman tradition would promulgate. See, in general, Ann Fitzpatrick, "Ezra, Nehemiah, and Some Early Greek Lawgivers," in *Rabbinic Law in Its Roman and Near Eastern Context,* ed. Catherine Hezser, TSAJ 97 (Tübingen: Mohr Siebeck, 2003), 17–48. For specific examples of *dāt* in Persian contexts, see Matthew W. Stolper, *Late Achaemenid, Early Macedonian and Early Seleucid Records of Deposit and Related Texts,* AIONSup 77 (Naples: Istituto Universitario Orentale, 1993), 60–61; Michael Jursa, "Nochmals Akka," *WZKM* 87 (1997): 101–10, esp. 104; Joseph Blenkinsopp, "Was the Pentateuch the Civic and Religious Constitution of the Jewish Ethnos in the Persian Period?," in *Persia and Torah: The Theory of Imperial Authorization of the Pentateuch,* ed. James W. Watts, SymS 17; Atlanta: Society of Biblical Literature, 2001), 41–62, esp. 42; and, in the same volume, L. S. Fried, "'You Shall Appoint Judges': Ezra's Mission and the Rescript of Artaxerxes," 63–89, esp. 81–83.

[25] Plato, *Epist.* vii.332b; Xenophon, *Oeconom.* 14.6-7. Darius's sweeping reform was called the *data sha sharri* of the empire, and it included the appointment of new judges throughout his satrapies.

[26] Briant, *From Cyrus to Alexander,* 183–95; A. T. Olmstead, "New Year's Day at Persepolis," in *History of the Persian Empire* (Chicago: University of Chicago Press, 1948), 272–88, esp. 274–77; John Razmjou and Shahrokh Razmjou, "The Palace," in *Forgotten Empire: The World of Ancient Persia,* ed. John E. Curtis and Nigel Tallis (Berkeley: University of California Press, 2005), 50–55, esp. 52. Interestingly, the Shah of Iran designated Persepolis as the ceremonial center for the birthday celebration of the Iranian monarchy and staged his own representation of Persian grandeur in the 1970s.

references in the accompanying inscriptions, on excavated tablets, or from Greek sources, there is very strong corroborating and in situ evidence.[27] First, Darius explicitly lists in his Behistun inscription nations that bear him tribute, the very ones listed as tributaries at Persepolis.[28] Second, according to Babylonian documents, tax agents regularly visited Susa (one of the four capitals of the Achaemenids) to make their deposits at the New Year season, that is, between the months of Shebat (the last month) and Nisan (the first month).[29] Finally, and most importantly, the relief at the base of the Apadana staircase in figure 2 shows a lion mauling a bull. This is a very specific astrological signal understandable to Mesopotamians that the occasion is the vernal equinox, the Persian New Year.[30]

On a broader ideological level, Persepolis offers some striking parallels to Ezra's task. Darius must refashion the Persian Empire in its Achaemenid form, just as Ezra (and Nehemiah) also must reinvent the national identity of Israel. In the case of the Apadana reliefs, the original highest central panel of the platform depicted the king in audience before a bowing official who seems to be recognizing the *novum ordinem* of the Achaemenids. Yet, in contrast to most Greek, Near Eastern, or Roman genres of political propaganda, the king here is not a particular individual—not Darius, Xerxes, or Artaxerxes, or any other.[31] The art rather depicts a generic image of dynastic order that de-emphasizes the particularities of any specific royal personality or fact of history in favor of re-presenting a pervasive royal ideology or experience of ecumenical order.[32] The Apadana staircase reliefs (and other visual manifestations at Persepolis) conjure an idealized vision of a world empire. This imperial world is made up of cooperative peoples from many lands speaking many languages and practicing varied customs—divinely ordained, eternal, and yet not entirely autocratic.

The reliefs on one side of the platform show envoys and officials from twenty-three subject lands who are lined up and proceeding up the stairs of the Apadana, led by Persian marshals. Each group is led solemnly by a Persian marshal, who

---

[27] My gratitude here goes to the Midwest Region of the American Oriental Society, especially to JoAnn Scurlock and Rich Beal, for their contributions on this point.

[28] See Roland G. Kent, *Old Persian: Grammar, Texts, Lexicon*, 2nd rev. ed., AOS 33 (New Haven: American Oriental Society, 1953), 109, 119, 136–38.

[29] See Caroline Waerzeggers, "Babylonians in Susa: The Travels of Babylonian Businessmen to Susa Reconsidered," in *Der Achämenidenhof/The Achaemenid Court: Akten des 2. Internationalen Kolloquiums zum Thema "Vorderasien im Spannungsfeld klassischer und altorientalischer Überlieferungen," Landgut Castelen bei Basel, 23.-25. Mai 2007*, ed. Bruno Jacob and Robert Rollinger, Classica et Orientalia 2 (Wiesbaden: Harrassowitz, 2010), 777–813, esp. 800–809.

[30] Willy Hartner, "The Earliest History of the Constellations in the Near East and the Motif of the Lion–Bull Combat," *JNES* 29 (1965): 1–16, esp. plate 1, "Lion and Bull at Persepolis, Sixth Century B.C."

[31] Root, "Achaemenid Imperial Architecture," 7.

[32] Thomas Harrison, *Writing Ancient Persia*, Classical Essays (London: Bristol Classical Press, 2011), 85–89.

holds the hand of the forward-most member of the delegation. The marshals arguably have the role of familiarizing foreign peoples with imperial ways and organizing the parade so that the subject peoples proceed according to Persian protocols. The marshals therefore are the guardians and communicators of the new Persian order.

On the other side of the platform, the relief shows Persians and Medes together advancing as teams, though some look back and some ahead, compared to the chains of gift-bearing subjects, pulled by individual nobles resolutely forward and upward. The implication is that the Achaemenid order has empowered its ministers and teachers, that royal authority is invested in them to make the empire work.

This rather gingerly and participatory approach to nation building can similarly be apprehended from the Nashq-i-Rustam relief, where the subjects support the royal platform almost effortlessly on their fingertips even from several layers below.[33] Contrast this presentation with typical reliefs of Egyptian subjects exhaustively laboring for the pharaoh by thrusting their shoulders and bodies in support. The *novus ordo* involves teamwork that almost floats by itself in tribute to Ahuramazda.

The fundamental question is whether the ceremonies and cultural performances of imperial ideology on the Apadana and on the other monuments had any conscious and definitive impact on Ezra's gathering. Did the Jews have access to the imperial program of visual art that stressed this ecumenical message in variant manifestations? We are, in effect, again questioning the presupposition made at the beginning of this article: Do the two sources actually share the same historical space? The blatant claim of the biblical text is that the Jews had access to Persian court culture and the ideologies underpinning its performative presentations.[34]

---

[33] Margaret Cool Root calls the image "a divinely sanctioned ... covenant of rulership" with the participants on the "verge of apotheosis" ("The Parthenon Frieze and the Apadana Reliefs at Persepolis: Reassessing a Programmatic Relationship," *AJA* 89 [1985]: 103–19, esp. 113), while Bruce Lincoln says that the art propaganda of Apadana "constituted the reversal of the [Zoroastrian] Lie's primordial assault and the reunification of previously sundered humanity ... by reversing the fragmentation and strife that had characterized existence" ("The Role of Religion in Achaemenian Imperialism," in *Religion and Power: Divine Kingship in the Ancient World*, ed. Nicole Brisch, rev. ed. OIS 4 [Chicago: Oriental Institute of the University of Chicago, 2012], 221–41, esp. 232).

[34] Recent research has shown that the Judean residents in Babylon would have had ample direct exposure to Persepolis. First, the Persepolis Fortification Texts show the employment of vast groups of various peoples during the reign of Darius who must have been doing construction work as laborers and skilled craftsmen. The lists include Babylonians. Second, the Achaemenids in general recruited dependent personnel from local temples (as well as military dependents) to carry out their building projects in other parts of the empire. Specifically the evidence points to holdings of the royal family in Persia as the location of the construction. See Wouter F. M. Henkelman and Kristin Kleber, "Babylonian Workers in the Persian Heartland: Palace Building at Matannan during the Reign of Cambyses," in *Persian Responses: Political and Cultual Interaction*

The program of propaganda (and presumably the actualized performances that accompanied the art) devised under Darius I were sent out far and wide across the entirety of the empire well beyond the heartland capitals of Persepolis and Susa.[35]

Ezra says that he was a recognized Persian delegate to Yehud, and Nehemiah claims that he was the king's confidant and cupbearer. As Darius, Xerxes, and Artaxerxes built their cities to accommodate their festivals, the biblical texts give strong clues that the subsidiary Jewish agents and culture did the same.

## IV. The Implications of Nehemiah 8:1–8 as a Persianized Liturgy

Due to the vast sway of the Persian Empire, it is not surprising that Jews returning from eastern domains should engage its rubrics and ideologies. Recognizing the specific expression of that Persian worldview and then drawing out its implication for Second Temple nationalism and liturgy is a different story. Nehemiah 8:1–8 is a deliberately crafted performance to express a restorationist agenda. The background context of Persian culture is instructive for interpreting this passage. The problem is that the texts and imperial artwork are propaganda and therefore may well belie the historical and archaeological record. Moreover, in the case of the Achaemenids, scholars often are most acquainted with them through non-Persian eyes. Nevertheless, if Neh 8:1–8 is a Persianized liturgy, there are a few unique insights that the text conveys about social hierarchy and government policy.

First, the reliefs and the biblical passage communicate that political authority is mediated or distributed throughout the institutions or bureaucracies they represent. Rulings, judgments, and standards are not sharply hierarchical but rely on intermediaries and guides for their subjects. The royalty depicted at Apadana is at the top of the social ascent, but power sharing characterizes his modus operandi. The same is true for Ezra, who is elevated above the assembly yet is not alone in this position or in his function of disseminating the law. He is like a master of ceremonies, prominently standing in front as the reader; yet to his right and left stand others associated with the Torah's authority. The text implies that leadership is a cooperative venture rather than a dictatorial position. As the rest of the chapter unfolds, Ezra's univocal recitation fades into the background of institutionalized

---

*with(in) the Achaemenid Empire*, ed. Christopher Tuplin (Swansea: Classical Press of Wales, 2007), 163–76.

[35] See Margaret Cool Root, "Defining the Divine in Achaemenid Persian Kingship: The View from Bisitun," in *Every Inch a King: Comparative Studies on Kings and Kingship in the Ancient and Medieval Worlds*, ed. Lynette Mitchell and Charles Melville, Rulers and Elites 2 (Leiden: Brill, 2013), 23–65.

transmission rather than top-down government—just as we would expect for Persian administration.[36]

Second, both the Persian king and Ezra in Neh 8:1–8 claim that their rule is one that is easily endured and utilizes a minimum of coercion. The king's rule rests lightly on the fingertips of his supporters. His Persian and Median subjects help one another up the stairs, as well as guide their charges gently by the hand. Meanwhile, the accompanying inscriptions assure subjects that the king's duty is to enforce *dāt* and to vindicate "Truth." Ezra's commission is similarly one of setting up and enforcing the Torah (or *dāt*, according to Ezra 7:25–26). His colleagues who share the dais patiently interpret the Torah so that the people will understand. While Ezra is initiating this process of keeping Torah, it is other Jews at many pastoral levels who keep the process going. The rabbis later find in this scene justification for their role as teachers.[37]

Third, neither the performance of Neh 8:1–8 nor the Apadana democratizes the government, as if rank and birth no longer mattered. Authority is still a privilege exercised by elites in both groups. It is always the Medes and Persians who serve as guides for the gift bearers. According to the reliefs of the north platform, they consult with one another as much as they look up to the king. Ezra's role is similarly ambiguous: he fades away from the text shortly after he gives the reading in Neh 8:1–8, and in his place his helpers come into view. Who are these helpers? They are the ones who naturally lead and teach the restored community. Yet even here the authority never ends up in the hands of the rank and file.

Fourth, the task of leadership of both groups involves nation building among diverse factions and conflicting interests. For the early Achaemenid rulers, it meant efforts to work with nonruling minorities and perhaps remnants of earlier Persian dynasties. For Jews in Yehud, the task was to bring together a people divided by claims to Jewish and apparently non-Jewish identities and those who were residents and those who were returnees. The performative quest for unity reverberates in later reconstructions of both the Jews (the rabbis) and the Persians (the Sassanids).

Fifth, and more speculatively, the performative dimension of Neh 8:1–8 and Persepolis seems to privilege sacrosanct languages, yet these languages require explanations in secondary and more popularized tongues.[38] Intriguingly, Darius

---

[36] See Gordon F. Davies, *Ezra and Nehemiah*, Berit Olam (Collegeville, MN: Liturgical Press, 1999), 114: "The effect of these syntactical and grammatical vagaries is to preserve the traditional hierarchies but flatten any accent on personalities or command structures. Placed together, Ezra and Nehemiah are seen to share success in their reforms, but their rhetorical presence is muffled."

[37] See Japhet, "Ritual of Reading," 187–90.

[38] Although the Achaemenids prioritized their own language, the pragmatics of imperial administration necessitated linguistic diversity if the rulers were to achieve stability and permanence. See Harrison, *Writing Ancient Persia*, 83–85. Matthew W. Stolper declares that the multilingual inscriptions found at Persepolis undergird the Old Persian word *vispazana*, "having

had probably introduced a new cuneiform script and idiom for Old Persian to impress the subjects who would view his Persepolis monuments. The new script was reserved for monuments, especially for royal display inscriptions.[39] The vague terms of Neh 8:1–8 were tantalizing enough for later rabbis to claim that the Aramaic script was introduced in this "Great Assembly." In this context, alternate translations of the sacred language were justified as legitimate substitutes.

Finally, for Ezra to fit into his reputed historical context among Achaemenid overlords, he could not pose as a royal figure or rival to Persian hegemony as he exercised a restorationist form of propaganda. At the same time, he had to appeal to his fellow Jews. In order to carry out this balancing act, in a brilliant play on the Persepolis symbolism, Ezra raises the book—the *dāt* to Persians and Torah to Jews—instead of promoting himself. Rather, in much the same way that Ahuramazda hovers ahead of the outstretched salute of the Achaemenid king, so Ezra implies that he offers support to the "God of heaven" while not threatening the established Achaemenid hierarchy. This is Ezra's answer to suspicious Achaemenid subjects who wonder what he is attempting to do in this nationalistic enterprise, and perhaps it is the answer throughout history of how those of Jewish ancestry acculturate to dominant civilizations.

---

all kinds of people"; that is, they embody the ecumenical esprit de corps that identified the Persians as dealing with various languages, races, ethnicities, and occupations.

[39] This new script was abandoned after Artaxerxes III (ca. 338). Extant inscriptions often offer three or four translations to accommodate the languages of observers as well as to impress them.

# Creation, Destruction, and a Psalmist's Plea: Rethinking the Poetic Structure of Psalm 74

NATHANIEL E. GREENE
ngreene@wisc.edu
University of Wisconsin–Madison, Madison, WI 53706

This article proposes a tripartite structure of Psalm 74. The proposal is based on various lexical and syntactic features of the psalmist's lament and sheds light on both the interpretation of the psalm as a whole and the interpretation of verses 12–17 in particular. It argues that these verses were interpolated to express a particular cosmogonic temple theology. When the psalm is viewed alongside comparable ancient Near Eastern literature from loci such as Ugarit, potential motives for this interpolation become evident. The interpolator sought to sharpen the petition to God by drawing on older, Canaanite mythology in hopes that such rhetorical maneuvers might occasion an acceptable solution to the psalmist's lament.

The relationship has long been established between ancient Near Eastern creation narratives and the *Chaoskampf*—the motif of divine struggle between patron deities and "watery-chaos" deities.[1] Creation imagery is pervasive throughout the biblical corpus (e.g., in Gen 1, Isa 27 and 51, Pss 74 and 104, and Job 3 and 41),

---

I am deeply indebted to Jeremy Hutton for looking over several different permutations of this article. His assistance was vital to the development of my thoughts on the issues addressed as well as to the final form of what appears here. Thanks are also due to Ronald Troxel, Jason Bembry, David Tsumura, Heather Dana Davis Parker, Adam Bean, Jack Weinbender, and my colleagues in the CANES department at UW–Madison, from whose thoughts and input I benefited greatly. Their influence can be seen here, but any mistakes that remain are my own. Thanks are due also to Kiersten Neumann and the Oriental Institute of the University of Chicago for their graciousness in allowing me to use their image and for their help in tracking down more information on the Assyrian cylinder seal discussed below.

[1] The full history of scholarship on the biblical text's dependence on ancient Near Eastern sources need not be rehashed here. A concise description of the evolution of thought on this topic may be found in Jeremy Hutton, "Isaiah 51:9–11 and the Rhetorical Appropriation and Subversion of Hostile Theologies," *JBL* 126 (2007): 271–303, here 272 n. 1.

often appearing with some reference to conflict between the deity and creatures such as Behemoth (בהמות), Leviathan (לויתן), Yamm (ים), Rahab (רהב), or "dragons" (תנין/תנינים). Recently, the presence of creation-oriented *Chaoskampf* imagery in Ps 74 has been questioned by David Tsumura.[2] He has argued that such imagery is, in fact, entirely absent from the biblical corpus and that Ps 74:12–17 exhibits different concerns (namely, destruction rather than creation).[3] I contend, however, that the presence of creation-oriented *Chaoskampf* imagery in Ps 74 is integral to the primary thematic concern of the psalmist (i.e., the destruction of the temple).

This study will be centered on the poetic function of the mythological hymn in Ps 74:12–17. Comments on the surrounding material in verses 1b–11, 18, and 19–23, however, are merited, because the larger structure of the psalm serves as an *Ausgangspunkt* for elucidating the relationship between the hymn in verses 12–17, the lament over the destruction of the temple in verses 1–11 and 18, and the final petition in verses 19–23.

## I. Structure

In order to assess the relationships between the constituent parts of the psalm, an analysis of its structure is required. The structure of Ps 74 proposed here consists of three primary sections:

I. Lament over the destruction of the temple (vv. 1b–11, 18)
II. Mythological hymn detailing the contest between אלהים and mythological beasts (vv. 12–17)
III. Petition for God to act on behalf of the poor (vv. 19–23)

The following discussion will provide a defense of this proposed structural outline with special attention paid to the pragmatic role of the placement of section II between sections I and III.

The opening exhortation in verses 1–2 is mirrored in verses 11 and 18. After the superscription (משכיל לאסף, "a psalm of Asaph"), Ps 74 opens the lament in verse 1b with the interrogative particle "why?" (למה). The initial question is immediately followed in verse 2 by the imperative "remember!" (זכר). Verses 3–10 carry on with the lament, providing details on the historical situation of the psalmist and

---

[2] David Toshio Tsumura, "The Creation Motif in Psalm 74:12–14? Reappraisal of the Theory of the Dragon Myth," *JBL* 134 (2015): 547–55, http://dx.doi.org/10.15699/jbl.1343.2015.2780.

[3] See also David Toshio Tsumura, *Creation and Destruction: A Reappraisal of the* Chaoskampf *Theory in the Old Testament* (Winona Lake, IN: Eisenbrauns, 2005). Tsumura thinks that the *Chaoskampf* motif is not as pervasive as many have suggested, and he concludes that the motif is not to be found in the creation account in Gen 1 (among other places).

what, precisely, the enemies and foes of God have done and, apparently, continue to do. Like verse 1, verse 11 begins with the particle "why?" (למה).[4]

Several commentators have noted that the second appearance of למה and the rest of the question that follows in verse 11 *conclude* the first major portion (or in some schemes, third portion) of the psalm.[5] Graeme E. Sharrock has suggested that verses 10–11 make up the "pivotal paragraph" of the psalm and are "the hinge of the whole psalm in its synthesis of prior arguments and its punctuation of [vv. 18–23]."[6] Erhard S. Gerstenberger's structural analysis is similar in that he, too, reads verses 10–11 as a section distinct from the preceding complaint. Gerstenberger suggests that these verses make up a "new element" in the psalm "because [they leave] behind the description of evil machinations and want [*sic*], challenging God to act immediately on behalf of his followers."[7] Gerstenberger omits, however, the very opening of Ps 74 (למה אלהים זנחת לנצח) as he cites the repeated למה in verse 11 as his evidence. Furthermore, verses 10–11 do not "[leave] behind the description of evil machinations and want"; rather, they continue the description of the result of the actions of the enemy's reproach (inability to see the native, presumably Yahwistic, "signs," lack of prophets, and so on).

Samuel Terrien suggests that the psalm be broken down into three parts (vv. 1b–8, vv. 9–17, and vv. 18–23), with each part consisting of three strophes. Terrien goes on to state, "[Parts One and Two], with regular strophes of three bicola, precede and prepare for Part Three, also made up of three strophes, each of which contains only two bicola, for it appeals bluntly to the Deity and requires a swift pace of definite urgency."[8] Terrien's analysis breaks the psalm up into awkward portions, separating comparable thematic strophes from one another only to enjoin them to different sections that do not fit together nearly as well. Hans-Joachim Kraus merely states, "And at the end of the first major section of lament, the למה-question is heard again in v. 11."[9]

---

[4] The morphological difference between למה (v. 1) and למה (v. 11) might readily be explained by the rhythmic phenomenon known as hiatus: "When a mil'el word ending with a vowel is followed by a word beginning with one of the gutturals, namely ה, א, and ע, the stress becomes mil'ra. The phenomenon is attested especially with לָמָּה, which becomes, לָמָה (without gemination), e.g. לָמָה אַתֶּם 2Sm 19.11" (Joüon, §33a).

[5] Frank-Lothar Hossfeld and Erich Zenger, *Psalms 2: A Commentary on Psalms 51–100*, trans. Linda M. Maloney, Hermeneia (Minneapolis: Fortress, 2005), 241; Graeme E. Sharrock, "Psalm 74: A Literary-Structural Analysis," *AUSS* 21 (1983): 211–23, here 213, 216.

[6] Sharrock, "Psalm 74," 216.

[7] Erhard S. Gerstenberger, *Psalms, Part 2, and Lamentations*, FOTL 15 (Grand Rapids: Eerdmans, 2001), 78.

[8] Samuel Terrien, *The Psalms: Strophic Structure and Theological Commentary*, ECC (Grand Rapids: Eerdmans, 2003), 539.

[9] Hans-Joachim Kraus, *Psalms 60–150: A Continental Commentary*, trans. Hilton C. Oswald (Minneapolis: Fortress, 1993), 99.

Frank-Lothar Hossfeld and Erich Zenger have also suggested that "the boundaries of this section are marked by the 'why?' in v. 1b and v. 11a.…[These 'why?' questions] function as a frame (*inclusio*)."[10] While the second appearance of למה in verse 11 does indeed hark back to the beginning of the lament in verse 1, Hossfeld and Zenger (among others[11]) have chosen to read the imperative "remember!" (זכר) in verse 18 as belonging to the final section of the psalm. למה and זכר, however, seem to be paired in verses 1b and 2a so that זכר functions as an immediate solution to the problem presented by the emphatic למה. God's remembrance of the "congregation [which God] acquired" (עדתך קנית) in verse 2 would seem to be the antidote for an act of rejection (זנחת) in verse 1b. It seems reasonable to conclude, then, that the זכר of verse 18 might function as an originally immediate (although now interrupted!) response to the למה of verse 11. Entreating the deity to remember the blasphemic acts of the enemy (זכר זאת אויב חרף, v. 18) is an attempt on the psalmist's part to adjure the deity to bring forth his hand to smite those who have reproached his name and destroyed his appointed places. This adjuration would reverse the destruction that has occurred since YHWH restrained his hand from worldly action (למה תשיב ידך, v. 11). Furthermore, the lexical parallels between verse 10 and verse 18 are striking. In both verses the psalmist points out that the enemy has "reproached" (√חרף) the deity and "despised" (√נאץ) the deity's name:

<sup>10</sup>עד מתי אלהים יחרף צר ינאץ אויב שמך לנצח
<sup>18</sup>זכר זאת אויב חרף יהוה ועם נבל נאצו שמך

<sup>10</sup>How long, O God, will [the] adversary reproach? Shall [the] enemy despise your name unto the end?
<sup>18</sup>Remember this: [the] enemy has reproached, O YHWH, and a foolish people have despised your name!

Kraus is therefore correct in asserting that "verse 18 takes up the theme of v. 10b again," and this is no minor point.[12] The fact that verse 18 maintains the primary concern of the actions of the enemy (אויב) and the foolish people (ועם נבל) suggests that it is actually verse 18 that closes off the lament portion of the psalm. Furthermore, the close lexical affinity between verse 10 and verse 18 suggests that the hymn of verses 12–17 was forcibly (and even violently[13]) inserted and was not a part of

---

[10] Hossfeld and Zenger, *Psalms 2*, 241.

[11] Ibid., 249; Kraus, *Psalms 60–150*, 100; Terrien, *Psalms*, 541; Gerstenberger, *Psalms*, 77. Mitchell Dahood, however, makes no mention of the structure of Ps 74 (*Psalms 51–100: Introduction, Translation, and Notes*, AB 17 [Garden City, NY: Doubleday, 1968], 198–208).

[12] Kraus, *Psalms 60–150*, 100. There is a possible wordplay between forms of √חרף in verses 10 and 18 and וחרף in verse 17. The wildly different thematic concerns of the hymn, however, suggest to me that any possible paronomasia was unintentional.

[13] By "violently" I mean that the five-verse hymn inserted between verse 11 and verse 18 harshly interrupts the למה/זכר sequence, further delaying the antidote to the psalmist's problem.

the original lament/petition. Jon Levenson has come closest to suggesting the kind of structure indicated here: "The context shows that God's primordial victory is recalled at the moment when he seems to be suffering defeat from a historical foe. The continuity between v. 11 and v. 18 strongly suggests that the hymn in vv. 12–17 has been interpolated."[14] Levenson, however, notes continuity strictly between verses 10–11 and 18–20 and does not detail the relationship of this block to the first nine verses of the psalm, where the psalmist first queries God and details the actions of his/God's enemy.

If we read verse 18 as beginning the third section of the psalm, we are left with three pairs of verses, alternating between second person masculine singular imperatives and imperfect verbs negated by אל ("negative order [prohibition], negative wish, negative prayer"[15]). In isolation this would be a noteworthy construction. Another structure for this section is possible (and even preferable), however. If we instead read verse 18 as the concluding verse to the lament in verses 1b–11, as suggested above, then the final five verses of the psalm are left as a separate, chiastic unit:

A   <sup>19</sup>אל־תתן לחית נפש תורך חית עניך אל־תשכח לנצח

B   <sup>20</sup>הבט לברית כי מלאו מחשכי־ארץ נאות חמס

C   <sup>21</sup>אל־ישב דך נכלם עני ואביון יהללו שמך

B′   <sup>22</sup>קומה אלהים ריבה ריבך זכר חרפתך מני־נבל כל־היום

A′   <sup>23</sup>אל־תשכח קול צרריך שאון קמיך עלה תמיד

A   <sup>19</sup>Do not give to the wild beast the vital-essence of your dove,
do not ever forget the life of your poor ones!

B   <sup>20</sup>Look to the covenant,
because the dark places of the land are full of dwellings of violence!

C   <sup>21</sup>Do not let the crushed one return humiliated,
let the poor and needy praise your name!

B′   <sup>22</sup>Arise, O God, contend your case!
Remember, your reproach is from the fool all day long!

A′   <sup>23</sup>Do not forget the voice of your foes,
[nor] the noise of your adversaries which arises continually!

Both A and A′ begin with אל plus a second person masculine singular prefixed verbal form, beseeching God not to give (אל תתן) and not to forget (אל תשכח). The latter prohibition appears in both verses, although with different objects. The objects of the verbs in verses 19 and 23 are matched with opposite gender and opposite semantic value (feminine objects חית נפש תורך and חית עניך in verse 19 // masculine objects קול צרריך and שאון קמיך in verse 23—although compare לנצח

---

[14] Jon D. Levenson, *Creation and the Persistence of Evil: The Jewish Drama of Divine Omnipotence* (Princeton: Princeton University Press, 1988), 18.

[15] Joüon, §114i.

// תמיד). Opposition in gender as well as in semantic quality may "be used to reinforce antithesis or contrast."[16] Gender inversion and parallel word pairs, moreover, are often used "to express reversal of state *or to produce chiastic pattern*."[17] We find not only gender inversion between verse 19 and verse 23 but semantic inversion as well.[18] Furthermore, B and B′ seek immediate positive action from God with the driving impetus for each petition in the second half of their respective verses (clause initial זכר in v. 22 would then function in a fashion similar to clause initial כי in v. 20). If we take Wilfred Watson's five-part pattern (address, lament, statement of trust, petition, and vow of praise[19]) as typical for lament psalms, then this would mean that the vow of praise (עני ואביון יהללו שמך) would be embedded in the very center of the chiastic structure amid the psalmist's petition to God. The proposed chiastic structure of verses 19–23 sets the vow of praise in bold relief in a position of emphasis within the psalm rather than simply presenting it toward the end of the piece in what would be a seemingly random position.

What we are left with, after setting aside the hymn in verses 12–17, comprises two major sections: (1) a lament in verses 1b–11 and 18 bracketed by two pairs of verses beginning with למה and זכר that form an *inclusio* around verses 3–10, and (2) a chiastic petition in verses 19–23 to God by the psalmist for God to act on behalf of the poor, anchored by the vow of praise in its center. The question remains, however, why the ancient mythological imagery in verses 12–17 would be connected with a lament over the destruction of the temple. What would cause the psalmist to reach back into the depths of his textual heritage to retrieve such powerful (and empowering!) literature?

## II. Evoking the Resurgent YHWH and Temple as *Axis Mundi*

With this structural outline in mind, we now turn to address the relationship between the thematic concerns of the hymn in verses 12–17 and the surrounding lament and petition. As noted above, Tsumura has argued that the theme of creation is absent from Ps 74:12–14 and, by extension, from the entire hymn of verses

---

[16] Wilfred G. E. Watson, *Classical Hebrew Poetry: A Guide to Its Techniques*, JSOTSup 26 (Sheffield: JSOT Press, 1984), 125.

[17] Ibid., 356 (emphasis added).

[18] Semantic opposition appears often with word pairs such as "rich/poor," "wicked/righteous," and so on. Although there are no formal contrastive word pairs in verses 19 and 23, the objects denoted by the lexemes are contrastive. Cf. Prov 10:15, where "wealth/poverty" (הון/ריש), "rich/poor" (דלים/עשיר), and "strength/ruin" (עזו/מחתת) are paired chiastically. See, e.g., Adele Berlin, *The Dynamics of Biblical Parallelism* (Bloomington: Indiana University Press, 1992), 94–95.

[19] Watson, *Classical Hebrew Poetry*, 167.

12–17.[20] He suggests instead that destruction imagery prevails at the expense of creation-oriented *Chaoskampf*, not only in texts such as Pss 18, 29, and 49, and Hab 3 but in Ps 74 as well.[21] That is to say, Tsumura argues that the ultimate goal of *Chaoskampf* is destruction rather than creation. Tsumura's discussion, however, fails to consider the full context and content of the material he purports to address. His argument is founded on discussion of the meaning of √פרר, displays overly rigid understandings of creation and destruction, and is driven by a misunderstanding of metaphor.[22] Furthermore, loosening the literary connections between Ps 74 and comparable literature from the ancient Near East (specifically, the Enuma Elish) is vital to Tsumura's argument. Though he does perceive similarities between Enuma Elish and Ps 74, he restricts these similarities "to common linguistic expressions based on a common literary tradition of ancient warfare."[23] I agree with Tsumura that battle imagery pervades the initial portions of the hymn in verses 12–14, but I disagree with his suggestion that what follows in verses 15–17 lacks the creative acts that result from the *Chaoskampf* of verses 12–14. Once the combat against the water creatures concludes in Ps 74:15, explicit creation imagery is used in 74:16–17:

> [16]Yours is the day; yours too, the night.
>     You established both light and sun.
> [17]You erected all of the borders of the earth.
>     As for summer and winter, you formed them.

Tsumura attempts to explain this portion of the text as expressing "the idea of creation by the *resultative*, that is, the outcome of a creative action, like 'house' in the phrase 'to build a house.'"[24] Conveniently, Tsumura really addresses only verse 15 (nowhere in his analysis of this portion of the psalm does Tsumura address any of the content of vv. 16–17), suggesting, "Verses 16 and 17 describe the organization

---

[20] Tsumura, "Creation Motif?" I should note that verse 12, while clearly distinguished from the subsequent second person address/hymnic material, is here taken as part of the textual unit of verses 12–17. The conjunction *waw* that opens verse 12 (ואלהים) can be seen as a topicalizer for all of the material that follows. Bruce K. Waltke and M. O'Connor note, "Interclausal *waw* before a non-verb constituent has a disjunctive role.... A disjunctive-*waw* clause may also shift the scene or refer to new participants; the disjunction may come at the beginning or end of a larger episode or it may '*interrupt*' one" (*IBHS*, 650–51; emphasis added).

[21] Tsumura, *Creation and Destruction*, 196.

[22] Tsumura's work on the meaning of √פרר is a welcome and thorough corrective to the somewhat rampant mistranslation of the verb. I am in agreement with his conclusion that √פרר means "to break" (Tsumura, "Creation Motif?," 550). Yet his consideration of possible meanings of √פרר, while helpful, is only loosely connected to the remainder of his discussion on the presence of *Chaoskampf* in Ps 74 and does not bolster his claims made therein.

[23] Ibid., 552.

[24] Ibid., 553.

of the earth *with springs and brooks* rather than the origination of the earth itself."[25] These verses, however, are not concerned with springs (מעין) and brooks (נחל), lexemes that appear only in verse 15a. Verses 16–17 are actually concerned with "day" (יום), "night" (לילה), "luminary" (מאר), "sun" (שמש), "earth" (ארץ), "summer" (קיץ), and "winter" (חרף). These are all lexemes that evoke thoughts of creation, with the vast majority appearing in Gen 1.[26] Furthermore, given the verbs and objects in verses 16b–17, it is rather clear that this portion of the psalm is indeed concerned with the organization of the earth itself. After all, what else could establishing the borders of the earth and forming summer and winter imply? Especially important is the final verb of the hymn, יצרתם ("you formed them"). This same root √יצר is used in Gen 2:7–8 detailing the creation of humanity:

> Gen 2:7a  And YHWH Elohim formed [√יצר] the man with dust from the ground.

> Gen 2:8  And YHWH Elohim planted a garden in Eden to the east, and he set there the man whom he had formed [√יצר].

Tsumura distinguishes two different uses of the English word *creation*: "the English term 'creation' is used to mean either an 'originating' action or 'a created order.'"[27] Describing the psalm in its entirety, he suggests, "The psalm, however, has nothing to do with creation, that is, origination, of the earth itself, unlike Enuma Elish."[28] This is a rather difficult position to sustain, however, in view of the explicit use of "originating" action verbs like √יצר in verse 17 and the strong lexical affinity of the psalm with the creation accounts in Genesis. Moreover, the creation accounts in Genesis make no distinction between the formation of the earth and its subsequent arrangement by the deity. These accounts take the deity's acts of both origination and organization as part of one action.

The appearance of a noun derived from the root √יבש in Gen 1:9 (היבשה, "the dry land") is also significant, since it demonstrates lexical connections to the text at hand: the final verbal form before the creation imagery begins in Ps 74:16 is הובשת ("you dried up") in 74:15.[29] Despite the appearance of √יצר and √יבש,

---

[25] Ibid. (emphasis added).

[26] While neither "summer" (קיץ) nor "winter" (חרף) actually appears in Gen 1, they are seasons of the year. As such, they evoke creation imagery by their relationship not only to the calendar and weather but to festivals, planting, and harvest as well. All of these things might readily remind one of creation—most notably Gen 1:14 (ויאמר אלהים יהי מארת ברקיע השמים להבדיל בין היום ובין הלילה והיו לאתת ולמועדים ולימים ושנים, "And God said, 'Let there be lights in the firmament of the heavens in order to divide between the day and between the night, and let them be as signs for appointed times and for days and years'").

[27] Tsumura, "Creation Motif?," 554 n. 31.

[28] Ibid., 554.

[29] The biblical image of drying up chaotic waters is not without comparable literary parallels. Bernard F. Batto suggests, "For the biblically attuned reader, Baal's smashing of Yam's head evokes similar images of Yahweh as he 'who smashed the heads of the dragon on the water, who crushed

however, Tsumura argues that verses 15–17 "simply describe the created order brought about by YHWH, rather than YHWH's creative actions ... the psalmist simply explains the saving act of YHWH, who is the lord of creation."[30] Ultimately, Tsumura's detachment of creative result from creative act draws too fine a distinction in view of the deity's creative acts as depicted in the text. The very fact that the created order is the result of YHWH's creative acts links the notions indefinitely. Unfortunately, Tsumura's reading of the hymn of verses 12–17 misses some of the deeper theological implications likely perceived by the psalmist. Notably, Tsumura divorces verses 12–14 from the whole hymn (vv. 12–17) in his assessment. When verses 12–14 are separated from the latter half of the hymn, many of these thematic connections are lost. These six verses certainly function as a unit:

¹²ואלהים מלכי מקדם פעל ישועות בקרב הארץ:
¹³אַתָה פוררת בעזך ים שברת ראשי תנינים על־המים:
¹⁴אַתָה רצצת ראשי לויתן תתננו מאכל לעם לציים:
¹⁵אַתָה בקעת מעין ונחל אַתָה הובשת נהרות איתן:
¹⁶לך יום אף־לך לילה אַתָה הכינות מאור ושמש:
¹⁷אַתָה הצבת כל־גבולות ארץ קיץ וחרף אַתָה יצרתם:

¹² Now, God is my king of old,
   working salvation in the midst of the land.
¹³ You broke, with your strength, the Sea,
   you shattered the heads of the dragons upon the waters.
¹⁴ You crushed the heads of Leviathan,
   you gave it as food to people, to desert wanderers.
¹⁵ You split the spring and wadi,
   you dried up mighty rivers.
¹⁶ Yours is the day, as well as the night.
   You established light as well as the sun.
¹⁷ You erected all of the borders of the earth.
   As for summer and winter, you formed them.

The sevenfold, emphatic use of the second person masculine singular independent personal pronoun אתה bolsters the link between the defeat of the cosmological beasts in verses 12–14 and the creation imagery of verses 16–17.[31] Not only is אתה fronted before the suffix form of the verb each time it appears in the destruction of the mythological beasts in verses 12–14, but it is also used in the same fashion in

---

the heads of Leviathan' ... while Baal's drinking up Yam evokes images of Israel's creator 'who dries up of [sic] the sea' (Isa. 51:10)" (*Slaying the Dragon: Mythmaking in the Biblical Tradition* [Louisville: Westminster John Knox, 1992], 134).

[30] Tsumura, "Creation Motif?," 553–54.

[31] I cite Ps 74:12–14 here rather than 74:12–15 because Tsumura did not include verse 15 in his primary object of investigation. He does address the verse, but it was not part of his main focus. The *Chaoskampf* imagery, however, does continue in verse 15.

the latter half of the hymn, which details creation.³² Furthermore, the use of אתה seven times in this pericope may be a function of traditions surrounding the Leviathan character. Leviathan was thought to have seven heads, as depicted in the Baal Cycle (*KTU* 1.5 I 1–4):

| ktmḫṣ . ltn . bṯn . brḥ/ | When you killed Litan, the Fleeing Serpent, |
| tkly . bṯn . ʿqltn . [ ]/ | Annihilated the Twisty Serpent, |
| šlyṭ . d . šbʿt . rašm/ | The Potentate with Seven Heads, |
| ṯṯkḥ . ttrp . šmm | The heavens grew hot, they withered.³³ |

Nor is the seven headed creature destroyed by deities a stranger to ancient Near Eastern iconography. An oft-cited cylinder seal from Tell Asmar portrays two deities slaying a seven-headed dragon (figs. 1 and 2).³⁴

---

³² Hutton, "Isaiah 51:9–11," 283–84. Note, however, that Hutton focuses strictly on Ps 74:13–15 in his analysis, which leads him to list only four occurrences of אתה out of the total seven (אתה פררת, אתה רצצת, אתה בקעת, אתה הובשת).

³³ All Ugaritic transliterations and translations are taken from Mark S. Smith, trans., *Ugaritic Narrative Poetry*, ed. Simon B. Parker, WAW 9 (Atlanta: Society of Biblical Literature, 1997; emphasis added).

³⁴ This particular cylinder seal exemplifies the commonness in the ancient Near East and the antiquity of the motif of deities slaying seven-headed dragons. Note the seven heads of the creature, one being struck by the two deities. Hossfeld and Zenger also note that "flames of fire ascend from the back of the monster. Here the multiplicity of forms in the ancient Near Eastern notion of chaos is visible; the destructive power was seen especially as a flood of water and an arid desert (flames of fire = heat). The two can also stand alongside one another in the OT (cf. Gen 1:2: the primeval waters and the *tohuwabohu* desert)" (*Psalms 2*, 274). The drawing originally appeared in Othmar Keel, *The Symoblism of the Biblical World: Ancient Near Eastern Iconography and the Book of Psalms*, trans. Timothy J. Hallett (New York: Seabury, 1978), 54. The original cylinder seal was discovered at Tell Asmar and dates to the late third millennium BCE. It was first published by Henri Frankfort in 1934 in *Iraq Excavations of the Oriental Institute, 1932/33: Third Preliminary Report of the Iraq Expedition*, Oriental Institute Communications 17 (Chicago: University of Chicago Press, 1934), 49–50. It was published again by Frankfort in *Stratified Cylinder Seals from the Diyala Region*, OIP 72 (Chicago: University of Chicago Press, 1955), no. 478. The seal also appears in James B. Pritchard, ed., *The Ancient Near East: An Anthology of Texts and Pictures* (Princeton: Princeton University Press, 2010), no. 171. Most recently, it seems the cylinder seal had been in the collections of the Iraq Museum (accession number IM15618) and had been identified by Frankfort with the excavation number "As. 32:738"; however, the University of Chicago's Oriental Institute's tracking of lost/stolen Iraqi antiquities suggests that the cylinder seal is feared to be stolen. See online at http://oi-archive.uchicago.edu/OI/IRAQ/dbfiles/objects/1065.htm. This website has not been updated since 14 April 2008. Gary Rendsburg offered an analysis of the seal and its impact on interpretation of *UT* 68 (= *CTU* 2.4) ("*UT* 68 and the Tell Asmar Seal," *Or* 53 [1984]: 448–52). The looting and pillaging of both archaeological sites and museum collections persist as a serious problem throughout the Near East, both in Iraq and, most recently, in Syria. Thankfully, this cylinder seal has a well-documented provenance and can be counted as authentic.

FIGURE 1. Drawing of IM15618 by Hildi Keel-Leu, as reproduced in Hossfeld and Zenger, *Psalms 2*, 247. Reproduced here by permission.

FIGURE 2. Photo of IM15618. Photo courtesy of the Oriental Institute of the University of Chicago.

The three appearances of אתה in verses 15–17 are then necessarily linked to the initial four occurrences in verses 12–15. When one considers the fact that Leviathan was conceptualized as having seven heads, the parallels become all the more striking. This creature appears two times in Job (3:8, 40:25) and once in Isa (27:1)—all with the name לויתן. The appearances in Job are noteworthy, as Job (along with the broader genre of wisdom literature) has a preoccupation with the creation of the world (cf. Job 9:8, 13; 26:12–13; 38:8–11, where actions such as "stretching out the heavens" [נטה שמים] are coupled with the destruction of Yamm and Rahab).[35] Tsumura, however, seeks a different explanation for the use of the seven-headed dragon in Ps 74:12–14:

---

[35] See John Day, *Yahweh and the Gods and Goddesses of Canaan*, JSOTSup 265 (Sheffield: Sheffield Academic, 2002), 100. These references mention Yamm (ים) and Rahab (רהב), but not Leviathan; however, Stuart Weeks suggests that "some of the wisdom literature is interested in using [creation] as a way to affirm the significance of wisdom or the power of God, but it would be difficult to maintain either that this interest reflects some single, defining set of ideas, or that much of it is especially distinctive." Furthermore, Weeks believes that wisdom literature is more

In Psalm 74, an actual battle is described *metaphorically* in terms of natural phenomena, that is, two stages of the calming down of the raging sea.... It is probable that in Israel this multi-headed dragon was used as an image for powerful enemies in general. Thus, for the author of Ps 74, "to crush the heads of dragons or Leviathan" meant "to destroy the enemy completely." In this psalm, therefore, highly *metaphorical* expressions with literary clichés are used to present YHWH's battle, which ends in his complete victory.[36]

Tsumura's relegation of the psalmist's use of dragon imagery to mere metaphor, however, is problematic.[37] He cites no comparable texts where dragon imagery is used in such a manner, and he fails to take into consideration the broader context of the psalm (namely, the concern of the lament in vv. 1–11, 18: temple destruction). Psalm 74:12b (פעל ישועות בקרב הארץ) is his only supporting text. Furthermore, claiming that a text utilizes salient metaphorical language requires discussion of cognitive metaphor and blending theory. Zoltán Kövecses notes, "Conceptual metaphors involve two concepts and have the form A is B, where concept A is understood in terms of concept B."[38] This means that, in a given metaphor, concept B functions as a *source domain* for qualities and characteristics that are cognitively mapped onto concept A (the target). Cognitive metaphor theory highlights *unidirectional* relationships between constituent parts of a given metaphor. Thus, Tsumura's approach allows for only *unidirectional* mapping (i.e., conceptual metaphor) at the expense of the larger context of the entire psalm. His relegation of this text to metaphor flattens the rich and complex nature of temple theology and its connection to creation, combat, chaos, and YHWH's enthronement in ancient Israel. In contrast, blending theory recognizes that thinkers combine (or "blend") multiple "input spaces"—ideas or concepts—in order to construct a new paradigm of reality.[39] Accordingly, aspects of both concepts infuse the new paradigm, creating a *new* reality in which the author or reader exists. That is to say, the person

---

concerned with the way in which the created world is ordered than with the act of creation itself. See Stuart Weeks, *An Introduction to the Study of Wisdom Literature*, T&T Clark Approaches to Biblical Studies (London: T&T Clark, 2010), 112.

[36] Tsumura, "Creation Motif?," 552–53 (emphasis added).

[37] Furthermore, the battle depicted in verses 12–14 does not merely end with YHWH's "complete victory," as Tsumura purports. Rather, the battle concludes with yet another act of YHWH: "you gave it [i.e., לויתן] as food for people, for desert wanderers." While the interpretive quagmire of the lexeme ציים is beyond the scope of the current discussion, it is clear from Ps 74:14b that the battle does not end only with complete victory or destruction. The battle (and its conclusion) serves a rather distinct purpose: to provide food for people. This could be an implicit (not explicit) reference to the earth and its productive value as the source of food for all living creatures in the created order. Discussion of Ps 74:14b remains a conspicuous lacuna in Tsumura's study.

[38] Zoltán Kövecses, *Metaphor: A Practical Introduction* (Oxford: Oxford University Press, 2010), 45.

[39] For more on cognitive blending, see Gilles Fauconnier and Mark Turner, *The Way We*

responsible for the presence of verses 12–17 in the midst of a lament about the temple's destruction found himself living in two "worlds," each in tension with the other. The first was the reality of the temple's destruction and the concomitant defeat/absence of YHWH; the second was the author/redactor's temple theology (part and parcel of his cosmogonic, theological worldview). Verses 12–17 are connected to the surrounding lament in verses 1–11 and 18–23 not simply because they form a single psalm but because of intimately related thematic and theological concerns.[40]

The depiction of divine combat in Ps 74 by no means exists in a textual vacuum (i.e., there are other texts in the biblical corpus that use similar imagery that must be considered). Two other texts share similar concerns—Ps 89:9–10 and Isa 51:9–11.[41]

> Ps 89:9–10
> O YHWH, God of hosts, who is strong like you, O Yah?
>     Your faithfulness surrounds you.
> You reign over the majesty of the Sea,
>     When its waves rise you still them.

> Isa 51:9–11
> Arise, arise, put on strength, O Arm of YHWH!
>     Arise, as in days of old, as in previous generations!
> Was it not you who cut Rahab to pieces?
>     [Was it not you who] pierced the dragon?
> Was it not you who cut the Sea? The waters of the great deep?
>     The one who set the depths of the Sea as a way for the redeemed to walk?

Again, Tsumura wishes to explain away the creation imagery embedded in these texts: "Similarly, in these [i.e., Ps 89 and Isa 51] biblical passages there is no allusion to the 'creation' of the heaven and the earth as in the case of Enuma elish.... The

---

*Think: Conceptual Blending and the Mind's Hidden Complexities* (New York: Basic Books, 2002), 39–50.

[40] The Targum of Psalms expands verse 12 with an explanatory plus of דשכינת קודשיה ("of the holy temple"). It seems likely that the targumist perceived a weak connection between the lament and hymnic material and expanded the text in an attempt to establish a stronger connection between the first and second sections of the psalm. David M. Stec points out that the Targum of Psalms is overwhelmingly characterized by the type of targum that "consists of a base translation plus explanatory explanations" where "the base translation follows the Hebrew very closely and corresponds on the whole one to one with it" (*The Targum of Psalms*, ArBib 16 [Collegeville, MN: Liturgical Press, 2004], 2).

[41] Hutton has convincingly shown the close relationship between these three biblical texts (i.e., Pss 74:13–15, 89:10–11, Isa 51:9–11) as well as *KTU* 1.3 III 38–46, noting both "lexical and syntactic repetition." He goes on to suggest that an intermediary text is necessary due to "the [dubious] degree to which *KTU* 1.3 was available to the Israelite audience" (Hutton, "Isaiah 51:9–11," 302).

biblical authors of the Iron Age could use these already-antiquated expressions to describe *metaphorically* Yahweh's destructive actions toward his enemies."[42] Simply ascribing the mythological imagery of Ps 89:9–10 and Isa 51:9–11 to the category of metaphor, as noted above, is tenuous and fails to take into account the depth of connection between the biblical authors and the Canaanite traditions they inherited. An author (especially an author of poetry!) need not explicitly state every image he or she wishes to create in the mind of the reader.[43] These passages, as well as Ps 74:12–17, are rehearsing theological history in the form of myth.[44] Hutton, noting the connection between creation and the exodus narrative, has suggested that "in the ancient mind-set, the two [i.e., creation and exodus] are inseparable—especially since the exodus is perceived and perpetuated in the community as a divine act of re-creation!"[45] This being the case, the presence of the creative-*Chaoskampf* motif in Ps 74 is then doubly marked by both creative language (i.e., language depicting the act of creation) and language and ideologies reminiscent of the exodus tradition as well (as is evident in the treatment of Ps 74 by the Targum of Psalms).[46]

Psalm 74:12–17 exhibits close thematic affinity with the Ugaritic Baal Cycle (*KTU* 1.1–1.6, specifically here 1.2 IV, lines 23–40).[47] One of the primary characteristics of the Baal Cycle is the contest between Baal and the mythological beings [Prince] Yamm (*zblym*) and Judge River (*ṭpṭ.nhr*), whom he fights and defeats. Yamm is then proclaimed king:

| | | |
|---|---|---|
| 27 | *yqṯbᶜl . wyšt . ym.* | Baal drags and dismembers (?) Yamm, |
| | *ykly . ṭpṭ . nhr* | Destroys Judge River |
| 28 | *bšm . tgᶜrm . ᶜṯtrt.* | By name Astarte rebukes (him): |
| 28–29 | *bṯlaliyn . b[ᶜl]/* | "Scatter, O Mighty Ba[al,] |
| | *bṯ . lrkb . ᶜrpt.* | Scatter, O Cloudrider. |
| 29–30 | *kšbyn . zb[l . ym.]* | For our captive is Prin[ce Yamm,] |
| | *[k(?)]/šbyn . ṭpṭ . nhr* | [For (?)] our captive is Judge River." |
| 32 | *ym.lmt.* | "So Yamm is dead! |
| | *bᶜlm.yml[k ]* | Baal rei[gns! (?)] |
| 33 | *ḥm . lšrr . w* | ... so he rules!" |

[42] Tsumura, *Creation and Destruction*, 192 (emphasis added).

[43] It is possible that the stacking up of the objects of creation in Ps 74:16–17 constitutes what Watson sees as a list with final total (the final total being expressed by יצרתם in v. 17) (*Classical Hebrew Poetry*, 352).

[44] Batto highlights the value of myth (especially myth appropriated from cognate cultures), noting that "myth has been found to be an appropriate medium for theologizing about the most profound issues" (*Slaying the Dragon*, 148).

[45] Hutton, "Isaiah 51:9–11," 283 n. 48.

[46] For the text and translation of the Targum of Psalm 74, see Stec, *Targum of Psalms*.

[47] Hutton suggests that *KTU* 1.3 III 38–46, Ps 74:13–15, Ps 89:9–10, and Isa 51:9–11 all originated with the same hypothetical *Urtext* and "point to a deliberately allusive intention on the part of the authors." Hutton dubs his suggested *Urtext* the "Hymn of 'Anat" ("Isaiah 51:9–11," 278).

It should be noted here that there is formally no creative act performed by Baal in the extant portions of the Baal Cycle, despite the fact that Baal does indeed battle monsters very similar to those subdued by YHWH in the biblical text. The function of the battle between Baal and the water deities Yamm and Judge River, though, seems to function as the impetus through which Baal's reign was established and his temple built. After Baal had secured his victory and had been enthroned, Kothar wa-Ḥasis constructed a temple for him (*KTU* 1.4 VI 16–38), a process that apparently took seven days to complete. It is certainly possible that the seven-day "building" motif expressed in Gen 1 came from the same literary stock as that found here in *KTU* 1.4 VI 16–38. Similarly, shortly before Marduk defeats Tiamat in the Enuma Elish and subsequently creates the world from her body, the assembly of the great gods builds a palace/temple for him as remuneration for his engagement with and defeat of the watery-chaos deity: "They set out for him a princely dais, / He took his place before his fathers for sovereignty."[48] For Baal, a palace/temple was the reward for the defeat of the watery-chaos deity, while Marduk constructed his temple upon completion of the creation event and his subsequent enthronement.

The relationship between creation and the temple may be borne out in the text of Ps 74 as well. That the psalm is concerned with the temple is suggested by the content of the lament in verses 1–11 and 18. Most notably, בקדש ("in the sanctuary") at the end of verse 3 is undoubtedly a reference to the temple,[49] and מועדך ("your appointed place"[50]) also suggests temple connections (cf. Lam 2:6, Zeph 3:18).[51] Levenson persuasively argues for understanding the temple as a "microcosm," "a rich and powerful re-presentation of creation" through nuanced understandings of the creation account in Gen 1 and the construction of the Jerusalem temple in 1 Kgs 6–7.[52] He further suggests that "the Temple has been assimilated phenomenologically to cosmogony."[53] The destruction of the temple as described in the opening verses of Ps 74 would then be an assault not simply on the physical

---

[48] "Epic of Creation," trans. Benjamin R. Foster (*COS*, 1.111.390–402, here 396). One might also readily compare Enuma Elish V:120–124: "As counterpart to Esharra, which I built for you, / Below the firmament, whose grounding I made firm, / A house I shall build, let it be the abode of my pleasure. / Within it I shall establish its holy place, / I shall appoint my (holy) chambers, / I shall establish my kingship" ("Epic of Creation," *COS* 1:400).

[49] BDB provides "the temple and its precincts" as one of the many glosses for קדש. While scholars are divided on the exact historical context for Ps 74 (e.g., Babylonian invasion and destruction of the temple in 586/587), they seem largely agreed that the situation that caused the psalmist to compose the lament was some kind of destruction or defilement of the temple (Terrien, *Psalms*, 539–40; Gerstenberger, *Psalms, Part 2*, 79–80; Kraus, *Psalms 60–150*, 97–98; Dahood, *Psalms 51–100*, 199–200.

[50] Or perhaps "your appointed *places*," if the MT is to be emended to מועדיך. Cf. מועדי אל בארץ in Ps 74:8.

[51] BDB, s.v. מועד.

[52] Levenson, *Creation and the Persistence of Evil*, 92.

[53] Ibid., 99.

building established for the worship of YHWH but on YHWH's very sovereignty and the entirety of the created order as well. It makes perfect sense that the author of Ps 74 would seek to connect creation imagery (the likes of which are found in Ps 74:12–17) to a lament over the destruction of the temple. As Bernhard W. Anderson has pointed out, the second half of the opening line of the hymn in Psalm 74 (פעל ישועות בקרב הארץ) "may reflect the view that the Jerusalem temple was located at the *omphalos* of the earth, where Israel remembered the Exodus and the other historical deeds of God."[54] If Levenson is correct in his conclusion that creation mythology served as enthronement literature (and I believe he is; cf. the Akitu festival in Mesopotamia), then by recalling much older creation mythology, the redactor of this psalm *re*-enthrones the recently dispossessed YHWH by calling upon him to *re*-enact his battle with his primordial enemies. This recollection of creation mythology then is a tacit call for YHWH to rebuild his temple, as enthronement and the construction of a temple seem to be the ultimate results of the *Chaoskampf* events.

One might question whether verses 12–17 are in fact an insertion by a redactor. After all, what is to say that the author himself did not compose that material as a part of the original psalm? In other words, is it possible that this is simply a case of a "disappearing redactor" who, in fact, never existed? I am not convinced that we are dealing with a potential "disappearing redactor," however. The structure of Ps 74 favors the view that verses 12–17 were secondarily added to the psalm, between verse 11 and verse 18. The interruption of the parallelism between למה/זכר in verses 11 and 18 suggests that the original psalm consisted of two sections (vv. 1–11 and 18, and vv. 19–23). This is further verified by the striking lexical parallelism between verse 10 and verse 18, as well as the chiasm in the final five verses of the psalm as a result of such a reading. The shepherd/flock metaphor for kingship in verses 1–2 and 12, moreover, does not connect the lament to the doxological hymn. Rather, the metaphor likely served as a trigger for the author/redactor. The redactor perceived the thematic/theological parallel, which then became the impetus for his insertion of the older mythological material into his lament.

## III. Conclusion

The hymn in Ps 74:12–17 is vital to the theological integrity of the entire psalm despite the fact that it was likely borrowed material inserted into the author's lament. This insertion violently interrupted the lament between the paired למה and זכר (vv. 11 and 18, respectively), much in the way the enemies of God acted violently against God's sanctuary. The author perceived a theological connection

---

[54] Bernhard W. Anderson, *Creation versus Chaos: The Reinterpretation of Mythical Symbolism in the Bible* (New York: Association Press, 1967; repr., Philadelphia: Fortress, 1987), 117.

between God's conflict with the mythological beasts and creation not only of the world but of a temple for God. To the author, the temple was a microcosm of creation[55]—the throne upon which God reigns, since "Israel [had] moved away from a cosmological model, in which the creative act had been performed only once, toward a model in which Yahweh's saving acts were continually performed for the benefit of the community."[56] The author likely hoped that the reuse of inherited creation mythology (so as to remind God of divine actions "of old") would cause the deity to engage in the battle once again, leading to the reestablishment of God's reign and the reconstruction of God's temple.

[55] Levenson, *Creation and the Persistence of Evil*, 86.
[56] Hutton, "Isaiah 51:9–11," 292.

# SBL PRESS

## New and Recent Titles

### THE FIRST URBAN CHURCHES 2
Roman Corinth
*James R. Harrison and L. L Welborn, editors*
Paperback $51.95, 978-0-88414-111-2   370 pages, 2016   Code: 064208
Hardcover $71.95, 978-0-88414-113-6   E-book $51.95, 978-0-88414-112-9
Writings from the Greco-Roman World Supplements 8

*Also Available*
### THE FIRST URBAN CHURCHES 1
Methodological Foundations
*James R. Harrison and L. L. Welborn, editors*
Paperback $34.95, 978-1-62837-102-4   360 pages, 2015   Code: 064207
Hardcover $49.95, 978-1-62837-103-1   E-book $34.95, 978-1-62837-104-8
Writings from the Greco-Roman World Supplements 7

### THE *PANARION* OF EPIPHANIUS OF SALAMIS
Books II and III; *De Fide*
*Translated by Frank Williams*
Paperback $89.95 , 978-1-62837-167-3   714 pages, 2017   Code: 069574
Brill Reprints 74   Nag Hammadi and Manichaean Studies 79

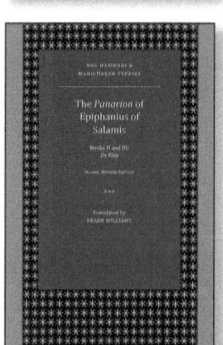

### EXPLORING SECOND CORINTHIANS
Death and Life, Hardship and Rivalry
*B. J. Oropeza*
Paperback $99.95, 978-0-88414-123-5   916 pages, 2016   Code: 067102
Hardcover $119.95, 978-0-88414-125-9   E-book $99.95, 978-0-88414-124-2
Rhetoric of Religious Antiquity 3

### RESURRECTION IN PAUL
Cognition, Metaphor, and Transformation
*Frederick S. Tappenden*
Paperback $37.95, 978-0-88414-144-0   310 pages, 2016   Code: 064519
Hardcover $52.95, 978-0-88414-146-4   E-book, $37.95, 978-0-88414-145-7
Early Christianity and Its Literature 19

SBL Press • P.O. Box 2243 • Williston, VT 05495-2243
Phone: 877-725-3334 (toll-free) or 802-864-6185 • Fax: 802-864-7626
Order online at www.sbl-site.org/publications

# A Shift in Perspective: The Intended Audience and a Coherent Reading of Proverbs 1:1–7

ARTHUR KEEFER
arthurkeefer@gmail.com
University of Cambridge, Cambridge CB2 1TN, United Kingdom

Two issues in Prov 1:1–7 have not been adequately accounted for in the interpretation of the passage as a whole: (1) the grammatical agent(s) of the infinitives in Prov 1:2–4, 6; and (2) the intended audience of Prov 1:1–7. By attributing a distinct agent to 1:4, most interpreters include the "simpletons" and "youth" of 1:4 in the audience of Proverbs, sometimes adding an ideal audience indicated rhetorically in 1:5—the "wise one" who hears. I argue that Prov 1:1–7 casts the "wise" as the ideal, intended audience rather than the "simpletons" and "youth" of 1:4. By addressing pertinent grammatical and rhetorical factors in Prov 1:1–7 in a consistent fashion, I offer a coherent reading of Prov 1:1–7 that views this passage as a tightly knit structure and addresses a single, intended audience.

Most interpreters agree that Prov 1:1–7 introduces a family of wisdom terms, identifies the intended audience(s), and states the book's purpose through a series of infinitive constructs (1:2–4, 6). Many commentators claim that the infinitives depend on the title (1:1) and indicate intended audiences: the simpletons and youth (1:4) as well as the mature reader referred to as the "wise" (1:5).[1] The reason is semantic: the title supplies the "proverbs of Solomon" as the agent required to complete the meaning of the infinitives. Read naturally as statements of purpose,

[1] See, among others, Ardnt Meinhold, *Die Sprüche*, 2 vols., ZBK.AT 16 (Zurich: Theologischer Verlag, 1991), 1:47–48; R. N. Whybray, *Proverbs: Based on the Revised Standard Version*, NCBC (London: Marshall Pickering, 1994), 16–17, 31; Michael V. Fox, *Proverbs 1–9: A New Translation with Introduction and Commentary*, AB 18A (New York: Doubleday, 2000), 53; Timothy Sandoval, "Revisiting the Prologue of Proverbs," *JBL* 126 (2007): 455–73, here 455, 459; Stuart Weeks, *Instruction and Imagery in Proverbs 1–9* (Oxford: Oxford Univeristy Press, 2007), 106; Christine Yoder, *Proverbs*, AOTC (Nashville: Abingdon, 2009), 2–5; Magne Sæbø, *Sprüche*, ATD 16.1 (Göttingen: Vandenhoeck & Ruprecht, 2012), 40, 43; William P. Brown, *Wisdom's Wonder: Character, Creation, and Crisis in the Bible's Wisdom Literature* (Grand Rapids: Eerdmans, 2014), 30–31.

103

the infinitives are often translated with a simple "to," indicating purpose. Hence, with a governing title and assumed linking verb, the phrases read, "The proverbs of Solomon (1:1) … [are] for the purpose of—."[2] Most commentators apply this pattern to verses 2b, 3a, and then also to verse 4, which would read, "The proverbs of Solomon . . . [are] for the purpose of giving to the simple ones prudence." It is therefore concluded that one of the intended audiences is the simple/youth.

## I. Proverbs 1:1–7: Translation

| | | |
|---|---|---|
| משלי שלמה<br>בן דוד מלך ישראל | 1:1 | The proverbs of Solomon,<br>son of David, king of Israel: |
| לדעת חכמה ומוסר<br>להבין אמרי בינה | 1:2 | to know wisdom and instruction,<br>to understand sayings of understanding, |
| לקחת מוסר השכל<br>צדק ומשפט ומישרים | 1:3 | to receive instruction in wise dealing:<br>righteousness, and justice, and equity, |
| לתת לפתאים ערמה<br>לנער דעת ומזמה | 1:4 | to give to the simple ones prudence,<br>to the youth knowledge and discretion. |
| ישמע חכם ויוסף לקח<br>ונבון תחבלות יקנה | 1:5 | Let the wise one hear and increase in learning<br>and the one who understands acquire guidance |
| להבין משל ומליצה<br>דברי חכמים וחידתם | 1:6 | to understand a proverb and an epigram<br>the words of the wise ones and their enigmas. |
| יראת יהוה ראשית דעת<br>חכמה ומוסר אוילים בזו | 1:7 | The fear of the Lord is the beginning of knowledge<br>wisdom and instruction fools despise. |

Between verses 2–3 and verse 4, the implied agent of the infinitives changes. In verses 2–3, it is consistently the reader, not the proverbs, who knows (v. 2a), who understands (v. 2b), and who receives (v. 3a). Yet in verse 4 it is the proverbs of Solomon, not the reader, that give. Michael V. Fox clarifies the shift at verse 4: "The verb [to give], may seem awkward because it describes something that book will do, whereas the parallel verbs in the series describe things the pupil will do (knowing, understanding, receiving)."[3] Fox assumes correctly that the infinitives imply an additional agent. Yet he, like many others, resolves the shift at verse 4 by claiming that the implied reader of verses 2–3 is now revealed in the direct objects of verse 4. Hence, verse 4 clarifies that the proverbs were written for the simple/youth, who might know, understand, and receive (1:2–3a). Interpreters then claim that

---

[2] See John Johnson, "An Analysis of Proverbs 1:1–7," *BSac* 144 (1987): 419–32, here 429. The minimalist translation implies "in order to" or "for the purpose of" or "for use in."

[3] Fox, *Proverbs 1–9*, 60–61.

verse 5 indicates a second audience, the "wise," with verse 6 resuming the style of verses 2–3. While views divide over the precise structure and relationship of the clauses, the shift at verse 4 has not been adequately addressed.[4]

The change at verse 4 relates directly to the question of audience. Who is or are the intended audience(s) as indicated by the introduction (1:1–7), particularly verses 4–5? Does Proverbs address the "simple/youth" or the "wise one" or both? In order to resolve these questions, I will account for structural, grammatical, linguistic, and rhetorical issues in Prov 1:1–7 and propose a coherent reading of the whole passage. In my reexamination of the section I undertake four tasks that will yield an alternative reading. I establish that (1) the title is independent of verses 2–6 and (2) that the infinitives depend on the finite verbs of verse 5. Then, (3) I demonstrate that the implied reader, or audience, is not the "simple" (v. 4a) but is indeed the "wise" (v. 5), who is the agent of verse 4 that gives prudence to the simple. I clarify the identity and literary-rhetorical function of the "wise," and (4) address the two terms in verse 4. My conclusions will not only reveal a tightly knit structure for Prov 1:1–7 but will also focus the identity of the book's intended audience, as I establish a singular audience, the "wise," rooted in the rhetorical-literary context of Proverbs in ways heretofore either overlooked or undeveloped by interpreters.[5]

## II. The Independent Title (1:1)

Most scholars assume that the infinitives of Prov 1:2–6 grammatically depend on the title (1:1),[6] but an examination of other biblical titles calls this assumed

---

[4] Compare a divided structure, where, for example, 1:5 links to 1:6 or 1:6 returns to 1:1.

[5] My goals concern the final, literary form of the text. I will therefore address only briefly matters of historical and redaction criticism. Rolf Schäfer extracts Prov 1:5 based on its distinction of style, content, and meter (*Die Poesie der Weisen: Dichotomie als Grundstruktur der Lehr- und Weisheitsgedichte in Proverbien 1–9*, WMANT 77 [Neukirchen-Vluyn: Neukirchener Verlag, 1999], 12). Proverbs 1:5, however, shares terms with 1:1–7, and on the basis of rare terms we could also extract 1:6. Schäfer seems to assume that the earlier author aimed for metric and stylistic conformity between 1:1–4, 6, but I will show that the differences of verse 5 cohere with verses 1–7 as a whole, supporting the views of many who accept verse 5 as original. See, among others, Fox, *Proverbs 1–9*, 62–63; Whybray, *Proverbs*, 31. While these issues are important, I must agree with Sandoval when it comes to Proverbs: "Compared with the hypothetical (though often plausible) theories of different oral and literary stages of the text that scholars imagine and often favor in interpretation, the final literary text (and context) of Proverbs is what is most unproblematically available to us. It thus merits at least as much attention as literary-historical interpretive endeavors" ("Revisiting the Prologue," 458–59).

[6] Hans F. Fuhs does note that the infinitives depend not on the title but on the main clause of 1:5, yet he offers no supporting evidence (*Sprichtwörter*, NEchtB [Würzburg: Echter, 2001], 23). James A. Loader identifies educators as the "first-tier users of the book" but does not consistently

connection into question. None of the other titles or subtitles in Proverbs connects grammatically to the verse or verses that follow (cf. Prov 10:1–2, 24:23, 25:1–2, 30:1, 31:1–3). Likewise, elsewhere in Old Testament writings most titles are not linked to the verses that follow; see, e.g., Eccl 1:1–2, Song 1:1–2; also Neh 1:1, most notably Eccl 1:1, which bears a striking similarity to Prov 1:1.[7] John Johnson notes the independence of Proverbs' title: "This construction is substantiated by the normal role of the title verses, which are not linked grammatically to what follows."[8] The independence of the title will be further supported by many structural and grammatical aspects of Prov 1:1–7.

The remaining verses of the introduction (1:2–7) cohere without the title and thus validate their own independence. The term משל (1:1a, 6a) seems to connect verses 1 and 6, creating an envelope that unifies Prov 1:1–6. R. N. Whybray notes, however, "The proverbs of Solomon (v. 1) for understanding a proverb (v. 6) is a tautology."[9] Over against the tautology stands an alternative linguistic envelope (1:2, 7). The terms *know*, *wisdom*, and *instruction* in verse 2a (לדעת חכמה ומוסר) appear in the same order in verse 7, where the fear of the Lord is the beginning of "knowledge / wisdom and instruction" (דעת חכמה ומוסר; an A–B–C / A–B–C pattern). While the single term in 1:1, 6 (משל) might structure verses 1–7, the envelope of three words at 1:2, 7 provides a stronger connection and, therefore, more likely structures the passage. In addition, the phrases in 1:2, 7 contrast conceptually and connect the introduction as a whole. As stated positively in verse 2, Proverbs intends for its audience to know wisdom and instruction (i.e., fear the Lord [v. 7a]). Stated negatively and by contrast in verse 7b, fools despise wisdom and instruction. In sum, 1:2–7 coheres linguistically and conceptually, standing apart from the title.

### III. Grammar: The Relationship of Infinitives and Verse 5

Instead of depending on the title, the infinitives may depend on the finite verbs of verse 5. That is, "in order to know … to receive … to give … Let the wise one hear." In another form, "Let the wise one hear in order to know…." Typically, infinitives precede the finite verb on which they depend when they occur with the prefixed prepositions -ב or -כ and carry temporal meaning (e.g., Prov 28:28; 29:2, 16). Yet an infinitive in construct, with the prefixed preposition -ל noting purpose as in 1:2–6, may also precede its governing verb, possibly for emphasis.[10] The

---

account for all aspects of Prov 1:1–7, most notably the title (*Proverbs 1–9*, HCOT [Leuven: Peeters, 2014], 51, 59–61).

[7] Consider also the prophetic literature (e.g., Isa 1:1–2, 15:1, Obad 1:1, Nah 1:1–2).
[8] Johnson, "Analysis of Proverbs 1:1–7," 429.
[9] Whybray, *Proverbs*, 34.
[10] GKC §114g (Gen 42:9, 47:4, Num 22:20, Josh 2:3, 1 Sam 16:2, all with בוא; and Judg 15:10,

grammatical style in 1:2-7, therefore, where the infinitive of purpose precedes its governing verb, is not only possible but attested. The style of Prov 1:2-6 is unique in the number of infinitives and in that they precede (1:2-4) and follow (1:6) their governing verb. Yet, based on the evidence presented here and despite the unique grammatical form of the passage, I see no reason why this combination is not possible.

Whybray translates the infinitive of 1:4 in the passive: "that [prudence, etc.] ... may be given."[11] Although he does not explain his decision, there is evidence that the infinitive construct, when active in form, can render a passive voice.[12] The verb נתן, however, occurs in the *qal* form here and regularly appears elsewhere in the *niphal* when an author wishes to use the passive voice, including the *niphal* infinitive construct (Esth 3:14, 8:13) and infinitive absolute (Jer 32:4, 38:3). Furthermore, why alter the use of infinitives, which are clearly active in Prov 1:2-3 and 6, when they can be read naturally and coherently in the active voice? The author had grammatical means to express the passive voice but chose otherwise.

Fox explains the change at verse 4 by means of a parallel in Egyptian literature, claiming that a similar grammatical shift occurs in the prologue of the Instruction of Amenemope. In Amenemope, he says, "some infinitives refer to what the book will do for the pupil (II. 7-12), and others indicate actions the pupil will learn to do (II. 5-6)."[13] This is indeed the way most commentators interpret Proverbs' introduction; and while the similarities between Amenemope's introduction and the introduction of Proverbs lend weight to Fox's case, the particular shift in perspective includes a notable dissimilarity. The lines in Amenemope indicate recipients other than the student/audience. They state that the student will know "how to answer one who speaks / to reply to one who sends a message" (I, 5-6).[14] In the Egyptian text, the direct objects—the one who speaks or sends a message—are not the audience; in Proverbs, according to Fox and most commentators, the direct objects are the audience (i.e., the simple/youth).[15] Thus, the categories do not match. It also includes no grammatical outlier, as does Prov 1:5, on which the infinitives can stably depend.[16] As I will show, these categories of instruction,

---

1 Sam 17:25, with עלה). See also Job 21:14, Prov 19:18, Isa 10:1-2, and 1 Sam 12:23. See esp. Prov 22:19.

[11] Whybray, *Proverbs*, 33.

[12] Joüon §124t.

[13] Fox, *Proverbs 1-9*, 61, 71-73.

[14] *AEL* 2:148. Fox translates, "to know how to return an (oral) answer to one who says it, to bring back a (written) report to one who sends it" (*Proverbs 1-9*, 71).

[15] Fox's comments that Amenemope actually supports the interpretation of Prov 1:2-6 proposed in this essay (ibid., 74). He claims that both Amenemope (XXVI, 10-12; cf. *AEL* 2:165) and Prov 1:2-4 orient the educated reader to teach the young and ignorant, while both also (XXVIII, 13-15; Prov 1:5-6) "extol the book's value to the wise man." Fox is not entirely clear on whom he identifies as Proverbs' audience (ibid., 53, 58, 62, 73, 349).

[16] When Amenemope wishes to indicate the audience, it may supply a pronoun to clarify

reader, and recipient actually argue against the accepted interpretation of Prov 1:4 and support an alternative reading. It seems, therefore, that the ancient Egyptian parallel does not justify a shift in grammar or perspective in Prov 1:4, and the issue becomes a matter of the audience of Proverbs' introduction.

## IV. Rhetoric: The Audience Identified

Most interpreters read 1:4 as a shift in subject from student (1:2–3a) to "proverbs" (1:4a), then view the recipients in verse 4 as an audience of the book, and then add a second audience in 1:5. Whybray claims verses 4–5 state that "the simple or inexperienced, the youth and also the experienced wise man and man of understanding will alike profit by the teaching which will be given.... [Verse 5] gives notice that the book as a whole was written not only for the young, but that it contains teaching from which even the experienced and wise adult can profit."[17] Timothy Sandoval, however, has redefined the traditional double audience and argued for an intended ideal audience. He summarizes: "Although simpletons and sage, and everyone in between, might read and learn something from the book, the text imagines its ideal addressee as one who is able, at one and the same moment, to occupy different subject positions vis-à-vis the book's instruction."[18] For the most part, I agree with Sandoval's case and conclusion. He does not, however, address the shift in perspective at verse 4, and he seems to assume that the title governs the infinitives and that the audience still includes, at least rhetorically, a form of the simpleton/youth. So he writes,

> The prologue, on the one hand, encourages an anticipated reader, whoever this might be, rhetorically to occupy the *readerly subject position* of a young, unlearned person [פתאים; נער] in need of instruction, as v. 4 implies. On the other hand, and at the same time, vv. 5–6 exhort the addressee to assume the subject position of the wise and understanding person [חכם; נבון (v. 5)] he in fact will become if he accepts the text's invitation, stays the course, and strives to understand Proverb's wisdom.[19]

Sandoval does not account for the shift at verse 4 and, in essence, along with many commentators, maintains two audiences, the unlearned and the wise. Yet he reveals a significant rhetorical strategy of Proverbs: the author intends to identify and align his audience with an ideal recipient.[20]

---

the meaning of its infinitive phrases, though the interpretation of the suffixes is debatable. For text and comments, see Vincent Pierre-Michel Laisney, *L'Enseignement d'Aménémopé*, StP.SM 19 (Rome: Pontifical Biblical Institute, 2007), 22–27.

[17] Whybray, *Proverbs*, 30–31. See others in n. 1 above.

[18] Sandoval, "Revisiting the Prologue," 466.

[19] Ibid. (emphasis original).

[20] Fuhs does assert a singular audience and begins to touch on the identity of the "wise" (*Sprichtwörter*, 23). He traces this conclusion, however, to its implications for the historical,

Although I build on Sandoval's insights, I suggest, rather, that this ideal audience is not both the youth and the wise but only the "wise one" of verse 5, where the subject functions rhetorically as a caricature for the interpreter to emulate. In his comment on verse 5, Crawford Toy describes the twofold sense in which we might understand the wise: "there is a certain incongruity in bidding a sage learn to understand the worlds of sages."[21] I resolve the incongruity by understanding how the "wise" in verses 5–6 has two distinct referents. The passage distinguishes between the sage as a historical figure and the sage as a literary figure, that is, the wise in real life versus the "wise one" in Proverbs.

In the titles and headings of Proverbs, the "wise" refers to particular persons living in the world, that is, the historical wise person, in contrast to the wise and foolish literary caricatures that appear throughout the teaching of Proverbs. Proverbs 1:6 links with 1:1 and 10:1 through the term "proverbs" (משלים). Furthermore, the "*words* of the wise" (דברי חכמים) appears in titles, superscripts, and postscripts in Proverbs and other biblical texts (Prov 22:17, 30:1, 31:1, Job 31:40, Eccl 1:1).[22] On 1:6, Fox notes that "*Ḥakamim* here seems to designate a specific group rather than simply men who are wise. The wise men mentioned so frequently in the proverbs are all who possess the skills for successful living. The headings in 22:17 and 24:23, however, apply the term to the learned authors of wisdom."[23] Hence, the term *wise ones* (1:6) denotes a historical referent. The historical reliability or exact referent of these titles does not affect my argument. The point is that on a literary level they function differently than the "wise" character in Proverbs. The "wise one" (1:5) refers to a caricature throughout the text of Proverbs, as the book typically portrays characters in extreme form. Thus, the "fool," the "one who understands," and the "simple" are respectively foolish, intelligent, and gullible in the extreme. Sun Myung Lyu argues that the righteous figure is Proverbs' prime pedagogical tool. The wise and righteous are coreferential for the ideal person who functions rhetorically as a model to emulate.[24]

---

familial context and does not consider its function at a rhetorical-literary level (24). Christopher B. Ansberry attempts to pare the simpleton from the fool and scoffer in the interludes and to align the youth with the son in chapters 1–9 (*Be Wise, My Son, and Make My Heart Glad: An Exploration of the Courtly Nature of the Book of Proverbs*, BZAW 422 [Berlin: de Gruyter, 2011], 65–69). Like Sandoval, he wishes to maintain the ideal reader position of the wise in verse 5 along with a primary audience of the youth yet adds that the youth fits the "courtly features" of Prov 1–9. If this is the case, however, how do we account for the nature of the wise person in relation to these courtly aspects of the discourse narrative?

[21] Crawford H. Toy, *A Critical and Exegetical Commentary on the Book of Proverbs*, ICC [Edinburgh: T&T Clark, 1904], 5.

[22] Bruce Waltke, *Proverbs: An Introduction and Commentary*, TOTC (Downers Grove, IL: InterVarsity Press, 1975), 180. While some of these passages are distant from Prov 1:6 and in distinct parts of Proverbs, they nevertheless reflect similar language and, as key structural markers, similar contexts (i.e., headings or introductions).

[23] Fox, *Proverbs 1–9*, 64.

[24] Sun Myung Lyu, *Righteousness in the Book of Proverbs*, FAT 2/55 (Tübingen: Mohr Siebeck,

The "wise" operates on this literary rather than historical level in the remainder of chapters 1–9, where it refers to one who is teachable and willing to learn (1:7, 9:8, 10:8). The verb to "hear" (שמע) in 1:5 and 1:8 connects the wise with the son, associating the ideal identity with the figurative, familial addressee. So Bruce Waltke concludes, "By using the volitional form of the word 'to hear,' the preamble subtly includes the son among the wise who are addressed in the volitional form of this word."[25] The son is directly addressed throughout the book (e.g., 19:27, 23:15, 24:13, 27:11) and appears in context with the wise (1:8, 10:1b–8, 13:1, 15:20; cf. 13:20, 17:25), supporting the view that in 1:5 the author addresses the "wise" as the intended audience in terms of the role that audience should assume.

The distinction that I have made between the literary wise and historical wise coheres with how the "fools" function in 1:7. Verse 7 introduces the "fool" as an antithesis of the successful student of Proverbs. Fools do not receive instruction, they despise it. Magne Sæbø's comment underlines both the parallel function of the wise and the fool, and the audience's place in relation to them. He notes that 1:7 poses "der Zweiteilung der Zuhörer, d.h. der Menschen, indem nun von den 'Toren,' die die 'Weisheit und Belehrung verachten,' als Antitypen zu den Weisen die Rede ist. Diese Art von Dichotomie wird im ganzen Buch der Sprüche öfter und vielfach fortgesetzt."[26] Thus, Prov 1:5–7 reveals a threefold distinction between the literary wise (1:5), the historical wise (1:6b), and the literary fool (1:7b), each supporting the existence and function of the other while further aligning the audience of Proverbs with the "wise" in 1:5.[27]

Even if the wise functions in 1:5 as proposed, that does not resolve the reference to the simpletons and the youth in 1:4, who are often tagged as one of the book's audiences. The simple ones (פתאים) are those not yet given to evil or committed to good.[28] At the outset of life, they need faculties of judgment and thoughtfulness in order to avoid folly and embrace wisdom; they are ethically, religiously, and intellectually malleable. Hence they need prudence (1:4a): "The simple believes everything; but the prudent gives thought to his steps" (Prov 14:15; cf. 8:5, 19:25). The age of a youth (נער) spans from an adolescent to a thirty-year-old, not only physically but experientially.[29] In parallel with the "simple," verse 4 emphasizes the youth's nascent approach to life. The youth appears only once more in chapters 1–9

---

2012), 53, 62–63. So also Waltke, *Proverbs*, 125.

[25] Waltke, *Proverbs*, 179.

[26] Sæbø, *Sprüche*, 44.

[27] The intent and function mirror those of Psalm 1, which contrasts the "blessed" man and the "wicked" in order to shape the faithful worshiper. Consider Derek Kidner's comments: "The tone and themes of the psalm bring to mind the Wisdom writings, especially Proverbs, with their interest in the company a man keeps, in the two ways set before him (cf. e.g. Prov 2:12ff., 20ff.), and in moral types, notably the scoffers" (*Psalms 1–72*, TOTC [Downers Grove, IL: IVP Academic, 1973], 63).

[28] Waltke's term *gullible* captures the sense (*Proverbs*, 173).

[29] Waltke, *Proverbs*, 178.

and is again joined to the simple in committing folly (7:7), which suggests little distinction between the two terms in 1:4.

If 1:4 was the only reference to the simple, whom the author refrained from developing later in the book, it would be plausible to view the simple as an intended audience. Yet the author develops an identity of the simpletons that dissuades the audience from aligning with then. The father consistently addresses the son but never addresses the simple. Furthermore, the simple are first addressed by the figure of Wisdom in chapter 1, where she includes them with the population of scoffers and fools (1:22) and then portrays the simple, along with the fool, turning away from her instruction (1:32). Likewise, in chapter 7, the youth who falls to the wiles of the seductress comes from the company of the simple (7:7), and in 8:4 the simple parallel fools, a negative portrait that Proverbs upholds throughout the book (9:4, 6, 16; 14:15, 18; 22:3; 27:12). In Proverbs 1–9, therefore, the father speaks to the son and associates him with the wise; Lady Wisdom addresses the simple and associates them with fools.

Although the appearances of the simple in Proverbs 1–9 suggest that they are beginners at the outset of their proverbial education, the author portrays the simple from a negative perspective and does not want the audience to identify with them. The distance between the interpreter and the simpleton becomes clear when we consider the context of the passages in which the simple appear.

In chapter 1, Lady Wisdom speaks in the public square and calls to the simple, the scoffer, and the fool with the pronoun *you* (v. 22). Yet she soon reveals that the audience, or the imagined city population, is not included among the threefold "you" group. Having addressed the fools/simple as "you" (vv. 22–27), she then claims, "Then they will call me and I will not answer / they will seek me diligently and will not find me" (v. 28). Thus, Wisdom points to the fools/simple as disobedient, distinguishing them from the remaining city population.[30] She thereby draws a lesson for the interpreter, saying to her intended audience, "Do not be like them, the simple, the fool, and the scoffer," and repeatedly mentions their folly (v. 32). Moreover, she concludes with an abstract, ideal audience by noting a response contrary to that of the fools: "But the one who listens to me dwells in security, and is at ease from the dread of evil" (v. 33). As Fox observes, "the speech is an apostrophe to an audience not present. The reader overhears a condemnation of categories of people in which he does not want to be included."[31]

---

[30] J. N. Aletti, "Séduction et parole en Proverbs I–IX," *VT* 27 (1977): 129–44, here 132. Likewise, Katharine J. Dell aligns the speech with prophetic texts and notes the perfect verbs in 1:24–31, "as if Wisdom's teaching has already been rejected, making judgement inescapable" (*The Book of Proverbs in Social and Theological Context* [Cambridge: Cambridge University Press, 2006], 96). This affirms the simpleton's association with a disfavored and unhopeful group.

[31] Fox, *Proverbs 1–9*, 98. See also Bálint Károly Zabán, *The Pillar Function of the Speeches of Wisdom: Proverbs 1:20–33, 8:1–36, and 9:1–6 in the Structural Framework of Proverbs 1–9*, BZAW 429 (Berlin: de Gruyter, 2012), 66–89, 99–109.

The scenes in Prov 7 and 8 function in a similar way. In chapter 7, the father recalls a moral story, and chapter 8 portrays Lady Wisdom again speaking in the city. Both scenes follow with identical phrases (7:24a, 8:32a): ועתה בנים שמעו לי, "And now, O sons, listen to me." The consequential grammatical note (ועתה) indicates a lesson for the audience to draw from the previous scene. Having viewed the foolish fate of the simpleton, the grammatical hook and following admonition—"O sons, listen to me"—encourages the interpreter to identify with the son. To summarize, the author uses the same strategy with scenes in Prov 1, 7, and 8, where the simple one never attains to wisdom but implicitly or explicitly stands condemned.[32]

The author employs a rhetorical strategy through the simpleton that mirrors the literary function of other characters, such as the wise and the fool. Throughout Proverbs, the simple appear not as a reading/listening audience but as literary figures portrayed in negative contexts. This negative caricature of the simple and the author's consistent use of literary exemplars, particularly in the wise and the fool of Prov 1:5 and 7, suggests that the "simpletons" function in the same way in 1:4. Thus, 1:5 commands and invites the audience to posture themselves not as the fool, simpleton, or youth but as the wise character who heeds instruction. It follows that the "wise," who can ideally give knowledge to the simple/youth, becomes the agent of verse 4, an implication to which I turn now.

I should briefly note that, based on these conclusions, the summons of verse 5 does not exclude the young or nascent student from the school of Proverbs. The introduction neither distinguishes nor exclusively invites "the wise in real life" or "the simpleton of real life"; rather, it distinguishes between literary types that

---

[32] I will comment briefly on Prov 9, since its coherence and redaction are debated. Fox extracts verses 7–12 and joins the two speeches (vv. 1–6 and 13–18) (*Proverbs 1–9*, 295–96; cf. 307, 317–18), but Waltke defends the final form (*Proverbs*, 438). Overall, the simpletons addressed by Lady Wisdom (vv. 4–6) and Lady Folly (v. 16) support the wise figure through contrast, who again appears attractive and ideal (vv. 7–9, 12). Most importantly, while Lady Wisdom addresses the simple (v. 4), the simple is later associated with the identity of Lady Folly herself. For she is "full of simpleness" and knows nothing (v. 13b), like the simpleton she addresses (v. 18a). Waltke finds in the final form of Prov 9 that verses 7–12 explain "why the gullible, who are still teachable, and not the mockers, who are incorrigible, are rebuked…. The first and last stanzas of this poem are invitations to the gullible; the middle insertion is instruction" (430). It is in this instruction (vv. 7–12) that we again see, in the words of Derek Kidner, "character-sketches of typical products of these opposing camps: the scoffer, with his closed mind, and the wise man, ever teachable and ever progressing" (*Proverbs: An Introduction and Commentary*, TOTC [Downers Grove, IL: InterVarsity Press, 1975], 77).

According to Fox, the discourse may focus more on the contrast of the women than on the contrast of their addressees: "The motive for the creation of this personification is rhetorical, to create a symmetry between wisdom and folly" (*Proverbs 1–9*, 300). Yet, for the interpreter, he notes, "The purpose of these sayings is not so much to assert a pedagogical tenet as to warn the reader that to resist chastisement is to be a fool" (316). To my point, Waltke claims, "The wise belong to the guests hosted by Wisdom, and the proud to the adherents of Folly" (*Proverbs*, 439).

function rhetorically to invite any interpreter. Thus, the book appears to address the student of wisdom at all levels of maturity.³³

## V. The Meaning of לקח and תחבלות

Thus far I have suggested that the "shift in perspective" at Prov 1:4 is not really a shift. The phrase naturally follows from the preceding verses, claiming that the interpreter will give prudence to the simple and knowledge and discretion to the youth. Furthermore, it seems that the author does not intend for the audience to identify with the simple or the youth, who appear as unattractive figures throughout the book. Rather the author invites the audience to assume the posture of the "wise" in 1:5. This interpretation, then, implies that the interpreter of Proverbs will actually teach, for it logically expresses, "Let the wise one [the interpreter] hear ... to give to the simple ones prudence." In addition to the evidence offered thus far, there are other reasons for such an interpretation. A close look at verse 5 will show not only grounds but positive support for understanding the intended audience of Proverbs as not only a learner but also a teacher.

Translations typically render 1:5a as, "Let the wise hear and increase in learning."³⁴ In light of the *vav* plus imperfect (ויוסף), the initial imperfect (ישמע) becomes a jussive and constitutes a command. It seems that the wise, regardless of whether we consider him "the wise in real life" or a literary figure, will simply accumulate further knowledge through the reading of Proverbs: "Whoever is wise is invited to add more learning [*doctrinam*] to that which he already possesses."³⁵ Yet, if we hold to the premise that the wise have been addressed from the outset (1:2–4), then verse 5a may simply repeat the admonition to attain knowledge and instruction (1:2a). The terms לֶקַח ("teaching") and תחבלות ("guidance") in 1:5 reveal that this is not a simple repetition but rather a fresh consequence of studying Proverbs, which reveals the teaching-role perspective of its intended audience and further supports my interpretation of 1:4.

The term לֶקַח stems from לקח ("to take") and refers etymologically to that which is received (Isa 29:24). It occurs most often in Proverbs and at times refers

---

³³ Richard J. Clifford, *Proverbs: A Commentary*, OTL (Louisville: Westminster John Knox, 1999), 36. The nouns in 1:4–5 themselves may also lend support. The wise and one who understands (v. 5) are singular, while the simpletons and fools (vv. 4a, 7b) are plural. The youth (v. 4b) is singular but may constitute a distributed hendiadys with the simpletons (so Fox, *Proverbs 1–9*, 61) or noun of species (Joüon §135c). While the youth occurs in the singular form in Proverbs, Franz Delitzsch claims that נער is usually collective (*Biblical Commentary on the Proverbs of Solomon*, 2 vols., CFTL 43, 47 [Edinburgh: T&T Clark, 1865], 1:56). Interestingly, BHS indicates a variant reading of the term in the plural.

³⁴ ESV, NASB, NIV, NRSV.

³⁵ Delitzsch, *Biblical Commentary*, 1:57. So also Whybray, *Proverbs*, 33.

not to received content but to persuasiveness or skilled eloquence. So the adulteress uses seductive speech (Prov 7:21), paralleling smooth talk. In the context of thoughtful speech (16:21–30), it joins the verb יסף ("to add") as in 1:5: "sweetness of speech increases persuasiveness" (16:21 ESV) and "the heart of the wise makes his speech judicious and adds persuasiveness to his lips" (16:23 ESV). A less-clear instance emphasizes gaining more לֶקַח: "teach a righteous man, and he will increase in learning" (9:9 ESV). Some interpreters apply the ambiguity of 9:9 to the term in 1:5.[36] Yet in 9:9 the word occurs in the context of verbal responses (cf. 9:7), not simply in receiving content, a pattern that will recur in other examples.[37]

In some cases, לֶקַח retains the nuance of "that which is received," as the father gives good precepts to the son (4:2a; parallel to תורה), and Moses nourishes the Israelites with לֶקַח or "teaching" (Deut 32:2). In Job, it is translated as "doctrine" (Job 11:4 ESV). In each of these cases, however, while the term maintains a sense of "that which is received," it appears in a context that emphasizes the quality either of verbal output or of content that is received and intended for dispensation. In Prov 4:2, the son does not simply receive לֶקַח; rather, the father recalls his own learning, which he now dispenses to his son (cf. 4:1–9). In reference to this passage, Whybray comments on 1:5: "[לֶקַח] together with *hear*, recalls the tradition of oral teaching in which the teacher hands on to the pupil what he himself has learned from his own teachers."[38] In Deuteronomy, Moses identifies his לֶקַח with dropping rain and parallels it to speech, which will shower the grass and herbs. This connotes not simply content but the quality of word and song that will follow. In Job, the term occurs in the context of varying qualities of speech, as Job's accusers claim that his self-proclaimed, pure לֶקַח (11:4a) is rather a multitude of words that amount to babble (11:2–3) and hold no parity to God's quality of instruction (11:5–6).[39]

The term's use in Proverbs and elsewhere suggests that it refers not simply to content received but to a fine quality of speech that includes a sense of passing on that which was received, a fitting emphasis for Prov 1:5. Thus, Franz Delitzsch

---

[36] Waltke, *Proverbs*, 179.

[37] Yoder affirms the wise role of the reader who is now ready to teach at Prov 9 (*Proverbs*, 106–7). Yet she later reverts to the audience as the youth who faces a final decision between wisdom and folly (109–10).

[38] Whybray, *Proverbs*, 33.

[39] William McKane supports this interpretation from the standpoint of verse 6, of which he concludes, "Wisdom embraces form as well as content, and it mattered that what is said should be said well and elegantly" (*Proverbs: A New Approach*, OTL [London: SCM, 1970], 467). The term also occurs in Sirach in contexts of reception for the sake of quality speech and dispensation (compare 8:8 and 8:9; 51:16 and 51:26, 28; and see also 37:22–23, where the wise man instructs). W. O. E. Oesterley notes the use of לֶקַח in rabbinic literature, particularly Pirqe 'Abot 2:11, where everything that the pupil "had received from his teachers he retained; the further implication being that he was therefore in a position to hand it down to others" (*The Book of Proverbs: With Introduction and Notes*, WC [London: Methuen, 1929], 4). See also Daniel J. Treier, *Proverbs and Ecclesiastes*, Brazos Theological Commentary on the Bible (Grand Rapids: Brazos, 2012), 11.

comments that לֶקַח here does refer to learning but "learning that has passed into the possession of the receiver."[40] Horst Seebass's definition does not apply to all occurrences of לֶקַח (cf. Isa 29:24, Prov 7:21), but it does pinpoint the sense captured in Prov 1:5 and the examples above. He concludes, "The term *leqaḥ* probably does not mean 'teaching' or 'persuasiveness,' but rather that which a person has been able to acquire in the way of wisdom or teaching and is thus in a position to pass on to others."[41] Proverbs 1:5, therefore, asks the interpreter to listen to the book's teaching and increase in לֶקַח, which would enable him or her "to give to the simple ones prudence / to the youth knowledge and discretion" (1:4). Mentioning a form of speech at the outset of the book coheres with the emphasis in the book on wise words (e.g., 13:14, 15:7).[42] Thus, my understanding of לֶקַח as "learning received for the sake of dispensation," supports the reading of 1:4–5a, where the ideal, wise interpreter learns and can thus teach the simple/youth.

Proverbs 1:5b–6 also supports this interpretation of 1:4–5a. The term תַּחְבֻּלוֹת ("guidance," but also translated "counsel" [NASB]) derives from a maritime context; the root חבל relates to "rope-pulling and hence steering (a ship), used figuratively of wise counsel."[43] It is an ethically neutral skill that emphasizes management or directing (Prov 11:14, 20:18, Job 37:12) and applies to the individual. Yet it is often applied by its possessor to others. For example, by "wise guidance you can wage your war" (Prov 24:6 ESV); as the thoughts of the righteous are just, so the "counsels of the wicked are deceitful" (12:5 ESV). Waltke notes that "the word connotes that the book's guidance enables the insightful to lead himself and others through life like a well-steered ship."[44] Guidance is not only received or applied to oneself but is meant for influencing others. This matches the dispensational sense of לֶקַח. Moreover, both terms are ethically neutral rather than inherently virtuous (cf. 7:7, 12:5). Therefore, the skills offered in 1:5 enable the interpreter to fulfill the purposes of 1:4.

## VI. Conclusions

The shift in perspective at Prov 1:4 has prompted a series of questions related to the rhetorical, grammatical, and linguistic features of the introduction to the book (1:1–7) and has challenged former understandings of the book's intended audience. Most notably, I have argued that the intended audience of Proverbs does

---

[40] Delitzsch, *Biblical Commentary*, 1:57.
[41] H. Seebass, "לקח," *TDOT* 8:21. Fox emphasizes the term's sense of eloquence and so concludes that "Proverbs 1:5a is offering to enhance the wise man's rhetorical skills in teaching" (*Proverbs 1–9*, 63). Despite this emphasis, his word study largely supports my interpretation.
[42] See Kidner, *Proverbs*, 43–45.
[43] G. van Groningen, "תחבלות," *TWOT* §596a.
[44] Waltke, *Proverbs*, 96.

not include the simpletons and youth of 1:4 or both the simple (1:4) and wise (1:5) but only the ideal "wise" person of 1:5, who functions rhetorically as a model for the interpreter to emulate. The reasons are as follows:

1. The purposes indicated by the infinitives of Prov 1:2–6 do not grammatically depend on the title (1:1); the title stands alone.
2. The infinitives grammatically depend on the finite verbs of command in 1:5.
3. The "simple" and the "wise" in Proverbs function as literary types rather than historical referents; the author dissuades the interpreter from aligning with the "simple" and encourages the interpreter to identify with the ideal "wise" one.
4. Learning and guidance (1:5) refer to content or skills received for the purpose of teaching and leading others in the way of wisdom; that is, they enable their possessor to carry out the task of verse 4.

These conclusions are not absolute, but they are favored by the evidence and, when taken together, fashion a possible, coherent reading of the passage. Proverbs 1:1–7 does enumerate the purposes and promises of the book. The fulfillment of these purposes, however, depends on the main clause of 1:5, which, it seems, does not add an alternative audience to the simple/youth of 1:4 but rather delineates a single, intended audience. The ideal interpreters of Proverbs should approach the book with a posture of ready reception, whereby they hearken to its contents and acquire wisdom, instruction, and hermeneutical faculties. Yet their task concludes not with learning but rather with the acquired knowledge and know-how they can give to those at the outset of wisdom education. Proverbs speaks to each interpreter as a learner-teacher, both roles requiring the fear of the Lord. The book opens with learning, where the fear of the Lord is the beginning of wisdom (1:7). Yet it closes with a competent, skilled, and wise woman who still "fears the Lord" (31:30).

# 2 Maccabees 10:1–8: Who Wrote It and Where Does It Belong?

**JONATHAN R. TROTTER**
jonathan.r.trotter@gmail.com
University of Notre Dame, Notre Dame, IN 46556

Many commentators agree on two points about the development of 2 Maccabees: (1) the letters in 1:1–2:18 were not written by the author of the rest of the history, and (2) the account of the rededication of the temple in 10:1–8 has been relocated or inserted into the text. In contrast to the positions of these scholars, the primary purpose of this article is to demonstrate that the author of 2 Maccabees deliberately composed 10:1–8 for its current position in the epitome. To this end, I will respond to the arguments against both the location of this passage and its composition by the author of the rest of 2 Maccabees, contentions that depend on finding evidence of narrative disruption, distinctive language and style, and conflicting content between 10:1–8 and its context. Finally, I will show how the account of the repossession and purification of the Jerusalem temple is essential in accomplishing one of the main goals of the history, namely, the explanation of the origin of Hanukkah, and is interconnected with the rest of the narrative with regard to its placement, language, style, and content.

---

Attempts to reconstruct the textual development of 2 Maccabees have had varying degrees of success. For instance, since 2 Maccabees claims to be an epitome of an earlier work by Jason of Cyrene (2 Macc 2:23), some scholars have tried to distinguish Jason's history from the rest of 2 Maccabees.[1] As this earlier work is no longer available, however, it is difficult to distinguish based on content and

I would like to thank the Dolores Zohrab Liebmann Fund for their support of my research on this project.
[1] For examples of the reconstruction of at least certain elements of Jason's history, see Jochen Gabriel Bunge, *Untersuchungen zum zweiten Makkabäerbuch: Quellenkritische, literarische, chronologische und historische Untersuchungen zum zweiten Makkabäerbuch als Quelle syrisch-palästinensischer Geschichte im 2. Jh. v. Chr.* (Bonn: Rheinische Friedrich-Wilhelms-Universität, 1971), 175–81; Jonathan A. Goldstein, *II Maccabees: A New Translation with Introduction and Commentary*, AB 41A (Garden City, NY: Doubleday, 1983), 55–70; Bertram Herr, "Der Standpunkt des Epitomators: Perspektivenwechsel in der Forschung am Zweiten Makkabäerbuch," *Bib* 90 (2009): 1–31, esp. 16–18; Daniel R. Schwartz, *2 Maccabees*, CEJL (Berlin: de Gruyter, 2008), 16–25.

language alone when the author of 2 Maccabees is making use of Jason's history, rewriting it for his own purposes, or using some other source. It makes most sense, therefore, to attribute the composition and perspective of 2 Maccabees to its author (cf. 2:23–31).[2] There also have been efforts to identify other sources underlying the epitome, such as those thought to be shared by 1 and 2 Maccabees,[3] but a comparison does not reveal any specific literary sources behind these two histories.[4] At this point, however, most commentators agree on two points concerning the development of 2 Maccabees: (1) the letters in 1:1–2:18 were not written by the author of the rest of the history, and (2) the account of the rededication of the temple in 10:1–8 has been relocated to its current position in the text.[5] A variation on this second point is proposed by Daniel Schwartz, who argues that 2 Macc 10:1–8 was not simply moved from a different location but was added to the text by the same individuals who appended the introductory letters.[6] These points depend on perceived discontinuities between 10:1–8 and its context.

In contrast to this near-consensus, my primary purpose in this article is to demonstrate that the author of 2 Maccabees deliberately composed 10:1–8 for its current position in the epitome. To this end, I will respond to the arguments against both the location of this passage and its composition by the author of the rest of 2 Maccabees. This study is divided into three sections corresponding to categories of data often used in identifying editorial work in ancient texts: narrative disruption, distinctive language and style, and conflicting content.[7] Those who maintain

---

[2] Robert Doran, *2 Maccabees: A Critical Commentary*, Hermeneia (Minneapolis: Fortress, 2012), 11; Reinold Zwick, "Unterhaltung und Nutzen: Zum literarischen Profil des 2. Buches der Makkabäer," in *Steht nicht geschrieben? Studien zur Bibel und ihrer Wirkungsgeschichte; Festschrift für Georg Schmuttermayr*, ed. Johannes Frühwald-König, Ferdinand R. Prostmeier, and Reinold Zwick (Regensburg: Pustet, 2001), 125–49, esp. 137–42.

[3] See, e.g., Bunge, *Untersuchungen zum zweiten Makkabäerbuch*, 207–63; Goldstein, *II Maccabees*, 37–48; Klaus-Dietrich Schunck, *Die Quellen des I. und II. Makkabäerbuches* (Halle: Niemeyer, 1954), 52–82.

[4] Robert Doran, *Temple Propaganda: The Purpose and Character of 2 Maccabees*, CBQMS 12 (Washington, DC: Catholic Biblical Association of America, 1981), 12–23.

[5] See, e.g., Diego Arenhoevel, *Die Theokratie nach dem 1. und 2. Makkabäerbuch*, WSAMA.T 3 (Mainz: Matthias-Grünewald-Verlag, 1967), 108; John R. Bartlett, *The First and Second Books of the Maccabees*, CBC (Cambridge: Cambridge University Press, 1973), 215, 296; Goldstein, *II Maccabees*, 24–26, 345–48; Christian Habicht, *2. Makkabäerbuch*, JSHRZ 1.3 (Gütersloh: Mohn, 1976), 199–200, 249–50; Gary Morrison, "The Composition of II Maccabees: Insights Provided by a Literary *Topos*," *Bib* 90 (2009): 564–72, esp. 564–65; cf. Victor Parker, "The Letters in II Maccabees: Reflections on the Book's Composition," *ZAW* 119 (2007): 386–402. In contrast, while they agree that the letters are later additions, Robert Doran and David Williams argue that 2 Macc 10:1–8 is in its correct location (Doran, *2 Maccabees*, 197; David S. Williams, "Recent Research in 2 Maccabees," *CurBR* 2 [2003]: 69–83, esp. 76–80).

[6] Schwartz, *2 Maccabees*, 8–10, 371–79; cf. Gerry Wheaton, "The Festival of Hanukkah in 2 Maccabees: Its Meaning and Function," *CBQ* 74 (2012): 247–62, esp. 248, 260–62.

[7] By structuring this study around these three basic categories of common indications of

the theory of the displacement of 2 Macc 10:1–8 are concerned almost exclusively with narrative disruption. In arguing for the secondary nature of the account of the rededication of the temple, Schwartz focuses additionally on distinctive language and style as well as conflicting content. Finally, I will show how the account of the repossession and rededication of the Jerusalem temple is essential for accomplishing one of the main goals of the history, namely, the explanation of Hanukkah, and is interconnected with the rest of the narrative with regard to its placement, language, style, and content.

## I. Narrative Disruption as Evidence of Editing

The most common reason for proposing that 2 Macc 10:1–8 does not belong in its current location in the text is that it interrupts the account of the death of Antiochus IV Epiphanes (9:1–29) and the final summary of his life (10:9). On this reasoning, the original text would have read:

> Therefore, the murderer and blasphemer suffered the worst evils, just like those he had inflicted upon others, and he died most piteously in the mountains in a foreign land. Philip, one of his courtiers, took his body home, and he went to Ptolemy Philometor in Egypt because he was afraid of the son of Antiochus.... Thus was the end of Antiochus, who was called Epiphanes. (9:28–29, 10:9 NRSV)

The coherence of this reconstructed text is the primary argument for viewing 2 Macc 10:1–8 as an intrusion into the summary of Antiochus's death. Scholars who hold this position must also determine the original location of this material.[8]

---

editorial activity, I also hope to contribute in a limited fashion to the discussion of the methods used for reconstructing the textual development of ancient Jewish literature. See, e.g., John S. Kloppenborg and Judith H. Newman, eds., *Editing the Bible: Assessing the Task Past and Present*, SBLRBS 69 (Atlanta: Society of Biblical Literature, 2012); Reinhard Müller, Juha Pakkala, and Bas ter Haar Romeny, *Evidence of Editing: Growth and Change of Texts in the Hebrew Bible*, SBLRBS 75 (Atlanta, Society of Biblical Literature, 2014), esp. 1–17; John Van Seters, *The Edited Bible: The Curious History of the "Editor" in Biblical Criticism* (Winona Lake, IN: Eisenbrauns, 2006). Since I am dealing with a small passage in an individual text, I cannot generalize about the value of applying these indicators in all cases. Nevertheless, this investigation highlights problems with these types of arguments that likely will apply to similar analyses of editing in other texts.

[8] To give an overview of one possible solution, Jonathan Goldstein suggests that 10:1–8 stood after 8:36, immediately before the story of Antiochus's death (*II Maccabees*, 347–48). First, Goldstein reasons that the displaced passage could not have come any later in 2 Maccabees. The ancient author notes that the next section of his work is concerned with "the calamities of the wars" of Antiochus V (10:10) and then introduces two such calamities—the appointment of Lysias (10:11) and Gorgias's attacks on the Jews (10:14). 2 Maccabees 10:15 describes the Idumeans' taking in those who were banished from Jerusalem, which suggests that the Jews occupied the city by this point. Therefore, the account of the repossession and rededication of Jerusalem and the temple must have come earlier in 2 Maccabees. According to Goldstein, it is clear that Judas

Instead of arguing against specific proposals for an alternative original location for these verses, it will be more convincing and efficient to focus on evidence that this text was placed intentionally in this context by the author of 2 Maccabees, which will render arguments of editing unnecessary.

Robert Doran has argued for a linguistic connection between 2 Macc 9:28 and 10:1. The particle μὲν οὖν introduces the summary of Antiochus's death (9:28). Doran, however, does not find an appropriate contrast in the δέ in the following verse detailing what one of Antiochus's companions does with Antiochus's body. Instead, Doran argues that the author of 2 Maccabees intended to draw a contrast between the blasphemous murderer Antiochus (9:28, ὁ μὲν οὖν ἀνδροφόνος καὶ βλάσφημος) and the savior of the Jewish people, Judas Maccabee (10:1, Μακκαβαῖος δὲ καὶ οἱ σὺν αὐτῷ). Doran puts it this way: "The striking contrast is between the dead body of Antiochus, the rebel against God, and the actions of Judas and his forces that revitalize the city and its traditions, a description that extends over three verses."[9] While it does not seem that the μὲν (οὖν) ... δέ construction must function in such a specific way, as Doran proposes, such a reading is supported by other features anchoring 2 Macc 10:1–8 to its current position in the epitome.

The most significant piece of evidence supporting the current location of 2 Macc 10:1–8 is the parallel structure of 2 Macc 10:8–9 and 15:36–37 (see chart on next page). These texts explain the institution of Hanukkah (10:8) and Nicanor's Day (15:36). The correspondences in language and content are striking. Both festivals were "decreed by public vote" (ἐδογμάτισαν μετὰ κοινοῦ ψηφίσματος) for all Jews (10:8, παντὶ τῷ τῶν Ιουδαίων ἔθνει; 15:36, πάντες), and the people decide to observe the festivals annually on specific days. As indicated in these two texts, the main purpose of 2 Maccabees is to provide an account of the origins of these two festivals and thus to encourage readers to celebrate Hanukkah and Nicanor's Day. The similarity in language is not surprising and highlights this dual intention. The affinities, however, do not stop there.

After the establishment of these festivals, each passage summarizes the death of an antagonist to the Jewish nation and the Jerusalem temple (10:9, 15:37). These

---

has not regained Jerusalem at the first defeat of Nicanor (8:29), and 8:30–32 is bound up with the preceding passage. Moreover, while 10:1–8 could have come before 8:33, which does mention the celebration of a victory in their πατρίς ("fatherland"), one would then expect a reference to the repossession of the temple in the summary of the preceding military victories in 8:36. So Goldstein concludes that 10:1–8 originally stood after 8:36 and immediately before chapter 9, the account of Antiochus's death. It was moved in order to line up with the chronology found in the second appended letter (1:11–18).

[9] Doran, *2 Maccabees*, 197. For a response to Doran's argument here, see Goldstein, *II Maccabees*, 346. Goldstein suggests that the μὲν ... δέ construction could signify a mere succession of events, such as Antiochus's death and then the provisions for his body made by Philip, or that an appropriate contrast is found between the living Antiochus (9:28) and his corpse (9:29).

| 2 Macc 10:8–9 | 2 Macc 15:36–37 |
|---|---|
| ἐδογμάτισαν δὲ μετὰ κοινοῦ προστάγματος καὶ ψηφίσματος παντὶ τῷ τῶν Ιουδαίων ἔθνει | ἐδογμάτισαν δὲ πάντες μετὰ κοινοῦ ψηφίσματος |
| κατὰ ἐνιαυτὸν ἄγειν τάσδε τὰς ἡμέρας. | (1) μηδαμῶς ἐᾶσαι ἀπαρασήμαντον τήνδε τὴν ἡμέραν, <br> (2) ἔχειν δὲ ἐπίσημον τὴν τρισκαιδεκάτην τοῦ δωδεκάτου μηνὸς … |
| καὶ τὰ μὲν τῆς Ἀντιόχου τοῦ προσαγορευθέντος Ἐπιφανοῦς τελευτῆς οὕτως εἶχεν. | Τῶν οὖν κατὰ Νικάνορα χωρησάντων οὕτως… |
| They decreed by public edict, ratified by vote, that the whole nation of the Jews | And they all decreed by public vote |
| should observe these days every year. | (1) never to let this day go unobserved, <br> (2) but to celebrate the thirteenth day of the twelfth month … |
| Such was the end of Antiochus, who was called Epiphanes. | This, then, is how matters turned out with Nicanor. |
| Single underline = same language; double underline = similar language; dotted underline = same content | |

summaries also share language with other statements that indicate the end of a structural unit (3:40, 10:9, 13:26, 15:37).[10] The affinity between 2 Macc 10:9 and 15:37 is not in question. The establishment of Hanukkah and Nicanor's Day are the final events depicted in their respective sections and are followed by similar summary statements. In other words, the strong correspondences between the language and content of 10:8–9 and 15:36–37 are complemented by their coordinated placement in the structure of the epitome. This further demonstrates the central importance of these two events as well as the intentional construction and integral connection of 10:8 and 10:9. In light of these parallels between 10:8–9 and 15:36–37, it is difficult to argue that the author did not compose 10:8 and 9 to be read together. What is most noteworthy about these parallels for my purposes is that they undercut the proposal that there is a noticeable seam between the narrative

---

[10] See Arenhoevel, *Theokratie nach dem 1. und 2. Makkabäerbuch*, 108 n. 28; Bunge, *Untersuchungen zum zweiten Makkabäerbuch*, 177; Doran, *2 Maccabees*, 5.

concerning the restoration of the temple (10:1–8) and the final summary of the death of Antiochus Epiphanes (10:9).

Not only are the parallels in language, content, and structural significance between 2 Macc 10:8–9 and 15:36–37 immediately apparent, but both of these pairs of verses are situated at the end of very similar stories that recount threats to the Jerusalem temple, the deaths of the antagonists, and the institution of a festival commemorating the divine restoration or protection of the temple and people. After Antiochus's campaign in Persia fails and he hears of the military successes of the Maccabees in Judea, he decides to head to Jerusalem himself in order to "make Jerusalem a cemetery of Jews" (9:4). Then Antiochus is afflicted by God with "sharp internal tortures, quite justly as he had tortured the bowels of others with many strange afflictions" (9:5–6; cf. 9:28). It is a common theme in 2 Maccabees that the opponents of the Jews die in a way that corresponds to the way they had persecuted the Jewish nation.[11] After the death of the one who had polluted the Jerusalem temple, it is fitting that the narrative transitions into an account of the repossession and rededication of the Jerusalem temple (10:1–8). With the divine punishment of Antiochus and the divinely orchestrated purification of the temple on the same day two years later (10:5), the God of the Jews finally had restored order and protected the temple in response to the obedience of the Jews and in direct contrast to the original desecration of the temple by Antiochus (5:17–20).

The end of Nicanor's life takes a similar course. After Judas eludes Nicanor's capture, Nicanor goes to the temple in search of Judas. When Nicanor does not find Judas there and the priests do not turn him over (14:31–32), Nicanor "stretched out his right hand toward the temple and swore these things, 'If you do not hand Judas over to me as a prisoner, I will level this shrine of God to the ground, destroy this altar, and build here a magnificent temple to Dionysus'" (14:33). In the end, Nicanor is killed in battle, but Judas finds his body, cuts off his head and arm, and takes them to Jerusalem. There he displays "the hand of the blasphemer, which he had stretched out and boasted against the holy house of the Almighty, [and] he cut out the tongue of the impious Nicanor" (15:32–33). So the story of Nicanor's death also ends with his punishment corresponding to his crimes. Moreover, Judas and his followers return to the temple in order to commemorate their victory and establish a festival.

---

[11] Andronichus is killed in the same place he killed Onias (4:38); Lysimachus dies near the temple treasury because he was a temple robber (4:42); Judas and his men burn those who set fire to the gates of Jerusalem (8:33); and Menelaus is pushed from a tower where it was customary to punish those guilty of sacrilege (13:6–8). See Beate Ego, "God's Justice: The 'Measure for Measure' Principle in 2 Maccabees," in *The Books of the Maccabees: History, Theology, Ideology; Papers of the Second International Conference on the Deuterocanonical Books, Pápa, Hungary, 9–11 June, 2005*, ed. Géza G. Xeravits and József Zsengellér, JSJSup 118 (Leiden: Brill, 2007), 141–54.

The identification of editing in 2 Macc 9:29–10:9 and the relocation of 10:1–8 based on the perception of narrative disruption alone is unconvincing.[12] Other factors, such as the language, content, context, and structure of the narrative overshadow and even explain what is perceived as an instance of interruption. In light of the deliberate construction of these corresponding narratives about the institution of two new festivals under the Maccabees, both in their overall construction (9:1–10:9, 14:1–15:37) and in their specific conclusions (10:8–9, 15:36–37), I conclude that 2 Macc 10:1–8 fits well in its current place in the epitome. It is portrayed as part of the divinely arranged conclusion of Antiochus's threat to the Jewish nation and temple.[13] Not only is he afflicted just as he had tortured others, but his desecration of the Jerusalem temple was undone as well. In this way, we see how 10:9 functions not simply as a summary of Antiochus's death—after all, such a summary is provided already in 9:28–29—but as the conclusion to this section of the epitome (4:1–10:9), which introduces the succession of Antiochus Epiphanes (4:7), moves to his desecration of the Jerusalem temple (5:11–17), and ends with his death and the rededication of the temple he had profaned (9:1–10:8).

## II. Distinctive Language and Style as Evidence of Editing

The previous section responds to scholars who argue that the narrative describing the restoration of the Jerusalem temple and establishment of Hanukkah originally belonged in another place in 2 Maccabees. Taking a different approach, Daniel Schwartz identifies 10:1–8 as an addition by drawing attention to examples of language, style, and content that he sees as discontinuous with the rest of 2 Maccabees. He suggests that the same people who appended the letters to the beginning of the epitome inserted this story in order to support the establishment of Hanukkah. In Schwartz's perspective, 2 Maccabees at first was concerned only with the institution of Nicanor's Day. In order to examine Schwartz's proposal

---

[12] It is also valuable to see if there are other places where the author "disrupts" the narrative and then returns to the earlier event or subject. The closest parallel would be Antiochus's desecration of the Jerusalem temple (5:16–21). Here the author describes how Antiochus "took the holy vessels ... and votive offerings" (5:16) before offering a theological reflection on why the God of the Jews would have allowed such a thing to happen (5:17–20). Then the narrative returns to the actions of Antiochus in the temple, saying, "So Antiochus carried away eighteen hundred talents from the temple" (5:21). At other points, the author also expresses awareness that he has interrupted the story and must return to the previous progression of events (6:17, 7:42; cf. 14:46). Though all of these individual examples have their own unique features, they support my basic contention that the author at times would intentionally disrupt the narrative.

[13] See Jan Willem van Henten. *The Maccabean Martyrs as Saviours of the Jewish People: A Study of 2 and 4 Maccabees*, JSJSup 57 (Leiden: Brill, 1997), 28.

that 10:1–8 is an addition to the text, I will focus on arguments concerning language and style.

Schwartz acknowledges that 10:1–8 in certain respects was composed to fit in its current position but in other respects shows signs of being an insertion. On this view, the editors who included the story of the purification of the temple "took care (as we saw in the comparison of the language of 10:8 to 15:36) to make their interpolation fit as best as possible into the book."[14] Put differently, on the one hand, whenever 10:1–8 seems to reflect the style and perspective of the rest of 2 Maccabees, this should be attributed to effective imitation by the editor. On the other hand, any instances of discontinuity between 10:1–8 and the epitome are evidence that this passage was an addition. The most basic problem with this approach is that it remains to be seen how one distinguishes between an author and an editor who can successfully imitate an author's language and perspective. Let us consider Schwartz's specific examples of discontinuities in the language and style of 10:1–8 in comparison with the rest of the epitome.

First, Schwartz identifies a number of particularities in the language of the story of the rededication of the temple. He points out the use of the "unadorned" κομίζομαι ("recovered") in 10:1, which "typifies the lower register" of 10:1–8, in contrast to the more "ornate" παρεκομίζομαι ("transport") and διακομίζομαι ("cross over") in 2 Macc 9:29.[15] The author, however, employs κομίζομαι at other points in 2 Maccabees (7:11, 8:33, 13:8), which argues against the significance of this variation in language. Schwartz highlights that ἀλλόφυλοι ("foreigners") "appears in our book only here and in v. 5—another indication of the special, Judaean, nature of this eight-verse section."[16] Yet we find the use of the related ἀλλοφυλισμός ("adoption of foreign customs") elsewhere (4:13, 6:24), which occurs only in 2 Maccabees in the Greek Bible. It is difficult to conclude that an author who uses ἀλλοφυλισμός would not also use ἀλλόφυλοι. Finally, according to Schwartz, the account of the rededication of the temple (10:1–3) recalls the parallel description of this event in the first letter (1:8), thus reaffirming that the same editor is responsible for the inclusion of both the letters and the restoration of sacrificial worship in 2 Maccabees. Each text contains a sacrificial offering, the lighting of lamps, and the setting out of loaves. These same details, however, are found also in the account of the

---

[14] Schwartz, *2 Maccabees*, 10.

[15] Ibid., 375.

[16] Ibid. See also David L. Balch, "Attitudes toward Foreigners in 2 Maccabees, Eupolemus, Esther, Aristeas, and Luke-Acts," in *The Early Church in Its Context: Essays in Honor of Everett Ferguson*, ed. Abraham J. Malherbe, Frederick W. Norris, and James W. Thompson, NovTSup 90 (Leiden: Brill, 1998), 22–47, esp. 23–34, http://dx.doi.org/10.1163/9789004267367_003; Daniel R. Schwartz, "The Other in 1 and 2 Maccabees," in *Tolerance and Intolerance in Early Judaism and Christianity*, ed. Graham N. Stanton and Guy G. Stroumsa (Cambridge: Cambridge University Press, 1998), 30–37, http://dx.doi.org/10.1017/cbo9780511659645.003; Lawrence M. Wills, *Not God's People: Insiders and Outsiders in the Biblical World*, Religion in the Modern World (Lanham, MD: Rowman & Littlefield, 2008), 87–98.

rededication of the temple in 1 Macc 4:48–51 (cf. Exod 40:23–27). In fact, the language of 1 Maccabees and that of the first letter in 2 Maccabees show the most similarities. It seems, therefore, that the events associated with the rededication of the Jerusalem temple by the Maccabees were well known. In short, Schwartz's examples of language unique to 2 Macc 10:1–8 do not support his conclusions.

Further countering Schwartz's claims are other similarities of language in 2 Macc 10:1–8 and the rest of the book, in addition to those mentioned in section II (10:8–9 // 15:36–37). The prologue of the epitome has notable correspondences with 2 Macc 10:1–3, an observation that would confirm that the same author wrote both passages.[17] In the introduction to his work, the author mentions specifically that his account will focus on "the purification of the greatest temple and the rededication of the altar [τὸν τοῦ ἱεροῦ τοῦ μεγίστου καθαρισμὸν καὶ τὸν τοῦ βωμοῦ ἐγκαινισμόν]" (2:19) as well as recount how the Maccabees "recovered the temple renowned throughout the whole world and liberated the city [τὸ περιβόητον καθ' ὅλην τὴν οἰκουμένην ἱερὸν ἀνακομίσασθαι καὶ τὴν πόλιν ἐλευθερῶσαι]" (2:22). In the recovery and rededication of the temple in chapter 10, the author analogously describes how Judas and his force "recovered the temple and the city [τὸ μὲν ἱερὸν ἐκομίσαντο καὶ τὴν πόλιν]" (10:1).[18] They also "purified the temple and made another altar [καὶ τὸν νεὼ καθαρίσαντες ἕτερον θυσιαστήριον ἐποίησαν]" (10:3; cf. 14:36). In light of these overlaps, it is apparent that in 10:1–3 the author is executing his plan to give an account of the repossession and restoration of the temple, as promised in the prologue. Providing another example of how the language of 10:1–8 is related to the rest of 2 Maccabees, the description of the activities of Judas and his followers during the period of the defilement of the temple lines up with the original description of their escape during the persecutions initiated by Antiochus (10:6, ἐν τοῖς ὄρεσιν καὶ ἐν τοῖς σπηλαίοις θηρίων τρόπον ἦσαν νεμόμενοι, "they had been wandering in the mountains and caves like wild animals" // 5:27, θηρίων τρόπον ἐν τοῖς ὄρεσιν διέζη, "… wild animals in the mountains live").

Consequently, (1) the examples provided by Schwartz of dissimilar language between 10:1–8 and the rest of the epitome are not convincing; (2) the language of 10:1–8 is no more closely associated with the introductory letters than with the rest of the history; and (3) there are a number of instances of language in 10:1–8 that reaffirm that this passage was composed by the author of the rest of 2 Maccabees. Thus, there is no linguistic evidence that 2 Macc 10:1–8 is an addition, let alone that it was added by the same editors who added the letters to the beginning of the epitome.

Turning briefly to the style of 2 Macc 10:1–8, this passage, according to Schwartz, is characterized by a "relatively simple Greek style, including even a good

---

[17] See van Henten, *Maccabean Martyrs*, 23.

[18] In this case, the composition by the same author is supported by the close parallelism in the structure of 2 Macc 2:22 and 10:1 (τὸ περιβόητον καθ' ὅλην τὴν οἰκουμένην ἱερὸν // τὸ μὲν ἱερόν; ἀνακομίσασθαι // ἐκομίσαντο; and καὶ τὴν πόλιν ἐλευθερῶσαι // καὶ τὴν πόλιν).

bit of parataxis (six occurrences of καί!) in v. 3."[19] Schwartz claims that this use of parataxis is similar to the usage in the first letter in 2 Macc 1:2–5, which may have been translated from a Semitic language, further supporting the attachment of the account of the rededication of the temple by the same editors who added the letters to the book. Schwartz himself, however, notes that there are two different occasions of similar style in the epitome (5:13, 8:2–4). The isolated and brief character of this example also cautions against giving it too much weight in identifying editorial activity. Moreover, there are other explanations for such a variation in style. It is possible for Jews writing in Greek to make use of Septuagintal style or Greek that looks as though it were translated from a Semitic language unintentionally or in order to lend authority to the text by mimicking biblical style.[20] Perhaps at this point the author of 2 Maccabees chose or slipped into a biblical style because of the nature of the topic being described, namely, the purification and rededication of the Jerusalem temple. In fact, the author is very concerned with providing details that lend authority to the rededication of the temple by the Maccabees, such as the divine coordination of the date of the profanation of the temple and its purification (10:5). Additionally, the celebration of an eight-day festival after the dedication of the temple most likely is meant to call to mind the celebration after Solomon's dedication of the First Temple (cf. 2 Chr 7).[21] Therefore, any examples of Semiticisms or biblicized language in 2 Macc 10:1–8 could be intended to contribute to the author's presentation of the legitimacy of the Maccabean temple.

## III. Conflicting Content as Evidence of Editing

Schwartz suggests that 2 Macc 10:1–8 does not belong in its current context and is at odds with the entire rest of the epitome with regard to its content and perspective. To a large extent, this type of reasoning explains why scholars identify the second introductory letter (1:10–2:18) as a later addition to 2 Maccabees. The primary example of this type of discontinuity comes in the descriptions of the death of Antiochus IV Epiphanes. In the second letter, Antiochus is lured into the temple of Nanea in Persia, locked inside with his men, stoned from an opening at the top of the temple, dismembered, and cast outside (1:11–17). In contrast, in 2 Macc 9

---

[19] Schwartz, *2 Maccabees*, 8.

[20] The most popular example of this is the Gospel of Luke (see Joseph A. Fitzmyer, *The Gospel according to Luke: Introduction, Translation, and Notes*, 2 vols., AB 28, 28A [Garden City, NY: Doubleday, 1981–1985], 1:114–25; William G. Most, "Did St. Luke Imitate the Septuagint?," *JSNT* 15 [1982]: 30–41). For another possible example of this in the book of Judith, see Jan Joosten, "The Original Language and Historical Milieu of the Book of Judith," *Meghillot* 5–6 (2008): *159–*176, esp. *162–*163.

[21] See James C. VanderKam, "Hanukkah: Its Timing and Significance according to 1 and 2 Maccabees," *JSP* 1 (1987): 23–40, esp. 32–34.

God afflicts Antiochus after he has left Persia and is on his way to destroy Jerusalem once and for all. Here Antiochus dies in the mountains (9:28). The story of Antiochus's death in the epitome lines up well with portrayals of nearly every opponent to the Jewish nation and the Jerusalem temple. Each enemy dies in a way that corresponds in some way to their oppression of the Jews. The account of the death of Antiochus in 2 Macc 9 fits well with the perspective of the rest of the epitome, while the depiction of Antiochus's demise in the second introductory letter provides an entirely different tradition. Scholars reasonably conclude, therefore, that the degree of divergence in these narratives provides evidence of two different authors.

Taking a related approach, Schwartz provides a number of possible examples of significant differences of perspective between 2 Macc 10:1–8 and the rest of the book. He notes the contrast in "the derogatory way [2 Macc 10:1–8] speaks about Gentiles, which is unusual for our book."[22] Here he is referring to the use of ἀλλόφυλοι in 10:2, 5. In general, it is true that 2 Maccabees as a whole emphasizes how Jews were at peace with and received the sympathy of their non-Jewish neighbors (3:2–3; 4:35–36, 49; 10:12), but it is not clear why Schwartz classifies ἀλλόφυλοι as an exceptionally negative term for non-Jews. We have already seen that the author uses ἀλλοφυλισμός elsewhere (4:13, 6:24). In addition, in the prologue the author describes the enemies of the Jews as τὰ βάρβαρα πλήθη, "the barbarian hordes" (2:21), which likely has a negative connotation (cf. 4:25, 5:22, 15:2). At another point the author prays that God not allow the Jews "to be given into the hands of the blasphemous Gentiles" (13:11, τοῖς δυσφήμοις ἔθνεσιν ὑποχειρίους γενέσθαι; cf. 15:32). Correspondingly, even within the account of the purification of the temple, Judas and the people pray for God to punish them for their sins and "not to be handed over to the blasphemous and barbarous Gentiles" (10:4, μὴ βλασφήμοις καὶ βαρβάροις ἔθνεσιν παραδίδοσθαι). Therefore, it does not seem that we can draw such a definite conclusion that the simple use of ἀλλόφυλοι demonstrates that 2 Macc 10:1–8 has a dramatically different perspective on non-Jews compared with the rest of 2 Maccabees.

Schwartz dissociates 2 Macc 10:1–8 from the author of the epitome and rather associates it with the Jerusalemite editors who added the letters for the following three reasons: (1) "its lack of worry about Dionysiac associations," (2) "the obscure reference to 'igniting rocks and extracting fire from them' in 10:3," and (3) "the precedence which it gives the Temple over the city (10:1) and its interest in cultic details, both of which depart from what is usual in our book."[23] According to Schwartz, the use of θύρσος (a special type of wand carried by the devotees of Dio-

---

[22] Schwartz, *2 Maccabees*, 8. Similarly, Erich S. Gruen suggests that 2 Maccabees does not have an entirely negative view of Hellenism or gentiles (*Heritage and Hellenism: The Reinvention of Jewish Tradition*, HCS 30 [Berkeley: University of California Press, 1998], 3–4; cf. Gruen, *Diaspora: Jews amidst Greeks and Romans* [Cambridge: Harvard University Press, 2002], 214–20).

[23] Schwartz, *2 Maccabees*, 8–9, 46–48, 374–79.

nysus) in the celebration of Hanukkah in 2 Macc 10:6–7 would have brought to mind the festival of Dionysus.²⁴ Since Schwartz thinks that 2 Maccabees was written by a diaspora Jew, he reasons that "any diasporan author would be sensitive about that, and take pains to avoid it" and thus that the author "was a Palestinian Jew who … was not so sensitive about what non-Jews think about Judaism."²⁵ The only other occurrence of θύρσος in a text from the Greek Bible is in Jdt 15:12, where similarly Judith and her companions are celebrating the deliverance of the Jewish nation and the Jerusalem temple. This is significant because there are a growing number of scholars who would argue that the book of Judith could have been composed in the diaspora.²⁶ In the end, then, it is difficult to be confident about any definitive distinction between how a diaspora Jew or a Palestinian Jew would have used such a term.

During the rededication of the Jerusalem temple, Judas and his followers make another altar and then offer sacrifices using fire that in some way comes from rocks (10:3, πυρώσαντες λίθους καὶ πῦρ ἐκ τούτων λαβόντες). Schwartz reasons that this "strange phrase" makes the best sense as reflecting the same image as the second opening letter, which describes the rededication of the temple under Nehemiah, during which liquid that had been taken from the altar in the First Temple is poured on stones (1:31).²⁷ Yet the connection between these two texts is not entirely clear.²⁸ Even if they were telling the same story, there was general knowledge about the rededication of the temple that could explain similar basic information. It does not follow that shared information about the source of the fire on the altar signifies that the same author composed both texts.

Finally, according to Schwartz, the concern in 2 Macc 10:1–8 with the temple and cultic details betrays a Judean rather than a diasporan author. This argument relies not only on 2 Maccabees but on Schwartz's understanding of diaspora

---

²⁴ See also Bartlett, *First and Second Books of the Maccabees*, 295.

²⁵ Schwartz, *2 Maccabees*, 378.

²⁶ See Helmut Engel, "'Der Herr ist ein Gott der die Kriege zerschlägt': Zur griechischen Originalsprache und der Struktur des Büches Judit," in *Goldene Äpfel in silbernen Schalen: Collected Communications to the XIIIth Congress of the International Organization for the Study of the Old Testament, Leuven 1989*, ed. Klaus-Dietrich Schunk and Matthias Augustin, BEATAJ 20 (Frankfurt am Main: Lang, 1992), 155–68; Joosten, "Original Language and Historical Milieu," *159–*176; Hans Yohanan Priebatsch, "Das Buch Judith und seine hellenistischen Quellen," *ZDPV* 90 (1974): 50–60; Claudia Rakel, *Judit—über Schönheit, Macht und Widerstand im Krieg: Eine feministisch-intertextuelle Lektüre*, BZAW 334 (Berlin: de Gruyter, 2003), 33–40; Barbara Schmitz, *Gedeutete Geschichte: Die Funktion der Reden und Gebete im Buch Judith*, HBS 40 (Freiburg im Breisgau: Herder, 2004), 2–3; cf. Jeremy Corley, "Septuagintalisms, Semitic Interference, and the Original Language of the Book of Judith," in *Studies in the Greek Bible: Essays in Honor of Francis T. Gignac, S.J.*, ed. Jeremy Corley and Vincent Skemp, CBQMS 44 (Washington, DC: Catholic Biblical Association of America, 2004), 65–96.

²⁷ Schwartz, *2 Maccabees*, 376.

²⁸ See Doran, *2 Maccabees*, 200.

Judaism in general and its distinctions from Palestinian Judaism. Schwartz has argued that the author of 2 Maccabees "has little interest in the Temple *per se* and in the sacrificial cult characteristic of it—a type of worship in which diasporan Jews can only rarely participate."[29] Along with other sources, 2 Maccabees shows that diaspora Jews were inclined to value the people principally or Jerusalem as a city, with the temple simply representing a regular institution of the city.[30] Diaspora Jews were not especially attached to the Jerusalem temple as the central cultic site of their religious identity but rather viewed Jerusalem as their mother city and the locus of their national identity in line with Hellenistic conventions. Therefore, any interest in the sacrificial cult in the Jerusalem temple in 2 Macc 10:1–8 is at odds with the diasporan perspective found elsewhere in 2 Maccabees. Schwartz's arguments concerning the perspective of diaspora Jews or 2 Maccabees as a whole on the Jerusalem temple cannot be considered here, it is important to point out that Schwartz unnecessarily severs the Jerusalem temple from Jerusalem as a city and unjustifiably treats diaspora Judaism as relatively monolithic in its perspective on the Jerusalem temple.[31] In brief, we should not categorize 2 Maccabees as a diasporan text and then excise any portions of it that would disqualify it as such. Related to this, one of the most perplexing elements about Schwartz's proposal that 2 Macc 10:1–8 is a later addition to the epitome is his claim that the original intent of 2 Maccabees was simply to explain the origin of Nicanor's Day and that the author had no interest in the sacrificial cult in the Jerusalem temple.[32] This is implied by his conclusion that the account of the repossession and rededication of the temple is secondary, but it does not explain the author's own claims about the contents of his history. In the first sentence of the prologue, the author declares that this story

---

[29] Daniel R. Schwartz, "Temple or City: What Did Hellenistic Jews See in Jerusalem?," in *The Centrality of Jerusalem: Historical Perspectives*, ed. Marcel Poorthuis and Chana Safrai (Kampen: Kok Pharos, 1996), 114–27, esp. 122–23; Schwartz, *2 Maccabees*, 46; cf. Michael Tuval, *From Jerusalem Priest to Roman Jew: On Josephus and the Paradigms of Ancient Judaism*, WUNT 2/357 (Tübingen: Mohr Siebeck, 2014), 55–57. Alternatively, Malka Zieger Simkovich suggests that, in comparison with 1 Maccabees, the temple is given more prominence in 2 Maccabees, while Judea and Jerusalem are marginalized in order to dissociate festival observance from Greek customs ("Greek Influence on the Composition of 2 Maccabees," *JSJ* 42 [2011]: 293–310, esp. 306–9).

[30] Schwartz, "Temple or City," 120; Schwartz, *2 Maccabees*, 46 n. 104. Cf. Arenhoevel, *Theokratie nach dem 1. und 2. Makkabäerbuch*, 126–29; Bernard Renaud, "La loi et les lois dans les livres des Maccabées," *RB* 68 (1961): 39–67, esp. 58–64. For a brief response to this argument of Schwartz, see Eyal Regev, *The Hasmoneans: Ideology, Archaeology, Identity*, JAJSup 10 (Göttingen: Vandenhoeck & Ruprecht, 2013), 86.

[31] See Noah Hacham, "Sanctity and the Attitude towards the Temple in Hellenistic Judaism," in *Was 70 CE a Watershed in Jewish History? On Jews and Judaism before and after the Destruction of the Second Temple*, ed. Daniel R. Schwartz and Zeev Weiss, in collaboration with Ruth A. Clements, AGJU 78 (Leiden: Brill, 2012), 155–79, esp. 158; and Jonathan R. Trotter, "The Jerusalem Temple in the Practice and Thought of Diaspora Jews during the Second Temple Period" (PhD diss., University of Notre Dame, 2016); Regev, *Hasmoneans*, 84–89.

[32] Schwartz, *2 Maccabees*, 8; cf. Wheaton, "Festival of Hanukkah," 248.

will describe "the purification of the greatest temple and the rededication of the altar" (2:19). On Schwartz's reconstruction of the development of 2 Maccabees, there would be no such account elsewhere in the epitome. In sum, there are no indications in 2 Macc 10:1–8 that it is discontinuous in language, style, and content with the rest of 2 Maccabees. Thus, this narrative cannot have been secondarily added by the same editors who appended the letters at the beginning of the epitome.

## IV. Conclusion

In this essay, I have drawn attention to the inadequacies of the arguments against both the current location of 2 Macc 10:1–8 and its composition by the author of the rest of 2 Maccabees. At the same time, a consideration of claims of textual disruption and discontinuity in language, style, and content between this text and its context demonstrates that the author of 2 Maccabees purposefully constructed and placed this account of the repossession and rededication of the Jerusalem temple. The account parallels the divine punishment of Antiochus Epiphanes and restores the order disrupted by the sins of the people and the arrogance of Antiochus earlier in the story. At the same time, the appropriately gruesome death of Antiochus and the establishment of Hanukkah celebrating the legitimacy of the sacrificial cult correspond to the later dismemberment of Nicanor and the institution of Nicanor's Day commemorating his defeat and the divine protection of the people and the Jerusalem temple. The intentional construction of these parallels is indicated most clearly in the affinities between the language and content of 2 Macc 10:8–9 and 15:36–37. Thus, if the author of 2 Maccabees is identified as a diaspora Jew, then the text complicates any proposal that diaspora Jews were generally disinterested in the Jerusalem temple cult.[33] The epitome encourages its readers to acknowledge the legitimacy of the temple restored by the Maccabees as well as to recognize the divine association with and protection of this sacred place.

---

[33] On the identification of the author as a diaspora Jew, see Bartlett, *First and Second Books of the Maccabees*, 218–19; Doran, *2 Maccabees*, 15–17; Schwartz, *2 Maccabees*, 45–51; Simkovich, "Greek Influence on the Composition of 2 Maccabees," 293–310; Solomon Zeitlin, *The Second Book of Maccabees*, trans. Sidney Tedesche, JAL (New York: Harper, 1954), 19–21.

# Her Memorial: An Alternative Reading of Matthew 26:13

WONGI PARK
wongipark1@gmail.com
Belmont University, Nashville, TN 37212

This article presents a case for an alternative reading of Matt 26:13. I argue that a subjective genitive reading of εἰς μνημόσυνον αὐτῆς is not only plausible based on Matthew's redaction of Mark 14:9 but also favorable, given Matthew's deliberate omission of the anointing of Jesus's body for burial in Mark 16:1 (cf. Matt 28:1). My proposed reading is as follows: "Truly I say to you, wherever this gospel is preached throughout the whole world, what she has done [to me] as her memorial will be mentioned." My argument appeals to three clues—the redactional, grammatical, and literary contexts of Mark 14:9, Matt 26:10–13, and Matt 16:8–9, respectively. Assuming Markan priority, I begin by examining the redactional changes of Mark 14:9 that make a subjective genitive reading possible. Next, I show how a subjective genitive reading fits favorably in the immediate context of Matt 26:10–13. Finally, I demonstrate how a subjective genitive reading underscores the verbal quality of the head noun μνημόσυνον based on its previous use in Matt 16:8–9. I conclude with two implications of the proposed reading.

---

In Matt 26:6–13, an unidentified woman performs an extravagant act that stirs up controversy among the disciples. Jesus defends the woman, declaring the underlying significance of her deed: ἀμὴν λέγω ὑμῖν, ὅπου ἐὰν κηρυχθῇ τὸ εὐαγγέλιον τοῦτο ἐν ὅλῳ τῷ κόσμῳ, λαληθήσεται καὶ ὃ ἐποίησεν αὕτη εἰς μνημόσυνον αὐτῆς (Matt 26:13).

In the history of scholarship, rendering εἰς μνημόσυνον αὐτῆς as an objective genitive—that is, interpreting the feminine pronoun αὐτῆς as the object of the head noun μνημόσυνον—is virtually unanimous.[1] Accordingly, Jesus's saying in Matt 26:13 identifies the woman as the object of memorial: "wherever this gospel is

---

[1] For representative examples in Matthean commentaries, see Craig A. Evans, *Matthew*, NCBiC (Cambridge: Cambridge University Press, 2012), 425–26; W. D. Davies and Dale C. Allison, *A Critical and Exegetical Commentary on the Gospel according to Saint Matthew*, 3 vols., ICC (Edinburgh: T&T Clark, 1997), 3:448; Ulrich Luz, *Matthew: A Commentary*, trans. James E. Crouch, 3 vols., Hermeneia (Minneapolis: Fortress, 2005), 3:338; David Turner, *Matthew*, BECNT (Grand Rapids: Baker Academic, 2008), 619.

preached throughout the whole world, what she has done will be told *in memory of her.*[2] On this reading, the anonymous nature of the woman's identity is called into question. Why, when Jesus intends to memorialize the woman, is she left unnamed by Matthew?

Recent answers have varied considerably. Mainstream scholarship of the 1980s and 1990s has generally downplayed the woman's anonymity by limiting her comprehension of the deed's scope and significance. Although the woman performed a generous act, she did not necessarily intend to anoint Jesus.[3] If the woman's act of pouring oil is differentiated from Jesus's interpretation of her act as an anointing, her role remains coincidental to the narrative. In this way, the problem posed by her anonymity is minimized.

Feminist biblical scholars have taken a much more critical stance on the issue.[4] That the woman is stripped of her identity, so it is argued, is clear evidence of androcentric bias. Not only does Matthew fail to record the woman's speech, but her actual name is also omitted, which precludes the possibility of a proper memorial.[5] These interpretations, however divergent, depend on reading εἰς μνημόσυνον αὐτῆς as an objective genitive.

The objective genitive, however, is not the only viable rendering of εἰς μνημόσυνον αὐτῆς. Another possibility is to take αὐτῆς as a subjective genitive—the probability for which, at least based on New Testament usage, is statistically greater than the probability for the objective genitive.[6] To be sure, what differentiates the two is not always obvious, nor does statistical probability necessarily settle the

---

[2] Other translations include "as a memorial for her" (R. T. France, *The Gospel of Matthew*, NICNT [Grand Rapids: Eerdmans, 2007], 972) and "in remembrance of her" (Thomas G. Long, *Matthew*, WeBC [Louisville: Westminster John Knox, 1997], 288). The consensus on the objective genitive reading is also reflected in various English Bible translations: "for a memorial of her" (KJV, ASV), "in memory of her" (NIV, NASB), and "in remembrance of her" (NRSV).

[3] See, e.g., Donald Hagner, *Matthew 14-28*, WBC 33B (Dallas: Word, 1995), 758. Leon Morris makes a similar observation about the anonymity of the woman: "Curiously both Matthew and Mark have this saying but do not name the woman, whereas John names her but does not have this saying" (*The Gospel according to Matthew*, PilNTC [Grand Rapids: Eerdmans, 1992], 650).

[4] Janice Capel Anderson provided one of the first feminist readings of Matthew's Gospel ("Matthew: Gender and Reading," in *A Feminist Companion to Matthew*, ed. Amy-Jill Levine and Marianne Blickenstaff, FCNTECW 1 [Sheffield: Sheffield Academic, 2001], 29, 40–41, 45). She argued that the woman at Bethany (Matt 26:6–13) and the women at the cross and tomb (Matt 27:55–56, 61; 28:1–10) play an important but limited role because of their gender. In the patriarchal world of the Matthean text, gender has a symbolic significance: discipleship is ultimately inscribed by male, not female, gender.

[5] Elisabeth Schüssler Fiorenza, *In Memory of Her: A Feminist Theological Reconstruction of Christian Origins Tenth Anniversary Edition* (New York: Crossroad, 1994), xliii.

[6] Daniel B. Wallace, *Greek Grammar beyond the Basics: An Exegetical Syntax of the New Testament* (Grand Rapids: Zondervan, 1996), 112–13.

matter. Herein lies the tension. A. T. Robertson explains, "[The subjective genitive] can be distinguished from the objective use only by the context. Sometimes the matter is not clear. This genitive is the common possessive genitive looked at from another angle. In itself the genitive is neither subjective nor objective, but lends itself readily to either point of view."[7] Robertson's point is especially relevant for this study since it supplies the basic premise for the argument that follows: identifying the use of the genitive in Matt 26:13 should ultimately appeal to evidence in the surrounding context.

Despite the pliability of the genitive, most translations and commentaries on the First Gospel do not give any indication that a subjective genitive reading of εἰς μνημόσυνον αὐτῆς is a possibility. There are a few exceptions that are worthy of mention.[8] In *New Testament in Modern English*, J. B. Phillips offers the following rendering: "this deed of hers will also be recounted, as her memorial to me."[9] A. T. Robertson's translation also gestures toward a subjective genitive: "For a *memorial of her*.... This *monument to Jesus* fills the whole world with its fragrance, greater than even permanent memorials."[10] But the scholar who has most explicitly argued for a subjective genitive reading is J. Harold Greenlee. His remarks are suggestive, if underdeveloped, in a one-page note published in 1960.[11] The paucity of references in the history of interpretation and the brevity of Greenlee's remarks provide the occasion for the present study. Building on Greenlee's suggestion but departing slightly from his translation, I present a case for an alternative reading of Matt 26:13.

I argue that a subjective genitive reading of εἰς μνημόσυνον αὐτῆς is not only plausible based on Matthew's redaction of Mark 14:9 but also favorable, given Matthew's deliberate omission of the anointing of Jesus's body for burial as in Mark 16:1

---

[7] A. T. Robertson, *A Grammar of the Greek New Testament in the Light of Historical Research* (New York: Hodder & Stoughton, 1914), 499. Similarly, Stanley Porter, on the difficult case of deciding between the objective and subjective genitive in Rom 3:22, writes: "Semantic or syntactical analysis alone will not solve the problem; context must decide" (*Idioms of the Greek New Testament*, Biblical Languages: Greek 2 [Sheffield: JSOT Press, 1992; repr., London: Sheffield Academic, 2005], 95).

[8] A handful of commentaries suggest that a subjective genitive reading is possible but unlikely. Davies and Allison briefly comment, "αὐτῆς is an objective genitive ('a memorial to her'), not a subjective genitive ('her memorial [to me]')" (*Critical and Exegetical Commentary*, 3:448). R. T. France acknowledges the possibility of a subjective genitive reading but asserts that it is unlikely (*Gospel of Matthew*, 972).

[9] J. B. Phillips, *The New Testament in Modern English* (New York: Macmillan, 1958), ad loc.

[10] A. T. Robertson, *Word Pictures in the New Testament*, ed. James A. Swanson (Nashville: Holman Reference, 2000), 25 (emphasis added). See also Joachim Jeremias, *The Eucharistic Words of Jesus* (New York: Scribner's Sons, 1966), 235.

[11] J. Harold Greenlee, "εἰς μνημόσυνον αὐτῆς, 'For her Memorial': Mt xxvi.13, Mk xiv.9," *ExpTim* 71 (1959–1960): 245.

(cf. Matt 28:1). My proposed reading is as follows: "Truly I say to you, wherever this gospel is preached throughout the whole world, what she has done [to me] as her memorial will be mentioned."[12] In support of this alternative reading, I appeal to three clues—the redactional, grammatical, and literary contexts of Mark 14:9, Matt 26:10–13, and Matt 16:8–9, respectively. Assuming Markan priority, I begin by examining the redactional changes of Mark 14:9 that make a subjective genitive reading of Matt 26:13 possible. Next, I show how a subjective genitive reading fits favorably in the immediate context of Matt 26:10–13. Finally, I demonstrate how a subjective genitive reading underscores the verbal quality of the head noun μνημόσυνον based on its previous use in Matt 16:8–9. I conclude with two implications of the proposed reading.

## I. Mark 14:9: "This gospel"

There is general agreement that the redactional changes of Mark 14:9 in Matt 26:13 are stylistic, not substantive. Commenting on Matthew's redaction of Mark 14:9, Adela Yarbro Collins observes, "Matthew reproduces this verse almost verbatim (Matt 26:13). He changed the order of the words in the last clause, a change that does not affect the meaning of the statement."[13] Ulrich Luz's assessment of Matt 26:6–13 is virtually identical.[14] A closer analysis of Matthean redaction, however, reveals a subtle nuance that modifies the Markan account. Greenlee succinctly expresses the difference between the two sources as a rhetorical question: "Is it possible that Mark's intended meaning is 'shall be told as a memorial' and that Matthew, by changing the word order of λαληθήσεται, has intended to convey the meaning, 'what she has done as a memorial to me shall be related'?"[15] In fact, as we shall see, Matthew's redaction of Mark 14:9 reveals a specification of meaning that provides an important contextual clue to the use of the subjective genitive. The two texts read as follows:

---

[12] The translation I am proposing has a minor difference from Greenlee but follows the gist of his subjective genitive reading. In my translation, the phrase "to me" is better located after "what she has done," rather than Greenlee's rendering ("what she has done as a memorial to me shall be related"). The phrase should also be placed in brackets since it is implied by the Greek. A defense for supplying the implicit phrase "to me" and locating it following "what she has done" will be offered in the second section of the article.

[13] Adela Yarbro Collins, *Mark: A Commentary*, Hermeneia (Minneapolis: Fortress, 2007), 643–44.

[14] Luz, *Matthew*, 3:335: "In many cases the Matthean changes are stylistic improvements of the text. The new formulations reflect almost completely the vocabulary preferred by the evangelist."

[15] Greenlee, "εἰς μνημόσυνον αὐτῆς," 245.

*Mark 14:9*
(a) ὅπου ἐὰν κηρυχθῇ τὸ εὐαγγέλιον εἰς ὅλον τὸν κόσμον
(b) καὶ ὃ ἐποίησεν αὕτη λαληθήσεται εἰς μνημόσυνον αὐτῆς

*Matt 26:13*
(a) ὅπου ἐὰν κηρυχθῇ <u>τὸ εὐαγγέλιον τοῦτο</u> ἐν ὅλῳ τῷ κόσμῳ
(b) <u>λαληθήσεται</u> καὶ ὃ ἐποίησεν αὕτη εἰς μνημόσυνον αὐτῆς

The two underlined changes are noteworthy. The first change is the addition of the demonstrative pronoun τοῦτο in Matt 26:13a, qualifying Mark's τὸ εὐαγγέλιον. The second change is the position of λαληθήσεται in Matt 26:13b. In Mark 14:9b, the word order is such that the verb λαληθήσεται is sandwiched between the relative clause ὃ ἐποίησεν αὕτη and the prepositional phrase εἰς μνημόσυνον αὐτῆς. In Matthew, however, λαληθήσεται is relocated to the first position of the main clause.

The first change is difficult. Several interpretations have been offered to determine the meaning of τὸ εὐαγγέλιον τοῦτο in Matt 26:13. One possibility is that this phrase refers to Jesus's preaching, the good news as expressed in the Gospel of Matthew as a whole.[16] Another is that it pertains to the good news about the messiah as revealed by the events of the passion narrative.[17] The best explanation is the simplest explanation—one that makes sense of the phrase in the redactional context of verses 6–13. For this reason, I regard "this gospel" as alluding to the preceding verse, where Jesus says that the woman's deed is a preparatory act of anointing for his death and burial.[18]

Reading "this gospel" (v. 13) as parallel to "this ointment" (v. 12) makes sense in view of the brevity of Mark's account and the strong undertones of Jesus's imminent death. That is to say, Matthew's redaction clarifies an ambiguity in the Markan text—which gospel will be proclaimed? Matthew is emphatic: *this* gospel (τὸ εὐαγγέλιον τοῦτο), namely, the good news concerning Jesus's death, which is prepared for and memorialized by the woman's act of anointing. The connection is further supported by the parallel syntactical construction of τὸ μύρον τοῦτο + prepositional phrase in verse 12 and τὸ εὐαγγέλιον τοῦτο + prepositional phrase in verse 13—along with the earlier τοῦτο of verse 9 in the disciples' initial objection. Indeed, the repetition of τοῦτο anticipates not only the woman's memorializing of Jesus's death but also the proclamation that will follow by the male disciples (Matt 28:18–20). In other words, what is left unspecified in Mark is made explicit in

---

[16] So Graham Stanton, *Studies in Matthew and Early Christianity*, ed. Markus Bockmuehl and David Lincicum, WUNT 309 (Tübingen: Mohr Siebeck, 2013), 96–97; and Yarbro Collins, *Mark*, 644.

[17] So Donald P. Senior, *The Passion Narrative according to Matthew: A Redactional Study*, BETL 39 (Louvain: Leuven University Press, 1982), 40.

[18] So Davies and Allison, *Critical and Exegetical Commentary*, 3:448; Luz, *Matthew*, 3:338.

Matthew. In the redactional context of Mark 14:9, then, "this gospel" is the good news as foreshadowed by the woman's anointing of Jesus's body.

An analysis of the second change—the position of λαληθήσεται—further elucidates the plausibility of this reading. W. D. Davies and Dale C. Allison, like Yarbro Collins, explain the second change stylistically: Matthew repositions λαληθήσεται in order to reflect the parallelism of the preceding clause (e.g., verb + subject + prepositional phrase). This change, they are quick to point out, does not significantly alter the meaning of verse 13.[19] Yet I submit that the change slightly alters the meaning; the change is best understood as coinciding with the previous Matthean addition of τοῦτο. By placing the verb at the beginning of the clause, Matthew specifies the content of τὸ εὐαγγέλιον τοῦτο, which includes not only the woman's action (ὃ ἐποίησεν αὕτη), as in Mark, but also the deed's attributed significance (εἰς μνημόσυνον αὐτῆς). In Matthew, the phrase τὸ εὐαγγέλιον τοῦτο glances back to verse 12 and looks forward to what follows in verse 13b. Placing λαληθήσεται in the first position of the main clause, therefore, is not merely stylistic. The repositioning of λαληθήσεται opens up the possibility for ὃ ἐποίησεν αὕτη εἰς μνημόσυνον αὐτῆς to be taken as a single nominal element. Within such a construction a subjective genitive is better suited than the objective genitive.

Together, both redactional changes point to the possibility of reading εἰς μνημόσυνον αὐτῆς as a subjective genitive. Matthew's first change—the addition of τοῦτο—clarifies Mark by specifying the content of proclamation: "This gospel" looks back on "this ointment" and looks forward to λαληθήσεται in 26:13b. Matthew's second change—the repositioning of λαληθήσεται—gives credence for the entire phrase (ὃ ἐποίησεν αὕτη εἰς μνημόσυνον αὐτῆς) to be read as a single nominal element, and therefore, as an elaboration of λαληθήσεται. Since τὸ μύρον τοῦτο and τὸ εὐαγγέλιον τοῦτο are the work of Matthean redaction, each phrase can be seen as reinforcing the other. On the one hand, the preaching of "this gospel" is made possible by "this ointment," which prepares Jesus's body for burial; on the other hand, the woman's deed, which memorializes Jesus's death, will be spoken of in the preaching of "this gospel." Matthew can be seen as deliberately repositioning λαληθήσεται to clarify the nature and content of Mark's εὐαγγέλιον. For Matthew, then, the proclamation of "this gospel" does not memorialize the woman per se; the content of proclamation, rather, acknowledges her instrumental agency in the Matthean passion narrative.

## II. Matthew 26:10–13: "What She Has Done [to Me]"

Reading εἰς μνημόσυνον αὐτῆς as a subjective genitive is supported by situating the phrase within the progression of Jesus's speech in Matt 26:10–13. The repetition

---

[19] Davies and Allison, *Critical and Exegetical Commentary*, 3:442.

of "what she did to me" is perhaps the most relevant evidence for a subjective genitive reading of Matt 26:13:

*Matt 26:10–13*

| v. 10 | ἔργον γὰρ καλὸν <u>ἠργάσατο</u> εἰς <u>ἐμέ</u> |
| v. 11 | <u>ἐμὲ</u> δὲ οὐ πάντοτε ἔχετε |
| v. 12 | ἐπὶ τοῦ σώματός <u>μου</u> |
| v. 12 | πρὸς τὸ ἐνταφιάσαι <u>με ἐποίησεν</u> |
| v. 13 | ὃ <u>ἐποίησεν</u> αὕτη εἰς μνημόσυνον αὐτῆς |

| v. 10 | a good deed <u>she did to me</u> |
| v. 11 | <u>me</u> you will not always have |
| v. 12 | on <u>my</u> body |
| v. 12 | she <u>did it to me</u> to prepare for burial |
| v. 13 | what <u>she did [to me]</u> as her memorial |

The progression begins in verse 10: "She did a good deed to me." In verse 12, the description of her deed is repeated and expanded; Jesus says, "In pouring this ointment on my body, she did it to prepare me for burial." In other words, the good deed performed in verse 10 was to do yet another thing: to make burial preparations. The woman's deed is then repeated and expanded a final time in verse 13. Here, the significance of her deed, marked by the substantival use of the relative pronoun, is fleshed out. Jesus says, "What she did [to me] as her memorial will be told." Although the phrase "to me" in verse 13 is not explicit in the Greek, it should be supplied based on the twofold repetition and progression of the preceding verses. In verses 10–12, "me/my" occurs four times: "to me" (v. 10), "you will not always have me" (v. 11), "my body" (v. 12a), and "prepare me for burial" (v. 12b). Moreover, *pace* Greenlee, the phrase "to me" should modify ὃ ἐποίησεν αὕτη mirroring verse 10 (ἠργάσατο εἰς ἐμέ) and verse 12 (με ἐποίησεν). The repetition underscores the proper object of the woman's action: she did what she did to anoint Jesus for burial. In the context of verses 10–12, verse 13 functions as a summary statement that brings the progression to its culmination.

In view of the repetition and progression of verses 10–13, a subjective genitive reading is to be preferred over an objective genitive reading. First, a subjective genitive reading makes sense of and completes the development of verse 12. In contrast, an objective genitive reading fails to account for but instead interrupts the repetition and progression of verses 10–13. Second, Matthew omits any reference to the anointing of Jesus's body as in Mark 16:1, making her anointing of Jesus in the opening scene of chapter 26 pivotal to the Matthean passion narrative. On a subjective genitive reading, the woman administers a proper burial, which, according to Jewish piety and custom, is deemed of superlative value—equal to, if not more important than, almsgiving since it cannot be repaid.

The juxtaposition between almsgiving to the poor (i.e., what the disciples advocate) and burial preparations (i.e., what the woman does) draws special attention to the crucial agency of the woman's "good deed" (v. 10). Here, Tob 12:12–14 and Acts 10:4, 31 provide illuminating parallels to Matt 26:6–13. Both texts not only make explicit reference to good works of charity, including burial practices and almsgiving, but also effectively underscore the agency of the one who performs the memorial.[20] In the case of Tob 12:12, the angel Raphael identifies Tobit and Sarah, who perform a memorial by way of prayer: ἐγὼ προσήγαγον τὸ μνημόσυνον ὑμῶν, "I brought the record of your prayer" (NRSV).[21] In the case of Acts 10:4, an angel identifies Cornelius, who performs a memorial by way of prayers and almsgiving: Αἱ προσευχαί σου καὶ αἱ ἐλεημοσύναι σου ἀνέβησαν εἰς μνημόσυνον, "Your prayers and your alms have ascended as a memorial" (NRSV) (cf. Κορνήλιε, εἰσηκούσθη σου ἡ προσευχὴ καὶ αἱ ἐλεημοσύναι σου ἐμνήσθησαν, "Cornelius, your prayer has been heard and your alms have been remembered" [Acts 10:31 NRSV]). In the case of Matt 26:13, by comparison, Jesus identifies the woman who performs a memorial by pouring expensive nard on Jesus: ἀμὴν λέγω ὑμῖν ... ὃ ἐποίησεν αὕτη εἰς μνημόσυνον αὐτῆς. In all three texts, the respective acts of prayer, almsgiving, and anointing are deemed memorial acts.[22]

Third, a subjective genitive reading is likely in view of Jesus's imminent departure and death highlighted in verses 11–12. The woman memorializes Jesus, since it is he, not the woman, who will soon be handed over to death. These considerations demonstrate how a subjective genitive reading is preferable in the context of verses 10–13. To paraphrase verses 12–13, it is as if Jesus says: "When she poured this ointment on my body, she did it to prepare me for burial. Her memorial to me will be included when this good news is proclaimed in the whole world."

### III. Matthew 16:8–9: "Her Memorial Will Be Mentioned"

Finally, a subjective genitive reading is intelligible insofar as it accentuates what the woman perceives in contrast to how the male disciples view her act. In response to the woman's anointing of Jesus, the male disciples become indignant.

---

[20] For a discussion of the importance of burial, almsgiving, and acts of charity in Judaism, see Davies and Allison, *Critical and Exegetical Commentary*, 3:446; see also 2:53 n. 157.

[21] For a discussion of acts of charity, burial, and almsgiving in Tobit, see Carey A. Moore, *Tobit: A New Translation with Introduction and Commentary*, AB 40A (New York: Doubleday, 1996), 166–67, 176–77. For a synopsis of textual variants in Tob 12:12 in Codex Vaticanus, Codex Sinaiticus, Biblioteca Comunale, Ferrara, 187 I, Oxyrhynchus 1594, see Stuart Weeks, Simon J. Gathercole, and Loren T. Stuckenbruck, eds., *The Book of Tobit: Texts from the Principal Ancient and Medieval Traditions; With Synopsis, Concordances, and Annotated Texts in Aramaic, Hebrew, Greek, Latin, and Syriac*, FSBP 3 (Berlin: de Gruyter, 2004), 292–93, http://dx.doi.org/10.1515/9783110897029. My thanks to the JBL reviewer for alerting me to Tob 12:12–14.

[22] For other examples that underscore the agency of the one who performs μνημόσυνον and its cognates in the LXX, see Exod 12:14, Sir 23:26, 35:6, and Ps 108:15; in the New Testament, see Matt 5:23, Mark 8:18, Luke 17:32, Phil 1:3, 1 Thess 1:2, 2 Pet 1:15.

They regard the woman's act as a waste, reasoning in financial terms that it would have been put to better to sell the expensive nard for a large sum of money to give to the poor. Jesus defends the woman's act adumbrating his death. The value of the woman's deed is expressed in the form of antithetic parallelism.[23] Verse 11 can be represented as follows:

*Matt 26:11a*
   A  πάντοτε γὰρ
      B  τοὺς πτωχοὺς
         C  ἔχετε μεθ' ἑαυτῶν
*Matt 26:11b*
   $A_1$  ἐμὲ δὲ
      $B_1$  οὐ πάντοτε
         $C_1$  ἔχετε

*Matt 26:11a*
   A  For you always
      B  the poor
         C  you have with you
*Matt 26:11b*
   $A_1$  but me
      $B_1$  not always
         $C_1$  you have

Mapping the verse in this way visually reveals where the parallelism breaks down: if $A_1$ and $B_1$ were switched, parallelism would be achieved. The breakdown of the parallelism where it does, however, accentuates ἐμὲ δέ in the story. The use of the adversative δέ adds further emphasis to ἐμέ. It is as if Jesus were exclaiming, "But you will not always have *me!*" The juxtaposition of Jesus with the poor gives the reason why the woman's act is timely: his imminent death requires and justifies the woman's costly memorial. Yet this is precisely what the male disciples fail to understand.

Further supporting this connection is the language of μνημόσυνον in Matt 26:13, which echoes Matt 16:9. In Matt 16:6–9 Jesus warns the disciples of the leaven of the Pharisees and Sadducees as a metaphor for their teachings. The disciples, however, misread the situation, thinking that Jesus is speaking about literal bread. Jesus responds: οὔπω νοεῖτε, οὐδὲ μνημονεύετε τοὺς πέντε ἄρτους τῶν

---

[23] A comparison of this verse with Mark 14:7 further underscores the antithetic parallelism Matthew's redaction achieves. Matthew omits Mark's phrase καὶ ὅταν θέλητε δύνασθε αὐτοῖς εὖ ποιῆσαι, "You can show kindness to them whenever you wish" (NRSV). See Elaine Wainwright, *Towards a Feminist Critical Reading of the Gospel according to Matthew*, BZNW 60 (Berlin: de Gruyter, 1991), 275, http://dx.doi.org/10.1515/9783110877106; see also Davies and Allison, *Critical and Exegetical Commentary*, 3:447.

πεντακισχιλίων καὶ πόσους κοφίνους ἐλάβετε, "Do you still not perceive? Do you not remember the five loaves for the five thousand, and how many baskets you gathered?" (Matt 16:9 NRSV). Here, the parallelism of νοεῖτε with μνημονεύετε highlights the dimensions of mind and intellect, of insight and understanding. But the term signifies not only the cognitive activity of calling a fact to mind but also the act of responding appropriately in the present moment.[24]

Despite three passion predictions, the disciples' failure to understand Jesus continues in Matt 26:6–13. Notably, the same word that Jesus uses negatively to describe the disciples failure in 16:9 is now applied positively to the woman in 26:13b. The repeated failure of the disciples to understand Jesus, therefore, serves to highlight the woman's insight. In other words, implicit in Jesus's exaltation of the woman's memorializing in 26:13b is an affront to the male disciples, who have misread the situation yet again. To acknowledge the woman's insight, Jesus declares that wherever this gospel is preached, what the woman has done (i.e., her memorial of Jesus) will be told when the disciples will proclaim the good news of Jesus's death and burial. Read as a subjective genitive, then, the phrase εἰς μνημόσυνον αὐτῆς explicitly praises the woman's perceptive understanding even as it implicitly critiques the male disciples' misunderstanding—a juxtaposition that is all the more striking in light of Matthew's explicit naming of the disciples (οἱ μαθηταί, Matt 26:8; cf. τινες, Mark 14:4).

The disciples' misunderstanding, however, does not end with Matt 26:6–13. In 26:75, Peter, after vehemently denying any association with Jesus, "remembers" (ἐμνήσθη) what Jesus had predicted earlier. Similarly, after his death in 27:63, the Judean leaders "remember" (ἐμνήσθημεν) Jesus's saying that he would rise again in three days. The sequence of cognate terms across Matt 16:9, 26:75, and 27:63 bolsters the proposed subjective reading. The woman properly comprehends and calls to mind what the disciples fail to grasp time and again.

## IV. Rethinking the Problem of the Woman's Anonymity

Two implications may be deduced concerning the interpretation of Matt 26:6–13. In the history of scholarship, feminist biblical scholars have taken issue with the woman's identity or lack thereof. Feminist scholars have uncovered gender

---

[24] According to Wainwright (*Towards a Feminist Critical Reading*, 135) μνημονεύετε means "to see, to understand, and possibly even to participate in the power of the βασιλεία manifest in the deeds of Jesus," which the disciples fail to do. So when Jesus rebukes his disciples for not remembering the bread, it is not as though they simply forgot. Rather, their actions in Matt 16:7 are not commensurate with the knowledge of Jesus they should have acquired based on the miraculous feeding of the five thousand (Davies and Allison, *Critical and Exegetical Commentary*, 2:591).

bias in Matthew by paying attention not only to what the text says but also to how it constructs what it says and does not say.[25] In this regard, Elisabeth Schüssler Fiorenza's classic text *In Memory of Her* deserves proper acknowledgment. For Schüssler Fiorenza, the namelessness of the woman is not incidental but a politically motivated act: that her name was deleted from the historical record is clear evidence of patriarchal bias in the biblical tradition. Consequently, Schüssler Fiorenza notes that Jesus's prophecies of Mark 14:9 and Matt 26:13 go unfulfilled because, even though her deed is remembered, the woman's name is lost in history and therefore she is forgotten in her individuality.[26] Schüssler Fiorenza writes, "The name of the betrayer is remembered, but the name of the faithful disciple is forgotten *because she was a woman*."[27] The influence of Schüssler Fiorenza's interpretation is reflected in recent scholarship on Matthew's Gospel—particularly Luz's reading of 26:6–13, which relies both on Schüssler Fiorenza and on Elaine Wainwright.[28] Luz draws a sharp distinction between the intention of the woman's act and the interpretation of that act, citing the omission of the woman's name as proof of the patriarchal character of the biblical tradition.[29]

Given the many instances of anonymity in Matthew, however, the woman's namelessness may not be as problematic as originally thought. In fact, according to Carol L. Meyers, anonymity cannot be reduced to sexism: "The omission of women's names may result from literary strategy, biblical androcentrism, concern with patrilineality (tracing descent through the male line), or some other reason. Because many male characters also remain anonymous, the absence of women's names cannot be simply attributed to biblical sexism."[30] According to the proposed reading, the focus of the story is less on the woman's identity per se than on the timely preparations she makes for Jesus's burial. This reading does not fully explain why the woman remains anonymous; perhaps this will never be known. The proposed reading does, however, offer an alternative view of the problem as originally posed by Schüssler Fiorenza. In stronger terms, the proposed reading alleviates the perceived tension surrounding the woman's anonymity. In other words, the identity

---

[25] Schüssler Fiorenza, *In Memory of Her*, xx.

[26] R. T. France concludes, "Current preaching of the Christian gospel seldom gives to the woman's act the place which Jesus says it deserves. In her anonymity she is not much remembered" (*Gospel of Matthew*, 976).

[27] Schüssler Fiorenza, *In Memory of Her*, xliii (emphasis added).

[28] Citing Wainwright and Schüssler Fiorenza, Luz writes, "At the same time the story shows how in primitive Christian tradition this woman's story was 'depoliticized' so that the woman loses her own name while her act is interpreted exclusively by men. My exegesis will have to show how valid these interpretations are" (*Matthew*, 3:335).

[29] Ibid., 3:338.

[30] Carol L. Meyers, Toni Craven, and Ross S. Kraemer, eds., *Women in Scripture: A Dictionary of Named and Unnamed Women in the Hebrew Bible, the Apocryphal/Deuterocanonical Books, and the New Testament* (Boston: Houghton Mifflin, 2000), xi.

of the woman is beside the point, and her anonymity may be no more noteworthy than the anonymity of any other female or male character in the First Gospel. In this way, the tensions superimposed on Matt 26:13 are removed.

A second implication concerns the significance of the woman's act of anointing for Jesus's burial. Regarding the virtues demonstrated by her deed, scholars are quick to point out the love, devotion, and prophetic symbolism of her deed,[31] but with regard to her agency, only a small degree of intentionality is attributed to the woman. Donald Hagner goes so far as to say that the woman did not intend to anoint Jesus for burial.[32] Luz's explanation of verse 12 is more generous but still one that I do not find to be satisfactory:

> As seen by Jesus (or the post-Easter church that is speaking here) her anointing was the anointing of a corpse. Jesus' explanation is somewhat surprising, since the woman anointed only his head. It may be that the readers notice that Jesus, who is aware of his own future, here gives the woman's act a *new* meaning of which she probably had not been thinking. We no longer learn what the woman herself intended by anointing Jesus' head. The men, especially Jesus, have taken over the interpretation of her deed.[33]

Differentiating what the woman intended from the significance attributed to her action by Jesus may not be necessary. Luz, of course, is not alone in making this distinction.[34] According to the reading proposed here, Matthew gives more credit to her than has been previously acknowledged.

---

[31] Thus, Daniel J. Harrington writes, "The action of the unnamed woman is in the long run more important as a positive model of Christian faith. Nothing is said about her sinfulness (see Luke 7:36–50). Rather she is simply a model of enthusiastic love for Jesus. Her devotion leads her to do precisely the right thing at the right time" (*The Gospel of Matthew*, SP1 [Collegeville, MN: Liturgical Press, 1991], 365). The majority of biblical scholars interpret the anonymous woman as a model disciple. Ben Witherington III, for example, comments, "In Mark and Matthew the act is described as a beautiful deed—which may indicate to the Evangelists' audiences that such extravagant devotion should be seen as an example for all disciples" (*Women in the Ministry of Jesus: A Study of Jesus' Attitudes to Women and Their Roles as Reflected in His Earthly Life*, SNTSMS 51 [Cambridge: Cambridge University Press, 1984], 109), In addition, Davies and Allison write, "The merit of the woman's good work, with its christological orientation, is not a general act of almsgiving without knowledge of its recipients but a personal act of devotion to Jesus" (*Matthew: A Shorter Commentary* [London: T&T Clark, 2004], 465). On the prophetic symbolism of the woman's action, see, e.g., Amy-Jill Levine, "Matthew," in *Women's Bible Commentary*, ed. Carol A. Newsom and Sharon H. Ringe, expanded ed. (Louisville: Westminster John Knox, 1998), 348: "The action has a twofold meaning: Jesus equates it with the rituals that accompany burial (26:12) and so acknowledges women's traditional role. But anointing the head is also a sign of a royal commission, and thus the woman is cast here in the untraditional position of priest and/or prophet."

[32] Hagner, *Matthew 14–28*, 758.

[33] Luz, *Matthew*, 3:338.

[34] Too much has been made of the woman's anointing Jesus's head (ἐπὶ τῆς κεφαλῆς, v. 7)

Stated positively, a subjective genitive reading of 26:13b accords the woman insight into Jesus's imminent death and departure. The proposed reading suggests that the woman's significance lies not merely in her love or devotion, as important as these virtues are, but in the integral role she played in Jesus's passion. Her act of anointing prepared Jesus's body to be buried. Furthermore, her understanding stands in sharp contrast to that of the male disciples; she alone understood what was necessary in light of Jesus's imminent departure. The woman's anointing of Jesus is a prototypical memorial act; she is the first person to remember Jesus's passion, and Matt 26:13 codifies the significance of her remembrance as a performative invitation to do precisely what the woman had done. Read as a subjective genitive, then, εἰς μνημόσυνον αὐτῆς contains a double entendre: Jesus's saying acknowledges the woman's remembrance or understanding and invites her remembering of Jesus to be remembered.[35]

V. Conclusion

In this article, I have presented a case for an alternative translation of Matt 26:13b. I have argued for the plausibility of reading εἰς μνημόσυνον αὐτῆς as a subjective genitive based on Matthew's redaction of Mark, as well as on the immediate context of 26:10-13 and 16:8-9. Reading the text as "what she has done [to me] as her memorial" heightens the reason why Jesus praises the woman: only the woman perceives, understands, and remembers Jesus. With this reading, the interpretation of the woman's identity and significance necessarily shifts, adding an alternative

---

versus anointing his body (ἐπὶ τοῦ σώματός μου, v. 12). For instance, Barbara Reid writes, "By anointing Jesus' head, the woman takes on the role of priest and prophet. She both prepares Jesus for burial (v. 12) and commissions him as messianic king (see 1 Sam 16:12-13; 1 Kgs 1:39).... Her pouring of oil on Jesus' head (v. 6) prefigures Jesus' pouring out of his blood for all (v. 28). While her action is remembered (v. 13), her identity is not" (*The Gospel according to Matthew*, New Collegeville Bible Commentary, New Testament 1 [Collegeville, MN: Liturgical Press, 2005], 128). While the two Hebrew Bible/Old Testament texts Reid cites do in fact refer to the anointing of kings, neither text actually specifies the head. 1 Kings 1:39 identifies Solomon as the object of anointing: וימשח את־שלמה (in contrast, see Ps 132:2 LXX: ὡς μύρον ἐπὶ τῆς κεφαλῆς). Even so, the emphasis in Matthew is not so much on where Jesus is anointed as on the appropriate timing and manner in which he is anointed. The proposed subjective genitive reading, then, not only minimizes the distinction between Jesus's head (v. 7) and body (v. 12) but also refocuses the significance of the woman's memorial act.

[35] On a related note, Joel Marcus, citing Lev 2:2, 9, 16, says that εἰς μνημόσυνον αὐτῆς may contain a liturgical nuance of a memorial sacrifice (*Mark 8-16: A New Translation with Introduction and Commentary*, AYB 27A [New Haven: Yale University Press, 2009], 937). Such sacrifice is made with the intention of invoking God to remember the individual who makes the offering. A New Testament example that fits the liturgical interpretation is Acts 10:4, in which prayers and alms are ascending as a memorial before God, that is, as a reminder.

understanding of the woman's role in the Matthean passion narrative. According to the proposed reading, the woman is more than a model disciple over and against the male disciples, as is generally noted in previous scholarship.[36] Hers is the very first act of remembrance, preparing the way for Jesus's death. Jesus in turn acknowledges the woman's insight, declaring that what she has done will be referred to as her paradigmatic act of remembrance—her memorial.

---

[36] See, e.g., Ronald F. Thiemann, "The Unnamed Woman at Bethany," *ThTo* 44 (1987): 179–88.

# The Open Horizon of Mark 13

MICAH D. KIEL
kielmicahd@sau.edu
St. Ambrose University, Davenport, IA 52803

Stephen O'Leary's theory of apocalyptic rhetoric proves helpful for understanding Mark's intentions for the apocalyptic motifs employed in his Gospel. The details of the discourse in Mark 13 ought not be correlated with specific historical events but should be understood as rhetorical ornaments that underscore watchfulness and wakefulness. O'Leary's comic framework of apocalyptic rhetoric provides new exegetical insight into how Mark uses apocalyptic topoi to jolt an audience that had grown complacent. Mark's apocalyptic components serve the Gospel's broader theological agenda, to profile a God for whom there is an open horizon for dramatic future action.

---

Despite its popularity, the scholarly consensus about apocalypticism and suffering in Mark has not satisfied everyone. Prominent among the dissenters was Donald H. Juel. In Juel's view, many of the Second Gospel's themes—its focus on fear, its depiction of the disciples, and particularly its ending—implied an audience that had grown complacent and needed a jolt, not an audience that was being persecuted.[1] For this reason, Juel rejected interpretations of Mark as a quintessentially apocalyptic text along the lines of the book of Daniel.

Juel's profile of Mark's intended audience has much to commend it, even if few scholars have been convinced. Nevertheless, Juel's corollary opinion, that scholars overemphasize the role of apocalypticism in Mark, is open to question. In this article, I argue that Juel was both right and wrong. He was correct in his profile of the audience but wrong about apocalypticism. If the role of apocalypticism in Mark is properly understood, especially its rhetorical dimension, then Mark's aims become clear: the apocalyptic motifs are employed toward his end of shaking up a complacent community, one that increasingly ignored the idea of God acting freely and dramatically.

---

[1] See esp. Donald H. Juel, *A Master of Surprise: Mark Interpreted* (Minneapolis: Fortress, 1994).

## I. Mark 13 and Apocalyptic Rhetoric

The starting point for understanding Mark's intended audience and its use of apocalypticism is Mark 13. Yet there is little agreement among scholars on a variety of fundamental issues including the redactional history of the apocalyptic discourse, its historical referents, and its rhetorical forms and function.

One significant approach to Mark 13 is to treat this chapter in its rhetorical context. C. Clifton Black argues that much of the oration in chapter 13 can be understood in light of the conventions of ancient rhetoric.[2] He concludes that the variety of rhetorical devices evident in Mark 13 is "striking" relative to the length of the discourse. For Black, the discourse is an example of epideictic speech. His main point, however, is not so much to defend this classification as to show that Mark "creatively adapts or even flouts" ancient rhetorical norms.[3]

Adela Yarbro Collins, by contrast, argues that Mark 13 does not fit any of the ancient categories of rhetoric particularly well.[4] Instead, she views this passage as a "rhetorically shaped esoteric instruction of a prophetic and apocalyptic nature."[5] Yarbro Collins shows how Mark's historical context helped shape the apocalyptic discourse—messianic claimants presented an exigence that spurred its creation.

Stephen D. O'Leary provides some new insights into the rhetorical dimension of Mark 13.[6] O'Leary's methodological categories and language address the rhetorical and apocalyptic dimensions simultaneously, showing how study of rhetoric and apocalypticism can inform one another. He argues that to ascertain the rhetorical import of a discourse properly, one must be able to "conceive of time not only as an external fact to which discourse must adapt itself, but as an experience that is perceived through symbols, and hence is subject to discursive manipulation."[7] The author of an apocalyptic text who wants the audience to come to certain conclusions must build the traditional materials, the "eschatological topoi," into "lines of argument."[8] When discussing early Christianity specifically, O'Leary uses Adela Yarbro Collins's book *Crisis and Catharsis: The Power of the Apocalypse* as a starting

---

[2] C. Clifton Black, "An Oration at Olivet: Some Rhetorical Dimensions of Mark 13," in *Persuasive Artistry: Studies in New Testament Rhetoric in Honor of George A. Kennedy*, ed. Duane F. Watson, JSNTSup 50 (Sheffield: Sheffield Academic, 1991), 66–92.

[3] Ibid., 88, 92.

[4] Adela Yarbro Collins, "The Apocalyptic Rhetoric of Mark 13 in Historical Context," *BR* 41 (1996): 5–36.

[5] Ibid., 13.

[6] Stephen D. O'Leary, *Arguing the Apocalypse: A Theory of Millennial Rhetoric* (New York: Oxford University Press, 1994).

[7] Ibid., 13.

[8] Ibid., 203.

point.⁹ O'Leary agrees with Yarbro Collins's reading of the book of Revelation as a "tragedy." His exploration of other examples of apocalyptic movements and their rhetoric leads him to another category—"comedy." These different frames of reference are explored rhetorically, O'Leary argues, through a series of questions and hypothetical answers between the rhetor and the intended audience.

In the tragic frame, the reader asks, "How shall we account for our present ills?" The answer comes, "The end is near."[10] O'Leary claims that, in the tragic frame, apocalypse is a "closed symbolic system in which each element of the myth signifies a particular historical or political referent."[11] The tragic frame puts evil in supernatural terms with history temporarily in the control of the demonic powers "that can only be overthrown by catastrophic divine intervention." This scenario also includes a well-calculated time for the end; time has been reduced to a "linear structure of necessity." The tragic frame and its accompanying calculation of the end "impart a dramatic urgency that transforms the audience ... into spectators and participants in a drama of cosmic redemption." Thus, the tragic frame of apocalyptic argument shifts the emphasis from "persuasion to enactment."[12]

In the case of the book of Revelation, the author answers questions through a proper alignment and reference to time, authority, and evil in a way that is comprehensible to the audience. For example, the author introduces the work as a prophecy (Rev 1:3; see also 22:18) and then arranges apocalyptic topoi to structure the audience's experience of evil in order to offer some resolution to their plight. The tragic frame of apocalypse attempts to pinpoint the timing and to personify a demonic presence in a particular historical figure or ruler. One can see an example of this in Revelation's symbolic references to the Roman Empire (e.g., Rev 17:9–18) and Nero (Rev 13:11–18). O'Leary summarizes the tragic frame by saying that it "defines evil in supernatural terms, placing history temporarily in the control of demonic powers that can only be overthrown by catastrophic divine intervention. Such argument structures time by the expectation of a predestined End in the immediate future."[13]

---

⁹ Adela Yarbro Collins, *Crisis and Catharsis: The Power of the Apocalypse* (Philadelphia: Westminster, 1984).

[10] O'Leary, *Arguing the Apocalypse*, 203.

[11] Ibid., 201. O'Leary here uses the word *apocalypse* as a noun. In doing so, he challenges the rigor called for by John J. Collins, who claims that the word is "burdened by a history of usage as an all-embracing term that includes literary form, worldview, eschatology and anything else that one might associate with this [i.e., apocalyptic] literature" (John J. Collins, "Prophecy, Apocalypse, and Eschatology: Reflections on the Proposals of Lester Grabbe," in *Knowing the End from the Beginning: The Prophetic, the Apocalyptic, and Their Relationships*, ed. Lester Grabbe and Robert Haak, JSPSup 46 [London: T&T Clark, 2003], 44–52, here 46).

[12] O'Leary, *Arguing the Apocalypse*, 201, 205.

[13] Ibid., 205.

O'Leary's "comic" frame of apocalyptic discourse offers symbolism that is "open rather than closed, emphasizing the multivalence of symbols and repudiating their simplistic identification with historical referents." The comic frame of apocalypse does not intend to read "ultimate historical meaning" into the present moment; the signs of the time do not indicate "imminent catharsis" but are instead "episodic setbacks to the progress of God's people." O'Leary uses the example of Augustine, who eschewed any correlation between the imagery of the Apocalypse and real historical scenarios. The text was to be read not as a prophecy but as a "parable of the historical church."[14] Augustine goes so far as to suggest that Christians should not look for portents in world events, for fear that someone who knows of more dramatic events will laugh at them or that their predictions will turn out to be wrong.

While O'Leary is careful to point out that these two modes of apocalyptic rhetoric (tragic and comic) exist on a continuum, it is not hard to see initially that most treatments of Mark and apocalypticism have read the Gospel, particularly chapter 13, through the "tragic" frame.[15] Such readings insist that Mark intended to address a suffering community through the apocalyptic topoi in his Gospel. This reading implies an intentional correlation between details of chapter 13 and real historical events that the audience either had experienced or were about to experience. O'Leary's comic frame allows us to rethink this assumption by showing how Mark employed an apocalyptic rhetorical argument, adapting traditional material toward new ends. In the comic frame, "the absolute necessity of history is replaced by an open horizon of possibility."[16] This open horizon is for God's activity, which can be demonstrated by analyzing exegetically selected portions of chapter 13 and coordinating the results with broader themes of the Gospel.

## II. Mark 13:5–13: "Watch!" (and Nothing More)

Because of its interaction with the book of Daniel and descriptions of tribulation and predictions of the future, Jesus's discourse in Mark 13 has long been read through the lens of ancient Jewish and Christian apocalypticism. The discourse opens with a question from four disciples (13:4).[17] At the outset, Jesus informs the

---

[14] Ibid., 201, 205, 203.

[15] Not all scholars are in agreement that Mark should be read as apocalyptic in some way. See, e.g., Richard A. Horsley, *Hearing the Whole Story: The Politics of Plot in Mark's Gospel* (Louisville: Westminster John Knox, 2001), 122–48.

[16] O'Leary, *Arguing the Apocalypse*, 201.

[17] Joel Marcus notes that such questions are common in apocalyptic texts (*Mark 8–16: A New Translation with Introduction and Commentary*, AYB 27A [New Haven: Yale University Press, 2009], 874). Although four disciples form the initial narrative audience, the discourse later expands its implied audience in verses 14 and 37.

disciples that the temple will be torn down (13:2), and they logically request a sign and time frame for when this will happen. Jesus does not immediately answer their question. This disjunction between the question and the extended discourse has led to redaction-based theories about the chapter, which spawned its common title: the "Little Apocalypse."[18] It may be, however, that Mark intended to stress the inappropriateness of Jesus's response. After hearing of the imminent destruction of the temple, the disciples asked the wrong question. Jesus tells them what they need to know regardless of the query that instigated the discussion in the first place.

The discourse itself begins in 13:5 with the word βλέπετε. This call to "watch out" becomes programmatic for the entire discourse, repeated in verses 9, 23, and 33.[19] The opening statement, "watch out that you are not deceived," governs the discourse up to verse 13.[20] Jesus warns about messianic pretenders (v. 6); geological and geopolitical phenomena (vv. 7–8); and the more personal beatings, arrests, and interrogations (vv. 9–13) so that the people will not be led astray. The section concludes in verse 13b with the comment that the one who endures unto the end will be saved. Mark's Jesus proscribes drastic action during the calamities; he highlights only endurance and watchfulness.

Yarbro Collins treats the various scenarios of this part of the discourse in divergent ways. Jesus's warning that the disciples keep watch because others will come in his name (13:6) refers to "specific historical events."[21] The evidence leads her to conclude that it is the word *Christ* that is in question and that messianic leaders, especially Simon bar Giora and John of Gischala, are the likely figures to whom Jesus refers.[22] In the next section (vv. 7–8), the references to wars and earthquakes do not have specific historical events behind them. Yarbro Collins calls them "apocalyptic commonplaces."[23] The events described in verses 9–13—deliverance

---

[18] In 1864, T. Colani proposed the "little apocalypse" theory, that Jesus himself bears no responsibility for the discourse; it is instead a later interpolation of an independent written source. For a fuller discussion, see George Beasley-Murray, *Jesus and the Future: An Examination of the Criticism of the Eschatological Discourse, Mark 13, with Special Reference to the Little Apocalypse Theory* (London: Macmillan, 1954). More recent analyses suggest that, although Mark used traditional sources, it is "unlikely" that he used a preexisting written source. See Adela Yarbro Collins, *Mark: A Commentary*, Hermeneia (Minneapolis: Fortress, 2007), 596.

[19] Marcus refers to the repetition of this word as a *leitmotif* (*Mark 8–16*, 879).

[20] This delineates the discourse into larger sections than many treatments of it. For instance, Yarbro Collins finds smaller units, marked by the use of δέ in verses 7 and 9 (*Mark*, 605–6).

[21] Yarbro Collins, "Apocalyptic Rhetoric," 19.

[22] See ibid., 15–18. Yarbro Collins recapitulates this argument in the more recent commentary, *Mark*, 602–5. Marcus argues differently, that the claimants in question are more likely "Christians claiming to *be* the returning Jesus" (*Mark*, 875; italics original).

[23] Yarbro Collins, *Mark*, 606. Marcus claims that these events "belong to the recent past" (*Mark*, 876). It is not clear if Marcus intends to suggest that Mark and/or his audience would have had specific referents in mind when these phenomena are mentioned. The broader point for Marcus here is that these events "did not lead *immediately* to the end" (*Mark*, 876; italics original).

to governors, beatings in synagogues, trials before kings, and intrafamily betrayals—Yarbro Collins treats as future events. The job of Jesus's followers will be to preach the gospel in the midst of the upheaval. The "occasion for this *will be* the official interrogation by Jewish and various Gentile authorities."[24]

One might ask: on what basis does one determine whether Mark's words are (1) a reference to a real historical situation, (2) apocalyptic boilerplate, or (3) events yet to happen?[25] Josephus mentions messianic claimants during the first century CE.[26] The existence of that evidence, however, does not necessarily mean that it is relevant to Mark 13. There is nothing in the discourse itself that justifies divergent treatments of the different sections in terms of their historical background.[27] The same word, βλέπετε, is used to introduce both sections (vv. 5 and 9), and grammatical tense does not distinguish them either. All of the events—that messianic pretenders will come (ἐλεύσονται), that there will be (ἔσονται) earthquakes, and that they will be handed over (παραδώσουσιν)—are future tense. Yarbro Collins reads Mark's apocalyptic discourse in a "tragic" frame by coordinating some of his words with a plausible piece of contemporaneous historical information.

If one reads the discourse to this point without reference to specific historical circumstances, it has a much more consistent rhetorical force. If Mark intends to repudiate "identification with historical referents," then Jesus offers a panoply of warnings, things to watch out for, and future occurrences whose rhetorical effect is emotional rather than cognitive.[28] The discourse, to this point, seems intended to set a mood and create an emotive response rather than to engender some cognition that correlates with actual historical events. If read this way, the beginning of Jesus's speech becomes disquieting at best, terrifying at worst. Mark's Jesus limits his exhortations to the need for watchfulness and endurance. No specific temporal markers have been given that might begin to answer the original question of the disciples: "When?" The symbolism of the imagery remains "open rather than closed."[29]

---

[24] Yarbro Collins, "Apocalyptic Rhetoric," 20 (emphasis added).

[25] Yarbro Collins does say that it is possible that the community's experience of persecution could have led them to think the prediction of persecution had already been fulfilled among them ("Apocalyptic Rhetoric," 20), but there is no specific evidence of this.

[26] For the stories of Menahem and Eleazar, see *B.J.* 2.17. John of Gischala's career is described in *B.J.* 4.7; Simon bar Giora, in 4.9.

[27] Mark does return to the topic of messianic claimants in 13:21–23, which raises a question about how these figures fit into the temporal divisions outlined by Yarbro Collins. Is it a revisiting of the original discussion, and thus still part of the first stage (ἀρχὴ ὠδίνων), part of the second stage (θλῖψις), or the start of a third stage? She ultimately claims that these are to be thought of as temporally separate but that the first experience should "provide a model for the second" ("Apocalyptic Rhetoric," 27–28).

[28] O'Leary, *Arguing the Apocalypse*, 201.

[29] Ibid.

## III. Mark 13:14–23: Calculated Obscurity

The opening of the next section of the discourse, verses 14–23, differs from the first section in that it points to a temporal designation. In verse 14 Jesus says, "But when you should see…" (ὅταν δὲ ἴδητε), at which point one expects a specific historical event or sign that would indicate it is time to begin some prescribed activity.[30] In this case, Jesus directs those in Judea to flee to the mountains (v. 14b). The situation will be dire. Any hindrance, be it winter weather or nursing child, will bring woe (vv. 17–18). As if this were not clear enough, the following verse claims that the suffering will be so severe that the earth has never seen and never will see its equal (v. 19). The sign of this suffering's imminent arrival is the desecrating sacrilege (τὸ βδέλυγμα τῆς ἐρημώσεως) that will be erected where it ought not be (v. 14). The referent of this phrase, which is from the book of Daniel, is the "notoriously difficult *crux interpretum*" of the entire discourse.[31] Beyond the fact that Daniel inspired the phrase, "commentators have despaired of precisely identifying to what or to whom Mark intends this epithet to refer."[32]

Most commentators focus specifically on what the reference to Daniel in Mark 13:14 says about the "historical context" of Mark.[33] According to Joel Marcus, "scholars have generally assumed" that Mark has in mind a specific historical referent.[34] Even commentators who take a narrative-critical approach often revert at this point in Mark to specific historical circumstances to explain the reference to Daniel.[35] Martin Hengel argued that the phrase τὸ βδέλυγμα τῆς ἐρημώσεως does not refer to a specific historical event during the Jewish war with Rome but instead refers more generally to the antichrist.[36] Marcus correlates the directions to flee

---

[30] A similar phrase is used in verse 7 (ὅταν δὲ ἀκούσητε), but the difference is that in verse 14 one clearly "should be alarmed" (Yarbro Collins, *Mark*, 607), whereas in verse 7 there is not yet a need for grave concern.

[31] Black, "Oration at Olivet," 89.

[32] Ibid.

[33] Yarbro Collins, "Apocalyptic Rhetoric," 22.

[34] Marcus, *Mark*, 890.

[35] See, e.g., John R. Donahue and Daniel J. Harrington, *The Gospel of Mark*, SP 2 (Collegeville, MN: Liturgical Press, 2002), 371–72. See also Francis J. Moloney, who claims that the members of Mark's audience "know what Jesus is talking about" (*The Gospel of Mark: A Commentary* [Peabody, MA: Hendrickson, 2002], 259), which he explains as Titus's activities in the temple. Mary Ann Tolbert also concludes that the masculine participle suggests a "personal agent" (*Sowing the Gospel: Mark's World in Literary-Historical Perspective* [Minneapolis: Fortress, 1996], 263), but she says we do not have enough information to pinpoint Mark's referent, even though it would have been clear to Mark's audience (263–64).

[36] Martin Hengel, "Entstehungszeit und Situation des Markusevangeliums," in *Markus-Philologie: Historische, literargeschichtliche und stilistische Untersuchungen zum zweiten Evangelium*, ed. Hubert Cancik, WUNT 33 (Tübingen: Mohr Siebeck, 1984), 1–45.

with a specific point in the war: Eleazar's movement into the temple before Vespasian's surrounding of the city.[37] Yarbro Collins disagrees with both of these arguments, suggesting instead that Mark expected the Romans to erect a statue in the temple, thereby defiling it and incurring a response from God "analogous" to that brought on Sodom.[38] This scenario, she argues, fits better the type of apocalyptic thinking that drives the discourse in chapter 13. While these treatments differ about the referent of the phrase τὸ βδέλυγμα τῆς ἐρημώσεως in Mark, they all agree that the evangelist intended to refer to one specific event (or series of events) that the readers would be able to identify. Modern interpreters agree further that Mark intended to employ the phrase in a way similar to its usage in the book of Daniel —as an identifiable temporal marker that signifies a shift from one phase to the next in an apocalyptic scenario. To return to O'Leary's language, these scholars read this part of the apocalyptic discourse as a "closed symbolic system," even if they cannot agree on the referent some two thousand years later.[39]

One would analyze this portion of the discourse (13:14–23) differently if one does not assume that Mark intended to connect the phrase τὸ βδέλυγμα τῆς ἐρημώσεως with any specific historical occurrence. One might suggest, for example, that the symbols are meant to be multivalent and not coordinated with specific events. O'Leary claims that "apocalypticism cannot be understood only as a series of movements with discrete and identifiable causes in historical events"; apocalypticism must also be understood as a "tradition, a textually embodied community of discourse ... augmented by the production of new revelations and interpretive strategies."[40] These interpretive strategies O'Leary extends to what are sometimes "new interpretations of canonical texts."[41] Clearly, we ought to think of Mark 13 as a discourse that has appropriated language and images from Daniel and employed them in a new way appropriate for Mark's situation. Yet how new is Mark's appropriation of Daniel? O'Leary's assessment of how apocalypticism functions rhetorically in specific situations provides a point of departure for revisiting how Mark employed his references to the book of Daniel.[42] A close examination of Daniel's

---

[37] Joel Marcus, "The Jewish War and the *Sitz im Leben* of Mark," *JBL* 111 (1992): 441–62, http://dx.doi.org/10.2307/3267261.

[38] Yarbro Collins, "Apocalyptic Rhetoric," 26. Yarbro Collins distinguishes her argument here from that of Lars Hartman, who suggests a more full-blown typological connection between the discourse in Mark 13 and the story of Sodom and Gomorrah (*Prophecy Interpreted: The Formation of Some Jewish Apocalyptic Texts and of the Eschatological Discourse Mark 13 Par.*, ConBNT 1 [Lund: Gleerup, 1966]).

[39] O'Leary, *Arguing the Apocalypse*, 201.

[40] Ibid., 10.

[41] Ibid., 11. O'Leary examines apocalyptic rhetoric in the Millerite movement in the early to mid-1800s and Hal Lindsay in the twentieth century before coming back to the book of Revelation as a touchstone for evaluating his theory of apocalyptic rhetoric.

[42] A seminal work on this specific topic is Hartman's *Prophecy Interpreted*. This very detailed

use of the phrase τὸ βδέλυγμα τῆς ἐρημώσεως and Mark's appropriation of it reveals a significant dissimilarity in how the two authors use the phrase.

### *Greek Daniel's Use of* τὸ βδέλυγμα τῆς ἐρημώσεως

The book of Daniel refers to the "abomination of desolation" three times but never makes explicit its likely historical referent.[43] Comparison with 1 Macc 1:54 and Josephus (*A.J.* 12.5.4) shows that Daniel refers to the offense of the Seleucid ruler Antiochus IV Epiphanes and the establishment of an altar that defiled the temple in Jerusalem.[44] In Dan 9:27, the reference to the desolation is surrounded by calculations pinpointing when it will happen. Verse 24 introduces the seventy weeks, which are then divided into smaller units in verses 25–26. In verse 27, the temporal prophecies become very specific:[45]

> And the covenant will rule over many. And it will return again and be rebuilt wide and long. And at the completion of time, even after seven and seventy times and sixty-two years, until the time of the end of the war, even the desolation will be taken away in which the covenant prevails for many weeks. And at the end of the week the sacrifice and the drink offering will be taken away, and in the temple there will be an abomination of desolations until the completion, and completion will be given to the desolation. (Dan 9:27 LXX)

A second reference to the abomination, in Dan 11:31, does not have the same extensive speculation as seen in 9:27, but the whole chapter does divide time into specific segments in its prophetic scenario (see the temporal determinacy hinted at in vv. 14, 27, 29, 35, and 40). The reference to the abomination is situated in the broader context of the things that will happen at their appointed times (referred to variously with the words ὥρα and καιρός). At the end of verse 35, the phrase εἰς ὥρας introduces the outrageous activities of the king (vv. 36–39). Although the temporal speculations in chapter 11 are not as specific as those in chapter 9, the activities in the temple (v. 31) are actually more specific. An army will enter and defile the temple and set up the abomination.

---

study shows that the apocalyptic discourse is an extended midrash (174) on Daniel and that the two texts share many similarities of both content and intention (147).

[43] The prophecy in Daniel is *ex eventu*. Nevertheless, specific calculation seems to be a major aspect of the references to the abomination.

[44] See further Yarbro Collins, *Mark*, 608.

[45] We cannot know for certain what form of Greek Daniel was available to Mark. Both the Old Greek and Theodotion are attested in the New Testament. See Pierre Grelot, "Les Versions grecques de Daniel," *Bib* 47 (1966): 383–91. I translate here from the Old Greek, not Theodotion. See also R. Timothy McLay, "Daniel (Old Greek and Theodotion)," in *The T&T Clark Companion to the Septuagint*, ed. James K. Aitken, T&T Clark Companions (London: Bloomsbury T&T Clark, 2015), 544–54.

The third reference to the desolation, in Dan 12:11, again is in the context of temporal speculation. In 12:6, one of the robed men in Daniel's vision asks, "When will be the completion of these things which you have spoken to me…?" Daniel deems the response too cryptic; he heard, but he did not understand about "the time itself." When the reference to the abomination arrives in verse 11, it is little more than a marker in a very specific time frame. From the time that the regular burnt offering is taken away and the abomination that desolates is set up, there will be 1,290 days. The very next verse offers yet a different calculation, 1,335 days.

Greek Daniel employs the phrase τὸ βδέλυγμα τῆς ἐρημώσεως with varying degrees of temporal specification. In chapters 9 and 12, the calculation is specific. In chapter 11 it is less so, but temporal markers still frame the phrase. It seems, therefore, that there is a tendency in Greek Daniel to make the specific timing of the end paramount as it relates to this phrase and to Antiochus's activities in the temple.[46]

## Mark's Interpretation of Daniel

Returning to Mark, we see a significant contrast. Compared to Greek Daniel, which tends toward temporal specificity, Mark shrouds the phrase τὸ βδέλυγμα τῆς ἐρημώσεως. Mark co-opts Daniel's repeated references to the abomination but employs them with "calculated obscurity" by providing none of the accompanying temporal references.[47] The phrase signals the turning point in the discourse's division of time, the point at which flight should begin, but Mark renders it powerless as a temporal trigger because its historical referent is indecipherable. If that to which the phrase refers is shrouded, then the temporal specificity of the scenario can no longer be the rhetorical point of the discourse. Mark's method here builds on the rhetorical force of the first section of the discourse (vv. 5–13) by adding further to the tension and not providing a starting point, a definitive and recognizable sign as the disciples had originally requested. If Mark's intention in the first section of the discourse was to cause disquiet and discomfort, here he has redoubled his efforts.

The grammatical details of how Mark uses the phrase from Daniel increase its obscurity. The phrase τὸ βδέλυγμα τῆς ἐρημώσεως is grammatically neuter, while the attributive participle paired with it, ἑστηκότα, is masculine. Such inconcinnity could be due to lack of attention to detail or lack of proficiency in Koine Greek.[48]

---

[46] First Maccabees 1:54, a very different genre of literature from that of Daniel, goes even further, pinpointing the exact date: the fifteenth day of Chislev in the 145th year.

[47] Black, "Oration at Olivet," 84.

[48] Mark is notorious for grammatical infelicities. For just one example, note the use of ἄν with an indicative verb (ἐσώθη) in 13:20. In Mark's defense on this point, Black points out that, for Mark, an ideal "standard of Attic purity is arguably as unrealistic as it is unsuited" ("Oration at Olivet," 84).

On the other hand, having suggested that the "obscurity" of its historical referent may be "calculated" on Mark's part,[49] is it not possible that Mark mismatched the grammar to underscore the phrase's incalculability? Perhaps the perceived grammatical solecism simply emphasizes obscurity, especially in comparison with the specificity in the parent text, Daniel. In this way, Mark misdirects anyone who would connect the phrase with a specific historical referent (whether a person or an event) and therefore view it as a turning point in the eschatological scenarios.[50] While Daniel and its Greek translator(s) were working in a tragic frame of reference with a closed system of possibility, Mark writes in the comic frame. O'Leary suggests that in a tragic frame, predictions polarize the audience, who are forced to choose whether to join the apocalyptic frenzy. Those who choose not to join view "every expression of apocalyptic urgency as an opportunity for further ridicule."[51] Such a view might illuminate Mark's motives; the evangelist clearly does not find in Daniel a helpful template with an apocalyptic scenario that has begun and whose end is imminent. Rather, he finds an evocative rhetorical resource for his aims. His employment of Daniel's phrase, ambiguous and grammatically illogical, serves to obfuscate any attempt to correlate it with an actual event or person in history.

Mark further erodes the audience's ability to pinpoint the βδέλυγμα τῆς ἐρημώσεως with the even more enigmatic directive "let the reader understand." This parenthetical statement seems to be "rhetorically inept," but it may make more "provocative" this whole section of the discourse.[52] Mark's readers would have wanted to understand, as the Greek of Dan 9:25 indicated that Daniel himself would (γνώσῃ καὶ διανοηθήσῃ). The point, however, becomes the opposite of the message of Dan 9: there are no temporal signposts that will allow the specific pieces to fall into place. In light of the interpretation offered here, Black's words seem appropriate: within the rhetorical framework, the significance of the phrase τὸ βδέλυγμα τῆς ἐρημώσεως "resides largely in its provocative mystery and its concomitant resistance to clear interpretation."[53] Mark's calculated obscurity in 13:14 is part of a larger rhetorical agenda throughout the discourse. The antecedent apocalyptic traditions, especially from Daniel, are reinterpreted toward new goals. In the words of O'Leary with which we began, Mark has availed himself of a

---

[49] Black, "Oration at Olivet," 84.

[50] Ernest Best has argued that the phrase "let the reader understand" was a cue for the reader of the Gospel meant to draw attention to the mismatched grammar in verse 14 ("The Gospel of Mark: Who Was the Reader?," *IBS* 11 [1989]: 124–32). In other words, the solecism was intentional and not to be corrected orally by the reader. Yarbro Collins says that Best's "ingenious" scenario should not be adopted because the grammatical infelicity here does not necessarily pose a problem; *constructio ad sensum* was common in ancient Greek (*Mark*, 597). Best's analysis, however, stands as one of the few treatments of the phrase that considers Mark's solecism to be intentional.

[51] O'Leary, *Arguing the Apocalypse*, 205.

[52] Black, "Oration at Olivet," 90.

[53] Ibid. He coordinates this phrase with the ancient technique of *controversiae*.

"textually embodied community of discourse" but augmented it by way of "new interpretive strategies," namely, to prod the very activities the discourse itself calls for: watchfulness and wakefulness.[54]

Verses 21–23 return to a discussion of messianic claimants, and the unit ends with Jesus's charge ὑμεῖς δὲ βλέπετε προείρηκα ὑμῖν πάντα ("Watch out, I have already foretold you everything"). The imperative βλέπετε concludes this section of the discourse, forming an *inclusio* with its beginning (v. 5) by prescribing an identical course of action: "Keep watch!" The list of things Jesus says will happen in Mark 13—the tribulation, earthquakes, and desolations—should not be correlated with actual historical circumstances because the overriding exhortation is simply to keep watch, and Mark has obfuscated the starting point for the next course of action (taking flight). The flight and severe tribulations in verses 14–20 loom on the horizon, but Mark employs them as little more than a shocking, imminent portent. The tribulations are meant to engender the more consistently advocated watchfulness.

## IV. Mark 13:32–37: Keep Alert! But Why?

The final section of the discourse offers a parable about a man who leaves on a journey.[55] Those who stay behind, the servants and the doorkeeper, do not know when the master will return. Their job in his absence is to wait and stay awake, lest they be found asleep upon the master's return. Scholars tend to perceive a tension at the end of the discourse. As Morna Hooker notes, the tension results from the fact that most of the chapter has been presenting an order of the events that are to occur, but "the final section [13:32–37] suggests that the End may come at any time."[56] Juel more broadly observes that "the little parable, in fact, sets a tone quite different from what one might have expected from an 'apocalyptic' discourse."[57] Even Lars Hartman, whose reading strategy is not primarily narrative-critical, notes a disjunction between the admonitions of the "midrash" earlier in the

---

[54] O'Leary, *Arguing the Apocalypse*, 10.

[55] Space constraints prevent a full discussion of 13:24–31. The content of these verses fits with the overall argument being made here. The prediction of the coming of the Son of Man continues Mark's employment of apocalyptic topoi and motifs, but again with no specific time frame for when this will happen. The parable of the fig tree also reinforces the idea of watchfulness; the fig tree has not broken into leaf, but it will. Again, however, Mark gives no indication what time of the year it is, just that some change is coming. It is clear that the audience will know the sign when they see it, but no starting point is provided.

[56] Morna D. Hooker, *The Gospel according to Saint Mark*, BNTC (Peabody, MA: Hendrickson, 1991), 301.

[57] Juel, *Master of Surprise*, 85.

discourse and the concluding parable. His redaction-critical methodology leads him to suspect originally separate sources and causes him to reassess whether these two disjunctive parts of the discourse "belonged together from the beginning."[58] Yarbro Collins attempts to alleviate this tension by saying that Mark does not end with antiapocalyptic sentiment; his belief in imminent expectation is clear in verse 30. Rather, the parable counteracts attempts to calculate the date of the end.[59]

All of these treatments of the parable at the end of the discourse share one assumption: that some earlier parts of the discourse ought to be correlated with specific historical events. This accounts for the scholarly confusion when presented with a concluding parable that suggests that the timing is unknowable. If we read the discourse without correlation with historical events—an open rather than closed system—then the rhetorical force of the parable (vv. 32–36) coheres with what came before. Nor is the concluding parable the only part of the discourse that advocates wakefulness and watchfulness. The word βλέπετε runs like a refrain throughout the discourse (in vv. 5, 9, 23, and 33). At the beginning, this word seems best translated as "watch out" or "guard (yourselves)." By the end of the discourse it becomes almost synonymous with the need simply to stay awake (γρηγορεῖτε). The parable actually does not stand out at all; Mark's Jesus seems consistently to have urged "inaction rather than action."[60]

While the tragic frame of apocalyptic argument shifts the emphasis from "persuasion to enactment,"[61] as we have seen, Mark's intentions seem to be the opposite: to engender no action apart from wakefulness and wariness. If Mark did not have specific historical referents in mind, then O'Leary's description of a comic frame of apocalyptic rhetoric becomes applicable and helpful. Mark is playing with the traditional apocalyptic folderol, its images and topoi, with a very specific rhetorical aim: the desire to keep open a "horizon of possibility." The rhetorical aim of the discourse becomes a repudiation of the calculation of the end—not, as Yarbro Collins claims, to repudiate such activity per se but rather to orient the entire discourse differently, toward an open rather than a closed system of possibility.

---

[58] Hartman, *Prophecy Interpreted*, 176. Hartman relieves this tension by revisiting connections between the two sections of the discourse and concluding that the midrashic section "had at least some of its paraenetic elements connected with it from the beginning" (177).

[59] Yarbro Collins, "Apocalyptic Rhetoric," 36.

[60] Hooker, *Gospel according to Saint Mark*, 300. Marcus calls Mark's end to the discourse "radical eschatological indeterminacy" (*Mark*, 921). The problem is that this does not fit the very specific circumstances Marcus coordinated with earlier parts of the discourse, which would provide a pivot point from which Mark's scenarios would start to fall into place and become decidedly determined.

[61] O'Leary, *Arguing the Apocalypse*, 205.

## V. The Open Horizon of Mark's Gospel

The conclusions reached thus far, that reading Mark 13 in light of O'Leary's comic frame of reference highlights Mark's intentions for the openness of the discourse, can be confirmed by a brief look at other sections of Mark's Gospel.[62]

### *Unclean Spirits and Jesus's Identity*

According to O'Leary, in the tragic frame of apocalyptic discourse, time and human history lie temporarily outside divine control.[63] The opposite is true in Mark. Jesus, as God's agent on earth (a fact known more clearly by the unclean spirits in the story than by most human characters), is the one strong enough to bind the strong man and plunder his house (3:20–30).[64] In 5:1–20, Jesus can handle a legion of demons with dispatch, binding the one whom no one could keep tied up. The miracles are narrated with the same language as the exorcisms: Jesus "rebukes" the wind (4:39). There seems to be little doubt, from beginning to end in Mark, who is in control. True opposition in the story comes from human institutions that are opposed to Jesus and his revelation of God's kingdom and its graciousness (e.g., 1:40–45, 2:23–28, 7:1–23, 15:1–20). Even the "institution" of the Twelve, its members hand-picked by Jesus, are oppositional, slow, and reticent (4:13, 40; 6:52; 8:14–21).[65] Such ignorance does not come from supernatural forces unless that supernatural opponent is God (e.g., 4:1–20, 6:52, 8:14–21). The details in Mark seem a better fit for O'Leary's description of the comic frame of apocalyptic discourse, which "tends to locate the cause of evil in human error and to postpone the date [of the end] or render it irrelevant."[66]

### *Suffering in Mark*

Reading the discourse of Mark 13 through the comic frame of reference will also shed some light on the situation of the Markan community.[67] Mark's Jesus is

---

[62] Juel argues for "interpretations of the chapter whose primary focus is the function of the discourse within the Gospel narrative" (*Master of Surprise*, 79). One should also include here the work of Timothy J. Geddert, *Watchwords: Mark 13 in Markan Eschatology*, JSNTSup 26 (Sheffield: JSOT Press, 1989), who takes a narrative-critical approach to understanding the function of the discourse within the overall narrative.

[63] O'Leary, *Arguing the Apocalypse*, 194–206.

[64] There are obvious exceptions to this, most notably 8:27–33, although even there Peter's correct answer is subverted by the fact that he does not properly ascertain its meaning.

[65] The disciples do occasionally show promise. They follow initially (1:16–20), and they have some missionary success (6:7–13).

[66] O'Leary, *Arguing the Apocalypse*, 205.

[67] Dwight N. Peterson makes a helpful point: "The Markan community is not the fiery brook

preoccupied with suffering and suggests that a life lived on his model will produce the same. H. N. Roskam has argued on redaction-critical grounds that texts such as 4:16–17, 8:34–35, 10:29–30, and 13:9–13 reveal Mark's emphasis on suffering.[68] Christopher Tuckett has shown, however, that at many of these points there are exegetical reasons to question whether they evince a suffering community behind the Gospel.[69] Form and redaction criticism, Tuckett argues, tend "to assume a simple one-to-one positive correlation between a text and a community's experience."[70] Thus, if Mark's Jesus talks about suffering, then this must mean that the community was suffering. Texts, however, can do more than simply reflect what is happening in a community. Tuckett points out, for instance, that "texts can function just as much to *address* readers and make them *change* their minds, re-evaluate their positions and *alter* their lifestyles."[71]

Mark's narrative frustrates the conclusion that suffering and its consolation drive his story of Jesus.[72] In 1:21–28, the unclean spirit knows Jesus as the "holy

---

through which interpretations of Mark must pass" (*The Origins of Mark: The Markan Community in Current Debate*, BibInt 48 [Leiden: Brill, 2000], 196). Despite such a caveat, Peterson's conclusion is not entirely negative, as he also suggests that such reconstructions can "produce provisional vantage points for some readers under some conditions in the service of some purposes" (196).

[68] H. N. Roskam, *The Purpose of the Gospel of Mark in Its Historical and Social Context*, NovTSup 114 (Leiden: Brill, 2004). The "Mark is addressing suffering" trope has become such a part of the scholarly consensus that one reviewer of Roskam's book suggests that arguments in this area are not "worth the work" (Zeba A. Crook, review of *The Purpose of the Gospel of Mark in Its Historical and Social Context*, by H. N. Roskam, *JBL* 124 [2005]: 553.) Crook's critique reflects the fact that most scholars were in agreement that Mark addresses suffering. At the same time, Crook also critiques Roskam's redaction-critical methodology.

[69] Christopher Tuckett, "Gospels and Communities: Was Mark Written for a Suffering Community?," in *Jesus, Paul, and Early Christianity: Studies in Honour of Henk Jan de Jonge*, ed. Rieuwerd Buitenwerf, Harm W. Hollander, and Johannes Tromp, NovTSup 130 (Leiden: Brill, 2008), 377–96, http://dx.doi.org/10.1163/ej.9789004170339.i-470.102.

[70] Ibid., 385.

[71] Ibid. (italics original).

[72] See Timothy Radcliffe, "The Coming of the Son of Man: Mark's Gospel and the Subversion of 'The Apocalyptic Imagination,'" in *Language, Meaning, and God: Essays in Honour of Herbert McCabe OP*, ed. Brian Davies (London: Geoffrey Chapman, 1987), 176–89; and Bas M. F. Van Iersel, "Failed Followers in Mark: Mark 13:12 as a Key for the Identification of the Intended Readers," *CBQ* 58 (1996): 244–63. Radcliffe argues that one of Mark's goals was to collapse the traditional boundaries that "characterized" apocalyptic literature (187). Van Iersel picks up Radcliffe's argument, which he claims has "gone practically unnoticed" (244), and expands on it. Both of these essays are helpful for the way in which they pay attention to narrative elements of the Gospel in seeking answers to questions that are traditionally given historical answers. Both authors are plagued by an overly simplistic understanding of apocalypticism and rely exclusively on Wayne Meeks's discussion of the three dualities inherent in apocalypticism ("Social Functions of Apocalyptic Language in Pauline Christianity," in *Apocalypticism in the Mediterranean World and the Near East: Proceedings of the International Colloquium on Apocalypticism, Uppsala, August 12–17, 1979*, ed. David Hellholm [Tübingen: Mohr Siebeck, 1983], 687–705). Radcliffe and Van

one of God" who has "come to destroy." The legion of demons in 5:1–20 knows similarly, calling Jesus "son of the most high God" and adjuring Jesus not to cause them torment. This is a fundamental irony in Mark's story that commentators have long noticed: the demons understand Jesus's true identity, while the disciples, those who are on the inside (see 4:10–11), often do not. Why does the opposition understand Jesus better than the disciples? Why do the disciples not understand the parable of the sower (4:13)? Why are they rebuked as having no faith (4:40)? Why are their hearts hardened (6:52)? Rarely are these questions allowed to intrude on an understanding of Mark's apocalyptic perspective as it relates to the situation of the people in his community and their purported suffering. The fact that the narrative gives rise to these questions suggests that Mark is dismantling any notion that God's kingdom relies on human power and ingenuity. The Gospel as a whole, like chapter 13, is more a proper profile of God than a manifesto for specific action.

Returning to the observations of Juel with which we began, the open horizon of chapter 13 makes more sense if "directed at insiders whose problem is indifference or a tired lack of perception about the way things are."[73] At stake is nothing less than the character of God in the Gospel. Mark 13 seems intended for a community that had grown complacent, "whose problem is not persecution as much as an inability to be surprised by the God who is both more dangerous and more promising than they can have imagined."[74] Mark need not fully believe the apocalyptic scenarios in order to use them for his rhetorical purposes. The warnings, calls for flight, disorder, and persecution may simply be intended to shock and scare the community into being serious, awake, and engaged.[75]

## *The Ending of Mark's Gospel*

If Mark's rhetoric in chapter 13 was intended to create an open horizon, not a closed one, then this view would seem to fit with the open ending of his Gospel as well. The abrupt ending at 16:8 does little to provide what a deprived or suffering community would want or need. Mark colors the traditional apocalyptic belief of an imminent change in the structure of the universe with disappointment. The fleeting postresurrection account starts off well: Jesus has been raised, the stone has

---

Iersel treat Meeks's heuristic categories as so entrenched in all forms of ancient apocalypticism that they could be subverted at every turn by Mark, almost as if Mark himself had read and appropriated Meeks's work.

[73] Juel, *Master of Surprise*, 145.

[74] Ibid., 146.

[75] Juel notes the observations of Nils Dahl ("The Purpose of Mark's Gospel," in *Jesus in the Memory of the Early Church: Essays* [Minneapolis: Augsburg, 1976], 52–65), whose profile of the implied reader in Mark suggests a community "that has tasted success and found it satisfying," envisioning believers "who have taken the gospel for granted, who no longer see the world painted in dramatic colors" (*Master of Surprise*, 88).

been rolled away, and a young man robed in white proclaims the resurrection. Mark, however, does not leave the reader with this image. Instead, the women who had made their way to the tomb leave in fear and silence. A community unable to live in that new age has thwarted the millenarian expectation.

When discussing the ending of Mark, Juel claims that the open ending provides so little comfort that it should problematize the categories of apocalyptic thought that are applied to it. Juel wrongly assumes that apocalyptic literature carries with it a specific social setting: a marginalized community that needs divine intervention to reverse its standing.[76] According to Juel, "an accurate profiling of the implied audience" is indeed "crucial."[77] O'Leary's theories about the rhetorical aspects of apocalyptic literature show how chapter 13 actually helps support Juel's conclusions. The discourse calls for watchfulness and wakefulness in order to create an open horizon of possibility for what God will do. Juel sees the same thing at work in the ending. He claims that there is "something disquieting about [the] lack of control" left with the reader at the end of the story.[78] Mark wrests control from the reader throughout the Gospel. Assumptions about who is and is not the good soil are consistently upturned with examples of who succeeds (e.g., 5:1–20) and who does not (e.g., 4:35–41). In chapter 13, Mark exploits apocalyptic imagery for the same end: to undermine confidence in humans' ability to know and perceive properly because the kingdom of God is not dependent on humans. It grows without cultivation (4:26–29). It seems insignificant but then blossoms unexpectedly (4:30–32). It takes root best in those who are marginalized by society: the sick, the dying, or the dead (5:1–20, 21–43). Mark 13 is not the evangelist's interpretation of specific historical events surrounding his community but is instead about a God with an open rather than a closed horizon for divine activity. Chapter 13 fits with Mark's portrait of a God whose actions are not determined by a historical succession of events, a God who remains free and open in the future, who will continue to do whatever God wants to do.

There are obvious reasons to dissent from this picture of the implied audience of Mark's Gospel; primary among them is the focus in the Gospel itself on persecution and suffering. David Rhoads's review of Juel's work notes that the text is meant

---

[76] Juel here is probably influenced by the work of Howard Clark Kee (*Community of the New Age: Studies in Mark's Gospel* [Philadelphia: Westminster, 1977]), who reads the apocalyptic perspective in Mark by using the work of social scientists. The connection between apocalypticism and a suffering community should not be overdrawn. See the nuanced position of Stephen L. Cook, *Prophecy and Apocalypticism: The Postexilic Social Setting* (Minneapolis: Fortress, 1995). See also O'Leary, who thinks that studies of apocalyptic texts and movements have spent too much time discussing "audience predispositions based in conditions of social and economic class, in experience of calamity, or in psychological anomie" (*Arguing the Apocalypse*, 11).

[77] Juel, *Master of Surprise*, 144. Note also the objection of Dwight N. Peterson (*Origins of Mark*, 195–96), who quotes Juel. Peterson's objection is that scholars have overemphasized the importance of profiling Mark's audience.

[78] Juel, *Master of Surprise*, 145.

to "lead readers to deal with their fear, not their complacency."[79] Fear certainly echoes throughout the Gospel. In Mark, however, fear does not arise in the context of persecution. Characters fear the crowds (e.g., 11:18, 32; 12:12) or Jesus and the manifestations of the kingdom related to him (e.g., 4:41; 5:15, 33, 36; 6:50; 10:32; 16:8). Fear in Mark comes when characters gape at the kingdom of God, forced to ascertain its true nature. Fear arises when people are changed by a God who does not play by societal or religious rules. Mark's depiction of the kingdom of God and humans' reaction to it evinces a complacent community that sees but no longer comprehends, that has forgotten the way in which the kingdom of God will "surely surprise" because its horizon is alarmingly open.[80]

---

[79] David Rhoads, review of *A Master of Surprise: Mark Interpreted*, by Donald H. Juel, *CBQ* 59 (1997): 161–62, here 162.

[80] C. Clifton Black, "Mark as Historian of God's Kingdom," *CBQ* 71 (2009): 64–83, here 83.

# Fleshly Resurrection, Authority Claims, and the Scriptural Practices of Lukan Christianity

SHELLY MATTHEWS
s.matthews@tcu.edu
Brite Divinity School, Fort Worth, TX 76129

In this article, I argue that references to the fleshly resurrection of Jesus in Luke and Acts, both those that tell of Jesus eating with his apostles and those that assert that Jesus's flesh was "incorruptible" (Luke 24:36–53, Acts 1:4, 2:31, 10:40–41, 13:37), share thematic continuity and are best understood as stemming from Luke's concern for the exclusive authority of the twelve apostles. I assume that Luke has access not only to oral and written resurrection narratives but also to a collection of the Pauline Epistles and that Luke frames Lukan narrative as the result of the scriptural practices of one second-century textual community, among others. In mapping both divergences *and* convergences between Lukan understandings of resurrection and views often attributed to Marcionites and/or so-called docetists, I challenge the view that Luke's assertions of fleshly resurrection represent (proto)orthodoxy's incipient battle with heresy over the nature of the resurrection of Jesus.

---

Classic arguments concerning the question of fleshly resurrection and apostolic authority in early Christianity have been framed in terms of orthodoxy and heresy. Nearly forty years ago, Elaine Pagels identified "two lines of theological tradition" with respect to questions of resurrection and authority, one linked to emerging orthodoxy and one linked to gnostic sources. In this framing, Lukan resurrection accounts stand in line with the writings of Ignatius, Justin, Irenaeus, and Tertullian—and thus with emerging orthodoxy—in their insistence that only the successors to the twelve apostles, who had seen the resurrected Jesus on the earth before his ascension, had legitimate authority. The other line of theological tradition traced by Pagels was drawn from gnostic sources and valued continual revelation in the form of visions of the resurrected Jesus as a means of authorization.[1] As Pagels underscored, the question of whether one's authority to speak for

---

[1] Elaine Pagels, "Visions, Appearances and Apostolic Authority: Gnostic and Orthodox

Jesus derived from earthly encounter or from visions was entangled in early Christian gender wars. Affirmation of the apostolic succession based on the privilege of the Twelve produced an exclusively male leadership class, while those linking authority to visions privileged the witness of Mary Magdalene and imagined both women and men speaking legitimately on behalf of the resurrected Christ.

In a monograph completed in the decade before the work of Pagels, Walter Schmithals took up the question of the distinctively Lukan tendencies with respect to apostolic authority. Schmithals argued that Luke connects the exclusive privilege of the Twelve as apostles with their witness to the resurrected Jesus before his ascension. At the same time, Luke suppresses the (original) concept of apostleship associated with Paul according to which authority derived from direct calling by Christ through the medium of visionary encounter. In Acts, this tendency leads to the subordination of Paul to the Twelve, the stripping from Paul of his apostolic office, and the alignment of Pauline theology with that of the Jerusalem church. While Schmithals, like Pagels, identifies antignostic polemic at the heart of the development of apostolic tradition in orthodox circles more generally, he identifies "Marcionitism" as the specific motivation for Luke's distinctive framing of the apostolate.[2]

In this article, I engage the work of Pagels and Schmithals in two ways. First, I argue that the insights of these scholars, connecting the resurrection appearances to the apostolic authority of the Twelve, are the exegetical key to understanding the interest in the fleshly resurrection of Jesus in Luke 24 and Acts. While the general arguments of Pagels and Schmithals are widely known, exegetes working on Luke 24 and Acts have not employed them to address the five specific passages that invoke the fleshly resurrection of Jesus (Luke 24:36–53, Acts 1:4, 2:31, 10:40–41, and 13:37). Because scholars have not recognized the thematic continuity shared by these passages, they have tended to treat them in isolation. Suggestions for topics that illuminate one or more of these passages have included Luke's battles with Marcion or with "docetism," his knowledge of ancient Jewish burial customs, and his decision to depict Jesus as enduring a martyr's death.[3] I argue here that these

---

Traditions," in *Gnosis: Festschrift für Hans Jonas*, ed. Barbara Aland (Göttingen: Vandenhoeck & Ruprecht, 1978), 415–30; Pagels, *The Gnostic Gospels* (New York: Random House, 1979), 3–32.

[2] Walter Schmithals, *The Office of Apostle in the Early Church*, trans. John E. Steely (Nashville: Abingdon, 1969), 272–86. Schmithals's framing of Acts as anti-Marcionite polemic built on the scholarship of John Knox, *Marcion and the New Testament: An Essay in the Early History of the Canon* (Chicago: University of Chicago Press, 1942). For a discussion of the revival of this theory in recent scholarship, see pp. 180–82 below.

[3] See below for arguments with respect to Lukan assertion of fleshly resurrection in the context of Marcionism and docetism. For arguments pertaining to Jesus's "incorruptible flesh" (Acts 2:31, 13:37) in the context of ancient Jewish burial customs, see Bruce J. Malina and John J. Pilch, *Social Science Commentary on the Book of Acts* (Minneapolis: Fortress, 2008), 225–26; and further discussion below. For the argument that Luke's stress on fleshly resurrection relates to his concern to interpret Jesus's death in the context of martyrdom, see Outi Lehtipuu, *Debates over*

five passages share thematic continuity and are all shaped by Luke's distinctive concern to tie the appearance of the resurrected Jesus in the flesh to the exclusive authority of the twelve male apostles.

Second, I depart from the classic model of orthodoxy and heresy employed by Pagels and Schmithals and situate this text in a more variegated context of early Christian religious pluralism. In making this departure, I build on the scholarship of Karen King. King has been at the forefront of scholars critiquing the tendency to categorize early Christian texts according to the orthodox/heretical binary.[4] Her reading of early Christian texts outside of that framework has resulted in rich and innovative mappings of the intersections and divergences among various early Christian groups.[5] I am also in conversation with a recent proposal of David Brakke, who suggests that, rather than classifying early Christians and their writings in terms of insiders and outsiders, we think instead about how various Christian groups in the second century and beyond "used texts, and how they formed groups for using them."[6] Like King, Brakke moves away from the language of orthodoxy and heresy, along with the categories of canonical and noncanonical, to the work of describing what he refers to as the scriptural practices of textual communities.

The models proposed by King and Brakke might have their biggest payoffs for the study of late antiquity, when early Christian communities are represented by identifiable authors and larger corpora. These models, however, also serve as a useful lens for studying a particular set of biblical texts and the communities that produced them. This set consists of late-first- and early-second-century texts that eventually became part of the New Testament canon but were written in communities that were *already* reflecting on earlier writings of Jesus followers, *already* engaged in experiments in how to read these earlier writings, and *already*

---

the Resurrection of the Dead: Constructing Early Christian Identity, OECS (Oxford: Oxford University Press, 2015), 45, http://dx.doi.org/10.1093/acprof:oso/9780198724810.001.0001.

[4] See Karen King's programmatic essay, "Which Early Christianity?," in *The Oxford Handbook of Early Christian Studies*, ed. Susan Ashbrook Harvey and David G. Hunter (Oxford: Oxford University Press, 2008), 66–84.

[5] See, e.g., Karen L. King, "Christians Who Sacrifice and Those Who Do Not? Discursive Practices, Polemics, and Ritualizing," in *"The One Who Sows Bountifully": Essays in Honor of Stanley K. Stowers*, ed. Caroline Johnson Hodge et al., BJS 356 (Providence, RI: Brown Judaic Studies, 2013), 307–18; and King, "Martyrdom and Its Discontents in the Tchacos Codex," in *The Codex Judas Papers: Proceedings of the International Congress on the Tchacos Codex Held at Rice University, Houston, Texas, March 13–16, 2008*, ed. April D. DeConick, NHMS 71 (Leiden: Brill, 2009), 23–42. Compare also Daniel Boyarin, *Border Lines: The Partition of Judaeo-Christianity*, Divinations (Philadelphia: University of Pennsylvania Press, 2004), for discussion of orthodoxy and heresy as discourses rather than essences.

[6] David Brakke, "Scriptural Practices in Early Christianity: Towards a New History of the New Testament Canon," in *Invention, Rewriting, Usurpation: Discursive Fights over Religious Traditions in Antiquity*, ed. Jörg Ulrich, Anders-Christian Jacobsen, and David Brakke, Early Christianity in the Context of Antiquity 11 (Frankfurt am Main: Lang, 2012), 263–80.

embedding into their own texts the narrative details that signal fluency with literate technologies.[7]

Taking cues from King and Brakke, I resist framing the final form of Luke, along with the Acts of the Apostles, as texts that can stand *in a straight line* representing emerging orthodoxy and anticipating Justin and Irenaeus. I assume that these Lukan narratives owe much to scriptural practices of modifying, erasing, and/ or engaging polemically with understandings of the resurrection found in previously written Gospels and oral traditions. I take the more controversial position that this author has access to a collection of Pauline epistles and that, like several other late-first- and early-second-century textual communities, the Lukan community is reading those epistles creatively, without concern for transmitting in its own narrative an accurate or "historically reliable" representation of Paul's teachings.[8] Finally, I assume that Luke has some concern to construct dividing lines between those who follow Jesus rightly and those who do not (see Acts 20:29–30). I nevertheless recognize that those dividing lines do not directly anticipate the orthodoxy/heresy binary that will come to be established in centuries well beyond the author's own line of vision. This framework leads to the following observations that give texture to my thesis that Luke forecloses authority to the twelve men who witnessed the resurrected Jesus in the flesh. First, although linking apostolic authority to having seen a fleshly Jesus anticipates what will come to be known as Christian orthodoxy, Luke's depictions of fleshly resurrection constitute a radical

---

[7] For instances of the embedding of textual practices into New Testament texts that demonstrate the presence of early Christian reading communities, see John S. Kloppenborg, "Literate Media in Early Christ Groups: The Creation of a Christian Book Culture," *JECS* 22 (2014): 21–59. As Kloppenborg notes, specific attention is drawn to book culture in Luke's description of Jesus's inaugural sermon at Nazareth in Luke 4:16–30; 2 Tim 4:13 draws attention to Paul as an author employing the tools of the trade; Paul is depicted in Acts as an orator rather than a writer but still one who engages in literate technologies, including debating from Scripture and citing Greek poets.

While the focus of this study is on Lukan materials, other late-first- and early-second-century canonical materials that might profit from this approach include the Pastoral Epistles, 2 Peter, the final chapter of the Fourth Gospel, and the Markan appendix (Mark 16:9–20).

[8] The proposal that Luke had access to a collection of Pauline letters has received a renewed amount of interest among biblical scholars, especially in view of the arguments for this position marshaled in Richard I. Pervo, *Dating Acts: Between the Evangelists and the Apologists* (Sonoma, CA: Polebridge, 2006), 51–147. For a recent testing of the hypothesis that Acts draws from a collection of Paul's letters, which concludes in support of this position, see Ryan Schellenberg, "The First Pauline Chronologist? Paul's Itinerary in the Letters and in Acts," *JBL* 134 (2015): 193–213, http://dx.doi.org/10.15699/jbl.1341.2015.2837.

I accept Pervo's arguments pertaining to the dating of Acts in the early decades of the second century. For my own arguments that Luke 24 was composed within that time frame as well, see Shelly Matthews, "Does Dating Luke-Acts into the Second Century Affect the Q Hypothesis?," in *Gospel Interpretation and the Q Hypothesis*, ed. Heike Omerzu and Mogens Müller (London: Bloomsbury T&T Clark, forthcoming).

departure from Paul's resurrection teaching. Second, while Luke is often understood to be battling docetists and/or Marcionites with his assertions of Jesus's resurrection in the flesh, aspects of his depiction support, rather than resist, what will come to be known as "heretical" understandings of the nature of Jesus's resurrection.

### I. The Thematic Coherence of References to Jesus's Fleshly Resurrection in Luke 24 and Acts

We turn now to the Lukan passages that emphasize Jesus's resurrection in the flesh. I argue here that emphasis on fleshly resurrection in Luke 24 and the Acts of the Apostles establishes continuity between the pre- and postresurrection nature of Jesus and, concomitantly, the exclusive authority of the twelve apostles, owing to their witness to that continuity. It will be underscored here how close the connection between fleshly resurrection and authority is for this biblical author. Indeed, at every juncture in Luke 24 and Acts in which Jesus's fleshly resurrection is invoked, this invocation is tied to the insistence that the twelve apostles are the authoritative witnesses.

*Flesh, Bones, and Fish: The Distinctiveness of Luke 24 among Canonical Resurrection Narratives*

The Third Gospel is most explicit concerning the fleshly nature of the resurrection. As he stands before the eleven, Jesus says, "Touch me and see; for a spirit does not have flesh and bones as you see that I have" (24:39b, ψηλαφήσατέ με καὶ ἴδετε, ὅτι πνεῦμα σάρκα καὶ ὀστέα οὐκ ἔχει καθὼς ἐμὲ θεωρεῖτε ἔχοντα). Narrative details leading up to this invitation suggest that the author is entering a resurrection debate already in progress, even among those the author would cast within the inner circle. Before Jesus clarifies that he stands before them in flesh and bones, he is said to perceive the "disputes" (διαλογισμοί) that arise in the hearts of the eleven (24:38) concerning the nature of what they are seeing.[9] As further proof that he stands before them in the flesh, Jesus consumes grilled fish in their presence.[10]

To appreciate the distinctiveness of Luke's rhetorical assertion here, we must consider how it differs from the resurrection scenes in the Fourth Gospel, which

---

[9] Daniel A. Smith, "Seeing a Pneuma[tic Body]: The Apologetic Interests of Luke 24:36–43," *CBQ* 72 (2010): 752–72, here 753.

[10] I follow the vast number of exegetes who recognize the emphasis on eating here as a proof of Jesus's fleshly nature. See, e.g., Turid Karlsen Seim, "The Resurrected Body in Luke-Acts: The Significance of Space," in *Metamorphoses: Resurrection, Body and Transformative Practices in Early Christianity*, ed. Turid Karlsen Seim and Jorunn Øklund, Ekstasis 1 (Berlin: de Gruyter, 2009), 19–39, http://dx.doi.org/10.1515/9783110202991.19.

have often been recognized as affirmations of Jesus's physicality. Both ancient authors and modern scholars have read Thomas's conditional proposition in the Fourth Gospel, "unless I see in his hands the print of the nails and place my finger in the mark, I will not believe," and the subsequent accommodation by Jesus as an apologetic for fleshly resurrection.[11] Still, Luke's assertions concerning resurrection are more directly aimed at underscoring its fleshly nature for the following reasons. First, while Thomas is invited to touch the wounds of Jesus, the climax of the Johannine scene lies in the realm of identity rather than physicality.[12] Thomas is able to confess the resurrected Jesus as Lord because he has seen—a confession that serves as the third point of recognition in the Johannine narrative, after those of Mary (20:18) and the disciples (20:20). The need for Thomas to see the wounds may be a Johannine employment of a common topos in Greek literature evident as early as the Homeric tradition—as with Eurykleia in the *Odyssey*, who does not recognize Odysseus until she has touched his scar. Yet the high point of the recognition scene is not Jesus's affirmation that the body demonstrated to Thomas is fleshly but rather a rebuke of faith that requires sight. Thomas sees the wounded Jesus and confesses, "My Lord and my God," to which Jesus responds, "Have you believed because you have seen me? Blessed are those who have not seen and yet believe" (20:29).[13]

Second, that interest in the physicality of the resurrected Jesus is more heightened in the Third Gospel than in the Fourth is evident in these Gospels'

---

[11] Pseudo-Justin's *On the Resurrection* 9.5–9 weaves together both the invitation to touch the wounded hands (John 20:25) and the eating of fish (Luke 24:42) as proof of fleshly resurrection; Irenaeus reads the demonstration of nail and side wounds as proof (*Haer.* 5.7.1; 5.31.2; cf. Tertullian, *Res.* 34; Origen, *Cels.* 2.61). See further Gregory J. Riley, *Resurrection Reconsidered: Thomas and John in Controversy* (Minneapolis: Fortress, 1995), 100–126.

[12] This is argued by both Ismo Dunderberg ("John and Thomas in Conflict?") and April DeConick ("'Blessed Are Those Who Have Not Seen' (Jn 20.29): Johannine Dramatization of an Early Christian Discourse," both in *The Nag Hammadi Library after Fifty Years: Proceedings of the 1995 Society of Biblical Literature Commemoration*, ed. John D. Turner and Anne McGuire, NHMS 44 [Leiden: Brill, 1991], 361–80 and 381–98, respectively).

[13] In spite of early Christian readings of John that see the wounds as proof of fleshliness, sightings of the wounded dead do not constitute proof of postmortem fleshliness in other ancient narratives. Shades, ghosts, and even deified emperors appear in ancient narratives exhibiting the wounds received in earthly life. Consider Virgil, *Aen.* 1.355, 6.488; Apuleius, *Metam.* 8.8; Seneca, *Apol.* 5.

For observations concerning the impotence of the Greek gods to re-create or repair body parts, see Dag Øistein Endsjø, "Immortal Bodies, before Christ: Bodily Continuity in Ancient Greece and 1 Corinthians," *JSNT* 30 (2008): 417–36, esp. 433. Candida R. Moss argues for modification of that understanding in early Christianity; see her "Heavenly Healing: Eschatological Cleansing and the Resurrection of the Dead in the Early Church," *JAAR* 79 (2011): 991–1017.

In distinction from the Fourth Gospel, Luke invites the apostles to see Jesus's hands and feet but makes no remark concerning the wounds. In view of the assertions in Acts that Jesus's body did not experience corruption (see below), one wonders if Luke imagines the body of the resurrected Jesus as unscathed by his execution.

respective treatments of the grilled fish. In John 21, Jesus does not eat the fish but only distributes it along with the bread. That is, the final chapter of John employs the fish as evidence that Jesus provides for his disciples; only in Luke is the grilled fish utilized in a demonstration that Jesus, possessed of a fleshly body, partakes of human nourishment.

## Luke 24 as a Rewriting of Traditions in Which Women Saw the Resurrected Jesus

One of the driving forces in the composition of this final chapter of the Third Gospel is the deflection and/or rewriting of traditions authorizing others, aside from the Twelve, as witnesses to the resurrected Jesus. I suggest that this is the case not just with Luke 24:1–12, as is often argued, but also with the story of Emmaus in Luke 24:13–35. Furthermore, it is arguable that in both scenes we see traces of Luke's tendency to diminish and/or erase traditions highlighting women's roles in the Jesus movement.[14]

*Concerning the women (Luke 24:1-12).* Luke shares with other Gospel traditions (Mark, Matthew, John, Gospel of Peter; cf. Ep. Apos. 9–10) that Mary Magdalene was first to the tomb. In this telling, the Marys (Magdalene and the mother of James) witness only the empty tomb; a risen Jesus does not appear to them in any form. Granted, Luke does not explicitly denigrate the women here. He allows that the women have received a true report from the messengers at the empty tomb and that they have faithfully transmitted that message to the eleven and all the rest. Readers know that the women's witness is reliable and that the disciples are mistaken and unfair in their assessment that the report of the women is an idle tale (Gk: λῆρος, 24:11).[15] But, given the role that appearances of the risen Jesus play

---

[14] In addition to the authors cited below, who have argued that Luke's redactional tendency is to diminish women's roles in the Third Gospel, see also the general treatments of Jane Schaberg and Sharon H. Ringe, "Gospel of Luke," in *Women's Bible Commentary*, ed. Carol A. Newsom, Sharon H. Ringe, and Jacqueline E. Lapsley, rev. and enl. ed. (Louisville: Westminster John Knox, 2012), 493–511; Barbara E. Reid, *Choosing the Better Part? Women in the Gospel of Luke* (Collegeville, MN: Liturgical Press, 1996); Elisabeth Schüssler Fiorenza, "A Feminist Critical Interpretation for Liberation: Martha and Mary; Luke 10:38–42," *Religion and Intellectual Life* 3 (1986): 21–36. Although I find these arguments persuasive, the issue of Luke's redactional tendencies concerning women requires rehearsing, owing to perennial attempts to argue that Luke's depictions of female characters are distinctly positive. See, most recently, the sanguine evaluation of Luke's depiction of women in the otherwise exemplary commentary on the Third Gospel by Robert L. Brawley, "Luke," in *Fortress Commentary on the Bible: The New Testament*, ed. Margaret Aymer, Cynthia Briggs Kittredge, and David A. Sánchez (Minneapolis: Fortress, 2014), 217–63.

[15] Turid Karlsen Seim, "Conflicting Voices, Irony and Reiteration: An Exploration of the Narrational Structure of Luke 24.1–35 and Its Theological Implications," in *Fair Play: Diversity and Conflicts in Early Christianity; Essays in Honour of Heiki Räisänen*, ed. Ismo Dunderberg, Christopher Tuckett, and Kari Syreeni, NovTSup 103 (Leiden: Brill, 2002), 151–64.

in Luke's understanding of apostolic authority and legitimation, it should not be missed that the women are met only by messengers, not by the risen Jesus, and further that they receive no explicit commission to tell the male disciples what they have seen (cf. Mark 16:7). Joseph Plevnik is correct to note that, while Luke allows that a number of events in Jerusalem and its environs have led many to belief in the resurrection, including the women, he makes clear that *apostolic* faith can be traced only to the originary appearance of Jesus to Peter. No mere report to the women concerning the resurrection could provide that validation.[16]

It is possible to argue that Luke does not include a resurrection appearance to the Magdalene (and/or "the women") because he has no access to such a tradition and has nothing to add concerning the women beyond what lies before him in Mark 16:1–8. But given the multiple, overlapping traditions in John 20 and Luke 24, the difference between their stories of Mary Magdalene's agency is striking and is best understood as Luke's redactional choice to diminish her significance.[17] Especially if Luke 24 receives its final form in an early-second-century context, it is difficult to imagine that traditions privileging Mary Magdalene as witness to the resurrection (John 20:18) and primary spokesperson for the resurrected Jesus, as preserved in the Gospel of Mary and other gnostic sources, were unknown to its author.

The argument that Luke knows but omits a resurrection appearance to Mary Magdalene as a means of countering traditions of women's agency in transmitting this central detail of the kerygma receives support from a larger pattern in the Third Gospel: traditions concerning prominent women in the Jesus movement appear to be rewritten in the direction of subordination and silence. Luke alone among the evangelists characterizes Mary in defamatory language as the woman from whom seven demons were drawn out (8:2).[18] If this character defamation is understood as a redactional tendency, it is comparable to Luke's recasting of other instances of the canonical Gospel tradition in which women are made signature witnesses to

---

[16] Joseph Plevnik, "The Eyewitnesses of the Risen Jesus in Luke 24," *CBQ* 49 (1987): 90–103, esp. 93. Compare also Daniel A. Smith's argument that, in Luke 24:12, Peter supplants the women as the "controlling witness" to the empty tomb (*Revisiting the Empty Tomb: The Early History of Easter* [Minneapolis: Fortress, 2010], 112–14).

[17] For one argument that Luke uses John as a source, see Barbara Shellard, "The Relationship of Luke and John: A Fresh Look at an Old Problem," *JTS* 46 (1995): 70–98, http://dx.doi.org/10.1093/jts/46.1.71.

[18] Several scholars have noted Mary Magdalene's prominent role in some early Christian circles and Luke's role in privileging Peter while denigrating the Magdalene's witness. See, among others, Jane Schaberg, *The Resurrection of Mary Magdalene: Legends, Apocrypha, and the Christian Testament* (New York: Continuum, 2004), 76–77; Karen L. King, *The Gospel of Mary of Magdala: Jesus and the First Woman Apostle* (Santa Rosa, CA: Polebridge, 2003), 138–54; Ann Graham Brock, *Mary Magdalene, the First Apostle: The Struggle for Authority*, HTS 51 (Cambridge: Harvard University Press, 2003).

christological proclamation. In Luke, the woman who anointed Jesus on the head prophetically before his passion (Mark 14:3–9, Matt 26:6–13) becomes the weeping sinner anointing Jesus's feet, with her hair inexplicably reduced to a "scrub rag" (Luke 7:36–50).[19] Martha of Bethany, the woman who identifies Jesus as the Christ (John 11:27), an identification that is aligned with the expressed purpose for writing the Fourth Gospel (John 20:31), is reduced in Luke's telling to a busybody needlessly worrying her head with *diakonia* (Luke 10:38–42). The Syro-Phoenician woman, who challenges Jesus and prevails in the Gospels of Mark (7:24–30) and Matthew (15:21–28) in what Marianne Sawicki persuasively—if provocatively— names her "table-crashing agenda of Christian Bitch-Cynicism," has no place in Luke's narrative.[20] In short, even if the argument that Luke knows but omits the tradition of an appearance to Mary Magdalene must remain an argument from silence, the plausibility of the argument lies in its resonance with this larger Lukan pattern.

*The Emmaus encounter: Luke 24:13–35.* Luke's account of the encounter between Jesus and Cleopas and his companion on the road to Emmaus carefully circumscribes the story so that it falls into a category of encounters different from those reserved for the eleven. Here Jesus does not "appear" to Cleopas and his companion. Rather, Luke 24:16 notes, in an uncharacteristic nod to supernatural intervention, that "their eyes were kept from recognizing him [οἱ δὲ ὀφθαλμοὶ αὐτῶν ἐκρατοῦντο τοῦ μὴ ἐπιγνῶναι αὐτόν]" in their initial encounter. Their ultimate recognition of Jesus is relayed not as an "appearance" of Jesus but rather as the result of their participation in a liturgical (eucharistic?) meal, at the point when the bread is broken. That is, Cleopas and his companion "see" Jesus only in the way that Luke would have all subsequent and ordinary believers see Jesus—in the breaking of the bread, here distributed by Jesus and subsequently by his foreordained apostles (cf. Acts 2:42).[21]

---

[19] Even if Luke's story of the woman who was a sinner comes to him from oral tradition concerning the woman who anointed Jesus, as Marianne Sawicki suggests, the fact that the Third Gospel adheres closely to the Markan account of the plot to kill Jesus (Luke 22:1–2; cf. Mark 14:1–2) and the betrayal of Jesus (Luke 22:3–6; cf. Mark 14:10–11) suggests that this author also possessed Mark's written version of the episode between the plot and the betrayal (Mark 14:3–9) but declined to include it. On the development of the oral tradition concerning the anointing, see Marianne Sawicki, *Seeing the Lord: Resurrection and Early Christian Practices* (Minneapolis: Augsburg Fortress, 1994), 150–67.

[20] Sawicki, *Seeing the Lord*, 167.

[21] On the breaking of bread as evoking a eucharistic context, see Hans Dieter Betz, "The Origin and Nature of Christian Faith according to the Emmaus Legend (Luke xxiv 13–32)," *Int* 23 (1969): 32–46, http://dx.doi.org/10.1177/002096436902300103. For one argument against this view, see Bernard P. Robinson, "The Place of the Emmaus Story in Luke-Acts," *NTS* 30 (1984): 481–97, esp. 487–94. The concern to relay the story of the Emmaus encounter as something other than an "appearance" of Jesus is not shared by the author of the Markan epitome (Mark 16:12:

That for Luke this encounter on the Emmaus road is not to be taken as an appearance proper is supported by the assertion of Petrine primacy following immediately on the arrival of the two in Jerusalem. While the narrative logic of the Emmaus story could lead, arguably, to the dramatic announcement "The Lord has risen," and appeared to Cleopas and [named companion of Cleopas]!," we find instead the assertion of an event that has not been narrated: "the Lord has risen and appeared to Peter!" (24:34).

Sharon H. Ringe has proposed that behind Luke's story of a named and unnamed traveler on the Emmaus road lies the tradition of an appearance to Cleopas and a female companion. Cleopas is a Greek name, while Clopas, the name of the spouse of Mary in John 19:25, appears to be a Semitic form. Ringe suggests that the variation between these two forms of the name resonates with the name shifts that immigrants experience as they move across different language contexts. Thus, John and Luke may be referring to the same missionary couple, whom John knows as Clopas and Mary.[22] If Luke has omitted the name of a female companion from a source while inserting the assertion of Petrine primacy as the climax of the Emmaus story, such redaction conforms to the narrative strategy underscored above for Luke 24:1–12. In this way, women's agency is diminished, and Peter becomes the controlling witness to the empty tomb. Regardless of whether Luke works from a source that names a female companion of Cleopas, it is clear here that the climax of the pericope is the appearance to Peter, not the appearance to the two on the Emmaus road.

*The appearance to the eleven and their companions: Luke 24:36–53.* In the final segment of chapter 24, Luke states that the resurrected Jesus appears not just to the eleven to offer proofs of his fleshliness and to commission them as witnesses. Jesus stands before the eleven and also before "those who were with them" (καὶ τοὺς σὺν αὐτοῖς, 24:33).[23] The first chapter of Acts demonstrates why the narrative must allow for more than eleven as potential resurrection witnesses in this first telling of the story, a narrative detail to which we turn below.

---

μετὰ δὲ ταῦτα δυσὶν ἐξ αὐτῶν περιπατοῦσιν ἐφανερώθη ἐν ἑτέρᾳ μορφῇ πορευομένοις εἰς ἀργόν, "After this, he appeared in another form to two of them, as they were walking into the country" [NRSV].

[22] Sharon H. Ringe, *Luke*, WeBC (Louisville: Westminster John Knox, 1995), 286–67. For bibliography on the question, see Gillman, "Emmaus Story," 184 n. 65.

[23] Joseph Plevnik demonstrates that the two passages in Luke 24 that allow for the presence of other disciples besides the eleven (24:9 and 24:33) are Lukan redaction ("'The Eleven and Those with Them' according to Luke," *CBQ* 40 [1978]: 205–11).

## II. Eating as a Cipher for Fleshly Resurrection: Acts 1:4 and Acts 10:40b–41

Two references in Acts to Jesus's fleshly resurrection are indirect, employing the cipher of Jesus eating to invoke the fleshly nature of the resurrection in the context of assertions pertaining to the privilege of the twelve apostles. In Acts 1:4, the narrator notes that, during the forty days in which Jesus appeared on the earth after the resurrection, he "took meals with them," as indicated by the unusual verb συναλίζω (literally, "to take salt with").[24] As in Acts 1:4, so in Peter's speech before Cornelius in 10:41, fleshly resurrection is invoked through reference to meals. When Peter here asserts that the appointment of the twelve apostles as witnesses was foreordained, he sets those witnesses apart as those "who ate and drank with him after he rose from the dead."

*The restoration of the Twelve: Acts 1:1–26.* As in Luke 24, while the eleven apostles are here given special prominence as witnesses to the resurrection, the narrative does not insist that *only* the apostles witnessed Jesus's resurrection. We see why at the end of the chapter, when the requirements for those qualified to take the place of Judas are laid out. The replacement must come from among those who accompanied Jesus until the day he was taken up (1:21). While Luke 24 and Acts 1 privilege the eleven as witnesses to the resurrection, these texts cannot foreclose the appearances to the eleven alone because a twelfth is needed. Once Matthias is elected and the Twelve are reconstituted (1:26), there are no further references to the apostles explicitly in the company of associates (cf. Luke 24:9, 33).[25]

Further, a gender requirement is made explicit (Acts 2:21–22). Perhaps this would go without saying, as it is certainly the case that all references to "the Twelve" in the Synoptic Gospels pertain to a group of men. Yet it is said here—in a portion of Acts that is notable for its stark focus on the masculinity of those involved in the Jerusalem movement—explicitly for the first time that apostles must be men (ἄνδρες).[26] That the twelve male apostles are ultimately granted a singular position as witnesses is made clear in Peter's speech before Cornelius in Acts 10.

*The apostolic witnesses: Acts 10:34–43.* Beginning with 10:40, in his speech before the baptism of Cornelius, Peter offers an interpretation of the significance of the resurrection and subsequent events. Like Acts 1:4, Acts 10:34–43 invokes

---

[24] On this translation, see Richard I. Pervo, *Acts: A Commentary*, Hermeneia (Minneapolis: Fortress, 2009), 38.

[25] Plevnik, "Eleven and Those with Them," 206.

[26] Mary Rose D'Angelo, "The ANHP Question in Luke-Acts: Imperial Masculinity and the Deployment of Women in the Early Second Century," in *A Feminist Companion to Luke*, ed. Amy-Jill Levine, with Mariane Blickenstaff, FCNTECW (London: Sheffield Academic, 2002), 44–69.

fleshly resurrection appearances through the cipher of meals but emphasizes more clearly than the previous passage that these appearances were reserved for the twelve apostles alone. Peter asserts that, after God raised him on the third day:

> He made him manifest *not to all the people*, but to those witnesses who were foreordained by God, to us, we who ate together and drank together with him after he rose from the dead. (10:40b–41)
>
> καὶ ἔδωκεν αὐτὸν ἐμφανῆ γενέσθαι, οὐ παντὶ τῷ λαῷ, ἀλλὰ μάρτυσιν τοῖς προκεχειροτονημένοις ὑπὸ τοῦ θεοῦ, ἡμῖν, οἵτινες συνεφάγομεν καὶ συνεπίομεν αὐτῷ μετὰ τὸ ἀναστῆναι αὐτὸν ἐκ νεκρῶν.

There may have been associates with the eleven when Jesus first appeared in flesh and bones to commission them as witnesses, as Luke 24:33 and 24:48 make explicit, and while he ate and drank with the apostles during the forty days, as Acts 1:1–4 suggests. But the reference to the witnesses in Peter's speech is not meant to conjure up just any group of anonymous persons sanctioned to preach the coming of the judge of the living and the dead. Peter emphasizes the exclusivity of apostolic privilege by juxtaposing *the people* to whom God did not make Jesus manifest and *the witnesses* to whom he did.[27]

The assertions pertaining to early Christian authority and proclamation condensed into this succinct formula in 10:40–43 are weighty. The Twelve function as witnesses who have been foreordained (προκεχειροτονημένοις). They are authorized to preach a message to which all the prophets testify (10:43). Their status comes from having eaten and drunk with the resurrected Jesus in the flesh. The affirmation that Jesus is *judge of the living and the dead* (κριτὴς ζώντων καὶ νεκρῶν) is not one that Acts shares with the Gospels or with the Pauline tradition. It is, rather, the (pre-)creedal phrase that this text shares with many other late-first- and early-second-century writings, including 1 Peter, 2 Timothy, 2 Clement, Polycarp, and Barnabas.[28] Finally the force of the negative emphasis—*he did not appear to all the people* (ἐμφανῆ ... οὐ παντὶ τῷ λαῷ)—suggests a concern to delegitimize claims that any outside of the Twelve had comparable appearances.

This language of exclusivity might appear surprisingly restrictive for anyone who knows alternate traditions of resurrection appearances, whether from the tradition of resurrection witnesses Paul lays out in 1 Cor 15:5–8 or from traditions concerning Mary Magdalene and the women. It might also puzzle careful readers of the previous narratives of resurrection encounters in Luke or Acts, given the story of Cleopas and his companion and the larger group of companions associated

---

[27] As the narrative proceeds, the term *witness* (μάρτυς) will be slipped into authorizing speeches, granting the status to Stephen (22:20) and to Paul (22:15, 26:16). On Paul's status as witness, see p. 179 below.

[28] Compare 2 Tim 4:1: κρίνειν ζῶντας καὶ νεκρούς; 1 Pet 4:5: κρῖναι ζῶντας καὶ νεκρούς; Barn. 7:2: ὢν κύριος καὶ μέλλων κρίνειν ζῶντας καὶ νεκρούς; 2 Clem. 1:1: περὶ κριτοῦ ζώντων καὶ νεκρῶν; Polycarp, *Phil.* 2:1: ὃς ἔρχεται κριτὴς ζώντων καὶ νεκρῶν.

with the eleven in Luke 24 and Acts 1. What Luke has allowed in previous narrative details, he disallows in Peter's direct assertion.

The significance of Peter's assertion of apostolic authority is further illuminated by the imperial setting of the speech. Peter addresses a Roman centurion in Caesarea, a city renowned for its centrally located Temple of Roma and Augustus.[29] C. Kavin Rowe has suggested that Peter's affirmation of the universal lordship of Jesus Christ in 10:36 ("this one is Lord of all") sets up a contrast whereby the "overwhelming and intrusive power" of the Caesars is answered by a "reversal of the common understanding of power" in a "lordship of humility and service."[30] Justin R. Howell, supplementing Rowe's arguments, suggests that 10:36 serves to critique not just the power of the emperor but also the brokerage of centurions such as Cornelius who enact that emperor's power. Howell concludes that the authority of centurions as benefactors is "diametrically opposed to Luke's concept of κοινωνία."[31] These arguments focus rather narrowly on the slogan of 10:36 and thus fall short of answering to the power dynamics embedded in the contest of authority highlighted here with respect to Peter and the Twelve. Howell's arguments concerning the brokering role of centurions in the empire lead more obviously not to the conclusion that Luke contrasts this imperial leadership hierarchy with a form of egalitarianism and humility but that the Twelve are cast here in an analogously hierarchical leadership role. As the centurion Cornelius stands as broker between the emperor and Roman imperial subjects, so the Twelve are singled out as the "witnesses" mediating between Christ and the churches.

### III. "His Flesh Did Not Experience Corruption": Acts 2:31b and 13:37

Two additional references to Jesus's fleshly resurrection occur in missionary speeches of Peter and Paul and emphasize that the body of the resurrected Jesus (in Peter's speech, specifically the *flesh*/σάρξ) did not decay. In Acts 2:31b, Peter's

---

[29] On the significance of Cornelius's status, see Wendy J. Cotter, "Cornelius, the Roman Army and Religion," in *Religious Rivalries and the Struggle for Success in Caesarea Maritima*, ed. Terence L. Donaldson, ESCJ 8 (Waterloo, ON: Wilfrid Laurier University Press, 2000), 279–301, here 282–83. On the significance of the setting in Caesarea, consider Peter Richardson's suggestion that Herod may have conceived of Caesarea as a "one-cult city," analogous to Jerusalem ("Archeological Evidence for Religion and Urbanism in Caesarea Maritima," in Donaldson, *Religious Rivalries*, 11–34, here 30).

[30] C. Kavin Rowe, "Luke-Acts and the Imperial Cult: A Way through the Conundrum?," *JSNT* 27 (2005): 279–300; see also Rowe, *World Upside Down: Reading Acts in the Graeco-Roman Age* (Oxford: Oxford University Press, 2009), 103–16.

[31] Justin R. Howell, "The Imperial Authority and Benefaction of Centurions and Acts 10.24–43: A Response to C. Kavin Rowe," *JSNT* 31 (2008): 25–51, here 45.

inaugural speech at Pentecost includes Ps 16:9–11 among its proofs from Scripture concerning the resurrection. The constellation of motifs in Ps 15:9–11 LXX, "therefore my *flesh* shall rest in hope, because he will not *leave my soul in Hades, nor will your Holy One experience corruption* [ἔτι δὲ καὶ ἡ σάρξ μου κατασκηνώσει ἐπ' ἐλπίδι· Ὅτι οὐκ ἐγκαταλείψεις τὴν ψυχήν μου εἰς ᾅδην, οὐδὲ δώσεις τὸν ὅσιόν σου ἰδεῖν διαφθοράν]" is realigned so that David, remarkably, is made to foretell a resurrection of flesh that has escaped the process of decay: "he was not abandoned to Hades, *nor did his flesh experience corruption* [οὔτε ἡ σάρξ αὐτοῦ εἶδεν διαφθοράν]."

A second example is Acts 13:37. In keeping with Acts' concern that Peter and Paul share identical teaching, the confession of fleshly resurrection by Peter in Acts 2 is echoed by Paul in his inaugural missionary speech, where he also exegetes Ps 16:10 as proof of the resurrection of the flesh, asserting that "the one raised up by God experienced no corruption [ὃν δὲ ὁ θεὸς ἤγειρεν, οὐκ εἶδεν διαφθοράν]" (13:37).

Few biblical commentators have ventured an explanation for these assertions of incorruptibility. Bruce J. Malina and John J. Pilch suggest as an "Israelite understanding of death" that the rotting of the flesh of a corpse served an expiatory function. From this they conclude that this speech of Peter is an assertion that Jesus had no guilt in his flesh needing expiation.[32] But, although the assumption circulates widely in secondary literature that rotting flesh was understood by Pharisees in particular, and by Jews of this period in general, to be expiatory, no literary sources from the first or second century of the Common Era support such a claim.[33]

A better explanation for this striking insistence that Jesus's flesh did not decay lies in its connection to reminders that the Twelve are the authoritative witnesses to this incorruptibility. Peter's Pentecostal declaration that Jesus's flesh did not see corruption (2:31) is followed immediately by the claim: "This Jesus God raised up and of that we [the Twelve] are all witnesses" (2:32). Similarly, in Paul's first missionary speech, the affirmation that the one raised experienced no corruption (13:37) is prefaced by the reminder that, after he was raised, Jesus appeared for many days to "those who came up with him from Galilee to Jerusalem, who are now his witnesses to the people" (13:31). In short, both speeches make the link between flesh, authority, and continuity. As Jesus's bodily substances are impervious to change, so are the status and legitimacy of the witnesses to that unchanged body.

---

[32] Malina and Pilch, *Social Science Commentary,* 225–26. So also Ben Witherington III, *The Acts of the Apostles: A Socio-rhetorical Commentary* (Grand Rapids: Eerdmans, 1998), 145.

[33] Steven Fine, "A Note on Ossuary Burial and the Resurrection of the Dead in First-Century Jerusalem," *JJS* 51 (2000): 69–76, http://dx.doi.org/10.18647/2241/JJS-2000.

## IV. The Limits of Luke's Interest in Fleshly Resurrection

Finally, in support of the argument that Luke's primary rhetorical aim in invoking the fleshly resurrection of Jesus is the establishment of the exclusive authority of the Twelve, it may be noted that Luke's concern with the flesh does not extend to the general resurrection or to Jesus himself once he has ascended to the heavens (or, for that matter, to the nature of Jesus's appearance on the Emmaus road). None of the references to general resurrection in Acts makes mention of flesh (see 17:32, 23:6, 24:14–15, 26:23). Although some Christians writing after Luke will read the Lukan ascension narrative as proof that Jesus ascended fleshly into the heavens,[34] Luke does not say this explicitly. Though he offers no narrative details on how Jesus's body is transformed as it moves from earth to heaven—and the substance of that heavenly body is never a point of emphasis or contention—references in Acts to Jesus communicating from the heavenly sphere after the ascension assume that Jesus bears a body appropriate to this sphere.[35]

Having considered the distinctive nature of the Lukan concern for fleshly resurrection and how this compares with traditions known from other Gospels, I turn now to further reflection on Luke's scriptural practices. First, I consider how Luke rewrites Pauline teaching. Then I position Luke vis-à-vis two understandings of Jesus's resurrection that are regarded as antithetical to Luke's and anachronistically categorized as the heresy to his orthodoxy.

---

[34] E.g., Pseudo-Justin, *Res.* 9.8; Irenaeus, *Haer.* 1.10.1–2.

[35] Seim, "Resurrected Body in Luke-Acts." In support of the argument that Luke is not imagining Jesus to have taken a place in the heavens *in the flesh*, consider also apotheosis narratives of kings, emperors, and other heroes in the Greco-Roman world that tell of mortal flesh melting away as a body is transformed from the earthly to the heavenly sphere. See, e.g., Ovid, *Metam.* 15.824–828; compare also Philo's description of Moses's translation, *Mos.* 2.288; and Shelly Matthews, "Elijah, Ezekiel and Romulus: Luke's Flesh and Bones (Luke 24:39) in Light of Ancient Narratives of Ascent, Resurrection and Apotheosis," in *On Prophets, Warriors, and Kings: Former Prophets through the Eyes of Their Interpreters*, ed. George J. Brooke and Ariel Feldman, BZAW 470 (Berlin: de Gruyter, 2016), 161–82.

If we imagine Luke as staging a resurrection in two steps—first in flesh and then in a heavenly body—Luke's ideas of afterlife may be considered roughly analogous to those in 4 Ezra 7:26–115, and 2 Bar. 50–51. See Outi Lehtipuu, "Biblical Body Language: The Spiritual and the Bodily Resurrection," in *Anthropology in the New Testament and Its Ancient Context: Papers from the EABS Meeting in Piliscaba/Budapest*, ed. Michael Labahn and Outi Lehtipuu (Leuven: Peeters, 2010), 151–68, esp. 158; Lehtipuu, *Debates over the Resurrection*, 46. Yet it must be noted that Luke's Emmaus story calls into question such a neatly drawn, two-step resurrection schema, as there is no emphasis in that pericope on Jesus's fleshliness.

## V. Fleshly Resurrection, Authority, and the Pauline Epistles

Lukan assertions pertaining to resurrection depart from the Pauline Epistles in two significant ways, first, with respect to the nature of resurrection, and, second, with respect to Paul's status as apostle owing to his vision of the resurrected Lord.

First, the "flesh and bones" of Luke 24:39b stand in stark contrast to Paul's proclamation that "flesh and blood cannot inherit." If it is granted that Luke knows 1 Corinthians, this phrase may be explained as Luke's rereading of 1 Cor 15:50.[36] Understood in this way, the Lukan text reflects the concern of many in the second century who are intrigued by this particular Pauline verse, a verse that Irenaeus bemoans as adduced by all the heretics in support of their folly (*Haer.* 3.9.1–2). While Irenaeus's solution is to qualify Paul's words, arguing that flesh and blood *alone* cannot inherit unless they are absorbed by the spirit, Luke's solution involves a more direct rewrite. Daniel A. Smith is correct to observe that, whereas Paul teaches "continuity of corporeality, but discontinuity of essences," Luke asserts an absolute continuity of substances in the pre- and postresurrection Jesus.[37]

Further, it may be noted that Luke diverges from Paul not only concerning substances but also in terms of process. The resurrection teaching in 1 Cor 15:35–54 offers a veritable blur of verbs for motion and transformation. The body sown as one thing is raised as another (vv. 42–44); all shall be changed (v. 52). Much of that change is described through employment of the root φθαρ-, signifying decay and perishability. The corruptible (φθορά) does not inherit incorruptibility (ἀφθαρσίαν, v. 50); the dead will be raised incorruptible (ἄφθαρτοι, v. 52); the corruptible nature (τὸ φθαρτόν) will put on the incorruptible (ἀφθαρσίαν, v. 53). This understanding of resurrection as transformation employing the root φθαρ- is present also in 2 Cor 4:10–11, 16, where Paul speaks of his own flesh as in the process of decay (ὁ ἔξω ἡμῶν ἄνθρωπος διαφθείρεται, v. 16). Luke employs that same root, but in order to come to an opposite conclusion with respect to Jesus: his flesh experienced no corruption (οὐκ εἶδεν διαφθοράν, Acts 13:37).

With this assertion of Jesus's incorruptibility, Luke also stands apart from many subsequent Christian authors who argue that general resurrection will involve *regeneration* of human flesh rather than continuity of bodily substance. For instance, both Pseudo-Justin and Athenagoras concede that flesh rots in death, but they argue that, because the *stoicheia* from which flesh is composed are indestructible, they make possible a reconstitution of flesh on the last day.[38] Luke may align

---

[36] Smith, "Seeing a Pneuma(tic Body)," 765–72.
[37] Ibid., 768.
[38] Pseudo-Justin, *Res.* 5, 6.3–5, 8; Athenagoras, *Res.* 2.5. See Taylor Petrey, *Resurrecting Parts: Early Christians on Desire, Reproduction, and Sexual Difference*, Routledge Studies in the Early Christian World (London: Routledge, 2016).

against Paul and with other early Christian authors in landing on flesh as the substance of the resurrection, but Pseudo-Justin and Athenagoras lie closer to Paul than to Luke in conceptualizing resurrection as a process of transformation and movement.

Second, as many have noted, in foreclosing apostolic witness to the Twelve, Luke deprives Paul of his forcefully held convictions pertaining to his own apostolic identity evident in the letters.[39] The criteria established in Acts 1:21–22 for replacement of the twelfth apostle hold no weight in Paul's own epistles, where he asserts his apostolic authority in direct defiance of those valuing flesh over spirit, grounding it in a revelation of the resurrected Christ (Gal 1:1–12, 1 Cor 9:1).[40] Perhaps no passage in Acts demonstrates the departure from the epistles' understanding of resurrection and authority more than 13:31, where Paul himself *in direct speech* is made to grant special status to the witnesses as those to whom Jesus appeared after his resurrection, while remaining silent about his own authorization ("and for many days, he appeared to those who came up with him from Galilee to Jerusalem, who are now his witnesses to the people"). The speech reflects the sequence of events in Acts 1, in which Paul plays no part. By limiting apostolic authority to those to whom the resurrected Jesus appeared in the flesh, and having Paul accede to that limitation, Acts seems to cut the ground out from under Pauline assertions of apostolic privilege.[41]

## *Fleshly Resurrection and the Question of Impassivity*

Luke's assertion of fleshly resurrection does not appear to be part of a larger quarrel with those who believed that Jesus did not truly suffer in his crucifixion, a position often categorized as "docetic." This sets Luke apart from Ignatius, who

---

[39] See, e.g., Rom 1:1, 11:13, 1 Cor 1:1, 4:9, 9:1, 15:9, 2 Cor 1:1, 11:15, Gal 1:1. For discussions of how Acts treats Paul's apostleship, see Schmithals, *Office of Apostle*, 247–50; Joseph B. Tyson, "Acts and the Apostles: Issues of Leadership in the Second Century," in *Engaging Early Christian History: Reading Acts in the Second Century*, ed. Rubén R. Dupertuis and Todd Penner, BWo (Durham: Acumen, 2013), 45–58.

[40] For further insight into the difference between Galatians and Acts with regard to Paul, the Spirit, and authority, see Christopher Mount, "Religious Experience, the Religion of Paul, and Women in Pauline Churches," in *Women and Gender in Ancient Religions: Interdisciplinary Approaches*, ed. Stephen P. Ahearne-Kroll, Paul A. Holloway, and James A. Kelhoffer, WUNT 263 (Tübingen: Mohr Siebeck, 2010), 323–47.

[41] Limits of space prevent analysis here of how Paul's authority is recouped through direct speeches of Jesus in Acts 22:15 and 26:16–18. Especially through the announcement that Jesus has appeared to Paul (ὤφθην σοι) and appointed him as servant and witness (προχειρίσασθαί σε ὑπηρέτην καὶ μάρτυρα), Paul is elevated, if not to one of the Twelve then to one with the same status. See Christoph Burchard, *Der dreizehnte Zeuge: Traditions- und kompositionsgeschichtliche Untersuchungen zu Lukas' Darstellung der Frühzeit des Paulus*, FRLANT 103 (Göttingen: Vandenhoeck & Ruprecht, 1970), 136, http://dx.doi.org/10.13109/9783666532429.

preserves a saying similar to Luke 24:39 concerning the resurrected Jesus's eating as proof of his fleshliness as but one plank in a larger argument that Jesus truly suffered (ἀληθῶς ἔπαθεν).[42] Indeed, on the question of whether Jesus experienced torment either in Gethsemane or on Golgotha, Luke's passion narrative can be read as an argument for an answer in the negative, as the later interpolator who felt the need to add the pericope of Jesus sweating drops of blood in Gethsemane surely sensed.[43] The Lukan Jesus does employ the verb πάσχω both in predicting his fate (9:22, 17:25, 22:15) and in reflecting on that suffering as a component of prophecy fulfillment (24:26, 46; cf. Acts 1:3, 3:18, 17:3).[44] Yet, as is well known, narratives of Jesus's comportment both on the way to Golgotha and on the cross itself suggests that his "suffering" does not include human experiences of physical agony or emotional distress.[45] The impassiveness of the Lukan Jesus is further underscored by the assertion of incorruptibility in Acts 2:31 and 13:37. Luke's Jesus may bear a body of flesh, even after the resurrection, but this flesh is not the ordinary flesh of humankind, which agonizes when threatened, writhes when tortured, and decays in death. The emphasis here is on flesh that is thoroughly masculine, perhaps even divine.[46]

## Fleshly Resurrection and Marcionite Polemic

The argument that Acts was written, and the Third Gospel put into final form, in order to refute the teachings of Marcion is currently experiencing a revival among biblical scholars.[47] Part of this revival involves proposals that both the

---

[42] See Ignatius, *Smyrn.* 1–3; *Trall.* 9–10; and the commentary of William R. Schoedel, *Ignatius of Antioch: A Commentary on the Letters of Ignatius of Antioch*, Hermeneia (Philadelphia: Fortress, 1985), 220–29. For a useful discussion of scholars who see Luke 24:36–43 as "antidocetic" and the problem of defining docetism, see Smith, "Seeing a Pneuma(tic) Body," 759–61.

[43] For persuasive arguments that Luke 22:43–44 is a secondary insertion motivated by concern that Jesus be depicted as suffering anguish in Gethsemane, see Bart D. Ehrman, *The Orthodox Corruption of Scripture: The Effect of Early Christological Controversies on the Text of the New Testament*, rev. and enl. ed. (Oxford: Oxford University Press, 2011), 220–27.

[44] As Joel B. Green notes, the phrase "to suffer" in Luke is used to evoke the totality of the passion (*The Gospel of Luke*, NICNT [Grand Rapids: Eerdmans, 1997], 856).

[45] Jerome H. Neyrey, "The Absence of Jesus' Emotions: The Lucan Redaction of Lk 22:39–46," *Bib* 61 (1980): 153–71; John S. Kloppenborg, "Exitus clari viri: The Death of Jesus in Luke," *TJT* 8 (1992): 106–20.

[46] On the idea of immortal flesh in Greek thought, see Dag Øistein Endsjø, *Greek Resurrection Beliefs and the Success of Christianity* (New York: Palgrave Macmillan, 2009), 47–104, http://dx.doi.org/10.1057/9780230622562.

[47] Joseph B. Tyson, *Marcion and Luke-Acts: A Defining Struggle* (Columbia: University of South Carolina Press, 2006); Tyson, "Acts and the Apostles," 45–58; Matthias Klinghardt, "Markion vs. Lukas: Plädoyer für die Wiederaufnahme eines alten Falles," *NTS* 52 (2006): 484–513, http://dx.doi.org/10.1017/S0028688506000270; Klinghardt, "The Marcionite Gospel and the Synoptic Problem: A New Suggestion," *NovT* 50 (2008): 1–27; Klinghardt, *Das älteste Evangelium und die Entstehung der kanonischen Evangelien*, 2 vols., TANZ 60 (Tübingen: Francke, 2015). See also

emphasis on flesh in the final form of Luke 24 and the subordination of Paul to the Jerusalem apostles in Acts can be attributed to an anti-Marcionite redactional agenda.[48]

A key difficulty in understanding the final chapter of the canonical Gospel as stemming from anti-Marcionite concerns (or, for that matter, in understanding Marcion's *Evangelion* 24 as a *direct* refutation of Luke 24) is that considerable overlap exists between the resurrection narratives of Marcion and canonical Luke, insofar as the former can be reconstructed. Granted, the *Evangelion* at 24.39 seems to have included neither an invitation to touch nor the reference to flesh. Yet even in the *Evangelion*, the resurrected Jesus asserts that he retains his bones, a puzzling acknowledgment of solidity if the two communities are imagined to be dueling over the question of spiritual versus fleshly resurrection.[49] Further, the insistence in canonical Luke that the resurrected Jesus eats cannot be understood as a rhetorical counter to Marcion's understanding of the resurrection, since Marcion's Jesus eats as well.[50]

When themes associated with fleshly resurrection in Luke 24 are taken together with the elaboration of those themes in Acts, arguments for an anti-Marcionite backdrop become even less compelling. Marcion's view of the resurrected body as a spiritual body from which the fleshly body is sloughed off might stand in some tension with the affirmation of Luke 24:39,[51] but insofar as Acts asserts the fleshliness of Jesus *only* in his earthly appearances to the Twelve, and not after his ascension, Lukan and Marcionite views ultimately align.

At first glance, subordinating Paul to the Twelve in Acts may appear anti-Marcionite. But a broader consideration of early Christian sources leads to the recognition that Lukan materials linking apostolic authority to fleshly resurrection

---

Markus Vinzent, "Der Schluß des Lukasevangelium bei Marcion," in *Marcion und seine kirchengeschichtliche Wirkung / Marcion and His Impact on Church History: Vorträge der Internationalen Fachkonferenz zu Marcion, gehalten vom 15.–18. August 2001 in Mainz,* ed. Gerhard May and Katharina Greschat, TUGAL 150 (Berlin: de Gruyter, 2002), 79–94, http://dx.doi.org/10.1515/9783110905595.79; Vinzent, *Christ's Resurrection in Early Christianity and the Making of the New Testament* (Burlington, VT: Ashgate, 2011). See also two important recent reconstructions of Marcion's Gospel: Jason BeDuhn, *The First New Testament: Marcion's Scriptural Canon* (Salem, OR: Polebridge, 2013); and Dieter T. Roth, *The Text of Marcion's Gospel*, NTTSD 49 (Leiden: Brill, 2015), along with my contribution to the discussion of the relationship of Marcion's Gospel to canonical Luke, Matthews, "Does Dating Luke-Acts into the Second Century Affect the Q Hypothesis?"

[48] Tyson, *Marcion and Luke-Acts*, 108–9; Tyson, "Acts and the Apostles"; cf. Schmithals, *Office of Apostle*, 272–78; Klinghardt, *Das älteste Evangelium*, 1:166–71.

[49] For BeDuhn's reconstruction of *Evangelion* 24.37–39, see *First New Testament*, 127.

[50] According to Tertullian, Marcion holds that, while Jesus was not of the flesh, he, like the angels in Genesis, assumed a state of "putative flesh" and ate as they did (*Marc.* 3.9). BeDuhn, citing Eznik, *De Deo* 407, includes the eating of broiled fish in his reconstruction of the *Evangelion* 24.41–43 (*First New Testament*, 127.)

[51] As argued by Vinzent, "Der Schluß des Lukasevangeliums," 86.

appearances not only exclude *Paul* from the list of those receiving legitimating appearances but also exclude James, the five hundred, and "all of the apostles" (1 Cor 15:5–8); Mary and the women (Luke 24:1–11; Matt. 28:1, 9; Mark 16:1; John 20:11–18; cf. Gospel of Mary, Pistis Sophia); and Cleopas and his companion (Luke 24:13–35). Especially in the assertion that the risen Christ was not made to appear to all the people but only to the foreordained witnesses, these Lukan materials seem to be aimed beyond Marcion, who granted apostolic privilege to Paul alone. They challenge, rather, an idea expressed across a wide range of materials, including materials eventually canonized, that authority to speak on behalf of the resurrected Christ is granted to the visionary (cf. 1 Cor 9:1, John 20:14–17, Rev 1:10–19).[52]

Finally, the privileging of Peter among the apostles as the first to whom the fleshly Jesus appeared and as spokesman in three of the four passages in Acts in which fleshly resurrection is invoked does not point in any obvious way to a Marcionite backdrop. This feature, taken together with the diminishing of Mary Magdalene's agency in Luke, calls to mind a number of extracanonical texts in which quarrels are staged between Peter and Mary Magdalene concerning her vision and speech. That traditions pertaining to Mary and the women, and not Marcion, fuel Peter's assertion that Jesus was *not* made manifest *to all the people* is further suggested by redactional tendencies noted in the discussion of Luke 24:1–12 above.

## VI. Conclusion

The assertion in Luke 24 that Jesus stands before his inner circle in flesh and bone and eats fish is followed in Acts by four additional instances in which fleshly resurrection is invoked: twice through the cipher of meals that the apostles ate with Jesus after his resurrection (1:4 and 10:41) and twice in speeches in which midrashic arguments are employed as proof that the body of Jesus did not know corruption (2:31b, 13:3). References to eating with the resurrected Jesus pertain to apostolic privilege, with the final such reference underscoring the exclusive nature of that privilege. Both the speeches of Peter and those of Paul concerning incorruptibility include reminders that the Twelve, and the Twelve alone, were witnesses to the resurrection. Luke makes no explicit argument that Jesus appeared in the flesh on the Emmaus road or that he bore his flesh into the heavens. Luke makes no argument for the regeneration of the flesh at the general resurrection. His concern to

---

[52] For arguments that John 20:14–17 parallels Rev 1:10–19 in form and the Pauline appearance traditions of 1 Corinthians in function, see Mary Rose D'Angelo, "'I Have Seen the Lord': Mary Magdalen as Visionary, Early Christian Prophecy, and the Context of John 20:14–18," in *Mariam, the Magdalen, and the Mother*, ed. Deirdre Good (Bloomington: Indiana University Press, 2005), 95–122.

underscore the fleshly nature of the resurrection pertains only to the appearances Jesus makes to his apostles while he is on earth.

On the question of the exclusive link between apostolic authority and witness to a fleshly, resurrected Jesus, these materials align with what will become orthodox Christian justification for an exclusively male leadership structure. This argument alone, however, does not allow for the identification of Luke as the forerunner, in any unqualified way, of Christian orthodoxy. Luke's resurrection teaching stands at odds with the teaching of Paul and seems to include an intentional rewrite of Pauline teaching. Luke's peculiar understanding of the resurrected Jesus's *incorruptible flesh* aligns more closely with the impassive Christology often associated with "docetism" than with "antidocetic" polemic. Details of Luke's resurrection narrative, including Luke's assertions pertaining to Jesus's resurrected body, do not differ dramatically from those found in Marcion's *Evangelion*. Luke is neither orthodox nor "proto-orthodox."[53] It is important to recognize the anachronism inherent in assigning this author to one side of a binary that, in his own time, had not yet come into existence.

[53] See King, "Which Early Christianity?," 70.

# NEW *from* OXFORD

**The Hebrew Bible As Literature**
Tod Linafelt | **New!**
9780195300079 | $11.95

**Calvinism**
Jon Balserak | **New!**
9780198753711 | $11.95

**The Bible**
John Riches
9780192853431 | $11.95

**The New Testament as Literature**
Kyle Keefer
9780195300208 | $11.95

**Zionism**
Michael Stanislawski | **New!**
9780199766048 | $11.95

**Christianity**
Linda Woodhead
9780199687749 | $11.95

## GROW YOUR KNOWLEDGE

Combining authority with wit, accessibility, and style, **Very Short Introductions** offer an introduction to some of life's most interesting topics. Written by experts for a broad audience, they demonstrate the finest contemporary thinking about central problems and issues in hundreds of key topics.

To order or for more information, visit our website at **www.oup.com/vsi**

# From Eloquence to Evading Responsibility: The Rhetorical Functions of Quotations in Paul's Argumentation

KATJA KUJANPÄÄ
katja.kujanpaa@helsinki.fi
University of Helsinki, 00100 Helsinki, Finland

The purpose of this article is to highlight the variety of functions that quotations perform in Paul's argumentation in light of two modern theories on quoting. First, psycholinguists Herbert Clark and Richard Gerrig's Demonstration Theory describes various functions a quotation may perform in a discourse. Second, the Proteus Principle of Meir Sternberg sheds light on the process of recontextualizing quotations, which serves as a starting point for analyzing Paul's strategies in integrating quotations into his own argumentation. Both theories can be illustrated by textual examples from Rom 9–11, and they bring conceptual clarity to recent debates about Paul's use of Scripture. The final section addresses questions that arise when modern theories are applied to ancient texts and discusses the relevance of such approaches for the study of Paul's argumentation.

---

Removing all scriptural quotations in Rom 10 would shorten the chapter by one-third. It is an example of a passage in which quotations are an integral part of Paul's argumentation This essay addresses the following questions: What functions do the quotations have in the argumentation? How are they related to each other and to the parts Paul formulated? Does their original literary context still "echo" through them?

Some scholars label Paul's use of quotations "prooftexting."[1] This term raises objections among scholars and leads to apologetic assertions of Paul's serious theological wrestling with the Scriptures. Both this kind of labeling and apologetic approaches aimed at justifying Paul's use of Scriptures tend to apply a binary

---

[1] See, e.g., E. P. Sanders, *Paul, the Law, and the Jewish People* (Philadelphia: Fortress, 1983), 21–22, 53 n. 25; Heikki Räisänen, *Paul and the Law*, WUNT 29 (Tübingen: Mohr Siebeck, 1987), 68–69. For a slightly different use of the concept of prooftext, see Shiu-Lun Shum, *Paul's Use of Isaiah in Romans: A Comparative Study of Paul's Letter to the Romans and the Sibylline and Qumran Sectarian Texts*, WUNT 2/156 (Tübingen: Mohr Siebeck, 2002), 243 n. 195.

framework that obscures the wide variety of argumentative functions of quotations. My aim in this article is to shed light on these various functions by introducing two modern theories on quoting and thereby examining the argumentative roles of quotations beyond the category of proof.[2] These theories can also bring conceptual clarity to recent debates related to Paul's use of Scriptures.

First, Demonstration Theory, developed by psycholinguists Herbert Clark and Richard Gerrig, explains why direct quotations are used in a discourse. The theory describes various functions a quotation may perform and how they affect the communication situation.[3] Applied to Paul's argumentation, the theory serves to highlight the multifaceted rhetorical effects of his scriptural quotations. Second, Meir Sternberg, a literary critic, examines the recontextualization process of a quotation.[4] Given that there is always a transformation in meaning when a quotation is taken from its original context and inserted into a new one, Sternberg refers to the phenomenon as the "Proteus Principle" after the shape-changing sea god of Greek mythology.[5] This theory functions as a starting point for analyzing Paul's strategies in integrating quotations from different sources into his own argumentation. As I will show, Paul creates unity between the quotations and the rest of the discourse by actively framing them with elements that influence their interpretation. Both theories will be illustrated by textual examples from Rom

---

[2] Ancient discussions of rhetoric offer few guidelines on the matter of quotation. Aristotle remarks on the usefulness of appealing to "ancient witnesses" in court rhetoric, by which he means "the poets and all other notable persons whose judgments are known to all" (Aristotle, *Rhet.* 1.15 [Roberts]). Referring to maxims, that is, general sayings usually related to proper conduct, he observes that their use "is appropriate only to elderly men, and in handling subjects in which the speaker is experienced" (Aristotle, *Rhet.* 2.21 [Roberts]). According to Quintilian, quoting "the happy sayings of the various authors" is especially useful in court: "For phrases which have not been coined merely to suit the circumstances of the lawsuit of the moment carry greater weight and often win greater praise than if they were our own" (Quintilian, *Inst.* 2.7.4 [Butler, LCL]). In addition, quoting poets shows the learning of the speakers and enhances the eloquence of the speech, which gives pleasure to the audience (*Inst.* 1.8.10–12). Apart from these remarks, there are no well-known principles that could be applied to Paul's use of quotations. See also Dennis L. Stamps, "The Use of the Old Testament in the New Testament as a Rhetorical Device: A Methodological Proposal," in *Hearing the Old Testament in the New Testament*, ed. Stanley E. Porter (Grand Rapids: Eerdmans, 2006), 9–37, here 27–30.

[3] Herbert Clark and Richard Gerrig, "Quotations as Demonstrations," *Language* 66 (1990): 764–805.

[4] Meir Sternberg, "Proteus in Quotation-Land: Mimesis and the Forms of Reported Discourse," *Poetics Today* 3 (1982), http://dx.doi.org/10.2307/1772069.

[5] I am indebted to Christopher D. Stanley's article "Rhetoric of Quotations: An Essay on Method," in *Early Christian Interpretation of the Scriptures of Israel: Investigations and Proposals*, ed. Craig A. Evans and James A. Sanders, JSNTSup 148 (Sheffield: Sheffield Academic, 1997), 44–58. Stanley presents several modern theories on quoting (including those of Clark and Gerrig and Sternberg) and discusses their relevance to biblical studies. He broadens the scope of theories further in his monograph *Arguing with Scripture: The Rhetoric of Quotations in the Letters of Paul* (New York: T&T Clark, 2004), 22–37. Stanley does not, however, systematically apply these theories to the study of concrete passages or even illustrate them with textual examples.

9–11, in which quotations are frequent and form an integral part of the argumentation.[6] In the final part of the article, I address the questions that arise when modern theories are applied to ancient texts and discuss the relevance of the approaches for the study of Paul's argumentation.

I concentrate on "direct" or "explicit" quotations. A scriptural reference is defined as a quotation if it has (1) an introductory formula, or (2) an established formula used for textual interpretation (e.g., τοῦτ' ἔστιν in Rom 10:6), or (3) a clear syntactical or stylistic tension with the surrounding text (e.g., an abrupt change of personal pronouns or verb forms), or (4) significant verbal correspondence with a certain scriptural passage. The last criterion is disputed among scholars and open to various interpretations. More important than having a certain number of words quoted in a chain is the frequency of words and forms. All of the examples used here, however, fulfill at least one of the first three criteria.

## I. Quotations as Demonstrations

### Demonstration Theory

Clark and Gerrig's Demonstration Theory focuses on the question of how quotations function in a discourse.[7] Although some features of the theory apply only to spoken communication, many of the key observations can also be applied to written texts. According to Clark and Gerrig, direct quotations are used for stylistic and rhetorical reasons when the person doing the quoting wishes to show what the original communication situation was like. Quotations do not describe the situation but "demonstrate" it from a certain point of view.[8] Thus, "quotations are intended to give the audience an experience of what it would be like in certain respects to experience the original event."[9] A quotation, however, is not intended to relay all aspects of the original event; rather, the speakers quoting choose what to include and what to leave out according to what they wish to "demonstrate" with the quotation.[10]

---

[6] The field of quotation studies is fragmentary, since quotations are studied in different disciplines without a common theoretical framework. I concentrate on Clark and Gerrig's and Sternberg's theories in this article because they can be sensibly applied to research on written texts and they offer concrete tools for that. For other approaches to quotations, see Stanley, *Arguing with Scripture*, 22–37.

[7] Clark and Gerrig, "Quotations as Demonstrations," 764–805. The theory is adopted also by Elizabeth Wade; see Wade and Herbert Clark, "Reproduction and Demonstration in Quotations," *Journal of Memory and Language* 32 (1993): 805–19, http://dx.doi.org/10.1006/jmla.1993.1040.

[8] Clark and Gerrig, "Quotations as Demonstrations," 764–66, 769–74; Wade and Clark, "Reproduction and Demonstration," 807–8.

[9] Wade and Clark, "Reproduction and Demonstration," 808.

[10] Clark and Gerrig, "Quotations as Demonstrations," 774–75.

Clark and Gerrig divide the different functions of quotations into two main categories: "detachment" and "direct experience." When speakers indicate that they are quoting, they distance themselves from the contents of the quotation. This is useful if they need to relay someone's utterance word for word (such as in a law court), if they do not wish to take responsibility for the utterance, or if they wish to strengthen their rapport with the audience by quoting from a source that unites them with its members. "Direct experience" means that quotations enable the addressees to become engrossed in an event and even to reexperience it vividly. Quotations invite the audience to experience the situation from a certain perspective according to who is speaking. Part of the direct experience is that quotations in spoken discourse help to "demonstrate" elements of the communication event that would be difficult to describe, such as the tone of voice or an emotion.[11] In the following I elaborate on three functions defined by Clark and Gerrig that seem to be most applicable for examining Paul's quotations: dissociation of responsibility, lending vividness, and increasing solidarity.

## *Dissociation of Responsibility*

According to Clark and Gerrig, a quotation can be used "to convey information implicitly that it might be more awkward to express explicitly."[12] Quotations enable authors to create distance between themselves and the quotation so that they cannot be held responsible for it. Clark and Gerrig call this function "dissociation of responsibility."

Paul resorts to quotations for this purpose repeatedly in Rom 9–11, especially when making far-reaching theological claims about the intentions and purposes behind divine action. Formulating statements like these in his own words would make Paul an easy target of criticism. After all, who is he to analyze divine purposes and to explain God's reasons? When a statement is expressed through a quotation, however, the responsibility shifts to the cited text. Paul appears to make some of his most audacious claims through quotations, which can be an effective rhetorical strategy. When he gives the impression of positioning himself in the background and letting the quotations speak for themselves, the reader disinclined to agree with the argumentation is faced not with Paul's authority but with that of Scripture.[13]

The quotation from Deut 32:21 in Rom 10:19 is an example of this kind of

---

[11] Ibid., 792–94.

[12] Ibid., 792, citing Ronald K. S. Macaulay, "Polyphonic Monologues: Quoted Direct Speech in Oral Narratives," *International Pragmatics Association Papers in Pragmatics* 1 (1987): 1–34, here 2, http://dx.doi.org/10.1075/iprapip.1.2.01mac.

[13] The expressions "audience" and "readers" are generally used interchangeably in this article. In practice, of course, most of the audience of Romans were "hearers" of the letter, which was read aloud. Here, "reader" does not refer to how a member of the audience becomes acquainted with the letter.

dissociation of responsibility: "But I ask, did Israel not understand? First Moses says, 'I will make you[14] jealous [παραζηλώσω] of a non-nation, with a nation lacking understanding I will make you angry.'"[15] The quotation derives from the Song of Moses, in which Moses foretells the unfaithfulness of the people and describes its consequences. In the original context of the verse, God is provoked to jealous anger by the idolatrous behavior of Israel and, in turn, provokes jealous anger in Israel by allowing a hostile nation to harass them. Although this is a prophecy of doom for Israel, ultimately the goal of the provocation is to make the people turn back to their God (Deut 32:39).[16] Both the immediate context of the quotation in Romans and its original context in Deuteronomy indicate that "you" refers to Israel. In contrast, the "non-nation" that lacks understanding is given a new interpretation by Paul so that it refers no longer to hostile neighbors but to gentiles who have been called by God.[17] In Romans, therefore, the quotation suggests that God has turned to gentiles in order to provoke jealousy in Israel. At this stage of the argument it appears that provoking jealousy in Israel is God's reaction and solution in a situation in which the "disobedient and contrary people" (Rom 10:21) reject the gospel. Paul returns to this jealousy motif in 11:11–14, where he gives it a positive interpretation.

Paul does not express in his own words the idea that God intentionally provokes jealousy in Israel by using gentiles; rather, he allows the quotation to convey it. By using an introductory formula and placing the quotation in a certain context, he ensures that the quotation is read in the way he intends. Consequently, the reference to God's purposes and the roles of Israel and gentiles as part of the divine purposes, which could give rise to objections, appears to be not Paul's own invention but a scriptural prophecy. The potential offense lies in the sacred writing.[18]

---

[14] Paul changes the personal pronouns of Deut 32:21 from the third (αὐτούς) to the second person plural (ὑμᾶς). The substitution can be traced to Paul, for it finds no support in the manuscript tradition of the LXX, or in the MT, targums, Vulgate, or Peshitta. Nor is there any need to speculate with reference to extant textual traditions; in its original context (Deut 32:20–27) the third person plural is used consistently and is totally unproblematic. In Romans, however, the second person plural is used as a rhetorical device that highlights the quotation by distinguishing it from the preceding discourse, thus making it more impressive. See Christopher D. Stanley, *Paul and the Language of Scripture: Citation Technique in the Pauline Epistles and Contemporary Literature*, SNTSMS 74 (Cambridge: Cambridge University Press, 1992), 143, http://dx.doi.org/10.1017/CBO9780511896552; J. Ross Wagner, *Heralds of the Good News: Isaiah and Paul "in Concert" in the Letter to the Romans*, NovTSup 101 (Leiden: Brill, 2002), 190.

[15] The translations of biblical texts are my own.

[16] For the background and dynamics of "jealousy," see Richard H. Bell, *Provoked to Jealousy: The Origin and Purpose of the Jealousy Motif in Romans 9–11*, WUNT 2/63 (Tübingen: Mohr Siebeck, 1994).

[17] Cf. 9:25–26, in which gentiles are referred to as "Not My People" (οὐ λαός μου).

[18] That Paul was to some extent aware of the controversial nature of such a scheme is suggested by the careful and considerate manner in which he discusses the interdependence of gentiles and Israel in chapter 11 (11:11, 15, 28–32).

## Vividness and Drama

Ancient rhetoricians were conscious that quotations brought vividness and variety into a speech—a device to be used at the right time, in the right place, and by the right speakers.[19] Clark and Gerrig analyze this effect more closely, suggesting that the audience may become engrossed in an event through a quotation: "When we hear an event quoted, it is as if we directly experience the depicted aspects of the original event."[20] The addressees enter the scene from which the quotation derives. In oral communication, however, the speakers quoting can never reproduce all the aspects of the original event and rather select the aspects they wish to highlight. Thus, they have the power to decide which elements to include in their "demonstration" and which to leave out.[21] In the case of written texts, the authors quoting make similar choices when they delineate a certain passage and detach it from its original context. Many aspects of the original passages are not transferred to the new environment of the quoted words. The selective character of quoting is clearly visible in Paul's writing; he did not always quote a passage as a whole but frequently condensed it and sometimes even omitted words from the middle.[22]

The function of adding vividness and drama to the argument is especially relevant to the study of quotations in Rom 9–11, in a remarkable number of which God speaks in the first person singular. These quotations bring liveliness to the argumentation, for instead of speaking of God, they allow God to speak. For example, in Rom 9:17 Paul quotes Exod 9:16: "For the Scripture says to Pharaoh, 'For this very purpose I have raised you up, that I might show in you my power and that my name might be proclaimed in all the earth.'" Interestingly, although the introductory formula presents "the Scripture" as the speaker, it is obvious that the one who has raised Pharaoh up and whose name will be proclaimed is not Scripture but God. This phenomenon will be discussed in detail below.[23] God, speaking in the first person singular, addresses Pharaoh and declares the divine motives and plans. The dialogical element that is built into the quotation invites the audience of Romans to follow the confrontation between God and hardened Pharaoh. It enables the audience to enter the scene, experience the situation and "hear" God's own voice. Instead of quoting, Paul could have paraphrased the passage: "For the Scripture says that Pharaoh was raised because of God's very purpose to show his power in him and to make God's name proclaimed in all the earth." Paul, however, would have lost the drama and intensity inherent in the quotation. Moreover, quoting God

---

[19] See n. 2 above.

[20] Clark and Gerrig, "Quotations as Demonstrations," 793. See also Wade and Clark, "Reproduction and Demonstration," 808.

[21] Clark and Gerrig, "Quotations as Demonstrations," 774–75.

[22] On this phenomenon, see Dietrich-Alex Koch, *Die Schrift als Zeuge des Evangeliums: Untersuchungen zur Verwendung und zum Verständnis der Schrift bei Paulus*, BHT 69 (Tübingen: Mohr Siebeck, 1986), 115–32.

[23] See below under "The Introductory Formula."

speaking in the first person singular is an appropriate rhetorical device in Rom 9, where Paul consistently emphasizes the sovereignty of divine action. Allowing God to speak directly serves this emphasis because such quotations highlight God's active agency.

## *Increasing Solidarity*

Quotations can be used to strengthen rapport with the audience. Quoting from a source that unites the audience and the author confirms their common bond and renders the audience more favorable toward the author. This effect is widely recognized in New Testament studies: when Paul is addressing a Roman audience he has never met, it is natural that he appeals to a common body of texts. As quotations can "demonstrate" only some aspects of the original event (or in the case of written texts, they convey only some aspects of the original literary context), however, the audience commonly needs background information to interpret them in the intended way. This, in fact, enhances the rhetorical effect of strengthening the rapport, as Clark and Gerrig aptly explain: "When speakers demonstrate only a snippet of an event, they tacitly assume that their addressees share the right background to interpret it in the same way they do. In essence, they are asserting, 'I am demonstrating something we both can interpret correctly,' and that implies solidarity."[24]

Romans 9:7 is an example of a quotation that requires prior scriptural knowledge from the audience, since Paul does not provide many interpretative clues: "And not all are children because they are Abraham's descendants, but 'In Isaac shall offspring be named for you' [Gen 21:12]." That the latter half of the verse is a quotation from an external source is something the audience can deduce from the abrupt change in person ("for you"): someone is clearly being addressed. In this case, only very basic prior knowledge is needed. The audience is expected to know that Isaac is Abraham's son and thus one of the children mentioned in the sentence that precedes the quotation. In addition, they have to realize that the speaker here is God, giving a promise to Abraham; without this understanding, Paul's argument would be unintelligible. Referring to a shared tradition without the need to articulate the information reminds the audience that they are insiders together with the author. They share a common narrative that Paul can cite elliptically while trusting that the audience can follow him.

What Clark and Gerrig do not discuss is the commonsense observation that, if a quotation is too elliptical, obscure, or from an unknown source, the rapport between the audience and the person quoting will hardly be strengthened. The example from Rom 9:7 requires knowledge only of the basic features of a patriarchal narrative. The extent of scriptural knowledge that Paul presupposes from his

---

[24] Clark and Gerrig, "Quotations as Demonstrations," 793.

audience in Romans in general is debated. In maximalist terms, Paul is inviting his readers to make connections between different scriptural passages and to listen to subtle intertextual echoes from texts that he does not cite but which are situated in the original literary context of the quotations or have thematic or verbal links to them.[25] In this case, he would assume that his readers have high scriptural competence. On the other hand, it is possible to outline the minimum amount of scriptural knowledge the audience needs to be able to follow the argumentation. For example, although there are nine quotations in Rom 9:6–29, the argumentation is completely accessible to an audience whose members are aware that Isaac was not Abraham's only son, that Jacob and Esau were twins, that Pharaoh was hardened, and that Sodom and Gomorrah should be associated with destruction.[26] This does not imply that Paul pictured all of his audience as having only modest scriptural competence or that readers with modest competence necessarily represented Paul's ideal audience. It demonstrates only that, although Paul quotes Scripture frequently, he ensures that his argument is also intelligible to readers with fairly modest scriptural literacy.[27] The focus in the following section is on how Paul accomplishes this by giving his audience interpretative clues that help them to read the recontextualized quotations as he intended them to be read.

## II. From One "Network of Relations" to Another: Framing the Quotation

### *Inevitable Change*

Meir Sternberg examines the effect that recontextualization has on a quotation when it is detached from its original context and inserted into a new one.[28] Sternberg argues that a shift in meaning is *inevitable* in the recontextualization process because a quotation always belongs to "a network of relations." The quoted passage has a frame that encloses and regulates it. When it is extracted from the framing elements that influence its interpretation and inserted into a new frame with different regulating elements, there is bound to be a change in the meaning of the quotation.[29]

---

[25] For examples, see n. 45 below.

[26] See also Stanley, *Arguing with Scripture*, 145–70 and esp. 172–73, where he traces the reading experience of three hypothetical reader groups and estimates their capabilities of following Paul's line of thought.

[27] Compare this with Stanley's more straightforward suggestion that "Paul constructed his biblical arguments for an 'implied audience' that was incapable of consulting the original context of most of his biblical references" ("Paul's 'Use' of Scripture: Why the Audience Matters," in *As It Is Written: Studying Paul's Use of Scripture*, ed. Stanley E. Porter and Christopher D. Stanley, SymS 50 [Atlanta: Society of Biblical Literature, 2008], 125–55, here 155; see also Stanley, *Arguing with Scripture*, 174–76).

[28] Sternberg, "Proteus in Quotation-Land," 107–56.

[29] Ibid., 108, 131, 152.

## Changing the "Network of Relations"

Romans 10:6, in which Paul quotes Deut 30:12, serves to illustrate what Sternberg means by "a network of relations." In its immediate original context the question of going up to heaven is framed by the idea of observing the commandment (table 1).

TABLE 1. Deuteronomy 30:11–14

| For **this commandment that I command you** today is not immoderate nor is it far away from you. It is not above in the sky, | Context of observing the commandment (bold) |
|---|---|
| so that one should say, | Introduction |
| '*Who will go up to heaven* and get it for us. And after hearing it **we shall do it**.' (Deut 30:11–12) … The word is very near to you, in your mouth and in your heart and in your hands, **to do it**." (Deut 30:14) | *The passage quoted in Rom 10:6 (italics)* |

Paul detaches certain words (in italics) from this network of relations and inserts them into a new network in which they are framed with completely different elements (table 2).

TABLE 2. Romans 10:5–6

| For Moses writes concerning the righteousness that comes from the law, that "the person who does these things will live by them." [Lev 18:5] | Previous sentence: introduces the principle of righteousness from the law |
|---|---|
| But [δέ] | Contrast |
| the Righteousness from Faith speaks in this way, "Do not say in your heart, [Deut 8:17//9:4]: | Introductory formula |
| 'Who will go up to heaven?'" [Deut 30:12] | The quoted words |
| That is, | Interpretation formula |
| to bring Christ down.* | Paul's interpretation |

*Rom 10:6: ἡ δὲ ἐκ πίστεως δικαιοσύνη οὕτως λέγει, μὴ εἴπῃς ἐν τῇ καρδίᾳ σου· τίς ἀναβήσεται εἰς τὸν οὐρανόν; τοῦτ' ἔστιν Χριστὸν καταγαγεῖν·

I leave aside a number of interesting hermeneutical questions related to this quotation and concentrate on examining the framing elements, in which this example is exceptionally rich. The unique introductory formula presents the personified Righteousness from Faith as the speaker of the quotation. In this context, the particle δέ implies a contrast with the previous verse, 10:5, which presents the dynamics of the "righteousness from the law" (also using a quotation).³⁰ Paul now contrasts this righteousness with the dynamics of the "righteousness from faith." The quotation from Deut 30:12 is followed by an interpretation formula τοῦτ' ἔστιν, an expression used in both Jewish and Greco-Roman literature to begin an exegetical interpretation.³¹ The table shows only the most immediate framing elements, but the network of relations extends deeper. For example, 10:6 has verbal links to other parts of Rom 9–11, and in some sense the whole letter is part of the frame of the quotation. What the frame completely lacks are the commandment and its observance. Paul frames the quoted passage so that the idea of observing the divine commandment, a distinctive feature of the frame in Deut 30, is in no way transferred to Romans. In contrast, the new frame implies that the personified Righteousness from Faith introduces a principle that differs from law observance.

The influence of the "network of relations" on quotations is further exemplified in Rom 10:18, where Paul quotes from Ps 18:5 LXX. The words he quotes are in italics:

> The heavens tell of the glory of God, and the firmament proclaims his handiwork. Day to day declares the word and night to night proclaims knowledge. There are no speeches nor words the articulations of which are not heard. *To all the earth went their sound, and to the ends of the world their words.* In the sun he set his dwelling place. (Ps 18:2–5 LXX [19:1–4 MT])

In the psalm, the third person plural of the words Paul quotes refers to day and night, and possibly also to the heavens and the firmament. In Paul's argumentation, however, the quotation is related to the question of whether everybody has been able to hear the gospel. In the new frame, the third person plural appears to refer to the preachers of the good news:

> As it is written: "How beautiful are the feet of **those who preach** the good news!" [Isa 52:7]. But not all have obeyed the gospel. For Isaiah says, "Lord, who has believed our message?" [Isa 53:1]. So the faith comes from what is heard, and

---

³⁰ Richard B. Hays suggests that δέ only signifies a change of speaker (*Echoes of Scripture in the Letters of Paul* [New Haven: Yale University Press, 1989], 208 n. 84); likewise Wagner, *Heralds of the Good News*, 161 n. 132. The context of 10:4–8, however, and the way Paul modifies the quotation from Deuteronomy strongly suggest that he intended to create a contrast between the two principles of righteousness. See Koch, *Die Schrift als Zeuge*, 130–31; James D. G. Dunn, *Romans 9–16*, WBC 38 (Dallas: Word, 1988), 601; Wolfgang Reinbold, "Das Ziel des Gesetzes nach Röm 10,4–13," in *Judaistik und neutestamentliche Wissenschaft: Standorte, Grenzen, Beziehungen*, ed. Lutz Doering, Hans-Günther Waubke, and Florian Wilk, FRLANT 226 (Göttingen: Vandenhoeck & Ruprecht, 2008), 297–312, here 301, http://dx.doi.org/10.13109/9783666530906.297; Friedrich Avemarie, "Israels rätselhafter Ungehorsam: Römer 10 als Anatomie eines von Gott provozierten Unglaubens," in *Between Gospel and Election: Explorations in the Interpretation of Romans 9–11*, ed. Florian Wilk and J. Ross Wagner, WUNT 257 (Tübingen: Mohr Siebeck, 2010), 299–320, here 313–14.

³¹ Koch, *Die Schrift als Zeuge*, 28 n. 23.

what is heard comes through the word of Christ. But I ask, have they not heard? Indeed they have! "*To all the earth went **their** sound, and to the ends of the world **their** words*" [Ps 18:5]. (Rom 10:15b–18)

Paul does not change the wording of the quotation but renders it verbatim. Neither does he formulate an introduction in which to claim explicitly that the psalmist has prophesied the extent of the preaching of the gospel. Yet the recontextualization of the psalm's words into a new network of relations changes their meaning completely. In Sternberg's words, "to quote is to mediate, to mediate is to frame and to frame is to interfere and exploit."[32]

### III. Paul's Tools for Recontextualization: The Framing Elements

If Paul's scriptural quotations are detached from their new context in Romans and inspected without any framing whatsoever, they appear ambiguous, and occasionally their relevance to Paul's argumentation is far from obvious. Paul actively creates connections, however, between the quotations and his own formulations. When he integrates a scriptural passage into his argumentation, he frames it with elements that create consistency and make the quotation fit into its new context.

*The Introductory Formula: What, from Where, to Whom?*

Of the framing elements Paul uses, the introductory formula is of the greatest significance and precedes most of his quotations. Occasionally he uses established, formulaic expressions (e.g., "as it is written"),[33] but more often he tailors the introductions to his argumentative needs. Introductory formulae offer the audience additional information in specifying the content, speaker, addressee, or location of the quotation. Most of the formulae feature conjunctions (γάρ, ὡς, καθώς, δέ) that indicate how the quotation is related to Paul's own words or to other quotations, for example, offering confirmation or indicating a change of topic or speaker.

The introductory formula in Rom 11:2 contains an exceptional number of elements that guide the interpretation of the quotation: "Or do you not know what the Scripture says in Elijah [narratives], how *it* appeals to God against Israel?" (ἢ οὐκ οἴδατε ἐν Ἠλίᾳ τί λέγει ἡ γραφή, ὡς ἐντυγχάνει τῷ θεῷ κατὰ τοῦ Ἰσραήλ;). At

---

[32] Sternberg, "Proteus in Quotation-Land," 108.
[33] Paul uses the expression "as it is written" (καθὼς γέγραπται) eighteen times in his undisputed letters. The expression is rare in non-Jewish literature, but it is common usage in Jewish writings (e.g., 2 Kgs 14:6). The equivalent phrase in the Qumran scrolls is כאשר כתוב (see Koch, *Die Schrift als Zeuge*, 25, 29).

its core is a typical formulaic introduction, "The Scripture says" (λέγει ἡ γραφή),[34] but the other parts are carefully crafted by Paul. The introduction begins with a rhetorical question that is clearly related to Paul's claim that God has not abandoned his people (Rom 11:1): "Or do you not know…" This beginning anticipates proof or reasoning of some kind. It is characteristic of Paul to use a rhetorical question to advance the argument, but including it in the introductory formula is exceptional. He also specifies the location of the quotation: it is to be found in the Elijah narratives.[35] The rest of the introduction indicates to whom the words are directed and what they concern: they are addressed to God and contain an accusation "against Israel."

The subject of the pleading in this introductory formula is not Elijah but Scripture. In the following quotation, however, it is Elijah, not Scripture, who speaks about his experiences in the first person singular ("I alone am left"). Paul obviously expects his readers to identify this speaker with Elijah, although he crafts the introduction to make Scripture appeal to God against Israel. This inconsistency should not be attributed to careless formulation. On the contrary, it is a recurring feature of Paul's introductory formulae.[36] As the following examples show, it is characteristic of Paul to make Scripture or the assumed author of the writing (such as David) the subject of the introductory formula, although it is unequivocal that the actual speaker in the quotation is someone else, usually God: "First Moses says, '*I will make you jealous of a non-nation, with a nation lacking understanding I will make you angry*' [Deut 32:21]" (Rom 10:19). "And Isaiah is bold and says, '*I have been found by those who did not seek me, I have become visible to those who did not ask for me*' [Isa 65:1]" (Rom 10:20). In these quotations the person speaking in the first person singular is God, not Moses or Isaiah, both in the original context and in Romans. Another illuminating parallel with the curious introductory formula in Rom 11:2 is that in Rom 9:17: "For the Scripture says to Pharaoh, '*For this very purpose I have raised you up, that I might show my power in you and that my name might be proclaimed on all the earth*' [Exod 9:16]." Despite Paul's formulation of this introduction, it is God and not Scripture that brought Pharaoh to power. Therefore, the grammatical subject of Paul's introductory formulae does not always identify

---

[34] Paul uses the expression λέγει ἡ γραφή also in Rom 4:3, 9:17, 10:11, 11:2, Gal 4:30.

[35] Similarly Koch, *Die Schrift als Zeuge*, 27 n. 17. Paul usually mentions the name of the alleged author, not the "location" of the quotation, but this introductory formula has parallels in Rom 9:25 (ἐν τῷ Ὡσηέ) and 1 Cor 9:9 (ἐν γὰρ τῷ Μωϋσέως νόμῳ). Cf. also Mark 12:26 and Luke 20:37.

[36] Most translators and commentators do not take into account the fact that this inconsistency is characteristic of Paul, which is why they try to fix it in Rom 11:2. Note the NRSV: "Do you not know what the scripture says of Elijah, how *he* pleads with God against Israel?" Lutherbibel 1912: "Oder wisset ihr nicht, was die Schrift sagt von Elia, wie *er* tritt vor Gott wider Israel und spricht?" Edition de Genève 1979: "Ne savez-vous pas ce que l'Ecriture rapporte d'Elie, comment *il* adresse à Dieu cette plainte contre Israël?"

the actual speaker. Readers have to deduce who is speaking, though in most cases the new context of the quotations in Romans makes it fairly obvious.

Paul may have two reasons for formulating introductions in this manner. First, he appears to have systematically avoided writing "God says" when referring to quotations.[37] Second, introductions such as this underline the authority of the scriptural witness. Moses, David, and Isaiah are all authoritative witnesses for Paul's arguments. In a similar way, Scripture is also a witness, although less well specified. In this light, the introductory formula in 11:2 is completely understandable: Paul deliberately crafts the introduction to make Scripture his witness that appeals to God against Israel. From a rhetorical perspective, the sentence becomes more dramatic when Scripture utters the accusation, but the theological consequences were probably even more decisive. It is apparently important for Paul that Israel's own Scripture testifies against it. He interprets Scripture's accusations against Israel as prophecies of Israel's disobedience in reluctance to embrace the gospel, as is repeatedly implied in Rom 9–11 (Rom 9:33; 10:18, 19, 21; 11:8–10). On the other hand, Paul is likewise certain that Israel's future salvation is firmly founded in Scripture (see Rom 11:25–26).

Hence, in 11:2 Paul carefully crafts a detailed introduction around a short formulaic core, every part of which has a role to play. On the one hand, this practice helps the readers to connect the quotation to a certain narrative in explicitly mentioning Elijah, and, on the other hand, it connects the quotation to the recurring theme of Scripture's testimony against Israel. Paul's introductory formulae inform the audience how a quotation should be approached and read. Through these formulae Paul actively and deliberately guides the interpretation process of his audience.

## *Summaries and Conclusions*

Integral to the frame of some quotations are Paul's summaries, interpretations, and conclusions; most quotations, however, lack such explanatory remarks. Quotations are seldom the objects of exegesis in the argumentation of Romans, in the sense that Paul would pause to interpret them (as in Rom 10:6–10). Rather, they function as independent arguments or as confirmation of Paul's claims that he generally does not explain. Occasionally, however, he summarizes in his own words what he intends the quotation to communicate or draws a conclusion based on it. In Rom 9:15–16, for example, he apparently felt the need to articulate in his own

---

[37] In Romans, Paul never explicitly states in his introductory formulae that God is the speaker of the quoted words, although it is obvious in most cases. In Rom 9:15 and 9:25, however, the subject has to be God, but even then readers have to deduce this from the preceding verses. On this curious characteristic of Paul's introductory formulae, see Hans Hübner, *Gottes Ich und Israel: Zum Schriftgebrauch des Paulus in Römer 9–11*, FRLANT 136 (Göttingen: Vandenhoeck & Ruprecht, 1984), 42–43; Koch, *Die Schrift als Zeuge*, 31–32.

voice the message and relevance of the quoted passage: "For he says to Moses, 'I will have mercy on whom I have mercy and I will have compassion on whom I have compassion' [Exod 33:19]. Therefore [ἄρα οὖν], it depends not on the one willing or the one running but on God who shows mercy" (Rom 9:15–16). Paul uses the expression ἄρα οὖν to introduce his conclusion from the quotation. Willing and running both signify human exertion, which is contrasted here with God's mercy.[38] The quotation in itself, however, does not draw such a contrast between human action and divine mercy; the focus is solely on God's sovereignty. In his conclusion, Paul integrates the quotation into the juxtaposition of human achievements and God's sovereign calling that is at the core of Rom 9. In this case it is not necessary for readers to consult the original literary context and transfer into Romans the meaning the words have in Exodus, for Paul himself provides the interpretative framework in which the quotation should be read.

## *Catchwords*

The frame of a quotation may also contain catchwords that have a pivotal role in the argumentation and create verbal links between passages. Creating catchword connections has been described as a typical rabbinic method,[39] but the phenomenon is also well attested in non-Jewish literature.[40] Paul uses catchwords to strengthen the cohesion between the quotation and other parts of the argumentation.

The verb "to call" (καλέω), for example, functions as a catchword in Rom 9. In Rom 9:25–26 Paul introduces a quotation that is a combination of Hos 2:23 and 1:10, two verses that play with the prophetic names of Hosea's children: "I will *call* [καλέσω] 'Not My People' 'My People' and 'Not Beloved' 'My Beloved' [Hos 2:23]. And it will be that wherever they *are called* [κληθήσονται] 'Not My People,' there they *will be called* [κληθήσονται] 'sons of the living God' [Hos 1:10]."[41] The two parts

---

[38] Dunn, *Romans*, 553; Robert Jewett, *Romans: A Commentary*, Hermeneia (Minneapolis: Fortress, 2007), 582.

[39] See, e.g., E. Earle Ellis, *Prophecy and Hermeneutic in Early Christianity: New Testament Essays*, WUNT 18 (Tübingen: Mohr Siebeck, 1978), 214–16; William R. Stegner, "Romans 9:6–29—a Midrash," *JSNT* 22 (1984): 37–52, here 40, http://dx.doi.org/10.1177/0142064x8400702203; Jewett, *Romans*, 571.

[40] John S. Kloppenberg, *The Formation of Q: Trajectories in Ancient Wisdom Collections* (Philadelphia: Fortress 1987), 48, 268, 282. On catchwords in general, see Stephen J. Patterson, *The Gospel of Thomas and Jesus*, FF: Reference Series (Sonoma, CA: Polebridge 1993), 99–102.

[41] In 9:26, the witnesses for the wording of Romans are divided. Although the majority reading of NA[28] follows the LXX (οὗ ἐρρέθη αὐτοῖς), there are good reasons to assume that οὗ ἐὰν κληθήσονται (p[46] F G ar b d* sy[p]) represents the original Pauline formulation, which is why I follow it in my translation. See Günther Zuntz, *The Text of the Epistles: A Disquisition upon the Corpus Paulinum*, Schweich Lectures of the British Academy, 1946 (London: Oxford University Press, 1953), 174; Wagner, *Heralds of the Good News*, 84–85. The variant, however, makes little difference

of the combined quotation share the name "Not My People" and the verb "call." Calling also links the quotation with Paul's own formulation in the previous verse (9:24): "including us whom he also *called* [ἐκάλεσεν], not from among Jews only but also from among gentiles." Calling is also an essential motif at the earlier stages of the argumentation in Rom 9:7 ("In Isaac shall offspring be named [κληθήσεται] for you") and 9:12 ("not because of works but because of him who calls [ἐκ τοῦ καλοῦντος]"). Thus, the catchword καλέω enhances the coherence of chapter 9, for the repetition of the verb connects different passages and leads the reader to interpret them in light of one another. The quotations become more firmly rooted in their new surroundings and can therefore function as integral parts of the argumentation.

## IV. THE RELEVANCE OF QUOTATION THEORY FOR PAULINE STUDIES

After applying Clark and Gerrig's Demonstration Theory and Sternberg's Proteus Principle to quotations in Rom 9–11, it is time to assess what they contribute to Pauline studies. First, however, it is necessary to raise an essential question concerning the Demonstration Theory: can a theory based on modern communication be applied to ancient texts? As I see it, doing so is based on the observation that certain features of communication appear to be relatively timeless. Classical rhetorical devices that were systematically analyzed in ancient treatises on rhetoric are successfully applied to modern advertising and political rhetoric. Conversely, techniques of using quotations that are found effective today may also have been effective in antiquity. Studying the functions of quotations in the New Testament should not, however, be limited only to categories deriving from recent quotation theory, for it is possible that an ancient author also used quotations for purposes that have not been identified in research on modern communication.

What makes Clark and Gerrig's Demonstration Theory relevant for the study of Paul is that it offers new tools with which to analyze the functions of quotations beyond the limited concept of "prooftexting." Although quotations certainly often serve as proof in Paul's argumentation, confirming and supporting his own statements by showing that they are in accordance with Scripture, this is only one of the numerous argumentative functions they perform. A more comprehensive toolbox makes it possible to articulate the effects of Paul's quotations in more nuanced ways. Different functions of quotations are, obviously, not mutually exclusive; they do overlap, and one quotation may fulfill several functions that work on different levels, for example, rhetorical effect, stylistic matters, the structuring of the argument, or the

---

to my analysis in this article (although it further underlines the importance of the verb καλέω in chapter 9).

relationship with the audience. When the more subtle effects of quotations are analyzed, questions concerning intentionality arise. To what extent did Paul deliberately hope to create a certain rhetorical effect with a quotation? The question is more acute with respect to some functions analyzed in this article than with others. It is well imaginable that Paul intentionally used a quotation in place of his own statement when discussing a delicate matter, thus shifting the responsibility to the quoted text (e.g., 10:19–21). But did Paul intend the rhetorical effect that is created by the repeated use of quotations in which God speaks in the first person singular? Paul would hardly have explicated the reasons for his abundant use of quotations in the same way as they have been analyzed in this article, but this does not mean that he was not on some level conscious that the practice was appropriate and advantageous for his argument. It is valuable to make the rhetorical effects of quotations visible even in those cases in which the question of the extent to which Paul deliberately attempted to create the effects cannot be answered.

The question of intentionality also arises when Paul's techniques of recontextualizing quotations are examined. For example, a recent debate circled around the question whether Paul "respected" the original context of his quotations—a discussion characterized by disputes about what "respect" and "original context" essentially mean.[42] The concepts of "network of relations" and "framing" in Sternberg's Proteus Principle may offer a productive standpoint from which to view the debate. Sternberg concludes, "However accurate the wording of the quotation and however pure the quoter's motives, tearing a piece of discourse from its original habitat and reconstructing it within a new network of relations cannot but interfere with its effect."[43] Therefore, even if Paul did not intend it, he in any case interfered with the "meaning" of a quotation just by framing it with different elements. The interesting question is, to what extent did he *intentionally* detach the quotation from its original network of relations and to what extent did he aim at preserving continuity with the original frame?

This question relates to another recent debate among scholars studying Paul's use of Scripture. Formulated using Sternberg's terminology, which network of relations is decisive in terms of understanding the quotation as part of Paul's argumentation—the original context or the new frame of the quotation in Paul's letter?[44] Did Paul intend his audience to interpret the quotation on the basis of its original

---

[42] The collection from the Society of Biblical Literature's Paul and Scripture Seminar entitled *Paul and Scripture: Continuing the Conversation* (ed. Christopher D. Stanley, ECL 9 [Atlanta: Society of Biblical Literature, 2012]) devotes three articles to these questions; see Steve Moyise, "Does Paul Respect the Context of His Quotations?," 97–114 (see also his response to Kim, 131–39); and Mitchell Kim, "Respect for Context and the Authorial Intention: Setting the Epistemological Bar," 115–29.

[43] Sternberg, "Proteus in Quotation-Land," 145.

[44] See Steve Moyise's analysis of the recent discussion in his *Paul and Scripture* (London: SPCK, 2010), 111–25.

literary context or with the help of the interpretative hints he offers? Scholars such as Richard B. Hays and Ross Wagner often appear to assume that the original setting of the quotation "echoes" through the quoted words so that the audience hears much more than only the words that Paul quotes. Hays and Wagner argue that this also was Paul's intention: he built his argumentation so that the wider passage from which the quotation was taken would shed light on it.[45] In Romans, there are passages in which this might indeed, at least to some extent, be the case. For example, knowledge of the plot and inherent logic of Deut 28–32 would help the audience understand how God turns away from his people in order to make them return to him again (cf. Rom 10:19). On the other hand, there are numerous examples of Paul systematically ignoring important aspects of the original literary context of the quotation (see Rom 10:18). In such cases, he frames the quotation with elements that suggest the new interpretation. In general, Paul appears to take great care in framing quotations: he crafts an individual introductory formula for a significant number of his quotations, integrates the quotations into their new surroundings with catchwords, and makes his own summaries or conclusions about their relevance to the matter at hand. In addition, he modifies the wording of approximately every second quotation, mainly to make the quotation more compatible with his argument.[46] Together the repeated modification of the wording and the careful framing suggest that, rather than preserving continuity with the original literary context, Paul frequently disentangles the quotation from it and creates a new framework for its interpretation. Consequently, examining the original literary context is not automatically the key to understanding Paul's intention in quoting scriptural passages.

[45] See, e.g., Hays, *Echoes of Scripture*, 22–23, 36, 177; Wagner, *Heralds of the Good News*, 62–68.

[46] Suggesting that Paul modified the wording of his quotations necessitates careful text-critical analysis aimed at reconstructing the wording Paul knew and used (or sometimes perhaps wordings; see Jonathan D. H. Norton, *Contours in the Text: Textual Variation in the Writings of Paul, Josephus and the Yaḥad*, LNTS 430 [London: T&T Clark, 2011], 55–56). Although even the best reconstructions are probabilities rather than certainties, when all preserved text-critical material and the function and context of the quotation are taken into account, it is possible to trace certain deviations from the LXX to Paul's own redactional activity. See Florian Wilk, "Letters of Paul as Witnesses to and for the Septuagint Text," in *Septuagint Research: Issues and Challenges in the Study of the Greek Jewish Scriptures*, ed. Wolfgang Kraus and R. Glenn Wooden, SCS 53 (Atlanta: Society of Biblical Literature, 2006), 263–64. Koch's and Stanley's comprehensive studies on all the quotations in the undisputed Pauline letters indicate that deviations from the preserved readings of the source text should not be explained primarily with the assumption that Paul was quoting from memory and may not have got the wording quite right. Often it is obvious that the deviating wording is connected to the way Paul uses the quotation. The emerging overview is widely accepted among scholars: Paul regularly changed the wording of the quotations in order to make them more compatible with his argumentation (Koch, *Die Schrift als Zeuge*, 186–90; Wagner, *Heralds of the Good News*, 14). On the amount of changes, see Koch, *Die Schrift als Zeuge*, 186; and Stanley, *Paul and the Language*, 348–49.

In conclusion, Clark and Gerrig's Demonstration Theory and Sternberg's Proteus Principle both offer important perspectives on the process of quoting while approaching it from different angles. The Demonstration Theory provides concepts for analyzing the diverse functions of quotations; Sternberg's Proteus Principle, for examining the recontextualization process. The contributions of the theories are connected to two perspectives that deserve more attention among those studying Paul's use of Scripture. The first is the variety of functions quotations perform and the variety of rhetorical effects they bring about in Paul's argumentation. The second concerns Paul's techniques in framing quotations. Tracing intertextual links between Paul's letters and the original literary context of quotations means concentrating on what he left unsaid. In contrast, the framing elements are actively and deliberately created by Paul and therefore are more likely to reveal how he intended the quotation to be read.[47] Directing more attention to these two matters deepens our understanding of Paul's quoting practice, rhetoric, and argumentation.

[47] On this point, see Stanley, *Arguing with Scripture*, 175.

*The*
# JBL Forum,
## an Occasional Exchange

### Black Lives Matter for Critical Biblical Scholarship

In his 2014 presidential address to the Society of Biblical Literature, Fernando Segovia called for "a fusion of the critical and the political, the biblical and the worldly" (*JBL* 134.1 [2015]: 6). Segovia was not the first to do so; Elisabeth Schüssler Fiorenza had done the same in her 1987 address. Indeed, the question of how the *Journal*, and the field, should relate to the world outside the academy has been debated since the *Journal*'s inception in 1881 (see "Editor's Foreword: The *Journal of Biblical Literature* and the Critical Investigation of the Bible," *JBL* 134.3 [2015]: 457–70).

The events leading to #BlackLivesMatter and #SayHerName, such as the killings of Trayvon Martin (Miami, February 2012), Rekia Boyd (Chicago, March 2012), Michael Brown (Ferguson, August 2014), Freddy Gray (Baltimore, April 2015), Tanisha Anderson (Cleveland, June 2015), Sandra Bland (Hempstead, Texas, July 2015), Korryn Gaines (Baltimore, August 2016), among many others, have been felt deeply both inside and outside the United States. One does not have to be a biblical scholar, or an American, to recoil at the senseless loss of lives and to deplore the persistence of violence, racism, and fear in society. But insofar as themes such as race, equality, justice, and the rule of law are present in the biblical corpus, and in the history of biblical scholarship, it seems appropriate to consider how our practices as scholars of the Bible—wherever we are located—are affected by these events and by the deeper social currents they reflect.

In this Forum, six scholars reflect on how racial violence and the movements that attempt to eradicate such violence intersect with the field of biblical studies, both as an area of research and teaching and as an academic guild, on the complex relationship between scholarship and the larger historical and social context within which we experience ourselves as scholars, as members of intersecting groups and communities, and as human beings.

Adele Reinhartz
General Editor, *Journal of Biblical Literature*

# A Reflection on the Black Lives Matter Movement and Its Impact on My Scholarship

WIL GAFNEY
wil.gafney@tcu.edu
Brite Divinity School, Fort Worth, TX 76109

---

"... they do not love your flesh."
—Toni Morrison, *Beloved*

Black lives matter.

"Black lives matter" is a simple affirmative sentence. The need to affirm, explain, or qualify that affirmation stems from the fact that this statement is not universally accepted as a truthful or legitimate claim. Concomitantly, the inverse proposition is always present: Black lives do not matter. That proposition requires no amplification for explanation. It is the ground on which all other claims about black life seem to rest in this society (by which I mean in the Western world, including Europe, though I am confining my reflections to the United States).

I came into my teaching and scholarly career committed to unmasking the whiteness that is applied to the biblical text, through which it is often interpreted—including by many persons and communities of color—and decentering the white male scholarly voice that masquerades as normative and neutral.[1] These commitments have only deepened with the rise of the Black Lives Matter movement.

As a black woman living in the United States, I have long been aware of the disproportionately violent and lethal policing of black folk in comparison with other groups. The shooting of Amadou Diallo, forty-one times, by NYPD officers on 4 February 1999 was the shooting that raised the issue for me initially. As is the case with the majority of recent police and other shootings of black folk, the officers were acquitted of Diallo's murder, even though he was unarmed.

---

[1] In truth I had long worked to peel off the layer of whiteness that I describe as being spackled on biblical texts and characters, particularly in their representation in religious art and curricula in addition to portrayals in popular culture. I do some of that work at wilgafney.com.

The killing of Trayvon Martin on 26 February 2012 marked a turning point for me in my understanding of the degree to which black folk are not regarded as fully—if even at all—human. The ready proffer (and acceptance) of a defense for shooting an unarmed child walking in his neighborhood based on the terror evoked by the mere presence of black bodies communicated to me that there is a broad acceptance of the anti-black dehumanizing bigotry of George Zimmerman. Trayvon's killing, which I regard as a murder in spite of the legal verdict, provided the impetus that crystallized the Black Lives Matter (BLM) movement organized by three black queer women who know what it is to have one's humanity demeaned and despised: Patrisse Cullors, Alicia Garza, and Opal Tometi.[2]

My understanding of the utter disregard for black lives shared broadly in this country and the implication of policing in that disregard became fully heightened with the killing and demonization of Mike Brown on 4 August 2014. The repeated presentation of Mike Brown as a monster and demon, combined with the indignities visited upon his corpse, deeply underscored the degree to which the very humanity of black folk is doubted and denied as a matter of course by individuals and institutions in our social and civil frameworks. The killings of Aiyana Stanley-Jones (2012), Renisha McBride (2014), and the death of Sandra Bland while in police custody (2015) are part of an inescapable rising tide of black death. These deaths occurred and continue to occur in the same public square in which biblical interpretation takes place, and they and their implications must be accounted for in the work of interpreters of the biblical text who write, speak, teach, preach, and think to any degree in public. The public nature of much of this work has meant that a major venue for my work has been, like the groundswell of BLM, social media.

One of my projects has been to help preachers responsibly engage the biblical texts in light of the increasingly visible and ongoing killings of black folk, particularly by police officers, and the accompanying protests by BLM activists. That project made use of a hashtag,[3] #what2preach,[4] to organize hermeneutical and homiletical conversations around lectionary and other texts engaging BLM, addressing its aims, its claims, and the resulting anxiety experienced by many.

As a biblical scholar in a divinity school teaching texts that are received canonically (however that is understood and articulated) by my students, I am clear that I must address BLM in the classroom as the movement and the deaths it protests shape the context in which students interpret the biblical text.

---

[2] A Herstory of the #BlackLivesMatter Movement by Alicia Garza, posted to *The Feminist Wire*, 7 October 2014, http://www.thefeministwire.com/2014/10/blacklivesmatter-2/.

[3] The hash sign, #, marks terms, allowing them to be indexed, searched, and retrieved on social media, e.g. #BlackLivesMatter.

[4] I initially deployed the #what2preach hashtag in the immediate aftermath of the shooting at Sandy Hook in 2012.

My teaching in the age of the BLM movement is characterized by the following: (1) unmasking whiteness in biblical scholarship and interpretation, (2) asking which lives matter in the biblical text, including applying a BLM hermeneutic to the text, and (3) analyzing prophetic literature in light of the claims of BLM while analyzing BLM and its rhetoric and actions as prophetic.

In order to unmask whiteness in scholarly and ecclesial biblical interpretation, I must first help my students identify and name it. My introductory courses begin with maps of Africa and Asia. Naming the context, literature, peoples, and languages of the Hebrew Scriptures "Afro-Asiatic" immediately calls into question the white imagery applied to the biblical world. This depiction manifests in the construction and consumption of white images and icons produced for religious and popular audiences, which are often imposed on peoples of color by their conquerors and colonizers. We talk about the sanctification of whiteness by aligning with the biblical text and the inevitable subsequent demonization of blackness in an interpretive world given easily to binary thinking.

It should be easy to say which lives matter in the biblical text. The Hebrew Bible is the story of Israel's relationship with God. Which lives matter in the Hebrew Bible? Israelite lives matter, and the lives that collaborate to produce, propagate, and protect the people of Israel matter. I explore the question of which lives matter in the Hebrew Scriptures by contrasting the common origin story of humanity with the profound othering of non-Israelite peoples, which often results in calls for (and claims of) genocide. It cannot be said that all lives matter in the Bible, nor can it be said that, of those lives that do matter, they matter equally.

When I apply a Black Lives Matter hermeneutic to the biblical text, I look for those lives that are at risk, subject to oppression, relegated to the margins of the text, and/or discounted as disposable, particularly as a result of an intersecting element of identity. The intersecting identities I consider are largely gender and ethnic identity. While racism does not exist in the Hebrew Scriptures, there is vicious ethnic conflict that can function as an analogue for contemporary race-based conflict.

More recently, my doctoral students in biblical interpretation and I examined the prophetic corpus of the Hebrew Bible in light of BLM and the calls, claims, and actions of the BLM movement as prophetic. I invited the students to reflect on how our academic study of the Bible (scholarship), particularly the prophets, pertains to the issues raised by BLM (justice) in concrete terms (practice).[5] Together we reassessed lament as a prophetic genre and read the rhetoric and actions of the BLM movement as prophetic, specifically lament. We identified the protests and riots as performance prophecy accompanying proclamation prophecy, reading all as lament.

---

[5] Brite Divinity School, where I am currently employed, describes itself as "a community engaged in transforming scholarship, justice, and practice."

There is a significant difference in how I teach now, after the emergence of the BLM movement. I am more intentional in talking about whiteness and white supremacist culture and ideology and the roles of these elements in the founding and shaping of the West, of America, of public and private institutions, including those in which knowledge is constructed and passed on, and of the church and its institutions.

Finally, the BLM movement now shapes my academic scholarship. In my commentary on Nahum, I reflect, "Nahum's Iron Age value system is alive and well in the Digital Age. I am writing after the emergence of the Black Lives Matters movement and find parallels between the disregard for the lives of the people of Nineveh (and others in the canon) and the disregard for the lives of whole populations in the present age."[6] A second project, *Womanist Midrash: A ReIntroduction to the Women of the Torah and of the Throne*,[7] uses my own contemporary midrash drawn from the use of the sacred imagination in black preaching and from classical rabbinic midrash to offer a womanist hermeneutic of selected passages. I use the notion of the *metaturgeman*, a translator prophet, to describe the interrelated work of translation and interpretation.

I close by donning the mantle of the *metaturgeman* and offering a womanist targum of Isaiah 53:

> *Who has believed what we have said?*
> *We have majesty that you would not regard,*
>     *yet you coveted our appearance.*
>
> *We are despised and rejected by others,*
> *a people of suffering and acquainted with grief,*
>     *those from whom others hide their faces;*
> *we are despised and deemed of no account.*
> *Surely we have borne your infirmities*
>     *and carried your diseases;*
> *yet you have accounted us stricken,*
>     *struck down by God, and afflicted.*
>
> *But we were wounded for your transgressions,*
>     *crushed for your iniquities;*
> *upon us was the punishment that made you who you are,*
>     *and by our bruises you are also destroyed.*

---

[6] Forthcoming in the Wisdom Commentary series from Liturgical Press.
[7] Louisville: Westminster John Knox, forthcoming.

# The Scholarly Network

**NYASHA JUNIOR**
nyasha.junior@temple.edu
Temple University, Philadelphia, PA 10122

---

Service is the rent we pay for a room on earth.
—Unknown author

I instruct my students to answer the exam question directly. That is, they must answer the question as I wrote it and not as they wish to reformulate it. I also tell my students to do as I say and not as I do. The editor has asked me and others to offer "personal reflections on whether and how your own work has been affected by recent events (high-profile murders of black people, including Trayvon Martin, Michael Brown, and Freddie Gray, as well as other black men, women, and children assaulted and murdered by law enforcement officials and others in the United States), including, if possible, one or two concrete examples of past, current, or future work."

The editor asks "whether" my work has been affected by these events. This question presumes that my work and I are separate, but as I am a black woman academic, my work and life are intertwined. It is not possible for me to remain unaffected by the murders of black people. Although I do not personally know the individuals who have been murdered, they are my kin. Although I do not know their families, I grieve with them. My work includes more than the items detailed in my annual faculty productivity report. I do not judge my success or productivity solely by standard academic metrics. My work involves not only what I publish but how I operate in the world and in this academic discipline. In this personal essay, I reflect on my motivation and efforts to support black and other underrepresented scholars through networking and social media.

Data from the Society of Biblical Literature (SBL) indicate that there are relatively few black biblical scholars in the United States. According to the 2015 *SBL Society Report*, "Presently, 85% of members who claim to be United States citizens are of European descent, 3.8% are multiethnic, and 3.4% are of African descent. Members of Asian descent account for 2.3%, Latina/o descent totals 1.7%, and

Native American, Alaska Native, or First Nation descent is 0.2%."[1] Furthermore, the *Society Report* acknowledges, "Members of African descent have the highest representation of contingent faculty at 9.5% and the lowest representation of full-time tenured faculty at 47.4%."[2] As a group, black SBL members remain underrepresented and are least secure regarding tenure status.

Academia is not a warm, welcoming space, and it is much less so for underrepresented scholars.[3] In many conversations with nonblack academics, I find that I may be one of the few black scholars they know. According to the 2013 American Values Survey by the Public Religion Research Institute (PRRI), the social networks of whites are 91 percent white.[4] Just as our neighborhoods and faith communities are segregated, so are our scholarly networks. Academics rely on a host of informal communication networks for a variety of reasons. We may contact our graduate school cohort at "feeder" schools to ask if they have promising students who are applying for doctoral programs. We may e-mail our colleagues seeking names to include on lists of potential job candidates or keynote speakers. "I have never heard of her" is one of the worst things that can be said about a scholar. People need to know that you exist in order to invite you to collaborate on projects, contribute to edited volumes, or apply for fellowships. Black scholars who are not part of those networks may miss out on vital opportunities.

I am fortunate to have a tenure-track position, encouraging departmental colleagues, a wonderful therapist, and a loving family. I want to help other scholars who may not have the same support. I do not consider myself an activist; for me, that term suggests someone who is strongly committed to a particular organization, cause, or action on a regular basis. I do not consider myself a protester, although my family and I attend local meetings, protests, and vigils, including those in support of the #SayHerName campaign.[5] Instead, I feel an obligation to support others because my parents instilled in me the importance of "lifting as we climb."[6] That is,

---

[1] Society of Biblical Literature, 2015 *Society Report*, https://www.sbl-site.org/assets/pdfs/SR2015_online.pdf, 22.

[2] Ibid., 23.

[3] See Gabriella Gutiérrez y Muhs et al., eds., *Presumed Incompetent: The Intersections of Race and Class for Women in Academia* (Boulder: University Press of Colorado, 2012); and Patricia Matthew, ed., *Written/Unwritten: Diversity and the Hidden Truths of Tenure* (Chapel Hill: University of North Carolina Press), 2016.

[4] Daniel Cox, Juhem Navarro-Rivera, and Robert P. Jones, *Race, Religion, and Political Affiliation of American's Core Social Networks*, PRRI, August 3, 2016, http://www.prri.org/research/race-religion-political-affiliation-americans-social-networks/.

[5] #SayHerName seeks to bring attention to the violence and police brutality experienced by black girls and women (African American Policy Forum, http://www.aapf.org/sayhername/).

[6] "Lifting as We Climb" was the motto of the National Association of Colored Women, which began in 1896. This association later became the National Association of Colored Women's Clubs; http://www.nacwc.org/aboutus/index.html.

even as I attain some measure of individual success, I have a duty to assist other black people. My service to others does not have a particular label. I don't wear it on a t-shirt. It is simply an important and expected part of my work and life. Recent events have not affected my current research projects, but they have made me more resolute in operating within my sphere of influence as a black woman biblical scholar.

### *Networking*

I reject a king-of-the-hill model of academia by sharing opportunities with other scholars. When I receive an invitation from a colleague, I may not be able to accept. Yet I fear that I may be one of few black scholars to receive an invitation, since I may be one of the only black scholars in the invitee's scholarly network. If I cannot accept an offer to speak or to contribute to an edited volume, I have a standing policy to decline politely and give three names. As I discuss on my blog, I suggest the names of three other scholars, especially those who are from traditionally underrepresented groups.[7] By offering additional names, I expand opportunities for other scholars and create new connections in the field. I know that this strategy works because editors let me know that they appreciate the suggestions, and scholars let me know that they have accepted an invitation. I hope to model good citizenship by refusing to engage in competitiveness, greed, and backstabbing.

I try to facilitate networking among graduate students and scholars who are at earlier stages of their careers. Social gatherings can be difficult for many introverted academics, but especially for those from underrepresented groups. Still, getting to know scholars personally is an important part of being in the academy. When I am at meetings or conferences, I make a beeline for the person who looks most uncomfortable in the room or at the reception and introduce myself. I give her my business card and encourage her to contact me. If she seems receptive, I will invite her to join my table or offer to introduce her to a senior scholar who is present. As I develop relationships with these people, I let them know that I am available to listen confidentially and without judgment. I know the weariness and loneliness of being the only one like you in your department or institution. I am not a therapist or counselor, but, in my experience, it can be helpful just to have someone confirm that it's not all in your mind and to acknowledge and name the racism, sexism, and politics of the academy.

### *Social media*

In addition to face-to-face networking in seeking to make academia a better place and space for black academics, I have become more active and outspoken on

---

[7] Nyasha Junior, "Speak Three Names," No Extra Credit, http://www.nyashajunior.com/noextracredit/130820-speak-three-names.

social media, especially in support of black academics. As my social media platform has grown, I have been deliberate about using social media to share my opinion, to disseminate resources, to facilitate networking, and to amplify the work of black and other underrepresented scholars.[8] I have become more vocal in asking predominantly white institutions and white colleagues about their inattention to recent protests. For instance, after the murder of Michael Brown in Ferguson, Missouri, I tweeted several professional organizations asking how they planned to respond. The Wabash Center for Teaching and Learning e-mailed me immediately. [Disclosure: I am a Wabash Center grant awardee.] With none of the red tape or excuses I have come to expect from institutions, the Wabash Center began the Race Matters in the Classroom blog to convene conversations on issues of race in teaching theology and religion.[9] For over a year, a diverse group of scholars contributed blog posts, and Wabash continues to host the blog on its website. It is possible that Wabash might have done something similar on its own, but I was glad to be able to facilitate this development by pointing out the need for some action.

Since the mainstream media anoints only a few scholars as thought leaders or public intellectuals, the work of some marginalized scholars remains underappreciated. In order to combat this, I signal boost the work of black academics on social media. Signal boosting involves posting with the aim of garnering greater attention for a person, a publication, or an event. Influenced by #blktwitterstorians, a hashtag cofounded by Joshua Crutchfield and Aleia Brown for black historians, I created hashtag #blkaarsbl. I use this hashtag to make more visible the work of black academics in religion and biblical studies. When I tweet a link to a book, I include the Twitter handle of the publisher and the scholar or the scholar's institution along with the hashtag. The scholars are usually grateful for the shout out, and both academics and nonacademics thank me for sharing these publications. I hope that others will "read, review, engage, cite, and assign" the work of these scholars.[10]

Even when not using #blkaarsbl, I help to publicize events, calls for papers, and other articles and books related to religion and biblical studies that may be of interest to my social media community. I "tag" influential people on social media to bring things to their attention. I have created a "Black women of SBL" Twitter list that includes black women biblical scholars who are on Twitter. When I participate in Twitter chats, I focus on tweeting links to books and articles in religion and biblical studies. I use Pinterest to curate collections of these links. In addition,

---

[8] My Twitter account (@NyashaJunior) was included on a list of fifteen indispensable academic Twitter accounts (Andy Thomason, "Here Are 15 Indispensable Academic Twitter Accounts," *Chronicle of Higher Education*, March 22, 2016, http://www.chronicle.com/blogs/ticker/here-are-15-indispensable-academic-twitter-accounts/109598).

[9] See Race Matters in the Classroom blog, http://wabashcenter.typepad.com/antiracism_pedagogy/.

[10] Nyasha Junior, *An Introduction to Womanist Biblical Interpretation* (Louisville: Westminster John Knox, 2015), 131.

I live-tweet almost any conference or lecture that I attend. For me, it is a way to share the conversations that are taking place among scholars especially for those who would not or could not attend the conference. In addition, I post images of gatherings of black scholars on social media, including Instagram and Facebook. It is fun to see friends, but it also makes black scholars more visible. These images show students, scholars, and others that black scholars exist and are active in the guild. It says that we are here and that we belong within the wider scholarly network.

# At Exodus as the Door of (No) Return

KENNETH NGWA
kngwa@drew.edu
Drew University Theological School, Madison, NJ 07940

*Charting Paths and Maps*

In the wake of the elections in the United States—elections during which many issues were raised and debated, including race and ethnicity, migration and immigration, gender, masculinity and sexual assault, nationality and religion, ability and disability, exceptionalism and decency, healthcare and trade, criminal justice reform and police violence, environmental justice and income inequality, and so on—poets and political pundits; scholars, teachers, students, and clergy; psychologists and counselors; comics and playwrights have been working hard to "make sense" of it all. As I tried to argue after Michael Brown's shooting death, some practiced routines of communal responses to the traumas of deadly, racial animus are sadly becoming predictable: a funeral service where the Bible is read and referenced in search of hope and justice; and a legal process that rehashes the old, old question of equality before the law and the experience of that equality—if and when it comes—as a posthumous credo to console the weary hearts of victims. How that debate is formulated locally and globally is particularly poignant when specific bodies are always seeking and asking for justice, oftentimes feeling hollow from having witnessed how justice itself is *executed* in dead bodies lying motionless on the streets or in coffins.[1]

As I have interacted with many thinkers and students, I have found myself returning to Jan Assmann's concept of mnemohistory as a useful trope for grappling with the mental, physical, political, and emotional exhaustion that comes with activating distinct kinds of memories and traumas and losses and hopes and institutionalizing them through a public ritual (read: election process). Grounded in a history-of-religions approach to biblical studies, Assmann's concept deploys

---

[1] See Kenneth Ngwa, "Ferguson, Bible and the 'Long Division' of Race," http://wabashcenter.typepad.com/antiracism_pedagogy/2014/09/fergusson-bible-and-the-long-division-of-race.html.

methodological insights from literary and narrative theory, along with Freudian psychoanalysis on trauma and Halbwachsian social theories on structures of memory. A subfield of historical studies, mnemohistory is, in its most simplified formulation, "reception theory applied to history."[2] The hermeneutical vehicle that carries this theory is cultural memory—understood as probing the depths of time and the phenomenological "archive" of human existence; it is distinguishable from other forms of memory (e.g., bonding memory) by encompassing "the age-old, out-of-the-way, and discarded" events of the past. In other words, cultural memory "includes the noninstrumentalizable, heretical, subversive, and disowned."[3]

But what does it mean to institutionalize the "noninstrumentalizable, heretical, subversive, and disowned"? And what constitutes the heretical and noninstrumentalizable, in terms of content and process of identity formation? In other words, how have acts of racial violence in the United States and around the world contributed to assessments of what is heretical and what is not? These questions of endangered belonging; of racialized history, politics, religion, and culture strike me from multiple directions, often not in isolation but in tandem. This multipronged force of community fragmentation and formation, forged in response to violent genealogies to which my identity is linked by the force of political history or of narration or of education or of religious heritage or of membership and citizenship, compels me to make hermeneutical moves that grapple with the twin experiences of alienation and erasure and their rootedness in history and storytelling.

In her captivating book *A Map to the Door of No Return*, Dionne Brand remembers when, as a thirteen-year-old, she tried to help her grandfather remember "what people we came from." They worked through a few possible African ethnic names but settled on none. That unresolved search and conversation, on this side of the Atlantic, opened a small space in Brand and, over time, came to "reveal a tear in the world." In Brand's words:

> I would have proceeded happily with a simple name. I may have played with it for a few days and then stored it away. Forgotten. But the rupture this exchange with my grandfather revealed was greater than the need for familial bonds. It was a rupture in history, a rupture in the quality of being. It was also a physical rupture, a rupture of geography.[4]

More than physical spaces across several countries along the coast of the Atlantic Ocean, the doors of no return have become a powerful symbol of ruptured identity in African diasporic studies—not just for those who were forcefully removed from

---

[2] Jan Assmann, *Moses the Egyptian: The Memory of Egypt in Western Monotheism* (Cambridge: Harvard University Press, 1997), 9.

[3] Jan Assmann, *Religion and Cultural Memory: Ten Studies*, trans. Rodney Livingstone, Cultural Memory in the Present (Stanford, CA: Stanford University Press, 2006), 27.

[4] Dionne Brand, *A Map to the Door of No Return: Notes to Belonging* (Toronto: Vintage, 2001), 4–5.

their homes and placed on slave ships but also for those who remained, for whom the doors they never entered nevertheless represent a gateway to unclaimed and unclaimable loss of familial kin and community, captured and taken. Identity is forever fractured. And the fracturing is coded in bodies and stories—official and unofficial—but also in the structures that hold these doors. Diaspora is haunting. And its institutional embodiment in the constructed slave castle's architecture performs the story of fracture and its layers of nightmare premised on political, religious, and racial patronage: the governor's residence at the very top, a chapel at the middle level, and dungeons at the bottom, all designed to compel the captured mind and body to bend and even break (cf. Exod 6:9).

How does one look through these doors from either side of the Atlantic? Perhaps the more pressing questions in light of acts of violence against black and brown bodies on the streets and in churches, schools, nightclubs, and in light of the expanding prison and military industrial complex and ongoing drumbeats of war, and in light of environmental degradation and poverty—are these: How have/did the ideologies that governed these doors travel to the New World and define local and global politics today? And "what kind of citizen are we willing to be"?[5] And how does one engage the Bible, given its role in the construction of these haunting structures and narratives that populate global spaces?[6]

In *The Genesis of Liberation*, Emerson B. Powery and Rodney S. Sadler Jr. examine antebellum African American appropriations of the Bible as authoritative Scripture and the methodologies that allowed them to create alternative narratives about self and to participate in the political project of Western civilization, which used Scriptures to enslave them. For Powery and Sadler, the Bible was spiritual and political, and failure to interpret it in the context of religious and political imagination would have been "counterproductive" for African Americans.[7] Similarly, in *The Stolen Bible*, Gerald West provides a historical panoramic assessment of the complex processes by which Africans encountered the Bible as an imperial document but over time, through various stages of interpretation and embodiment, appropriated the Bible as a central document in their lives—indeed, as an icon.[8] These two publications represent long-standing creative engagements with hermeneutical doors of no return, carved out with the Bible and the gun.[9]

---

[5] Tim Lake, in a private conversation with me.

[6] See Tod Linafelt, ed., *Strange Fire: Reading the Bible after the Holocaust*, BibSem 71 (Sheffield: Sheffield Academic, 2000); and Danna Nolan Fewell and Gary A. Phillips, "Bak's Impossible Memorial: Giving Face to the Children," *ARTS* 20 (2009): 93–123.

[7] Emerson B. Powery and Rodney S. Sadler Jr., *The Genesis of Liberation: Biblical Interpretation in the Antebellum Narratives of the Enslaved* (Louisville: Westminster John Knox, 2016), 2–3.

[8] Gerald O. West, *The Stolen Bible: From Tool of Imperialism to African Icon*, BibInt (Leiden: Brill, 2016).

[9] See the intersections of Bible, religion, culture, and gun violence (war) in Akiki K. Nyabongo's *The Story of an African Chief* (New York: Scribner's Sons, 1935).

These hermeneutical moves are guided by rhythms of life that emerge from deep spaces and traditions. It is a merging of history and story through interpretive repositioning grounded in *having seen or encountered and somehow survived the formlessness of alienation and the void of erasure*: "I saw the earth/land and behold, formlessness and void" (Jer 4:23). Survival, regeneration, and even progress cannot be fully understood except in relation to that which is lost, not simply as transition but as trauma survived. Accordingly, methods of interpretation and structures of existence are developed and embraced as contingency mechanisms, because always in the shadows are pernicious threats to communal existence. The ancient biblical writer, faced with the traumatic act of geopolitical transition that created alienation and erasure, emerged as a subject-historian and perhaps even as a poet, not unlike a modern biblical scholar grappling with trauma—the physical and psychic wound of fragmentation and survival.[10] Jonathan Z. Smith has argued that the historian, unlike the philosopher or the theologian, has no places where to stand "apart from the messiness of the given world," so that, for the historian, there is "no real beginning, but only the plunge … at some arbitrary point to avoid the unhappy alternatives of infinite regress or silence."[11] Marginalized persons experience this plunge at some arbitrary point as traumatic, as the experience that makes engagement with the door of no return and the development of identity around alienation and erasure so compelling and haunting.

### Political and Biblical Worlds: Strange and Familiar Kin

In the 2007 movie *The Great Debaters*, the lead character (Professor Tolson, played by Denzel Washington) begins his education of the potential 1935 Wiley College debate team by quoting from Langston Hughes's poem, "I, Too."[12]

Set in the early 1930s, on the back end of the Harlem Renaissance and the emergence of the Negritude movement in Paris, the movie reflects shifts in black consciousness and intellectual creativity in the midst of major economic depression, racial segregation in the United States, emerging nationalist parties in Europe, impending war, and still ongoing colonial rule in Africa. Taken up and used to introduce and frame the movie, Hughes's poem functions as another engagement with that haunting door to America. The movie engages theology, biblical studies, homiletics, law, language, literature, and philosophy; its topics range from self-pity to beauty; from economics (child welfare) to cultural expression and carnival; from gender and race to the importance of credible "sources" and "evidence," both canonical/official (e.g., President Roosevelt's fireside chats) and canonical/

---

[10] David M. Carr, *Holy Resilience: The Bible's Traumatic Origins* (New Haven: Yale University Press, 2014).

[11] Jonathan Z. Smith, *Map Is Not Territory: Studies in the History of Religion*, SJLA 23 (Leiden: Brill, 1978), 288–90.

[12] See https://www.poetryfoundation.org/poems-and-poets/poems/detail/47558.

unofficial ("that look in a mother's eyes when she can't feed her kids"). Professor Tolson's words to his debate prep team are pointed and sharp: "Debate is blood sport. It's combat. But your weapons are words." Potential members of the debate team are invited to enter the "hot spot" where the rigor of intellectual research is matched with a critically embodied analysis of the effect of gender and race discrimination, politics, and history.

In one of these "hot spot" moments, reference is made to what might be the most famous line from James Joyce's novel *Ulysses*, spoken by the character Stephen Dedalus: "History ... is a nightmare from which I am trying to awake."[13] But what exactly is this nightmarish history? It is the history that gives rise, for example, to the Black Lives Matter (#BLM) movement, and to Standing Rock, and to the #RhodesMustFall and #FeesMustFall movements in South Africa, and to refugees fleeing wars in Syria and Central African Republic, and to school girls captured by Boko Haram in Nigeria, and to terrorist attacks and drone attacks, and to promises to build walls between peoples, and to profiling Muslims, and so on.

In this global geopolitical context of racial, ethnic, ecological, and gendered violence; of political alienation, terrorism, and erasure, I return to a hermeneutic of trauma-hope. It is a hermeneutic premised on the philosophy of Ubuntu, the complex Bantu-derived concept of political, social, psychological, and spiritual communal belonging most famously popularized and enacted by Desmond Tutu during the Truth and Reconciliation Commission's work in post-apartheid South Africa.[14] Much like the Jewish concept of Tikkun Olam, the notion of Ubuntu involves the hard work of piecing together fragmented and endangered identities into a web of interconnectedness and social bonding that strives toward healthy being and belonging.

### *Exodus: Community Formation around Alienation and Rupture*

In *Theorizing Scriptures*, Vincent Wimbush has argued for a "differently oriented interpretive practice" that is focused not on "the exegesis of texts but the fathoming of human striving and behaviors and orientations, with their fears, aspirations, low points and high marks, as they are represented in relationships to 'scriptures.' It has to do with excavating the work and the consequences of such that we make 'scriptures' do for us."[15] One such excavation revolves around a key verse in Exodus: "There arose a king who did not know Joseph" (Exod 1:8). Far from being a simple literary ploy connecting Exodus and Genesis, this phrase functions

---

[13] James Joyce, *Ulysses* (New York: Random House, 1961), 34.
[14] See Desmond Tutu, *No Future without Forgiveness* (New York: Doubleday, 1999); Michael Battle, *Ubuntu: I in You and You in Me* (New York: Seabury Books, 2009).
[15] Vincent Wimbush, "TEXTures, Gestures, Power: Orientation to Radical Excavation," in *Theorizing Scriptures: New Critical Orientations to a Cultural Phenomenon*, ed. Vincent Wimbush, Signifying (on) Scriptures (New Brunswick, NJ: Rutgers University Press, 2008), 1–20, here 1.

to demarcate an epistemological and hermeneutical fault line, carved or reopened by a dreadful circumstance! The emergence of a new governance premised on institutional amnesia triggers traumatic memories and anxieties among marginalized persons. The sense of alienation and erasure inherent in this new political structure is experienced not just in the form of Orientalism, which Edward Said named,[16] but also in the form of institutionalized and authorized violence. In his initial theorizing of the African postcolony, Achille Mbembe called this existential reality "illicit cohabitation" made fraught by the colonizer and the colonized sharing the same living space; in her contributions to the intellectual culture of the Harlem Renaissance, Zora Neale Hurston framed it as being "kinfolks to the Pharaohs."[17] Drawing on Michel Foucault's notion of biopolitics, Mbembe diagnosed and named this form of governance necropolitics: "the power and the capacity to dictate who may live and who will die."[18] To be on the receiving end of this power structure; to belong to a community political or otherwise where institutionalized necropolitics infuses and structures routine rhythms of life and citizenship; and to work toward survival, in spite of these challenges, is to inhabit and embody an epistemological and hermeneutical identity of trauma-hope.[19]

If disruptive social and political events create distortions that reshape identity through transformation (even erasure) and displacement, then the biblical myth of adoption constitutes a narrative expression of that profound shift and survival. To set the stage for such a myth, the biblical story portrays Pharaoh as the institutional embodiment of cultural amnesia—he did not know Joseph—and as the first character to theorize about an exodus, conceptualized as an event of wartime alliances and population movements that redefines geopolitical identity. Speaking to his counselors about the Hebrews, Pharaoh says, "in the event of war, they may join forces with our enemies, fight against us and go up from the land" (Exod 1:10). Pharaoh's hypothetical scenario, as the political embodiment of governing power, backed by institutional, deliberative, and legislative power, performs multiple social, political, and geographical functions. It ruptures Hebrew identity from "national" identity and history ("they" versus "us"); it links this ruptured or fragmented identity and history to alien adversaries ("our enemies"); and finally it remaps geopolitical existence and belonging ("go up from the land"). Pharaoh's

---

[16] Edward W. Said, *Orientalism* (New York: Vintage Books, 1978).

[17] Achille Mbembe, "Provisional Notes on the Postcolony," *Africa: Journal of the International African Institute* 62 (1992): 3–37, here 4 (in his later work *On the Postcolony*, Studies on the History of Society and Culture 41 [Berkeley: University of California Press, 2001], Mbembe dropped this expression); Zora Neale Hurston, *Moses, Man of the Mountain* (New York: Harperperennial, 1991), 31.

[18] Achille Mbembe, "Necropolitics," trans. Libby Meintjes, *Public Culture* 15 (2003): 11–40, here 11.

[19] Kenneth Ngwa, "The Making of Gershom's Story: A Cameroonian Postwar Hermeneutics Reading of Exodus 2," *JBL* 134 (2015): 855–76.

hypothetical scenario constitutes the founding and perennial political challenge for the marginalized community.

In the face of racialized necropolitics, exodus (as engagement with the door of no return) is fundamentally an act of rediscovery of otherwise forgotten experiences or erased identities. This rediscovery emerged in Sigmund Freud's *Moses and Monotheism* and is defined as much by a sense of deep loss as by obsessive search for the sublime—what Freud called intellectual progress—both of which reveal textures of individual and collective identity.[20] Exodus, as a motif and as a story, is rooted in rugged terrains of violently destroyed, abandoned, and remapped geographies, histories, and belief systems, as well as in the ingenuity of individual and collective brilliance, imagination, and innovation. This exploration at the interface of political constructions of racial/ethnic and national affinities has preoccupied studies on Freud's sense of identity as a Jew and his approach to Judaism, global geopolitics, and anti-Semitism.[21]

Freud's hermeneutic was historical, contemporaneous, and complex. Issues of religion, race, nationality, displacement, and survival intersect in *Moses and Monotheism* and found contextual urgency with Germany's annexation of Austria in 1938. Within months of that violent political reality, Freud and his family fled Vienna to London, where he published what turned out to be his last book. Two chapters had already been published in 1937, so Freud's thinking on Moses and the exodus was not completely new. But the third section of the book provides the religious and political context that fueled its composition:

> Formerly I lived under the protection of the Catholic Church and feared that by publishing the essay I should lose that protection and that the practitioners and students of psycho-analysis in Austria would be forbidden their work. Then, suddenly, the German invasion broke in on us and Catholicism proved to be, as the Bible has it, "but a broken reed." In the certainty of persecution now not only because of my work but also because of my "race" I left with many friends the city which from early childhood through 78 years, had been a home to me.[22]

Endangered and displaced, Freud returned to *Moses and Monotheism* and embarked on a daring project around trauma, memory, identity formation, religion, and survival. Attuned to historical-critical scholarship that flourished on the premise of identifying narrative fragments in the biblical text and using those fragments to postulate traditions about possible distinct communities, Freud made his hermeneutical move: narrative gaps and discrepancies in the biblical text are covert evidence of historical processes of violence and fragmentation. He then postulated an

---

[20] Sigmund Freud, *Moses and Monotheism*, trans. Katharine Jones (New York: Vintage Books, 1939).

[21] Yosef Hayim Yerusalmi, *Freud's Moses: Judaism Terminable and Interminable* (New Haven: Yale University Press, 1991); Edward Said, *Freud and the Non-European* (London: Verso, 2003).

[22] Freud, *Moses and Monotheism*, 69–70.

analogy between narrative violence and real violence: "The distortion of a text is not unlike a murder. The difficulty lies not in the execution of the deed but in doing away with the traces."[23]

The door of (no) return is carved, again. Its distortions are understood in the double sense of changing the appearance of something and wrenching apart or putting it in some other place, that is, as erasure and alienation.[24] In this scenario, legislation and narration are war by other means, repeatedly reenacting the door of (no) return but also seeking to ground resistance to oppression. The scholarship is activist, in the mode of Mr. Tolson's in *The Great Debaters*.

## Conclusion

The interpretive significance of probing exodus as a wartime scenario, that is, as a scenario in which stories are developed and decisions are made about who lives and who dies, raises critical questions for Exodus interpretation: How do violence and communal responses to violence shape the narrative content and significance of Exodus and exodus storytelling? Which bodies are dying, and how are they dying, and where are they dying—dying as a result of official discourse, policy, and practice? And which bodies are spatially displaced? As one gapes into this door of (no) return, adoption functions as a social act of counteralienation and survival that performs more than a singular political act of putting Moses and Pharaoh in the same house. Adoption also compels a conceptualization of the traumas of erasure and alienation as profoundly ironic and indeed tragic acts of self-amputation that bind the oppressor and oppressed across generations and geographical regions. To navigate and survive the dual threads and threats of communal *erasure* and *confinement*, evoked in Pharaoh's exodus scenario and anti-exodus policy, requires more than engagement with epistemological breaks with a past built on political and institutionalized oppression; to navigate and survive this dual thread and threat also requires hermeneutical repositioning—reengagement with biblical texts and reengagements with communities under duress, marginalized by episodic and systemic acts of alienation and erasure. This, for me, is an ideological project around trauma-hope. It works for communal regeneration and strives for improved quality of life.

[23] Ibid., 52.
[24] Ibid.

# The African American Bible: Bound in a Christian Nation

RICHARD NEWTON
newtonr@etown.edu
Elizabethtown College, Elizabethtown, PA 17022

At the 2015 National Prayer Breakfast, President Barack Obama delivered a sermon from his bully pulpit that garnered the ire of the Christian Right.[1] In retrospect, there were many moments from the speech that could have caused concern. The president's conciliatory gestures toward the Dalai Lama might have opened a diplomatic Pandora's box, for even the slightest bow of acknowledgment could tax relations with the Chinese government. Ultimately this hardly proved newsworthy, nor did Mr. Obama's description of the Islamic State as a "death cult." His denunciation of Islamicized violence in Paris, Pakistan, and the Middle East was as expected as his recitation of words attributed to the Prophet Muhammad, "None of you truly believes until he loves for his brother what he loves for himself."[2] At the time, "the golden rule" was a party line feigned by Democrats and Republicans alike.

Any contention from these statements paled next to this controversial presidential parable:

> So how do we, as people of faith, reconcile these realities—the profound good, the strength, the tenacity, the compassion and love that can flow from all our faiths, operating alongside those who seek to hijack religion for their own murderous ends? Humanity has been grappling with these questions throughout human history. And lest we get on our high horse and think this is unique to some other place, remember that during the Crusades and the Inquisition,

---

[1] Juliet Eliperin, "Critics Pounce after Obama Talks Crusades, Slavery at Prayer Breakfast," *Washington Post*, 5 February 2015, http://wapo.st/1ugu8JG.
[2] The Companion Anas ibn Malik is said to have heard this according to Sahih al-Bukhari, vol. 1, book 2, Hadith 15, https://sunnah.com/bukhari/2.

people committed terrible deeds in the name of Christ. In our home country, slavery and Jim Crow all too often was justified in the name of Christ.³

Much could be said about the identity politics at play in Mr. Obama's statement—the limits of his religious pluralism, his signification of 9/11, his social location of theodicy. But in this moment, I'd like to suggest that this event was proof positive that Americans are *bound in a Christian nation*.

To be clear, the United States of America is not made up solely of Christians, nor is it a theocracy. But America is a Christian nation. Those who protest with song of "the separation of church and state" forget that its refrain comes after a verse *not about whether* but *how* the one may operate in the other. Put differently, Americans would not argue about church–state relations were it not a central concern.

In terms of the "anthropology of Scriptures," I contend that black people's relationship with the Bible testifies to two aspects of the Christian nation paradox.⁴ America is a strange new world in which some are *bound in* (i.e., the enchained, the castigated, the conquered) just as it can be the promised land where others *are bound for* (i.e., the invigorated, the cheered, the conquerors). In theorizing about an African American Bible, members of the Society of Biblical Literature might re-cognize the category of Scriptures as indicative of the stories not only that we read but that also read us back.⁵ Within their binding, the astute begin to make sense of their worlds.

The following reflective essay recounts some of the lessons learned in studying the tension between the Bible and the very constitution of African American identity. There we see the ambivalence of this nation's Bible readers to the matter of black life—namely, that its import is far from sacrosanct according to America's hermeneutical posturing.⁶

## *In the Beginning*

At the crossroads of the "genetic turn" and the post–civil rights era, inclusion-minded Americans began to profess that we are all just part of one race, the human

---

³ Barack Obama, "Remarks by the President at the National Prayer Breakfast" (Washington Hilton, Washington, DC, 5 February 2015), https://www.whitehouse.gov/the-press-office/2015/02/05/remarks-president-national-prayer-breakfast.

⁴ The name for this approach comes from Wilfred Cantwell Smith's study of Scripture as a "human activity ... human propensity, and potentiality" (*What Is Scripture: A Comparative Approach* [Minneapolis: Fortress, 1993], 237).

⁵ My thesis regarding critical examination of Scripture is heavily informed by the work of two scholarly circles, the Institute for Signifying Scriptures and the Society for Comparative Research on Iconic and Performative Texts.

⁶ Shannel T. Smith's "hermeneutics of *ambiveilence*," suggests that scriptural engagement can simultaneously "signify victimization by, and ... participation in" dominance (*The Woman Babylon and the Marks of Empire: Reading Revelation with a Postcolonial Womanist Hermeneutics of Ambiveilence*, Emerging Scholars [Minneapolis: Fortress, 2014], 12).

race.[7] The Christian Pop/Rock/Rap group called DC Talk (Decent Christian Talk) made the statement into a creed.

> We're colored people, and we live in a tainted place.
> We're colored people, and they call us the human race.
> We've got a history so full of mistakes.
> And we are colored people who depend on a Holy Grace.[8]

The racial sentiment also reflects the scientism of the zeitgeist. The "Mitochondrial Eve" discourse has given moderns sufficient license to remark that we are all African from a certain point of view.

But we would be remiss if we forgot that scientific talk of primitive Africa convinced more than a few Europeans that Africans needed to be saved from themselves, by the hand of either a more civilized master or a more knowledgeable helpmate.

To recover the missing link, the African American Bible records the curse of Canaan, son of Ham, son of Noah (Gen 9:18–27 NRSV). After the flood, Noah is said to have planted a vineyard. After drinking the fruit of his labor, he falls into a naked, drunken stupor. When Ham stumbles upon Noah, this youngest son goes to his elder brothers, who cover Noah with a garment while backing away, eyes averted. After Noah comes to consciousness, he praises the discretion of the older brothers but, for whatever reason, stands ashamed of Ham, cursing the youngest's son, Canaan—"lowest of slaves shall he be to his brothers" (Gen 9:25).

This would be insignificant to the plight of black peoples had not slave masters found etiological value in denoting the origin of Ham's sons in the people of "Cush, Egypt, Put, and Canaan" (Gen 10:6).[9] The Dark Continent had scriptural grounds to receive the Enlightenment; Africa was an Eden waiting to be subdued by those made in God's image. In historicizing origins in Africa, the slave institution had further evidence for rendering black peoples as the "lowest of slaves."

Indeed President James Madison likened slavery to America's "original sin," but African Americans would long be made to sow the garden's seed without a taste of free will's fruits.[10] One might grant that all humans come from an Edenic Africa,

---

[7] Christopher Shea, "The Nature-Nurture Debate, Redux," *Chronicle Review: A Weekly Magazine of Ideas* 55, no. 18 (2009): B6–B9.

[8] DC Talk, "Colored People," lyrics by Toby McKeehan and George Cocchini, on *Jesus Freak*, Gotee Records, 1995.

[9] Emerson B. Powery and Rodney S. Sadler Jr., *The Genesis of Liberation: Biblical Interpretation in the Antebellum Narratives of the Enslaved* (Louisville: Westminster John Knox, 2016), 83–111.

[10] James Madison, "Letter to Marquis de Lafayette, November 25 1820," in *The Writings of James Madison*, vol. 9, *1819-1836* (New York: G. P. Putnam's Sons, 1910), 37, https://books.google.com/books?id=e5M5AQAAMAAJ&lpg=PA35&ots=D90wmyclE9&dq=james%20madison%20to%20lafayette%20november%2025%201820&pg=PA37#v=onepage&q=original%20sin&f=false.

though in my reading of the African American Bible, there is a qualifying clause—a paraphrase of George Orwell's famous riff in Animal Farm: "All humans are created equal, but some more equal than others."[11]

## *Let My People Go*

National lore need not depend on primeval pasts. Americans also take solace in deliverance from civil wars and emancipation from slavery. Working but a few miles from Gettysburg, I grow convinced of the country's haggadic memory of Lincoln's address, "that this nation, under God, shall have a new birth of freedom—and that government of the people, by the people, for the people, shall not perish from the earth."[12] As quick as we are to follow this New World Moses, the African American Bible would have us remember that Moses, too, worked in the court of Pharaoh. And, like Moses, Lincoln needed encouragement to proclaim release to the captives.

We should not struggle to imagine nineteenth-century black people envisioning the trappings of Washington, DC, as Egypt. Lest one think I exaggerate, the National Archives and Records Administration holds receipts in testament to the blood, sweat, and tears shed by the slaves who built the White House.[13] And in his 1829 "Appeal to the Coloured Citizens of the World," freedman David Walker bluntly commented, "In all probability, Moses would have … been seated on the throne of Egypt. But he had rather suffer shame, with the people of God, than to enjoy pleasures with that wicked people for a season." Walker's words stand in stark contrast to America's self-understanding as a chosen, freedom-loving people.

Frederick Douglass similarly denounced the nation's Independence Day as a grotesque "Passover for the emancipated people of God."[14] The abolitionist's famous jeremiad of 5 July 1852 condemned the Christian nation with prophetic fury.

> I do not hesitate to declare, with all my soul, that the character and conduct of this nation never looked blacker to me than on this 4th of July! … America is false to the past, false to the present, and solemnly *binds* herself to be false to the future. Standing with God and the crushed and bleeding slave on this occasion, I will, in the name of humanity which is outraged, in the name of liberty which is *fettered*, in the name of the constitution and the Bible, which are disregarded and trampled upon, dare to call in question and to denounce, with all the

---

[11] George Orwell, *Animal Farm* (1945; repr., New York: Mariner Books, 2009), 192.

[12] Abraham Lincoln, "Gettysburg Address," 19 November 1863, http://avalon.law.yale.edu/19th_century/gettyb.asp.

[13] Dennis Lewis, "The White House Was, in Fact, Built by Slaves," *Smithsonian.com*, 26 July 2016, http://www.smithsonianmag.com/smart-news/white-house-was-fact-built-slaves-180959916/.

[14] Frederick Douglass, "The Meaning of July Fourth for the Negro" (Rochester, NY, 5 July 1852), http://masshumanities.org/files/programs/douglass/speech_complete.pdf.

emphasis I can command, everything that serves to perpetuate slavery—the great sin and shame of America! "I will not equivocate; I will not excuse"; I will use the severest language I can command; and yet not one word shall escape me that any man, whose judgment is not blinded by prejudice, or who is not at heart a slaveholder, shall not confess to be right and just.[15]

Abraham Lincoln could only stand tall as Moses because of the backbreaking rhetoric that challenged America to no longer be Egypt.

In national memory it is Lincoln's tragic denouement that brought the commandments of freedom to this people. His Mosaic actions are retold with the gravity and mourning held together in (often in Paul Robeson's timbre) the words of the Negro spiritual:

> Go down, Moses,
> 'way down in Egypt's land.
> Tell ol' Pharaoh,
> Let my people Go![16]

In the African American Bible, Lincoln is remembered not simply for demonstrating the inalienability of freedom from the condition of black humanity but also for knowing the price for insisting so—"the last full measure of devotion."[17]

## *Thy Kingdom Come*

Still, why would African Americans follow a text that says "slaves obey your earthly masters" (Col 3:21)? Dr. King was "ashamed to affirm that eleven o'clock on Sunday morning, when we stand to sing 'In Christ there is no East nor West,' is the most segregated hour [in] America."[18] How could black people put their faith in the way of so many of their oppressors?

Because of the African American Bible, we know that this same faith gave black people a vocabulary for talking back to America. King called the nation to repent and to hear the good news, the fulfillment of what Lincoln had wrought. The dream he proclaimed baptized America into a land awaiting opportunity, where "every valley shall be exalted, every hill and mountain made low, the rough places will be made plains, and the crooked places will be made straight, and the glory of the Lord shall be revealed, and all the flesh shall see it together"

---

[15] Ibid. (emphasis added).

[16] Negro Spiritual, "Go Down Moses," in *The African American Experience: Black History and Culture through Speeches, Letters, Editorials, Poems, Songs, and Stories*, ed. Kai Wright (New York: Black Dog & Leventhal, 2001), 106.

[17] Lincoln, "Gettysburg Address."

[18] Martin Luther King Jr., Address before the National Press Club, 19 July 1962, in *Testament of Hope: The Essential Writings and Speeches of Martin Luther King, Jr.*, ed. James Melvin Washington (San Francisco: HarperOne, 1986), 101.

(Isa 40:4–5).¹⁹ King not only knew the Gospel of Luke, for many he would be the Gospel incarnate, turning the page on "Let my people go!" to "Thank God Almighty, we are free at last!"

But such an inspiring message and powerful transformation, in light of King's death, prompts us to wonder who in this nation could go on without knowing this chapter from the African American Bible? Who could see the Lincoln Memorial without recalling King televised in glory before it? I hope these inquiries are beginning to make clear that the African American Bible is not just "texts" but the social forces with which Americans must reckon—regardless of one's relationship to the color line.

## *The End-Times*

It is also to wrestle with the possibility that we are living in the end-times. Consider the lengths to which Americans have gone to cast Barack Obama as a false prophet, antichrist, Satan, or all of the above. Conservative pundit Glenn Beck saw evidence enough in the History Channel miniseries *The Bible*, linking Moroccan actor Mehdi Ouazanni's appearance as "the Devil" to the visage of President Barack Obama.

FIGURE 1. Glenn Beck sees "the Devil" in the History Channel's *The Bible*²⁰

Such racial profiling may not be worthy of attention in our flagship journal. But what of the fact that a white cop swore (on the Bible?) that an unarmed black

---

[19] Martin Luther King Jr., "I Have a Dream," 28 August 1963, in Wright, *African American Experience*, 531–33.

[20] Glenn Beck, Twitter Post, 16 March 2013, 9:52 PM, https://twitter.com/glennbeck/status/313120671297306624?lang=en.

teenager appeared like a demon who had to be stopped?[21] I am speaking of Ferguson police officer Darren Wilson's official testimony regarding his 2014 killing of Michael Brown.

Terror is casting a pall over black churches in this country in ways that my generation was only supposed to hear of in the past tense. But activists like performance artist Bree Newsome have used these last days to speak countermessages of hope and agency. In the aftermath of the massacre at Mother Emanuel AME Church, she took it upon herself to bring down the battle flag of the Confederacy from South Carolina's statehouse pole, proclaiming the words of the psalmist.[22]

> You come against me with hatred, repression, and violence. I come against you in the name of God. This flag comes down today.... "The Lord is my light and my salvation whom shall I fear. The Lord is the stronghold of my life, but whom shall I be afraid" (Ps 27:1).... "The Lord is my shepherd, I shall not want. He maketh me to lie down in green pastures. He leadeth me beside still waters; He restoreth my soul" (Ps 23:1–3a).

Upon her descent from the heavens she was met by two groups. The principalities of this earth stood at the bottom of the pole, standing ready with chains to put her in her place. And in the distance rang out a throng of supporters reciting the words of the former Black Panther Party and Black Liberation Army revolutionary Assata Shakur:

> It is our duty to fight for our freedom.
> It is our duty to win.
> We must love and protect each other.
> We have nothing to lose *but our chains.*
> Power to the people.[23]

For our scholarly body, I see this apocalypse not as a final moment but as an uncovering of a canonical world for view. In discussing the counts on which black lives matter, our situation appears more and more like a "scriptural economy," wherein we use texts to imprint values on our bodies.[24] It has never been clearer to me that every human person is a testament to others' God complexes, people's naming of how things are meant to be.[25]

---

[21] Josh Sanburn, "All the Ways Darren Wilson Described Being Afraid of Michael Brown," *Time*, 25 November 2014, http://time.com/3605346/darren-wilson-michael-brown-demon/.

[22] Bree Newsome, "This Flag Comes Down Today" (Columbia, SC), 27 June 2015. Video recording by The Tribe, YouTube, https://www.youtube.com/watch?v=gr-mt1P94cQ.

[23] Assata Shakur, "To My People," 4 July 1973, http://www.assatashakur.org/mypeople.htm (emphasis added).

[24] Michel de Certeau, "The Scriptural Economy, " in *The Practice of Everyday Life* (Berkeley: University of California Press, 1984), 131–53.

[25] I am thinking here of Christopher Driscoll's reflection on The Last Poets' 1971 song "The

So, going forward, what hermeneutic might the SBL apply to reveal more about these discourses? I am convinced that we need to be as astute as that nineteenth-century black woman who was given the name Isabella Baumfree. Our history books remember her saying, "I can't read little things like letters. I read big things like men."[26] Her taking of such texts into her own hands is what has us remember the name she gave herself, Sojourner Truth.

To that end, I ask, what does the African American Bible reveal to you about this Christian Nation, our guild, and the story we are bound in? What future are we bound for? What truths are we bound by? And how might we be bound to each other? In the African American Bible, that is the chapter calling to be written.

---

White Man's Got a God Complex" in his essay "On the Journey to White Shame," *Marginalia*, 8 December 2014, http://marginalia.lareviewofbooks.org/mrblog-journey-white-shame-christopher-driscoll/.

[26] Harriot Stanton Blatch, *Challenging Years: The Memoirs of Harriot Stanton Blatch* (New York: G. P. Putnam's Sons, 1940), 17.

# Research on the New Testament and Early Christian Literature May Assist the Churches in Setting Ethical Priorities

BERNADETTE J. BROOTEN
brooten@brandeis.edu
Brandeis University, Waltham, MA 02454

The hashtags #BlackLivesMatter and #SayHerName remind non-African Americans of issues that black communities in the United States have long faced: disproportionate police killings of black persons of all genders, mass incarceration of black and brown persons, economic and educational disadvantages, discrimination in housing, racial and sexual stereotypes that harm both rape complainants and defendants, and so on. I view these issues through a deep lens into history, extending back from Jim and Jane Crow through to religiously sanctioned legal slavery, behind that to the Vatican-approved onset of the Portuguese and Spanish slave trades with West Africa, canon-law sanctioned slavery going back from the Middle Ages to late antiquity, and to the Christian Bible, both testaments of which tolerate slavery. To be sure, Christians were at the forefront of opposing slavery in the eighteenth and nineteenth centuries, and many other factors have played a role in arriving at the current situation. Nevertheless, the Bible and the ancient sources of canon law served as justifications for the slavery whose legacies linger.

My mentor Krister Stendahl's concept of the "public health" aspect of New Testament studies has inspired me to undertake research that may limit harm caused to marginalized persons through specific uses of the New Testament and further the values of human dignity and equality as these interact with the Bible. To that end, most of my research has consisted of historically grounded, close analysis of New Testament, contemporaneous, and other ancient texts, each of which has some relevance for contemporary public and religious debates. I see my work as part of a broader mosaic of scholarly contributions that, together, can provide solid historical depth and religious literacy in contemporary policy discussions. I am reflecting here on how I, as a biblical scholar, respond to structural racism and other contemporary forms of inequality.

As I contemplated current racial and gender inequities and considered how I, as a scholar of the New Testament and of Jewish and early church history in the Roman period, could contribute to solving these pressing ethical problems, I determined that collaboration was the best way to observe connections and contrasts, thereby creating a deep historical picture. Within the Feminist Sexual Ethics Project that I direct, a group of outstanding scholars specializing in several religious traditions and periods of history and in ethics, theology, and law, and activists in the areas of US incarceration practices and contemporary slavery made that possible. In addition, artists in dance, music, and poetry, as well as musicologists, helped audiences to shift their vision, to see the world around them in new ways.

Collaborators sought to address the nexus of slavery, religion, and sexuality, especially as it has impacted women and girls. The collaboration resulted in *Beyond Slavery: Overcoming Its Religious and Sexual Legacies* (2010), as well as an archive of the public conference on the Feminist Sexual Ethics Project's website.[1] The team of scholars, artists, and activists investigated this issue beginning with the Bible and the ancient Near East and extending through to early Christianity; the Talmud; early Islamic jurisprudence; sixteenth-century Valencia; US slavery, including the use of the Bible in antebellum slavery debates; contemporary incarceration practices in the US; welfare reform; reparations for slavery; contemporary cultural depictions of slavery; a reading of the Bible and the Qur'an on slavery by a formerly enslaved woman; and poetry inspired by these themes.

The researchers ascertained that sexual access by masters to enslaved women and girls and, although far less frequently acknowledged, to men, boys, and persons of other genders, has de facto characterized the slavery systems analyzed. While the Qur'an and early Islamic jurisprudence explicitly allowed a master sexual access to his enslaved women and girls, which the jurists then regulated by obligating masters vis-à-vis the slave-woman or slave-girl and the child of such a union, the Jewish and Christian Bibles, the Talmud, and the ancient sources of canon law did not prohibit such sexual access even as they showed awareness that such contact occurred in their own communities. By discouraging, but not prohibiting, masters from having sex with their enslaved females, early Christian religious leaders created a tension between slavery and chastity and marital fidelity. That tension haunted Christian concepts of sexual morality until slavery's abolition. Much more seriously, Christian toleration of masters' sexual use of their enslaved laborers was always a potential part of these forced labor relations. In the Roman world, however, a master could normally manumit his slave-woman and marry her. That

---

[1] Bernadette J. Brooten, ed., with the editorial assistance of Jacqueline L. Hazelton, *Beyond Slavery: Overcoming Its Religious and Sexual Legacies* (New York: Palgrave Macmillan, 2010); Feminist Sexual Ethics Project, videos of the conference "Beyond Slavery: Overcoming Its Religious and Sexual Legacy," http://www.brandeis.edu/projects/fse/conferences/beyond-slavery/index.html.

drastically changed with the invention of slavery as a race-based institution in the early modern era, which eventually opened the way to antimiscegenation statutes that prohibited interracial marriage but not sexual contact. These statutes prevented a white man from entering into a serious relationship with a black woman that included mutual rights and responsibilities. Sexual exploitation reminiscent of slavery, however, remained a viable option. The Ku Klux Klan, a Christian terrorist organization, employed sexual terror against the African American population with impunity. Today, black women who experience rape are less likely to report it to law enforcement and, if they do report it, face greater hurdles than white women in the criminal justice system. A long view of history enables one to see in the current situation echoes of slavery and of Jim and Jane Crow.[2]

In addition to collaborative work, I have published on the severe challenges faced by enslaved families in early Christianity and on early Christian canons on sexual activity, rape, and/or choice of marital partner with respect to enslaved women, free married women, widows, and virgins dedicated to God.[3] I am currently extending this into a monograph on enslaved women and female slaveholders in early Christianity. The ancient sources burst the mold of early Christian slavery as a benign institution and of female slaveholders as kinder and gentler than their male counterparts. Medieval Latin canon law incorporated early canons on slavery, gender, and sexual behavior from the synods of Elvira and of Gangra and the canonical letters of Basil of Caesarea, thereby creating authoritative slave law for the Roman Catholic Church until 1918. Some Eastern churches likewise took up some of these canons, ensuring their long-term influence on churches' stances on slavery. I aim for this research to become a small tessera in a larger mosaic of the long history of enslaved women and female slaveholders that can inform contemporary discussions.

The African American Policy Forum, cofounded and directed by Kimberlé Crenshaw, draws attention, in general, to the plight of black girls and women in the United States and, through the #SayHerName campaign, to the killing, raping, and beating of black girls and women by police. Against the background of a slavery

---

[2] See video clips of the 2012 Feminist Sexual Ethics Project's conference, "Disrupting the Script: Raising to Legal Consciousness Sexual Assaults on Black Women," convened by Anita F. Hill and myself, as well as reviews of the research underlying the conference, http://www.brandeis.edu/projects/fse/conferences/disrupting-the-script/index.html; and http://www.brandeis.edu/projects/fse/sexual-violence/black-women.html.

[3] See Bernadette J. Brooten, "Early Christian Enslaved Families (1st–4th C.)," in *Children and Family in Late Antiquity: Life, Death and Interaction*, ed. Christian Laes, Katariina Mustakallio, and Ville Vuolanto, Interdisciplinary Studies in Ancient Culture and Religion 15 (Leuven: Peeters, 2015) 111–34; and Brooten, "Enslaved Women in Basil of Caesarea's Canonical Letters: An Intersectional Analysis," in *Doing Gender, Doing Religion: Fallstudien zur Intersektionalität im frühen Judentum, Christentum und Islam*, ed. Ute E. Eisen, Christine Gerber, and Angela Standhartinger, WUNT 302 (Tübingen: Mohr Siebeck, 2013), 325–55.

that was sanctioned by most nineteenth-century Christians and opposed by only a small number of active Christian Abolitionists, and against nearly a century of segregation tolerated by Christians, I view the current struggles of African Americans as a pressing ethical issue for the churches. Exegesis of biblical passages on slavery, viewed in the full context of what one can know about the life circumstances of slavery from a range of ancient historical sources, can provide the churches with tools for facing up to legal institutions that contributed to current inequities. Churches and other Christian institutions have also begun to investigate their own denominational histories, the histories of their specific congregations, and the histories of their universities and religious orders, all of which is salutary and gives hope for the future.

Both #BlackLivesMatter and #SayHerName are explicitly inclusive with respect to sexual orientation, gender identity and expression, and several other identities. This stance puts them at odds with a number of Christian groups, for whom a marriage consisting of a female and male defined as such at birth is the only biblically acceptable setting for sexual contact. Such Christians are increasingly defining marriage and a pro-life stance with respect to the unborn as the central questions of Christian ethics. Accordingly, many Christians see opposition to same-sex marriage and to any other rights accorded to lesbian, gay, bisexual, queer, and comparable individuals or groups and, most especially, to any rights granted to transgender individuals or groups as epitomizing Christian religious freedom to live according to the Bible and tradition. If groups of Christians define abortion and LGBTQ rights as the most foundational ethical questions, then issues such as racism and the long-term effects of slavery and its aftermath, sexual and other gender-based violence, massive incarceration, police killings, anti-Muslim and anti-immigrant sentiments, war and militarization, fair working conditions, climate change, and healthcare for all will be peripheral.

After having written *Love between Women: Early Christian Responses to Female Homoeroticism* (1996),[4] I turned to the topic of slavery, and especially to sexual violence and coercion within slavery, precisely in order to help shift church attention away from opposing consenting same-sex relations between adults and toward reflecting on sexual violence within slavery and on its long shadow over present society. Many more church people are now discussing the history of slavery than when my collaborators and I began our work and when other historians increasingly revised previous views through new archival research and new methodological approaches.

In *Love between Women*, I had examined Paul's condemnation of female homoeroticism in Rom 1:26–27. Paul defines sexual contact between females and between males as a result of human beings having "exchanged the glory of the immortal God for images" (Rom 1:23). He depicts these unnatural sexual

---

[4] Bernadette J. Brooten, *Love between Women: Early Christian Responses to Female Homoeroticism* (Chicago: University of Chicago Press, 1996).

encounters as "impurity," "degrading," "degrading passions," and "unnatural" (vv. 24, 26–27). Romans 1:32 states that all who do such things (i.e., the behaviors described in the vice list of vv. 29–31, as well as the same-sex sexual acts of vv. 26–27) "deserve to die." Considering both other Pauline statements on women and on marital relations and other Roman-period responses to female homoeroticism, nearly all of which were negative, I concluded that Paul likely condemned such relations for the same reasons as a number of others in the Roman world did. These reasons included the views that women are passive by nature and meant to subordinate themselves to men and that such relations overturn the social order and are monstrous and unnatural. I then tested my interpretation by examining early Christian writers' readings of Rom 1 and their discussions of female homoeroticism more generally and found that they confirmed my construal of the text. Unlike many others working hard to create acceptance within the churches for LGBTQ persons, I did not claim that Paul, properly understood, may well have accepted same-sex sexual intimacies and relationships of the type that we know today. Ancient sources depicted consenting relationships, including long-term ones, between adult women, and Paul, in his extensive travels, could have encountered such relationships. Similarly, unlike others, I did not claim that Paul could have had no concept of an inborn sexual orientation. Indeed, some in the Roman world, specifically in the realms of medicine and astrology, claimed that a same-sex orientation could be caused by the seeds mingling improperly with each other in the womb or by the configuration of the stars under which one was born. I engaged scholars from a number of backgrounds, including those who believe that the churches should not treat same-sex relationships on a par with heterosexual ones, and I agreed with them on some points. Similarly, I critically engaged scholars elsewhere on the theoretical and ideological spectrum. Subsequent to the book, many more Christians have come to accept LGBQ and, increasingly, transgender individuals as equals. Some of my arguments may have had an impact, although I think that the view that Paul, were he only here today to see loving same-sex relationships, would have accepted them, has probably swayed more people. That interpretation allows one to hold to the authority of these Pauline passages, even while arguing that they do not apply today. In contrast, my arguments challenged the authority of this text by illustrating the vision of gender relations embedded within it, a vision of female subordination that many Christians no longer hold. I consciously did not interpret these texts in such a way that they would line up with what I would have liked them to say. I tried instead to respect Paul by understanding his words as those from a stratified society in the distant past, one in which I would not wish to have lived. In pointing out, however, that some interpretations might be more comfortable to the Christian church audiences whom advocates for LGBQ equality wish to persuade, I am not on those grounds arguing against such interpretations. Because scholarship is critical engagement, debate, and the weighing of the respective merits of each argument, we need a range of interpretations.

Perhaps the single most important aspect of my research for what became *Love between Women* was that I continued to work on it in the face of very significant opposition to the topic itself. Whereas some tried to dissuade me through disciplinary means, others would simply ask whether I did not wish to go on to other topics. Both methods made me realize that I had my finger on the pulse of a topic that others wanted to avoid, not for scholarly reasons but for theological or ideological ones. I recognized that the very act of continuing to devote my best intellectual energies to this topic itself constituted activism and resistance. That, together with the comparable acts of many other scholars in a range of fields, may have had more impact on the move toward greater acceptance in the churches, in society, and under the law than any single argument in any of our publications.

Competing visions of the top priorities for Christian ethics gained prominence in the 2016 U.S. presidential election. Inner-Evangelical debates illustrate divergent paths, based at least in part on differing biblical interpretations. For some Evangelical leaders, the very top priorities are (1) creating marriages consisting of one man and one woman who were designated as male and female at birth as the only settings in which sexual contact should occur, and (2) protecting the life of the unborn at every stage. While these leaders might articulate such other political concerns as the right to bear arms, a more restrictive immigrant policy, repeal of the Affordable Care Act, school vouchers, and less government regulation, in this election the top priorities usually took center stage. In "Trump's Moral Character and the Election," leading white Evangelical ethicist Wayne Grudem delineates these:

> What if we fail to vote against the liberal support for abortion rights, government imposition of gender confusion on our children, hate speech laws used to silence Christians, and government-sanctioned exclusion of thousands of Christians from their lifelong occupations because they won't bow to the homosexual agenda—will our failure to oppose these evils also destroy our Christian witness for the future?[5]

Grudem can make a biblical case for these positions. In contrast to such other ancient texts as Ps.-Phoc. 184 ("Nor should a woman destroy the fetus growing in her uterus"), the Christian Bible nowhere proscribes abortion, but many believe that such passages as Luke 1:41 ("When Elizabeth heard Mary's greeting, the child leaped in her womb" [NRSV]) function as a prohibition. One could find biblical opposition to gender fluidity in Gen 1:27 ("male and female God created them") and Deut 22:5 (prohibition on cross-dressing). Further, the Bible forbids male–male (most likely anal) intercourse and sexual relations between females and

---

[5] Wayne Grudem, "Trump's Moral Character and the Election," *Townhall*, 9 September 2016, http://townhall.com/columnists/waynegrudem/2016/10/09/trumps-moral-character-and-the-election-n2229846.

between males (Lev 18:22; 20:13; Rom 1:26–27; and perhaps 1 Cor 6:9 and 1 Tim 1:10).

What moves to the periphery if abortion and LGBT acceptance are the lynchpins of Christian religious liberty? Grudem writes that Trump's "many years of business conduct show that he is not racist or anti-(legal) immigrant or anti-Semitic or misogynistic."[6] Many of the approximately 81 percent of white, born-again/Evangelical Christians who voted for Donald Trump may have had these same priorities. Perhaps some of the approximately 60 percent of white Roman Catholics and the approximately 61 percent of Mormons who voted for Trump did so, in part, based on comparable ethical priorities.[7]

In "A Declaration by American Evangelicals Concerning Donald Trump," a multiracial group of nearly eighty Evangelical Christian female and male leaders sets very different priorities: "racism strikes at the heart of the gospel," "[r]acism is America's original sin," and "Mr. Trump's racial and religious bigotry and treatment of women is morally unacceptable to us as evangelical Christians, as we attempt to model Jesus' command to 'love your neighbors as yourself.'"[8] For this group and the large number of persons who signed its petition, Matt 25:31–46, especially the "stranger" in the person of refugees and immigrants, is central. While many of the signatories may hold that acceptance of LGBT rights or a right to an abortion runs contrary to the Bible, racial bigotry, bigotry toward Muslims, lack of care for the poor and the vulnerable, public humiliation of persons with disabilities, and disrespect for women are the decisive factors. Although this statement does not name US slavery, its view of racism as "America's original sin" and the call for "a long-needed repentance from our racial sin" point in that direction.

In writing first *Love between Women* and then turning toward slavery, I hoped to help bring about precisely this shift toward what I view as the most pressing moral issues facing society to which Christians can and must contribute. Even though perhaps only a very small number of these Evangelical leaders have ever read anything that I have written or encountered our collaborative work, we participate together in a broader shift in ethical priorities. A conversation on an airplane or with a dean or my nephew may be as important as a book in helping to reorient these priorities. Similarly, seeing the discrepancy between a race-neutral

---

[6] Wayne Grudem, "Why Voting for Trump is a Morally Good Choice," *Townhall*, 28 July 2016; retracted on 8 October 2016; reinstated on 19 October 2016, http://townhall.com/columnists/waynegrudem/2016/10/09/trumps-moral-character-and-the-election-n2229846.

[7] Gregory A. Smith and Jessica Martínez, "How the Faithful Voted: A Preliminary 2016 Analysis," Pew Research Center, 9 November 2016, http://www.pewresearch.org/fact-tank/2016/11/09/how-the-faithful-voted-a-preliminary-2016-analysis/.

[8] "A Declaration by American Evangelicals Concerning Donald Trump," https://www.change.org/p/donald-trump-a-declaration-by-american-evangelicals-concerning-donald-trump; also reported upon in, among other places, *Los Angeles Times*, 7 October 2016, http://www.latimes.com/nation/politics/trailguide/la-na-live-updates-trailguide-more-than-75-evangelicals-call-trump-1475849049-htmlstory.html.

statute and its racist implementation has helped to reorient my scholarship. For example, I now view exhortations to enslaved persons in the New Testament or ancient canons concerning slavery more realistically.

The lives of black persons of all genders will only matter to all once non-black persons make it so. If I can learn to take the lead from scholars and activists of African origin and engage their scholarship and insights, I may be able to contribute to that project. Kimberlé Crenshaw has profoundly shaped my work, and I express deep gratitude to collaborators Adrienne Davis, Dorothy Roberts, Emilie Townes, Dwight Hopkins, Mia Bay, Barbara Savage, Sylvester Johnson, Frances Smith Foster, Florence Ladd, Nancy Rawles, Mende Nazer, Monique Moultrie, Anita Hill, Intisar Rabb, Traci West, Régine Jean-Charles, Jennifer Nash, Janice Liddell, Vanessa Adams-Harris, Jasmine Johnson, and, most of all, my dear friend Sheila Briggs, for your generosity in working with me and for all that each of you has taught me.

In closing, I want to note that the work of scholar-activists requires nonactivist research. In order to delineate the history of ancient Mediterranean responses to female homoeroticism, to interpret the sources of early canon law, and the like, I need the best editions of ancient texts and artifacts, the most precise dating, the most detailed commentaries, and so on. Furthermore, only the very best libraries contain all of the resources necessary to understand the arcane sources needed to write the history of marginalized persons. For any other period of history on which I or we work, we need both foundational research and innovative questions. Thus, many scholars may already be contributing to the larger project of the "public health" aspect of biblical studies.

# Black Scholarship Matters

TAT-SIONG BENNY LIEW
bliew@holycross.edu
College of the Holy Cross, Worcester, MA 01610

---

Frank Leon Roberts's website (BlackLivesMatterSyllabus.com) is brilliant in recognizing and promoting the connection between what one does in the academy and as an activist. Academic scholarship does not require neutrality. As Howard Zinn explains, academic "objectivity" does not mean that one should not "have strong opinions on which ideas are right and which are wrong," but only that one will be "fair to opposing ideas by accurately representing them."[1]

As the Black Lives Matter movement confronts society with the question, "Whose lives count as lives?" I find myself asking, "Whose scholarship counts as scholarship in my guild?"

Just as the African American civil rights movement in the 1960s helped open and pave the way for other racial/ethnic "minoritized" groups to fight for equal access to legal rights and protections, *Stony the Road We Trod*,[2] which I read as a doctoral student in the early 1990s, helped me consider if and how my specific location as a first-generation male immigrant from Asia could or would impact my practice of biblical interpretation. Cain Hope Felder's "Introduction" provided for me insights into the racialized dynamics of the US academy and words to express my own feelings. He talked about the structural factors (both economic and political) that kept most African Americans from pursuing higher education, the pervasive and inveterate whiteness of graduate programs in biblical studies, as well as black biblical scholars' experiences of isolation and pressure to assimilate.[3]

I read and reread that anthology in those early years. Womanist readings therein exposed me to intersectional analysis with their focus on both race and

---

[1] Howard Zinn, *Passionate Declarations: Essays on War and Justice* (New York: Perennial, 2003), 7.

[2] Cain Hope Felder, ed., *Stony the Road We Trod: African American Biblical Interpretation* (Minneapolis: Fortress, 1991).

[3] Felder, "Introduction," in Felder, *Stony the Road*, 1–14, here 1–2.

gender.⁴ I was especially intrigued by and indebted to the essay by Renita Weems, because it also emphasizes literary and interdisciplinary readings of the Bible by referring to the work of feminist literary critics in "linguistics, psychology, sociology, and philosophy."⁵ Weems's essay also points to the need for biblical scholarship to be methodologically rigorous, even or especially when reading processes "are both empirical and intuitive, rational and transrational, recoverable and unrecoverable."⁶ A sentence in her essay remains important to me today: "Texts are read not only within contexts; a text's meaning is also dependent upon the pretext(s) of its readers."⁷ Largely because of this anthology, I decided to make "identity politics" one of my comprehensive examination topics and started dipping my feet in African American studies and Asian American studies and learning from the writings of Barbara Christian, Henry Louis Gates, Patricia Hill Collins, Elaine Kim, Sau-ling Cynthia Wong, and Cheung King-kok. Though I was not ready to dive into anything that might be called Asian American biblical interpretation on my own for my doctoral dissertation,⁸ I did enough to sense that a group project similar to that of *Stony the Road* could be both desirable and feasible. Since (1) many among the already low number of Asian American biblical scholars at the end of the twentieth century were trained, as Felder pointed out, by white scholars in white institutions; and (2) I was just beginning my teaching career at the time and had little to no knowledge of how to organize or fund a gathering of scholars as the black colleagues did for *Stony the Road*, I decided to go beyond the biblical studies guild to see if and how scholars more familiar with Asian American studies might read the Bible. This resulted in a special double issue in the journal *Semeia*, entitled *The Bible in Asian America*.⁹

---

⁴ Renita J. Weems, "Reading *Her Way* through the Struggle: African American Women and the Bible," and Clarice J. Martin, "The *Haustafeln* (Household Codes) in African American Biblical Interpretation: 'Free Slaves' and 'Subordinate Women,'" in Felder, *Stony the Road*, 57–77 and 206–31, respectively. In addition to race and gender, both Weems and Martin also mention class as an important identity factor that functions to marginalize African American Women (Weems, "Reading *Her Way*," 58, 59; Martin, "*Haustafeln*," 208–9, 218 n. 55). I will return to the question of class in biblical interpretation later. For early articulations of intersectional analysis, see Kimberlé Crenshaw, "Demarginalizing the Intersection of Race and Sex: A Black Feminist Critique of Antidiscrimination Doctrine, Feminist Theory, and Antiracist Politics," *University of Chicago Legal Forum* 140 (1989): 139–67; and Crenshaw, "Mapping the Margins: Intersectionality, Identity Politics, and Violence against Women of Color," *Stanford Law Review* 43 (1991): 1241–99.

⁵ Weems, "Reading *Her Way*," 58.

⁶ Ibid., 59.

⁷ Ibid., 62.

⁸ In the published version of my dissertation, my explicit engagement with my reading contexts as an Asian American is limited to the concluding pages and only as a pointer for future explorations. See Tat-siong Benny Liew, *Politics of Parousia: Reading Mark Inter(con)textually*, BibInt 42 (Leiden: Brill, 1999), 150–58.

⁹ Tat-siong Benny Liew and Gale A. Yee, eds., *The Bible in Asian America*, special issue, *Semeia* 90–91 (2002).

While this *Semeia* volume would have been inconceivable to me without the example and inspiration provided by *Stony the Road*, its publication in 2002 was actually preceded by another important publication of black biblical scholarship: the encyclopedic *African Americans and the Bible*.[10] Despite differences not only in scope but also in direction (to which I will return in a moment), both of these volumes were intentional in involving scholars outside the biblical studies guild to talk about the Bible. In view of the temporal proximity of these two publications, a day-long symposium brought together a panel of African American and Asian American biblical scholars at Union Theological Seminary (New York) to discuss our different experiences in life and approaches to the Bible. Out of that came an essay that I coauthored with Vincent Wimbush, in which we talked about identities (problems of essentialism and effacement), communities (differences within and between our two communities of color), the guild of biblical interpretation (its dismissal of or disinterest in "minoritized" readings), and possible changes (such as displacement of the biblical texts and the ancient world as the beginning and centering foci of biblical interpretation, or collaboration of biblical scholars among and across communities of color).[11]

One of the African American scholars I met for the first time at the symposium was Randall C. Bailey. Since Fernando F. Segovia was also present at the symposium as a respondent, Bailey approached Segovia and me about a project involving biblical scholars from all three communities of color (African American, Asian American, and Latino/a American).[12] Bailey's insistence from the beginning that sexuality be a part of our conversation pushed me to widen and deepen my intersectional interrogations of biblical texts by not allowing me to put sexuality issues on a back burner. After trying but failing to recruit a biblical scholar of color who has self-identified as queer, Bailey proceeded to tell me that he *and I* must do some queering in our respective contribution to the publication project. I took up the challenge by writing an article that queers John's Jesus in terms of not only race/ethnicity but also gender and sexuality. In the process I learned much from queer studies done by scholars of color.[13] Bailey also taught me how solidarity could be

---

[10] Vincent L. Wimbush, ed., *African Americans and the Bible: Sacred Texts and Social Texture* (New York: Continuum, 2000).

[11] Tat-siong Benny Liew and Vincent L. Wimbush, "Contact Zones and Zoning Contexts: From the Los Angeles 'Riot' to a New York Symposium," *USQR* 56 (2002): 21–40.

[12] See Randall C. Bailey, Tat-siong Benny Liew, and Fernando F. Segovia, eds., *They Were All Together in One Place? Toward Minority Biblical Criticism*, SemeiaSt 57 (Atlanta: Society of Biblical Literature, 2009). The collaboration also resulted in the establishment of a new SBL program unit called "Minoritized Criticism and Biblical Interpretation."

[13] Tat-siong Benny Liew, "Queering Closets and Perverting Desires: Cross-examining John's Engendering and Transgendering Word across Different Worlds," in Bailey, Liew, and Segovia, *They Were All Together*, 251–88; in the same volume, see also Randall C. Bailey, "'That's Why They Didn't Call the Book Hadassah!': The Interse(ct)/(x)ionality of Race/Ethnicity, Gender, and Sexuality in the Book of Esther," 227–50.

practiced, promoted, and even pushed in the academy. Perhaps the most important lesson I learned from working with Bailey is that, when tempted to label a position or approach as "extreme," we would do well to reexamine our perception of what is "acceptable."

Second, while I was aware that race was a construct, my interaction with black colleagues gave me courage to try reading a biblical text as if I were an African American by using primarily African American resources. In another article on John's Gospel, I read Jesus and his awareness of—even obsession with—his death (what John calls Jesus's "hour") as a colonized Jew through the lens of what Abdul R. JanMohamed identifies as a "death-bound-subjectivity" of many African Americans.[14] Given Ruth Wilson Gilmore's definition of racism as "state-sanctioned ... premature death," it should not be surprising that death is a consistent subject in black scholarship.[15]

The directional difference between *The Bible in Asian America* and *African Americans and the Bible* can already be detected in their respective titles. Wimbush's "African Americans" puts the emphasis on a community of people in contrast to the more geographically sounding "Asian America." The conjunction *and* also implies a much more dynamic relationship with the Bible than the relatively static preposition *in*. Finally, the placement of the word *Bible* as the first or the second term is also telling.

In sum, while the *Semeia* project followed the more conventional disciplinary focus on reading for textual meaning (though from Asian American perspectives), Wimbush's project focused on how African Americans make social and cultural meaning with and through the Bible.[16]

This key difference also explains why Wimbush started the Institute of Signifying Scriptures in 2004 and then embarked in 2006 on a different consultation project, in which I was also fortunate enough to participate and from which I learned. Although this latter project, like the earlier project with Bailey and Segovia, involved various communities of color, it pushed me far beyond my comfort zone as a

---

[14] Tat-siong Benny Liew, "The Word of Bare Life: Workings of Death and Dream in the Fourth Gospel," in *Anatomies of Narrative Criticism: The Past, Present, and Futures of the Fourth Gospel as Literature*, ed. Tom Thatcher and Stephen D. Moore, RBS 55 (Atlanta: Society of Biblical Literature, 2008), 167–93. See Abdul R. JanMohamed, *The Death-Bound-Subject: Richard Wright's Archaeology of Death*, Post-contemporary Interventions (Durham, NC: Duke University Press, 2005).

[15] Ruth Wilson Gilmore, *Golden Gulag: Prisons, Surplus, Crisis and Opposition in Globalizing California*, American Crossroads 21 (Berkeley: University of California Press, 2007), 28. See also Dorothy Roberts, *Killing the Black Body: Race, Reproduction, and the Meaning of Liberty* (New York: Vintage, 1997); Sharon Patricia Holland, *Raising the Dead: Readings of Death and (Black) Subjectivity*, New Americanists (Durham, NC: Duke University Press, 2000); and Karla F. C. Holloway, *Passed On: African American Mourning Stories* (Durham, NC: Duke University Press, 2002).

[16] Vincent L. Wimbush, "Preface," in Wimbush, *African Americans and the Bible*, xiii.

biblical scholar. Instead of reading biblical texts or biblical interpretations, I was to engage in an ethnographic team project on how some Asian Americans make and negotiate meaning in their lives as racialized subjects in the United States by reading or believing in the Bible *literally*. It was an ambitious attempt to understand a segment of the Asian American communities in terms of not only what Michael Omi and Howard Winant call "racial formation" but also what Wimbush calls "reading formations" with and through the Bible.[17] Interviewing living persons is very different from reading texts by authors who were either literally dead or, as Roland Barthes taught me, who are at least theoretically dead.[18] Postmodern critiques of ethnography further increased my anxiety.[19] Again, what I learned in the process was much more important than the product.[20]

Gay Byron's proposal to extend the study of Christian origins and traditions beyond the Roman Empire to include "places and people south of the Mediterranean," such as Ethiopian civilizations and the Axumite Empire,[21] also prompted me to rethink the foregone conclusion that the Christian canon has been fixed and closed since the fourth century CE. Given Wimbush's understanding of "scripturalization" as "the use of texts, textuality, and literacy as a means of constructing and maintaining society,"[22] I found myself re-viewing (Chinese/American) culture itself as a kind of open canon, *changeable* social script, or scripturalization. Instead of thinking that cultures and the Bible are finished products only to be transmitted and received, I should *dis*-close that all scripts, scriptures, and scripturalizing processes are not only authoritative and abiding but also arbitrary and ever-altering.[23] Black scholarship has made me a more careful critic and a more broad-minded biblical scholar.

The recent US presidential election has made it clear that race, religion, and *class*, among other issues, remain contentious matters in this country. Several news

---

[17] Michael Omi and Howard Winant, *Racial Formation in the United States: From the 1960s to the 1980s*, 2nd ed. (New York: Routledge, 1994); Vincent L. Wimbush, "Introduction: Knowing Ex-centrics/Ex-centric Knowing," in *Misreading America: Scriptures and Difference*, ed. Vincent L. Wimbush (New York: Oxford University Press, 2013), 1–4.

[18] Roland Barthes, "Death of the Author," in *Image, Music, Text*, ed. and trans. Stephen Heath, Fontana Communications Series (London: Fontana, 1977), 142–48.

[19] See, e.g., James Clifford, "On Ethnographic Authority," *Representations* 2 (1983): 118–46; and Renato Rosaldo, *Culture and Truth: The Remaking of Social Analysis* (Boston: Beacon, 1989).

[20] Tat-siong Benny Liew, "Asian Americans, Bible Believers: An Ethnological Study," in Wimbush, *Misreading America*, 165–207.

[21] Gay L. Byron, "Ancient Ethiopia and the New Testament: Ethnic (Con)texts and Racialized (Sub)texts," in Bailey, Liew, and Segovia, *They Were All Together*, 161–90.

[22] Vincent L. Wimbush, *White Men's Magic: Scripturalization as Slavery* (New York: Oxford University Press, 2012), 87.

[23] Tat-siong Benny Liew, "Journey-s to the West: (Re)Writing Scripts, Scriptures, and Scripturalization," in *Refractions of the Scriptural: Critical Orientation as Transgression*, ed. Vincent L. Wimbush, Routledge Studies in Religion 48 (New York: Routledge, 2016), 121–38.

commentators and political pundits have even brought back the popularized slogan of Bill Clinton's presidential campaign in the 1990s to analyze this election: "It's the economy, stupid!" Black biblical scholars have generally done a better job than most others of pointing to the importance of class, though many, including myself, who spent hour after hour in the classroom—which is often "indeed a room of class"[24]— have proven to be slow learners. As Weems and Martin did in their respective contributions to *Stony the Road*, Raquel Annette St. Clair presents the challenges facing African American women in terms of "the tridimensional oppression of gender, race, and class" in her womanist reading of Mark's Gospel.[25] More recently, through her "hermeneutics of ambi*veil*ance, Shanell T. Smith's interpretation of the well-dressed and bejeweled Babylonian whore in Rev 17–18 and of herself, an educated and privileged black professor, both as victims and beneficiaries of empire brings up the issue of class to critique as well as for self-critique.[26] What this election and black scholarship suggest to me now is the importance of scrutinizing what bell hooks calls "imperialist white supremacist *capitalist* [hetero]patriarchy,"[27] in order to grapple genuinely with class, status, and economic issues in my own scholarship on the Bible.

Womanist scholars often express feelings of shame and anger, but let me point to St. Clair's articulation of "three key issues that shape the sociocultural location of African American women—suffering, shame, and surrogacy."[28] Those three words point to embodiment and feelings, thus what has now been called a new materialist turn within feminism and an affective turn in literary/cultural studies.[29] Black scholarship, biblical or otherwise, could have been an early precursor of *and* a continuing corrective to these trails of scholarly developments if I had been a quicker and better learner.[30]

---

[24] Miguel A. De La Torre, *Doing Christian Ethics from the Margins*, 2nd rev. ed. (Maryknoll, NY: Orbis, 2014), xi.

[25] Raquel Annette St. Clair, *Call and Consequences: A Womanist Reading of Mark* (Minneapolis: Fortress, 2008).

[26] Shanell T. Smith, *The Woman Babylon and the Marks of Empire: Reading Revelation with a Postcolonial Womanist Hermeneutics of Ambiveilence*, Emerging Scholars (Minneapolis: Fortress, 2014).

[27] bell hooks, *The Will to Change: Men, Masculinity, and Love* (New York: Atria, 2004), 17, 29, 51, 116 (emphasis added).

[28] St. Clair, *Call and Consequences*, 8–9. See also Martin, "Haustafeln," 221; and Smith, *Woman Babylon*, 3, 92, 174.

[29] Among womanist scholars, see Hortense J. Spilers, "Mama's Baby, Papa's Maybe: An American Grammar Book," *Diacritics* 17 (1987): 64–81; and Sharon Patricia Holland, *The Erotic Life of Racism* (Durham, NC: Duke University Press, 2012).

[30] See, e.g., Zakiyyah Iman Jackson, "Outer Worlds: The Persistence of Race in Movement 'Beyond the Human,'" *GLQ: A Journal of Lesbian and Gay Studies* 21 (2015): 215–18; and Diana Leong, "The Mattering of Black Lives: Octavia Butler's Hyperempathy and the Promise of the New Materialisms," *Catalyst: Feminism, Theory, Technoscience* 2 (2016): 1–35.

When hooks called the Chinese American film director Wayne Wang to task for casting a black actor in the role of the thief in the film *Smoke* (1995) and thereby perpetuating the racist and racializing stereotype of blacks as criminals,[31] she was pointing to the failure of many to learn from black experience and scholarship. Likewise, it is one thing to have black bodies showing up in the annual SBL meeting or even joining SBL committees and council and serving as SBL presidents. It is quite another to acknowledge and integrate black scholarship into our disciplinary discourse. If we have learned anything from Michel Foucault or from feminist standpoint theory, it is the intertwined nature of power and knowledge.[32] Of course, W. E. B. Du Bois might have said as much when he claimed to be "singularly clairvoyant" in his understanding of white people.[33] You always (try to) know what (you think) you need to know to survive. When one looks at the bibliographies and references of some of the most-used textbooks for introductory Hebrew Bible or New Testament courses, however, one will not see much indication about the importance of black scholarship.

To illustrate, let me use two introductory texts to the Hebrew Bible/Old Testament and two introductory texts to the New Testament.[34] Three of them were published by prestigious university presses and one by a well-known church-related publisher. All four were published within the last five years; two are updated editions that signify strong sales and popularity. Of a total of 114 chapters plus two unnumbered introductions and over 1,390 bibliographical entries, only four entries involve a black scholar. That would average out to be one single reference to black scholarship for each of these four introductory texts.

What does this practice of overlooking (at best) or excluding (at worst) suggest about the importance we, as a guild, place on the work of our black colleagues?[35]

---

[31] bell hooks, *Reel to Real: Race, Sex, and Class at the Movies* (New York: Routledge, 1996), 91, 157, 160–62.

[32] See, e.g., Michel Foucault, *Power/Knowledge: Selected Interviews and Other Writings, 1972–1977*, ed. and trans. Colin Gordon (New York: Pantheon, 1980); and Sandra Harding, ed., *The Feminist Standpoint Theory Reader: Intellectual and Political Controversies* (New York: Routledge, 2004).

[33] W. E. B. Du Bois, *Darkwater: Voices from within the Veil* (New York: Harcourt, Brace & Howe, 1920), 29.

[34] Since I am interested in making only a general comment and critique about the guild of biblical studies, I withhold the identity of these specific texts and their authors to prevent any misunderstandings.

[35] Referencing another scholar's work should signify, of course, real engagement rather than a polite exchange, though the lack of reference to black scholarship by non-black scholars (when the reverse is hardly the case) reminds me of the opening scene in Du Bois's *The Souls of Black Folk* regarding how a tall white female newcomer to the schoolhouse in New England refused to exchange visiting cards with him when he was a young boy, which led him to a deep sense of the "vast veil" that separated him from the white world (*The Souls of Black Folk: Essays and Sketches*, 3rd ed. [Chicago: A. C. McClurg, 1903], 2–3).

How is it possible that black scholarship remains so hidden in current—even revised—editions of texts used to introduce the academic study of the Bible? By saying in practice that black scholarship does not matter, we in the biblical studies guild are directly reflecting and indirectly ratifying—rather than rectifying—the dominant preconceptions of blacks as inferior and disposable.

Let me say, therefore, "Black Scholarship Matters." This, like "Black Lives Matter," is a statement that should not have to be made explicitly in 2017, but it obviously does. James Baldwin wrote back in 1955, "This world is white no longer, and it will never be white again."[36] It is far past time for the practices of our guild to reflect a broader awareness and acknowledgment of that reality.

---

[36] James Baldwin, "Stranger in the Village," in *Notes of a Native Son* (Boston: Beacon, 1955), 175.

# WISDOM COMMENTARY

## THE BIBLE THROUGH A FEMINIST LENS

Wisdom Commentary, a fifty-eight-volume feminist commentary on every book of the Bible, makes the **best of current feminist biblical scholarship** available in an accessible format to aid all readers in their advancement toward God's vision of dignity, equality, and justice for all.

**NEW VOLUMES!**

Each book is hardcover with dust jacket, 6 x 9. eBooks also available. Based on the NRSV translation.

> The offer of the Wisdom Commentary, with its accent on feminist reading, is welcome and much needed.
>
> **WALTER BRUEGGEMANN**
> Columbia Theological Seminary

> The series should become required reading for any serious engagement with the Bible.
>
> **ADELE REINHARTZ**
> University of Ottawa, Canada

To learn more about the series and its authors, visit **WisdomCommentary.org**

**LITURGICAL PRESS**  litpress.org • 1-800-858-5450

## IVP Academic
*Evangelically Rooted. Critically Engaged.*

THE RICHNESS OF ISAIAH

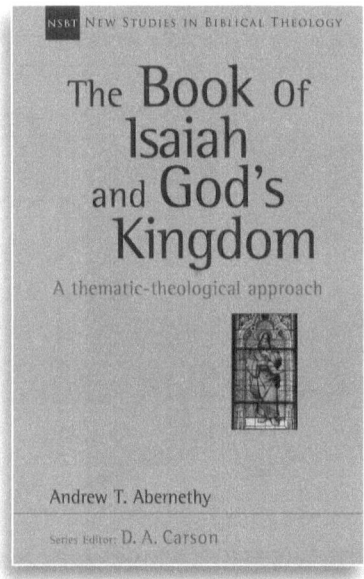

### THE BOOK OF ISAIAH AND GOD'S KINGDOM
*A Thematic-Theological Approach*
New Studies in Biblical Theology

**Andrew Abernethy**

Anyone who has attempted to teach or preach through the prophecy of Isaiah has felt a tension. In view of what the structure of the book of Isaiah aims to emphasize, this NSBT volume employs the concept of "kingdom" as an entry point for organizing the book's major themes, identifying the links to the broader biblical canon and ultimately to Jesus.

250 pages, paperback, 978-0-8308-2641-4, $25.00

Visit **ivpacademic.com/examcopy** to request an exam copy.

 800.843.9487 | ivpacademic.com

# eerdmans

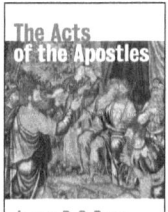

**THE ACTS OF THE APOSTLES**
James D. G. Dunn
Foreword by Scot McKnight

"In this little commentary by Dunn you have insight, measured judgment about history and theology and context, and suggestions that take the preacher to the heart of what the book of Acts can mean for us today."
— Scot McKnight

ISBN 978-0-8028-7402-3 • 421 pages • paperback • $32.00

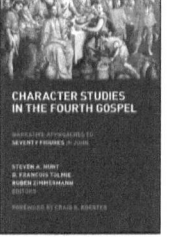

**CHARACTER STUDIES IN THE FOURTH GOSPEL**
*Narrative Approaches to Seventy Figures in John*
**Steven A. Hunt, D. Francois Tolmie,** and **Ruben Zimmermann,** editors
Foreword by **Craig R. Koester**

"This collection of studies of John's characters builds on the numerous literary studies of the Gospel that have been done in recent decades, offering the best in recent scholarship." —Craig R. Koester

ISBN 978-0-8028-7392-7 • 746 pages • paperback • $60.00

**A MAN ATTESTED BY GOD**
*The Human Jesus of the Synoptic Gospels*
**J. R. Daniel Kirk**

"Kirk ably demonstrates the wealth of Jewish material focused on an ideal, glorious humanity and its significance for the Gospels' portrayal of Jesus. Anyone working on the Gospels and New Testament Christology will now have to reckon with these arguments." — Crispin Fletcher-Louis

ISBN 978-0-8028-6795-7 • 656 pages • hardcover • $60.00

**WOMEN IN THE STORY OF JESUS**
*The Gospels through the Eyes of Nineteenth-Century Female Biblical Interpreters*
**Marion Ann Taylor** and **Heather E. Weir,** editors

"In this superb anthology we hear from a veritable cloud of witnesses. . . . These female biblical interpreters—most of them previously overlooked by scholars—can now be restored to their rightful place in the history of New Testament interpretation." — Joy A. Schroeder

ISBN 978-0-8028-7303-3 • 288 pages • paperback • $35.00

At your bookstore,
or call 800-253-7521
www.eerdmans.com

Wm. B. Eerdmans
Publishing Co.
2140 Oak Industrial Dr NE
Grand Rapids MI 49505

# NEW FROM
# BAKER ACADEMIC

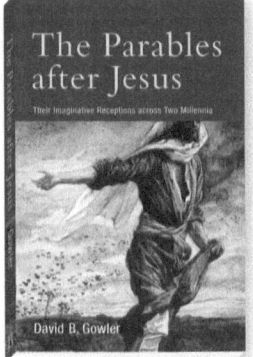

978-0-8010-4999-6 • 320 pp. • $29.99p

"David Gowler is a master of the reception history of the Bible, and he demonstrates his wisdom and experience in this wonderful book."—**Christopher Rowland**, University of Oxford

978-0-8010-9626-6 • 288 pp. • $29.99p

"Crowe shows the theological yield of attending to the Gospels' presentation of Jesus as the new Adam who redeems through his life as well as his death."
—**L. W. Hurtado**, University of Edinburgh

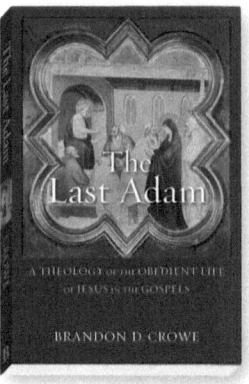

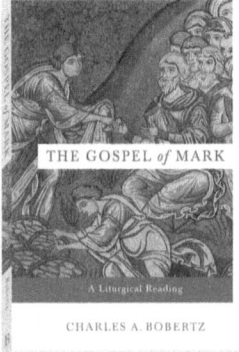

978-0-8010-3569-2 • 288 pp. • $27.99p

"Takes the bold but necessary step of restoring Mark's Gospel to its original context: the earliest Christian communities and gatherings, formed in the ritual crucible of baptism and Eucharist."—**Andrew McGowan**, Yale Divinity School

**ℬ BakerAcademic** | bakeracademic.com
Available in bookstores or by calling 800.877.2665

www.ingramcontent.com/pod-product-compliance
Lightning Source LLC
Chambersburg PA
CBHW051231300426
44114CB00032B/315